The Tainted Desert

The Tainted Desert

Environmental Ruin in the American West

· **Valerie L. Kuletz** ·

ROUTLEDGE   *New York   London*

Published in 1998 by
Routledge
29 West 35th Street
New York, NY 10001

Published in Great Britain by
Routledge
11 New Fetter Lane
London EC4P.4EE

LIBRARY OF CONGRESS CATALOGING-IN-PUBLICATION DATA

Kuletz. Valerie.
The Tainted Desert : environmental ruin in the American west /
    by Valerie Kuletz.
        p. cm.
Includes bibliographical references and index.
ISBN 0–415–91770–0 (hb). — ISBN 0–415–91771–9 (pb)
l. Indians of North America—Nevada. 2. Nuclear weapons—Nevada Testing—
Social aspects. 3. Radioactive waste disposal—Nevada —Social aspects.
4. Indians of North America—West (U.S.) 5. Nuclear weapons—West (U.S.)—
Social aspects. 6. Radioactive waste disposal—West (U.S.)—Social aspects.
I. Title.
    E78.N4K85   1998
    363.17'99'0978—dc21   97-3459
                                                                 CIP

DEDICATION

For my father, Edward Kuletz (1921–1995),
for Corbin Harney,
>*Spiritual Leader of the Western Shoshone*
>*and tireless antinuclear activist,*

for Richard Rawles,
>*who explored this sad and*
>*beautiful landscape with me, and*

for the people of the desert

Contents

List of Illustrations/Maps

Legend of Map Symbols

⊙ Government installation or National Laboratory

☢ Radioactive activity or proposed site for nuclear waste burial

✸ Nuclear explosion

╴╶╱╶ Regional desert boundary

▨ Military Reservation or Training Area

⊕ Mescalero Apache Indian Reservation

◉ Zone Two Indian Reservation or Colony

☢ Monitored retrievable storage (MRS) proposed site

Ⓤ Uranium production

✸Ⓤ Uranium production radiation accident

List of Acronyms

GOVERNMENTAL

ACOHP	Advisory Council on Historic Preservation
AEC	Atomic Energy Commission
AIRFA	American Indian Religious Freedom Act
ARPA	Archaeological Resources Protection Act
BLM	Bureau of Land Management
DOD	Department of Defense
DOE	Department of Energy
EIS	Environmental Impact Statement
EPA	Environmental Protection Agency
LANL	Los Alamos National Laboratory
MOA	Military Operations Area
NAGPRA	Native American Graves Protection and Repatriation Act
NAWS	Naval Air Weapons Station
NDRC	National Defense Research Committee
NEPA	National Environmental Policy Act
NHPA	National Historic Preservation Act
NOTS	Naval Ordinance Test Station
NPS	National Park Service
NRC	Nuclear Regulatory Commission
NWC	Naval Weapons Center
NWPA	Nuclear Waste Policy Act
OCRWM	Office of Civilian Radioactive Waste Management
OSRD	Office of Scientific Research and Development
WIPP	Waste Isolation Pilot Project
YMP	Yucca Mountain Project

NONGOVERNMENTAL

APC	All People's Coalition
CANAP	Citizen Alert Native American Project
CCNS	Concerned Citizens for Nuclear Safety
DRI	Desert Research Institute
NACE	Native Americans for a Clean Environment
NIEC	Nevada Indian Environmental Coalition
SAIC	Science Applications International Corporation
RAMA	Rural Alliance for Military Accountability
WSNC	Western Shoshone National Council
WSNDP	Western Shoshone National Defense Project

Preface

This book focuses on the social and environmental impact of nuclearism, from its inception in the 1940s through its escalation during the Cold War to the establishment of the first U.S. deep-geologic repository for high-level nuclear waste at Yucca Mountain, Nevada, in the late 1990s. In the process it illuminates some of the hidden and unacknowledged costs of the Cold War—both environmentally and socially—in the interdesert West. It also identifies competing claims to these lands by different actors in the region—Native Americans, antinuclear activists, Euroamerican scientists, and government officials. Because of their importance to the region, Native American elders and Euroamerican government-sponsored scientists are focused on as cultural groups that promote competing truth claims about this landscape. One group views areas within the region as sacred landscapes and aboriginal homelands, and the other sees these same areas as wastelands of little economic and productive value, suitable primarily for environmental experimentation and ultimately sacrifice.

Having grown up within a defense scientific community situated for purposes of secrecy and weapons testing in the desert, I have long been aware of the combined impact and power that science and the military have had on the U.S. Southwest landscape. Most people, however, are unaware of the extent to which this landscape has been sacrificed to the "national interest," and even scholars of the U.S. West until relatively recently have ignored the militarization of the region. This study serves as the first comprehensive account of the impact of nuclearism on Native Americans in the U.S. Southwest—an account that also points to a much larger problem of nuclear colonialism worldwide, in which nuclear activities continue on lands historically inhabited by indigenous people.[1] The practice of nuclear colonialism is only now gaining recognition as nations confront the toxic legacy of fifty years of military and commercial nuclear production.

The nuclear landscape began in secrecy with the discovery of uranium in the Four Corners area, the establishment of the Manhattan Project, its associated research enterprise "Project Y," and the construction of Los Alamos on New Mexico's Pajarito Plateau. Although the nature of secret installations such as Los Alamos has changed over the last fifty years, viewing this landscape still often entails navigation through a world of electric fences, military guards, watchtowers, and code names familiar to me from my youth at a similarly secretive weapons research center. I grew up as the daughter of a weapons scientist at China Lake Naval Weapons Center, now NAWS (Naval Air Weapons Station), in eastern California. Although not widely known, the Salt Wells Valley at China Lake was an early pilot plant for the Manhattan Project, producing and testing high explosives for the first atomic bombs.[2] Hidden in the upper Mojave desert, China Lake is one of the largest weapons research and testing facilities in the world. This home of my youth is bordered by the High Sierra to the west, the dry Owens Valley to the north, Death Valley to the east, and the lower Mojave Desert to the south. Like the other research and testing centers of this study, China Lake profoundly impresses itself upon the land. Its air space is twice as large as its million-acre land space. The work of its labor force is highly secretive, as are the fruits of the labor. Much about the place is meant to assure invisibility. There is no viable lake at China Lake, and a good deal of its workforce—its scientists and technicians—work hidden behind mountains and in desert territories that are strictly guarded. Throughout much of my youth the China Lake Naval Weapons Center did not appear on maps of the area; and besides, who would expect to find a naval base with a large and highly trained scientific civilian population in the middle of the desert?[3]

Throughout the period of above-ground nuclear bomb testing at the Nevada Test Site in the 1950s and early '60s, the mushroom clouds could be seen from the China Lake testing ranges—if one knew where to look and when, and people did. Fighter jets were common above us, with their ear-shattering, window-rattling sonic booms, as were the frequent sound of massive explosions resulting from missile tests, their accompanying plumes of smoke emanating from the Coso or Argus mountain ranges. What was *not* visible in this area were the Indians, those other occupants of desert valleys, mountains, and desert springs. As a youth, I had little real knowledge of the social history of that desert, or that Indian people claiming descent from those who left an abundance of artifacts and petroglyphs still lived there. Throughout my youth in the late '50s, '60s, and '70s Indians—Western Shoshone, Timbisha Shoshone, and Owens Valley Paiute—were invisible. They weren't *not* there, they were simply invisible to most (although not all) of the white scientific research community and their families.

Whether they exist alongside the uranium mining districts, the nuclear research and development centers with their testing grounds, or the nuclear waste dumps, Native people and their lands constitute an invisible presence in areas heavily occupied by the U.S. military and the Department of Energy. Part One of *The Tainted Desert* attempts to make visible the close proximity of Indians and military and nuclear regions and to show how a consistent pattern of internal nuclear colonialism—suggesting environmental racism—might emerge. In this part I introduce not only some of the political, economic, and institutional forces responsible for the creation of this landscape but also the mechanisms of exclusion that are used to silence Indian perspectives on nuclear and land-use issues. I employ several methodologies to accomplish these goals. Using narrative historical and visual mapping strategies in conjunction with the testimony of marginalized actors to demonstrate the existence of the hidden zones of nuclear contamination helps identify the institutions and practices that serve to "legitimate" the forces contributing to the creation of such "zones of sacrifice." Detailed ethnographic empirical data from both indigenous and scientific communities contribute to the environmental history of the region and establish land-use patterns. I use a socioecological approach to compare accounts by representatives of the contesting cultures, revealing in the process the political and cultural factors that inform both scientific and Native attitudes and practices, their representations of the natural world, and how these conflict with one another in the struggle for power in the desert region surrounding Yucca Mountain.

In order to get at the root causes of this clash of cultures, Part Two examines the relationship between human and nonhuman nature, looking at how the two cultural groups—Native elders and Western scientists—view this relationship. Using a phenomenological analysis, I argue that traditional Native culture can be characterized in part as possessing an intersubjective relationship with nature, whereas Euroamerican scientific culture tends to separate the human (subject) and the nonhuman "other" (nature/object). This analysis does not present Indian intersubjectivity as any more "natural" than Euroamerican objectivity. Rather, it locates intersubjectivity within material practices (long land tenure) and a particular mode of communication (orality) that help to explain how a distinctively Indian ecological ethos might emerge. Traditional indigenous practices of subsistence living among the three major Indian ethnic groups of the Yucca Mountain area (Western Shoshone, Southern Paiute, and Owens Valley Paiute), have shaped current Indian cultural views and representations of their natural environment. Twentieth-century intrusions by Euroamericans have disrupted these practices and modified Indian representations, introducing ecological language into Indian discourses. Oral culture, communicated through stories, songs, tribal histories, and tales, also contributes to an ecological ethos different from Euroamerican values, which have been shaped by exploitive technologies, property rights, capitalism, and fear of nature. Once subjectivity in relation to the environment is understood as culturally constructed (whether by Indians or scientists), we can begin to recognize how culture influences human material practices on the land, offering at least part of the answer to how the nuclear landscape (detailed in Part One) came into being and what it might take—from a cultural standpoint—to change it.

The region I study has become very much a scientific landscape—indeed, certain areas are often referred to as "outdoor laboratories"—and science helps designate the region not only as a weapons testing ground but also as a nuclear wasteland. Scientific discourses and representations legitimate the designation of areas within this region as toxic and nuclear-waste dumping grounds—a particularly brutal objectification of the non-human world. Cybernetic models of natural processes and, specifically, the subdiscipline of radioecology have historically contributed to scientific perceptions of certain areas as experimental landscapes. Legitimating such destructive practices has helped to further marginalize the indigenous inhabitants of the region, contributing to an unacknowledged practice of environmental racism.

An ethnoecological methodology such as I employ here that lends equal credence to both Native and Euroamerican perspectives on the natural world demonstrates how one cultural view comes to dominate the other. Recognizing difference and validating the perspective of the "other" are important strategies in assessing long-standing land-use conflicts involving separate cultures that also continue to profoundly influence each other in surprising ways. Although viewing Native American knowledge about nature as culturally and socially influenced is not unusual, examining scientific representations and perspectives as such disrupts the discourse on objectivity that places science beyond the influence of culture. Science, particularly environmental science as it is practiced in this region under the auspices of the U.S. Department of Energy, is composed of an array of culturally bound knowledge traditions and practices. The nuclear waste crisis, and the problem of nuclearism in general, thus has roots not only in Euroamerican political and economic institutions but in Euroamerican cultural knowledge regimes as well. Consequently the epistemological foundations that dominate how people understand the natural world and their relationship to it contribute to the ways in which they attempt to resolve environmental crisis.

The interconnections among politics, culture, and science show up in the relationship among nuclear culture, militarism, and environmental science in the postwar era. The discourses on nature that are the product of such interconnections are part of a complex web of social and cultural practices with real material consequences, such as radiation victims, radioactive waste dumps, and sacrificial landscapes. These practices constitute part of the unacknowledged price the United States pays for global military dominance, as well as for dominance in late-capital global markets. Because this study identifies and documents the reality of nuclear colonialism, it provides a rarely seen map of the Indian populations affected by nuclearism in this region—one that can then be used as a base map for comparative analyses and further investigations of nuclear colonialism internationally and in the twenty-first century.

The often dispossessed and marginalized people who inhabit these zones of sacrifice have a unique perspective stemming from their firsthand experience with nuclearism and nuclear colonialism. This book attempts to make the arguments of this marginalized minority heard over technical discussions of the feasibility of nuclear waste storage and, in some way, to lend credence to their forms of knowledge within the public debate on the nuclear waste crisis. I make no attempt to hide my bias in this debate—it is with those who have been silenced by the military occupation of the West.

When I started this project and began to investigate the way in which nuclear dumps, testing ranges, and military/scientific research centers tended to be on or near Native American traditional lands and reservations, I saw that my own homeland was part of a larger pattern of secrecy. This project for me has been more than academic, growing out of love for a landscape that I have experienced firsthand. It is also an attempt to come to terms with the social history of this interdesert region—a history denied me by the Euroamerican-centered culture of my youth, and of today.[4]

By documenting the stories of those who were and continue to be made invisible (American Indians) and naming those who choose to be invisible for reasons of power and so-called national security (the U.S. military and "private" nuclear commercial enterprises), I will show that two very different narratives about this desert land occupy the same place—one that, by implication, sees it as a landscape of national sacrifice and another that sees it as a geography of the sacred and a crucial link to cultural survival.

This book documents a contemporary problem, and the field of its investigation is constantly changing. Plutonium stockpiles are shifted from place to place, legal battles are ongoing, plans to open dumps for radioactive materials get delayed. Ending this story is therefore arbitrary but necessary. Though my investigation and account end in 1997 the struggle to contend with nuclear waste and the government's continuation of domestic military expansion continues. With the end of the Cold War and the reduction of arms and the growing recognition that commercial nuclear power is untenable, the United States has a unique opportunity to redress some of the wrongs committed during that long twilight conflict and to reconsider our reliance on nuclear power and move toward a nuclear-free future. This book is my contribution to that process of renewal and reconciliation.

Valerie Kuletz
Berkeley, 1997

Acknowledgments

I would like to acknowledge the University of California at Santa Cruz and the Board of Sociology at UCSC for help in funding parts of the fieldwork and in the writing of the dissertation that became this book. The "Dissertation Fellowship" I received from the Sociology Board proved especially helpful.

I would also like to thank my dissertation committee: Donna Haraway, Andrew Szasz, Robert Connell, John Brown Childs, and Raoul Birnbaum for their direction and encouragement. Special thanks go to Donna Haraway, who provided unfailing enthusiasm and commitment to the goals of this project.

For expertise on specific areas I would like to thank Chris Shuey and Don Hancock with the Southwest Research and Information Center in Albuquerque, N.M., for information on uranium mining and the Waste Isolation Pilot Project (WIPP); the people at Concerned Citizens for Nuclear Safety in Santa Fe, N.M.—particularly Susan Hirschberg—for information on WIPP and Los Alamos; Phil Klasky on Ward Valley; and Joe Masco on Los Alamos and the New Mexico region. For information on Yucca Mountain thanks goes to those working with the Yucca Mountain Project who made it possible to explore Yucca Mountain and the complexities of the project; also to Karl Johnson of Nevada's Nuclear Waste Project

Office, and to the people at Citizen Alert and Citizen Alert Native American Project in Nevada. I am especially grateful to Jared Dawson, who donated his considerable cartographic expertise to produce many of the maps in this book.

I also want to thank the many activists who talked with me about their work, sent me valuable information, and taught me by their actions about commitment in social justice; such as Jennifer Olaranna Viereck, Grace Bukowski, Heidie Black-eye, Helen Herrera, Corbin Harney, and Willie. I am indebted to the work of many tireless individuals who run watchdog organizations, create maps of contaminated areas, edit and write newsletters, distribute informational flyers, show up to speak at Department of Energy scoping sessions, and organize protests. Such people monitor and document government and industry activities in these out-of-the-way places, often working anonymously for change. Without their work there would be few threads to follow.

Friends and family who saw this long project to its end and supported me in numerous ways include Diana Drake Wilson, Patricia Allen, Giovanna DiChiro, Kathleen Boehm, Kathy Kuletz, Ivan Kuletz, Karl Kuletz, Robert Atkinson, Bryan Rawles, Janet McCandless, Cecelia Littlepage, and Bob Cowart. Special thanks goes to readers of the manuscript: Kai Erikson, T.V. Reed, Hal Rothman, Joe Masco, Jessie Lawson, and Sumner Carnahan. My editors at Routledge—Jayne Fargnoli, Heidi Freund, and Ilene Kalish—were helpful and encouraging, believing in the project and working to promote it.

I'd like to express my gratitude and respect to the Indian people of the interdesert region who graciously gave their time to discuss the important issues facing their communities, especially Pauline Esteves, Corbin Harney, William (Bill) Rosse Sr., Ian Zabarte, Dorothy Purley, Bertha Moose, Gaylene Moose, Clara Rambeau, Marion Zucco, Lalovi Miller, and the women elders at the Moapa Paiute reservation.

Most importantly, I would like to express my gratitude to my life partner, Richard Rawles, whose support made this project possible and whose encouragement, intellectual insights, and developmental editing skills were invaluable. His contributions are found throughout this book. Writing a book is always a collective endeavor, and Richard's contributions are extensive.

Our eyes
Are armed, but we are strangers to the stars,
And strangers to the mystic beast and bird,
And strangers to the plant and to the mine.
The injured elements say, "Not in us;"
And night and day, ocean and continent,
Fire, plant and mineral say, "Not in us;"
And haughtily return us stare for stare.
For we invade them impiously for gain;
We devastate them unreligiously,
And coldly ask their pottage, not their love.
—RALPH WALDO EMERSON
  from the poem *Blight*

I bless the mountain by asking the mountain to
bless us.
—CORBIN HARNEY
  Western Shoshone Spiritual Leader

PART ONE

Mapping the
Nuclear Landscape

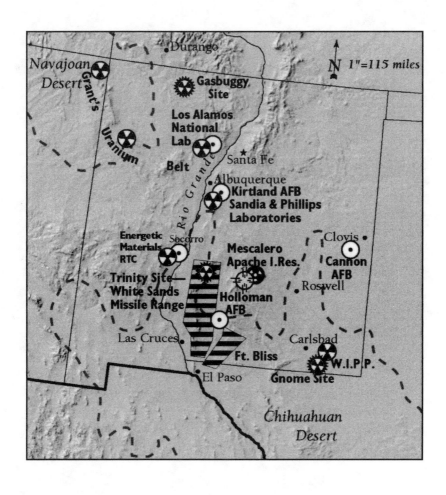

· 1 ·

Introduction

Mapping the Invisible Nuclear Landscape

In April 1995, while visiting a group of Southern Paiute women elders on the Moapa reservation in the desert 45 miles northeast of Las Vegas, Nevada, I was told how tribal members used to drive up into the mountains that separated the reservation from the Nevada Test Site and watch tests of atomic bombs. As one woman recalled:

> They didn't tell us how dangerous it was. They just said in the news media and the papers that there was going to be a test. So naturally, you know, a whole bunch of us after we got off work, away we'd go headed right toward that place. And we'd get on the road there, and there'd be miles and miles and miles of cars just going to see it. We'd all get out and get on the little hills, you know, all around there and we could see right across there where it was, this big beautiful cloud! Just all white and fiery, you know, and just gorgeous! They didn't tell us how dangerous it was. They just told us they were going to have it at such and such a time. And now I think, I think personally, that we're suffering—almost all of us have something wrong with us. I've had thyroid problems.[1]

No one at the time, or in the years that followed, thought to warn them that exposing themselves to fallout might prove dangerous to their health. The Moapa women told me stories about how they foraged for wild plants near the Test Site, ate rabbit and deer that roamed the Test Site, and, as was their custom during the hot summers, moved their beds outside to sleep in the cool night air:

> So in the summertime in the fifties . . . the reservation wasn't really that well established. Some of us didn't have electricities. So in the summertime when it got hot we moved everything outdoors into now what we call the little arbors. And every family made one of those in the summertime, and they took out the stove, table, and chairs. And we'd even take our beds out and sleep outside underneath the trees. All of our activities were outside during those times, during times that they were having the tests. And at that time we didn't have indoor plumbing or indoor water. Our water ran down in ditches along in front of the homes, so that was our water. I mean, like I say, we lived outdoors in the summertime. We never moved back in until the fall when it got cold. Everything went outdoors, and that's where we were in the summertime. So during the nuclear tests, well, we were still outside.[2]

These domestic activities were common long before the time of the nuclear testing, but they take on new meaning when we recognize how nuclear contamination moves through the food chain and water supply, and through the air in the form of radiation fallout. With their greater reliance on obtaining sustenance from the land, Indian communities may have been far more exposed than, for instance, people in nearby Las Vegas, or even other downwinders in Utah and Arizona. In recent years the 250-member tribe claims to have suffered from increased incidence of cancers. As eight of us were seated around a fold-up table in the tribal council hall, one Moapa elder woman said she had lost three nephews to cancer. Another described her own struggles with thyroid disease, and another with ovarian cancer. Others had similar stories.

With incomplete and inaccessible health records to rely on, no official epidemiological study has been undertaken of the tribe's past exposure to radiation.[3] The extent of official disregard for the health of Moapa tribal members was brought strikingly home to me when one of the elders told me that I had been one of the few people from outside the tribal community to ask about possible links between their health and the community's exposure to nuclear tests conducted on the Nevada Test Site—less than 60 miles from their homes. As noted by a Department of Energy publication: "Through 1992, when the President halted underground nuclear testing, the United States conducted 1,054 nuclear tests, of which 928 occurred at the Nevada Test Site. The remaining 126 nuclear tests were conducted at other sites in and outside Nevada."[4] From 1951, when a B-50 bomber dropped the first atomic bomb on the Nevada desert, to 1963 the U.S. government detonated more than 120 atomic bombs into the atmosphere over the Nevada Test Site.

The plight of "downwinders" in southern Utah, the use of soldiers in nuclear tests, and the recent Department of Energy revelations that civilians were used as subjects in nuclear medical experiments have received, if not extensive, at least partial media coverage.[5] Such reports only partly tell the story of the human cost of nuclear weapons development in the United States. Curiously, the vulnerability of Native Americans living near sites of nuclear weapons research, development, and testing has gone virtually unnoticed. Western Shoshone and Southern Paiute individuals, as well as individuals from other Indian tribes, have reported increased incidences of cancer on their reservations and "colonies." Increased numbers of birth defects have also been noted.

Most historians and government officials have ignored the presence of certain populations at risk in areas of nuclear weapons development and testing—populations whose subsistence economies depend heavily on land resources, including its flora, fauna, and water. This neglect is not accidental. When not deliberately part of official secrecy, it reveals an all-too-familiar pattern of disregard for the people that inhabit these desert areas, masking an exploitation of their land that goes back to the beginning of the so-called westward expansion. This is a landscape—a nuclear landscape—too often ripened by sacrifice, for sacrifice, shrouded in secrecy, and plundered of its wealth.

One method for piercing the veil of secrecy cloaking these landscapes is to listen to the stories of those who live on the land (those who are often invisible to Euroamericans) and to examine their "unofficial" maps that identify where and how nuclearism has affected them. This methodology relies on and uses local knowledge to make visible geographies of sacrifice—areas of the United States set aside for weapons testing and development, uranium mining, and military training that reveal a pattern of what several commentators have termed nuclear colonialism.[6] My use of the term "nuclear colonialism" attempts to situate the emergent nuclear landscape in the arid regions of the American Southwest within a larger history of U.S. internal colonialism,[7] that is, within the expropriation of native lands and the displacement of North America's indigenous population by their European conquerors.

The use of spatial coordinates (maps of designated areas) and historical and contemporary narratives locate and delineate the nuclear landscape that has emerged through time and space in the American Southwest of the late twentieth century. Fifty years of the unbridled pursuit of nuclear power have obscured a geography of sacrifice that, when mapped, shows how racism, militarism, and economic imperialism have combined to marginalize a people and a land that many within government and industry, consciously or not, regard as expendable.[8] Many of the same lands that have been used for weapons testing and development are currently being designated as waste repositories for the byproducts of America's headlong pursuit of nuclear power. For instance, if Yucca Mountain in Nevada is designated the United States's high-level nuclear waste repository, most of the waste from commercial reactors destined for this site will be transported by truck and by rail only a few miles from the Moapa reservation. Yucca Mountain is partially within the Nevada Test Site, on land claimed as traditional homeland by both Western Shoshone and Southern Paiute people. Thus, a tribe such as the Moapa Paiutes, or the Yomba band of the Western Shoshone, or the Timbisha Shoshone, encounter nuclearism at various stages of its life cycle (in both testing and waste disposal). Like radiation itself, nuclearism doesn't simply disappear once the combatants have called off the dogs of war.

Seeing and Deterritoriality

Naming and mapping the nuclear landscape opens a space for other critical narratives to emerge: narratives about science (and what constitutes objectivity), power (and the representations used to legitimate it), racism, and cultural marginalization. It provides an avenue to explore some of the ways human culture and politics transform place and "nature." Most importantly, mapping the nuclear landscape employs the political practice of *seeing* purposefully unmarked and secret landscapes; it makes visible those who have been obscured and silenced within those landscapes.

Once made visible, the zones of sacrifice that comprise these local landscapes can begin to be pieced together to reveal regional, national, and even global patterns of *deterritoriality*—the loss of commitment by modern nation-states (and even the international community) to particular lands or regions. Deterritoriality is a term used to explain the construction of national and international sacrifice zones. It is a phenomenon that is becoming an increasingly common feature of late twentieth-century industrialized societies, where extensive zones of sacrifice are allowed to emerge as the price for, and inevitable result of, a particular set of power requirements.[9] As such, deterritoriality is a particularly dramatic form of disembodiment—the perceived separation between self and nature. This pattern of land use, on such a massive scale, indicates one of the cultural differences between capitalist, late-industrial Euroamerican societies and many Native American and indigenous societies for whom land is linked not only more immediately to economic subsistence but also to their cultural viability and religious identity. With such cultural differences in mind, the practice of deterritoriality can be seen as a form of cultural imperialism.

Part One of this book provides an historical and spatial backdrop against which, in Part Two, I investigate the complex struggles—with their conflicting narratives and their corresponding cultural politics—currently being engaged over the siting of the world's first high-level nuclear waste repository at Yucca Mountain, Nevada. The Yucca Mountain story must be seen within the larger context of the nuclear landscape of the American Southwest interdesert region.[10]

The nuclear landscapes in this region began to emerge in the 1940s and have included many aspects of nuclear activity—from uranium mining and milling to the development, manufacture, and testing of weapons to the present activity of siting nuclear waste repositories.[11] Uranium mining, nuclear weapons testing, and nuclear waste dumps are not the only activities that have transformed the West and Southwest over the last fifty years, but they comprise significant activities that demonstrate how nuclearism can be understood as a form of internal colonialism. The concept of internal colonialism has been used by political scholars, such as Gramsci, to describe political and economic inequalities between regions within a given society. Like colonialism, where "core" countries in the "first world" exploit "peripheral" countries for their natural resources, internal colonialism is characterized by one region—usually a metropolis that is closely associated with state power—exploiting a colonylike peripheral region. In the case of nuclear colonialism, what is seen as usable, sparsely populated, arid geographic space is used as a dumping ground or a testing field to allow more powerful regions to continue their present form of energy production or to continue to exert military power globally. The relationship between core and periphery is typically one of exploitation, where the human populations in the periphery usually consist of people with a different cultural, racial, or class background. The presence of internal colonialism argues against the myth of an integrated and truly democratic society, and it argues that such regional inequalities are not temporary but necessary features of industrial society—features we choose not to see in order to maintain the myth of American equality and democracy.

Mapping the nuclear landscape in and around Native lands also provides an environmental and geosociological history of a region during our entry into the nuclear era, an era that in a very spectacular and menacing way ushers us into the realm of the "unnatural" with the transuranic elements.[12] As a cultural sociology of nature and its representation the story of the nuclear landscape describes both a literal and figurative transformation of nature and the profound consequences of this transformation on people, in particular, on American Indians in the interdesert Southwest.

The Emerging Landscape

Science and the military meet in the deserts of the Southwest literally to transform the landscape. While militarization plays a large part in the creation of the nuclear landscape, this landscape is the product of an even larger social and technological transformation that emerged most forcefully in the second half of the twentieth century. The emergence of nuclear culture occurred simultaneously with an escalation in technological knowledge and practices—nuclear power, commercial air travel, television, computers—that has profoundly changed our lives and our environment.

The technological transformations of the postwar era are themselves part of a process of rationalization—a particular kind of rationalization—that is hundreds of years old and that has always resulted in hardship for Native peoples:

> [I]t may be the central assumption of technological society that there is virtue in overpowering nature and native peoples. The Indian problem today, as it always has been, is directly related to the needs of technological societies to find and obtain remotely located resources, in order to fuel an incessant and intrinsic demand for growth and technological fulfillment. The process began in our country hundreds of years ago when we wanted land and gold. Today it continues because we want coal, oil, uranium, fish, and more land. . . . All these acts were and are made possible by one fundamental rationalization: that our society represents the ultimate expression of evolution, its final flowering. It is this attitude and its corresponding belief that native societies represent an earlier, lower form on the evolutionary ladder, upon which we occupy the highest rung, that seem to unify all modern political perspectives.[13]

Having emerged piece by piece over the last fifty years, the nuclear landscape constitutes as much a social and political geography as it does an environmental region. Because it is a rather recent phenomenon and has taken time to emerge in a recognizable form, because it exists in desert lands, and because it is the child of secret operations hidden behind the veil of national security, the nuclear landscape is to a large extent an invisible landscape. One could argue that it exists in many places throughout the continental United States, including Oak Ridge, Tennessee; nuclear processing centers in Kentucky and Ohio; Hanford, Washington; Rocky Flats, Colorado; and the Pantex plant in Amarillo, Texas.[14] Indeed, as a result of the Cold War, the soil of the North American Great Plains has been seeded with a thousand intercontinental ballistic missiles—sentinels of the nuclear age.[15] And the eastern United States contains a dense constellation of nuclear facilities of all kinds, including the majority of nuclear power plants in the country. With cooling ponds overflowing, these facilities have reached the limits of their storage capacity for the byproducts of nuclear-power generation. Thus, in order to continue production, utility companies must now find repositories for waste that remains dangerous for more than 240,000 years.[16]

Though the nuclear landscape can be said to exist throughout the United States, nowhere has it emerged as extensively as in the Southwest interdesert region. This is because the nuclear landscape is much more than a collection of weapons stockpiles and production facilities; it includes large land masses for uranium mining and milling, the testing of high-tech weaponry, and waste repositories—all found in the Southwest.

Originally chosen for its inaccessibility and inhospitable character—making secrecy easier to maintain—the interdesert region now stands as a testament to our entry into the nuclear age and to the dominance of the military-industrial complex in the late twentieth century. Encompassing most of the Southwest, the nuclear landscape covers a swath of land that includes much of New Mexico, Nevada, southeastern California, and parts of Arizona, Utah, Colorado, and Texas. (To the north, in the West, we can also add parts of the state of Washington and Idaho.) This region (see Figure 1.1) includes all five of the major North American deserts: the lower Great Basin desert in Nevada and the southeastern margins of California, the Navajoan desert in the Four Corners area, the upper Chihuahuan desert in New Mexico, the upper Sonoran desert in California and Arizona, and the Mojave Desert in California, Nevada, and Arizona.[17]

Within this region stand thousands of abandoned and unreclaimed open-pit and underground uranium mines and mills, two proposed national sites for deep geologic nuclear waste repositories of monumental proportions, all potential sites for the nation's above-ground temporary nuclear waste containment facilities, a constellation of other nuclear pollution points such as "unofficial" waste holding stations, and secret testing sites. The nation's largest nuclear accident—known as the Rio Puerco accident—took place in northern New Mexico.[18] Home to "downwinders," or victims of airborne radiation, this region also includes the site where the U.S. government has detonated more than 928 above-ground and below-ground nuclear bombs, as well as hundreds of secret and previously undisclosed nuclear tests. This region contains important nuclear research and development centers, with their own "private" on-site nuclear waste disposal areas of significant size. The region has seen more military land

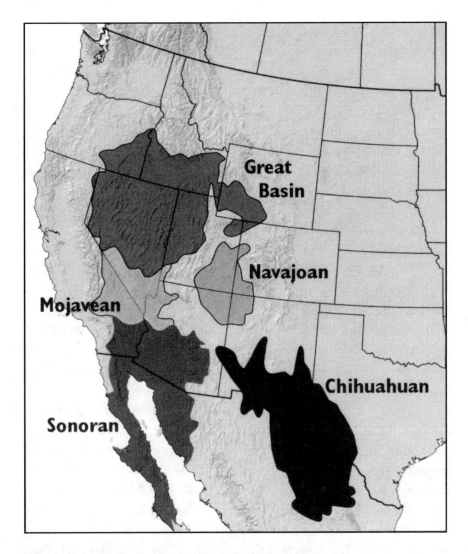

Figure 1.1 The North American interdesert region

Cartography production by Jared Dawson

withdrawals than any other region in the United States, eliminating many millions of acres of land from public access, transforming whole mountain ranges and desert valleys into massive weapons testing theaters. Finally, it contains a site where shallow burial of "low-level" nuclear waste is scheduled to occur. Significantly, this region is home to the majority of *land-based* American Indians alive today on the North American continent.

The Indian Landscape

In this Indian country two landscapes—Indian and nuclear—meet at nearly every point of the nuclear cycle, from uranium mining to weapons testing to the disposal of nuclear waste.[19] For example: Nuclearism in this large region began in the early 1940s with the mining and milling of uranium ore largely on Navajo, Hopi, Pueblo, and Ute Mountain Ute land in the Navajoan desert. This uranium fueled the atomic bomb developed at Los Alamos, located adjacent and near traditional Pueblo lands on the Pajarito Plateau of New Mexico. In 1945, the first testing of the atomic bomb occurred at Alamagordo (now White Sands), New Mexico, near the Mescalero Apache reservation. In the 1950s, ancestral lands of the Western Shoshone and Southern Paiute at the intersection of the Great Basin and Mojave deserts were seized by the federal government, in violation of the 1863 Treaty of Ruby Valley, for use as the nation's testing fields for nuclear weapons (the Nevada Test Site)—an area where more nuclear bombs have been detonated than on any other single, similar size region on the globe.

Today, the only above-ground, temporary nuclear waste storage facilities under consideration have been on the Nevada Test Site and the Mescalero Apache, Skull Valley Goshute, and Fort McDermitt Paiute-Shoshone reservations. The nation's moderate-level nuclear waste storage facility, called WIPP (for Waste Isolation Pilot Project), is in the same general region as the Mescalero Apache reservation in the Chihuahuan desert.[20] Radioactive waste from research at Los Alamos National Laboratory is now stored at "Area G," which borders the San Ildefonso Pueblo and is near the Santa Clara Pueblo's lands. Low-level nuclear waste is targeted for disposal in the Mojave Desert's Ward Valley, home of the Fort Mojave Indians and the Chemehuevi of the Colorado River Indian tribes. Finally, the proposed premiere site for the nation's high-level nuclear waste repository is Yucca Mountain—"holy land" to the Western Shoshone, Southern Paiute, and Owens Valley Paiute.

This discursive map demonstrates how the development, testing, and waste storage of nuclear materials in the highly militarized landscapes of the western United States might be understood as a form of environmental racism. At the very least, it sets the stage for asking how land use, racism, power, and internal colonialism intersect in this region. This mapping not only makes *visible* the millions of acres that were removed from access for weapons testing and development in the postwar years, it also reveals the peoples affected and displaced by these activities. Once revealed, the nuclear landscape can be perceived and experienced differently; it can be seen as one landscape superimposed upon another: a *landscape of national sacrifice*, an *expendable landscape*, over what many North American Indians understand as a *geography of the sacred*, a geography where spiritual and cultural life are woven directly into the landscape itself.

The Wasteland Discourse

Along with their Indian inhabitants, these dry, arid regions are perceived and discursively interpreted as marginal within the dominant Euroamerican perspective. Environmental science discourse often supports the pre-existing settler discourse about desert lands as barren wastelands by organizing bioregions within hierarchies of value according to productive capacity. In this scheme, deserts are placed at the bottom of the ladder. They become marginal lands. Similarly, American Indians in these regions tend to be placed at the bottom of the ladder of economic productivity. For example: Indians have the lowest per capita income of any population group in the United States, the highest rates of malnutrition, the highest rates of infant mortality, the highest rates of plague disease, death by exposure, and so on.[21]

These desert lands commonly referred to as wastelands, or badlands, are, ironically, very rich in energy resources. Indian reservations alone account for two-thirds of all U.S. "domestic" uranium reserves, one-quarter of oil and natural gas reserves in the United States, and one-third of U.S. low-sulfur coal reserves, not to mention substantial reserves of minerals such as gold, silver, copper, bauxite, and others.[22] The ironic and continuing designation of this resource-rich terrain as wasteland in fact represents a very important means of justifying the relentless plunder of the region through highly environmentally destructive extractive technologies. The wasteland designation also supports the region's use as a large-scale waste dump and weapons testing range in the minds of policy makers, government bureaucrats, and military officials. The wasteland discourse remains useful for private corporate energy and waste management industries as well.[23] Bolstering this wasteland perspective are a variety of scientific discourses that serve to legitimate these industrial practices. The "logical" outcome of such practices renders not only the land but the people who live on it expendable.

Indeed, today's version of the wasteland discourse has serious implications for the very real bodies that inhabit the zones of sacrifice within the nuclear landscape.[24] Within the context of a nuclear society that produces deadly byproducts that alter and transform the earth and living organisms, those paying the highest price for advanced technologies are often those for whom technology offers the least benefits.

Virtually unknown to the public at large, an alternative narrative exists about these dry desert places. Rather than a no man's land, or wasteland, many Indians describe these deserts as places of origin and emergence, as holy places, and sacred geographies. Much controversy surrounds these alternative discourses. Whether they represent resurgent Indian cultural identity or political postures stemming from an ingenuous "higher" moral understanding, or whether they articulate genuine, long-sustained indigenous wisdom founded on an earth-based, animistic cosmology—these alternative stories about this landscape are as much a part of the region's cultural history as any of those that have emerged in the past 500 years of European and American occupation and dominance. (The co-optation of such views by "New Age" sympathizers—largely white and middle class—demonstrates their power over the imagination.) To counterbalance the powerful wasteland discourse, these alternative Indian discourses on sacred geographies must be made continually visible, that is, discursively mapped in conjunction with the nuclear landscape. At the very least they provide a perspective from which to view the Euroamerican "frontier," "pioneer," and even scientific narratives about place in this region. They underscore the diversity of cultural constructions of place and nature and reinforce the view that ethnic groups, including whites, are often bound by their own cultural lenses, that different cultures create very different landscapes, both narratively and materially. While the Euroamerican narrative in this instance results in the nuclear landscape, these preexisting and continuing indigenous representations of nature and place refuse to remain silent, refuse to acquiesce to the wasteland discourse. The outcome of this dialogue between different representational systems for the land and our relationship to it will be explored in more depth in Part Two.

Interlocking Desires: Science, Industry, and the Military

Behind the sacrificial geography of the nuclear landscape lie the Cold War and the development of nuclear power, those who manipulated these events, and those who prospered by them.

The United States has paid a high price for "winning" the Cold War and for its use of nuclear energy in the pursuit of global economic and military superiority. But the actual price of the Cold War, and of "national competitiveness," hasn't even begun to be tallied. An exploration of the nuclear waste crisis reveals the inequitable distribution of payment, weighing most heavily on the disenfranchised, and thus contributes to a more accurate assessment of what "collateral" damage has been inflicted in the pursuit of capitalist political hegemony. The so-called "price" for "freedom" is paid for by those with the least power, the least chance to benefit from U.S. control of global order and the wealth it brings. If we look beneath the rhetoric of progress so common in the postwar twentieth century—a rhetoric that equates nuclear technology with unlimited clean power—we find a familiar triad: the military, science, and industry. These comprise the institutions that have most benefited from nuclearism and whose interlocking desires have resulted in, among other things, the emergence of a nuclear wasteland in the interdesert region populated by communities with far less prestige, privilege, and power.

What was needed for the nuclear industry and the military weapons complex at its inception in the 1940s was a landscape in which weapons development could be hidden and weapons testing could proceed undisturbed. As Hal Rothman notes about Los Alamos in *On Rims and Ridges*:

> Ironically, the very attributes that protected the Pajarito Plateau [home of Los Alamos] from the systematic colonization that engulfed much of New Mexico before the 1940s made it attractive for this secret project. Seeking a remote locale to hide those researching the possibility of creating the single most dangerous human weapon invented up to that time, federal and military officials wanted a place with minimal distraction and little chance of discovery or subversion. The Pajarito Plateau fit such requirements. It had never become thoroughly integrated into the economy of modern America, and in the 1940s it remained as it had always been: remote, peripheral, and marginal to the mainstream. . . . The region did not offer industrial society

enough to justify development. Before the 1940s, the Pajarito Plateau failed the measure of importance in modern Industrial society.[25]

By inverted logic, the landscape of much of the Southwest was viewed by the state as desirable because of its undesirability. This was true not just for the nuclear industry and the Atomic Energy Commission but also for various branches of the military that established centers of "conventional," or nonnuclear, weapons development here—a move that required the expropriation of millions of acres of land for "military reservations." (The desirability of "undesirable" land will also mark the nuclear waste era.) Secrecy played a crucial role in the inception of this landscape, particularly for two of the three powerful players in this terrain: the scientific establishment and the military. The story of the third player, transnational corporations engaged in uranium mining, concerns invisibility in another way. Rather than cultivate invisibility for reasons of secrecy, the uranium industry exploited the low visibility and lack of political power of the semisovereign Indian nations (reservations) to bypass environmental protection standards and job safety regulations, to bypass (for decades, and with the cooperation of federal agencies) their responsibility to inform uranium miners of the deadly hazards of their occupations, as well as to ensure a high profit margin in the extraction, processing, and sale of uranium ore to the secret scientific-military complex.[26]

The forces and players behind the promotion of nuclearism are often as invisible as the landscapes destined to hold its waste. Since the two primary sources of nuclear waste are commercial nuclear reactors for electricity and military activities such as weapons development, production, and testing, it stands to reason that the primary players are the nuclear industry and the military. (A very small amount of the total high-level nuclear waste stream—less than 1 percent—comes from medical uses.[27]) The technical knowledge to produce and run the nuclear programs, however, whether for weapons or commerce, comes from a third player, the scientific community, which provides nuclear researchers, engineers, and technicians. The first player—commercial industry—legitimates its involvement by claiming a desire to use nuclear power to fuel "national competitiveness." The second player—the military—legitimates its involvement through claiming a desire to maintain "national security."[28]

The third player—the scientific community—legitimates its involvement by donning the cloak of neutrality (insisting that science and technology are essentially neutral and not social or political practices) and arguing that *not* to research and develop nuclear technology somehow violates a basic human imperative to pursue knowledge. Indeed, for scientists lured by lucrative research grants in the postwar years, the pursuit of nuclear science proved absolutely seductive, and they responded by vigorously supporting the "Atoms for Peace" program that sustained nuclear technological research. And the seducer, in large part, was the military.

Atoms for Peace, however, could not be separated from Atoms for War. Hoping to ensure a steady supply of weapons-grade plutonium (a byproduct of nuclear fission energy from commercial nuclear reactors), the U.S. government launched, in 1951, a policy of promoting commercial nuclear power that—although nuclear power has become less popular in the United States—remains with us today, approximately forty years later.[29] As K. S. Shrader-Frechette notes in *Burying Uncertainty*:

> The top lobbyist for the nuclear industry, the president of the Atomic Industrial Forum, has confirmed what numerous government committee reports show. Commercial nuclear fission began, and was pursued, only because government leaders wanted to justify continuing military expenditures in nuclear-related areas and to obtain weapons-grade plutonium.[30]

To entice the utility industries to enter the nuclear arena required government subsidies and liability legislation. Because nuclear power posed serious economic and safety problems, U.S. corporations demanded indemnity legislation to safeguard their assets in case of catastrophic accidents. They also demanded subsidies for the huge overhead costs in development and research.[31] And they got what they wanted. Influenced by military interests, "fission-generated electricity began only because the government provided more than $100 billion in subsidies (for research, development, waste storage and insurance) to the nuclear industry."[32] In 1957, Congress passed into law the Price-Anderson Act, limiting the utilities' accident liability. Not until 1982, however, did Congress assume responsibility for finding "safe" waste burial sites by passing the Nuclear Waste Policy Act (NWPA), thereby relieving industry from responsibility for waste disposal. The belated legislation recognized that earlier optimistic projections for recycling waste were grossly exaggerated and served to shore up public confidence in the industry's ability to deal with nuclear waste, which—by the late 1970s—was becoming unraveled.

Today, the 19 percent of U.S. electricity needs that are met through nuclear power continues to be heavily subsidized by the federal government, thus weakening any claims that nuclear-generated electricity is an economically productive strategy for power generation. Some scientists have even claimed that current U.S. government subsidies for commercial reactors amount to more than $20 billion per year.[33] Such subsidies remain invisible to the general public and may come as a shock to those who believe that we live in a democracy governed by the "invisible hand" of the "free" market. The nuclear energy market appears to be driven—historically at least—by the "invisible hand" of the military.

In the end, both kinds of nuclear activity—atoms for peace and atoms for war—result in the same problem: high-level nuclear waste. By the year 2010, in the United States alone, the so-called peaceful use of nuclear power will have generated 70,000 metric tons of high-level nuclear waste.[34] Competing with this accumulation of lethal materials is the military's current weapons-grade plutonium stockpile; that weighs in at 33.5 metric tons, which is in addition to the military's 55.5 metric tons of plutonium in nuclear warheads, as well as its ever-increasing moderate and "low-level" nuclear waste. The powerful triad responsible for these materials have fundamentally interrelated interests. All of them—the nuclear scientific community, the nuclear (and uranium) industry, and the military—can be found in the uranium mining districts, the nuclear and military testing ranges, and the nuclear research and development facilities throughout the interdesert regions that make up the nuclear landscape.

· 2 ·

Tragedy at the
Center of the Universe

The Uranium Story

On a crisp autumn afternoon in 1995 my husband and I drove west from Albuquerque to the Laguna Pueblo and then to the small village of Paguate to interview Mrs. Dorothy Purley, a Laguna Pueblo woman who had worked in New Mexico's Grants uranium district when its mines were viable. Paguate is an old village, the requisite Catholic church at its center, with dirt roads winding around clusters of small, earth-colored adobe dwellings. To get to Paguate we had to drive through the recently capped-off Jackpile-Paguate uranium mine. The disrupted landscape appeared endless; one could not see where the mine began and where it ended—it was everywhere. From Mrs. Purley's kitchen, its walls painted a brilliant turquoise blue, I could see the massive mine stretching out in all directions. I could also see the enlarged thyroid on Dorothy's neck. She later confirmed she was suffering from cancer, which is not uncommon in this section of the nuclear landscape. As she told me:

> My mother died of it . . . my brother died of it! My aunt! How many aunts and how many uncles have died? And you know it's just a shame that DOE doesn't believe what's going on. . . .

I'm in that same situation right now. This cancer has really ruined my health. . . . You know it really hurts, and I'm standing here living on borrowed life right now. I don't know when my time is going to expire, but all I do is keep praying that God will continue to give me my strength. . . . I'm too young to die. I'm not ready to die. That's why I'm up and about, going here and there [speaking on behalf of radiation victims]. When they call me, I go![1]

At first, Dorothy stayed home because she felt ashamed of her sickness, but her sister convinced her to make her story public, even within her own community, to break the unspoken code of silence. As her sister said: "People have to *know* what's wrong, people have to *see* what's wrong, maybe that way our people will understand what is going on on the Laguna Reservation, mainly in Paguate."[2]

Dorothy said that a nineteen-year-old had recently passed away because of prostate cancer, as had a fifteen-year old with leukemia; that her brother-in-law had skin cancer; and that the number of miscarriages on the reservation had increased radically since the uranium mining began, as well as birth defects and serious respiratory and allergy ailments. She spoke of villagers finding rabbits riddled with internal tumors. The list of radiation-related incidents was not unlike that enumerated by the Moapa Paiute women living near the Nevada Test Site. Only the Laguna landscape was pitted with uranium mines instead of bomb craters.

Those who have attempted to inform the public about uranium mining and milling in the Four Corners area refer to the postwar period as a "hidden holocaust," a tragic legacy of the Cold War. Still, today, few Americans are aware of this particular story of national sacrifice. Most tourists speak about the Four Corners area with admiration for its beauty and share the colonist's fascination with its "picturesque" Indian cultures. Uranium fields aren't on the AAA road map of Indian Country.

The Four Corners area, where New Mexico, Arizona, Utah, and Colorado meet, contains two-thirds of U.S. uranium deposits, most within reservation boundaries. Located within much of the Navajoan Desert, or Painted Desert (also regarded as an extension of the Great Basin), this uranium-rich area of the Colorado Plateau is known as the Grants Uranium Belt. It is the first node on the network of pollution sites stretching out across the map of the nuclear landscape.

Arid-ecosystems geologists who promote hazardous waste disposal in desert regions describe the region this way:

> [The Navajoan Desert] is located in northeastern Arizona, southeastern Utah, and the northwestern corner of New Mexico and is best correlated with the exposure of the Chinle Formation, which contains variously colored clay shales. Most of the area is composed of valley slopes, plains, and badlands, located between sandstone hogbacks. *The Chinle Formation is of interest to the energy industry because of the naturally occurring deposits of uranium in the interbedded sandstone and conglomerate strata and the clays of the deep shale beds, as well as oil and gas deposits in deeper formations.* The clays were formed in swamplands and frequently have high concentrations of smectite (a swelling clay) that may reduce the hydraulic conductivity of the soil, an important consideration in waste disposal facility siting.[3] [My italics.]

This geologic discourse is typical of those that, while noting the importance of these formations for "the energy industry," leave out the existence of its human inhabitants, many of whom are Indian. What first appears as a purely objective scientific account upon closer examination is little of the sort; it is an account for use by the energy industry. However, living on the "Chinle Formation" is one of the largest concentrations of Indians in North America, as well as a significant number of Spanish-speaking people.

The Scale of the Uranium Operations

Because of the density of uranium deposits in this area and because a cheap and expendable labor force could be quickly mobilized there, "as much as *90 percent* of the country's uranium mining and milling have been undertaken on or immediately adjacent to Indian land since the mineral became a profitable commodity in the early '50s."[4] Indeed, Indian activists and their supporters cite just this kind of information when accusing the United States of nuclear colonialism (see figure 2.1).

In 1941 uranium was discovered by the U.S. Bureau of Indian Affairs in the Monument Valley and the Carrizo Mountains on the Navajo reservation in Arizona. "From 1942 to 1945 over 11,000 tons of uranium-bearing

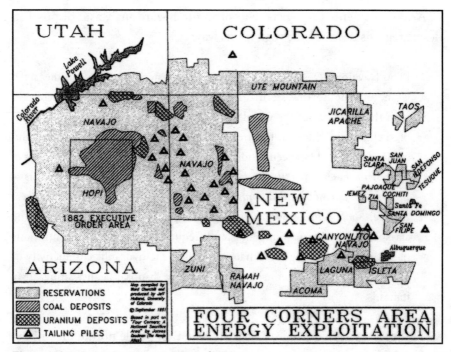

Figure 2.1 Four Corners uranium district

From: Churchill, *Struggle for the Land* (Compiled by Ward Churchill and Glenn Morris; produced by Jeff Holland)

ore were mined at Monument Valley by the Vanadium Corporation of America."[5] The yellow cake processed from this uranium was used by the scientists at Los Alamos to make the original three atomic bombs (the "Trinity" that signified the godlike powers of the new nuclear science), the first of which was exploded in 1945 at New Mexico's Alamagordo Bombing and Gunnery Range (now White Sands Missile Range).[6] From 1946 to 1968, more than 13 million tons of uranium ore were mined on the Navajo Reservation alone—all for use in nuclear weapons and nuclear reactors.[7]

The amount of acreage designated for uranium development was immense. The *Southwest Indigenous Uranium Forum* newsletter gives an idea of the monumental scale of these operations:

> In 1958, the Bureau of Indian Affairs reported that over 900,000 acres of tribal land were leased for uranium exploration and development. Today, there are over 1,000 abandoned and unreclaimed open-pit and underground uranium mines on the former nuclear reservation.

Figure 2.2 Aerial view of 2,800-acre Jackpile-Paguate uranium mine
From: Department of the Interior, *Jackpile-Paguate Uranium Mine Reclamation Project Environmental Impact Statement*

The heaviest uranium exploration, mining and milling activity occurred on predominately [sic] Indian lands in the Grants Mineral Belt and San Juan Basin in New Mexico. In 1976, the Department of the Interior called the New Mexico portion of the Grants Mineral Belt "the hottest uranium exploration area in the country." Two years later, 740,000 acres of Indian land in this region were leased for uranium exploration and development.[8]

At the height of the second uranium boom in the late 1970s, the Bureau of Indian Affairs "approved 303 uranium leases covering 250,000 Indian acres in the region, and the federal government estimated a total of 3.5 million acres, including federal uranium, were going to be developed."[9] Near the Navajo Reservation, at Laguna Pueblo, more uranium mining and milling occurred, most notably the Jackpile-Paguate mine—until 1980 the largest uranium mine in the world (and the largest ever in the United States), covering approximately 2,800 acres. During its 30-year operation, the mine produced 22 million tons of ore and removed 44 million tons of materials from three open pits and several underground mines.[10] This was the mine I gazed out upon from the window of Dorothy Purley's kitchen.

Fifty percent of the residents of the state of New Mexico live within a 50-mile radius of the Jackpile-Paguate mine, including those living within the Albuquerque metropolitan area and the city of Grants. The mine itself is larger than downtown Albuquerque. Two rivers run through it, the Rio Paguate and the Rio Moquino, which eventually run into the Rio Puerco and the Rio Grande.[11] The Jackpile-Paguate mine was owned by the Anaconda Copper Company, a subsidiary of the Atlantic Richfield Company. In fact, scattered over much of this portion of the nuclear map are the names of transnational corporations and federal government agencies. Some companies that contracted with the U.S. Department of Energy were: Kerr-McGee, Vanadium Corporation of America, Foote Mineral, AMEX, United Nuclear Corporation, Exxon, Mobil Oil, and Gulf. In addition to the big corporate mines, between 300 and 500 shallow uranium mines were opened by "independent" Native Americans with the encouragement of the U.S. Small Business Administration. Uranium ore from these mines was sold to the Atomic Energy Commission at the Kerr-McGee milling plant (by the 1970s the largest in the world) near Shiprock, New Mexico.

The Toll on the People

Indian lands under uranium mining and milling development were extensive, with the Navajo Nation, Laguna Pueblo, and Acoma Pueblo carrying some of the heaviest burden and consequently suffering some of the most severe health repercussions. Though the uranium booms helped the destitute Indian economy to some extent and for a brief time, they also transformed these Indian lands (almost overnight) from a pastoral to a mining-industrial economy, resulting in a mining-dependent population. Indians did not get rich off the uranium development on their lands because they lacked the capital and the technical knowledge to develop them and, at least initially, they were kept ignorant of the value of their land. Instead, development was contracted out to large energy companies. Because "national security" and energy consumption needs (read "national competitiveness") were at stake, Indians were not given the right to stipulate conditions for development and reclamation for decades, and this never sufficiently. Unchecked and unmonitored production were excused during World War II and the Cold War on the grounds of national security and, in the 1970s, on the basis of the energy crisis and the ongoing arms escalation that mushroomed in the 1980s.[12] Throughout the postwar period American Indian populations were exploited as a cheap source of labor. For example, Indian miners were paid at a rate two-thirds that of off-reservation employees.[13] In addition, Indians were not compensated adequately for the uranium taken from their lands. "As of 1984, stateside Indians were receiving only an average of 3.4 percent of the market value of the uranium extracted from their land."[14] The median income reported in 1970 (at a boom time for uranium mining) at the Laguna Pueblo was only $2,661 per year—a little more than $220 a month, or $50 per week. And Indians paid a high price for the right to work the mines. Uranium development's legacy has been one of a severely polluted environment, human and nonhuman radiation contamination, cancers, birth defects, sickness, and death. Health risks associated with uranium mining and milling have been identified and examined by different investigators and reported in a variety of sources including the Southwest Research and Information Center publications and the *New England Journal of Medicine* as well as others.[15]

Since large amounts of water are used in the mining process and mountains of uranium tailings are produced as a byproduct, uranium pollution poisons earth, air, and water. Radioactive particulates (dust particles containing uranium 238, radium 226, and thorium 230) blow in the desert winds, and radioactive elements travel in both surface and ground water. Radioactive materials from the mining of uranium produce radon and thoron gases, which combine with the molecular structure of human cells and decay into radioactive thorium and polonium. The dust irritates cells in the lining of the respiratory tract, causing cancer. Radioactive materials can also damage sex cells causing such birth defects as cleft palate and Down's syndrome.[16]

In seeking federal assistance to study the effect of low-level radiation on the health of their children, Navajo health officials called attention to at least two preliminary studies—one conducted by the March of Dimes (principal investigator Dr. L. Shields) and the other by the Navajo Health Authority (principal investigator Dr. D. Calloway). Calloway's study suggested that Navajo children may have a five times' greater rate of bone cancer and a fifteen times' greater rate of ovarian and testicular cancer than the U.S. average.[17] However, despite these preliminary findings, no funding was granted for extended epidemiological studies of the impact on Navajos living near uranium tailings and mines.[18]

Further extending the nuclear landscape and causing harm to those who live there, millions of gallons of water in the Four Corners area were subjected to radiation pollution by the extractive processes of uranium mining. Accidents, such as the Rio Puerco incident, cause serious water pollution in an already water-scarce environment.

Rio Puerco

On July 16, 1979, at Church Rock, New Mexico, the United Nuclear Corporation's tailings dam broke, sending at least 94 million gallons of radioactive water into the nearby Rio Puerco.[19] Said one resident of the Navajo Reservation:

> It had a terrible odor and a dark chocolatey color. Right away, we could tell it was unusual. It was a day later that it came over the radio about the spill, telling people to stay away from the river. *A week later* they put up those signs saying it was dangerous.[20]

The Rio Puerco accident has been called the worst single nuclear accident in U.S. history, far outweighing the well-reported Three Mile Island accident. Why wasn't this massive radioactive pollution reported in the national press? The Navajo people in the surrounding area were unable safely to use their single source of water, nor could they sell or eat the livestock that drank from this water. Acute toxicity caused by increased acidity of the water resulted in burns leading to infections that required amputations. No serious study of possible radiation contamination of soil sediment was ever conducted, and no large-scale study of exposure was ever initiated. Only an out-of-court settlement totaling $525,000 was offered as a collective payment to victims of the Rio Puerco disaster.

But, then, the Rio Puerco was not a clean river prior to this accident. As noted by one groundwater protection researcher: "Between 1969 and February of 1986, the Puerco flowed year-round, fed by millions of gallons of contaminant-laden water that poured daily into one of its tributaries (called the North Fork) from three underground uranium mines. . . . No one bothered to tell the Navajos that the water that poured from the mines during the uranium boom years of 1952–1964 and 1969–1981 was not safe for man or beast."[21] And the Rio Puerco disaster was not the only one. "Between 1955 and 1977, 15 tailings dams broke, releasing their contents into the wider watershed areas."[22]

Science as a Mechanism of Exclusion

Today—seemingly as invisible as the Rio Puerco accident—the uranium mines and tailings are, for the most part, left unreclaimed. Although a 1983 Environmental Protection Study confirmed that the Navajo Reservation alone had approximately 1,000 significant nuclear waste sites, the Environmental Protection Agency (EPA) deemed them all "too remote" to be of "significant national concern."[23] A 1978 study by Los Alamos National Laboratory (LANL) concerning rehabilitation of land and water contaminated by uranium mining and milling offered one solution: to zone such areas as forbidden to human habitation.[24] A report in 1972 by the National Academy of Science suggested that the Four Corners area be designated a "national sacrifice area."[25] Other scientific accounts, as noted below, were completely contrary to these findings and denied that any significant pollution problems existed or that adverse health effects could be associated with living in the region. Though seemingly different in content, all these reports belie the same prejudice: The land, and by implication the people living on the land were better left ignored. That is, neither was worth saving.

To understand how an entire society could ignore an environmental disaster on the scale of the Rio Puerco incident or the open-pit uranium mines, it is necessary to examine some of the ways scientific discourse can be used as a mechanism of exclusion, particularly when it is marshaled against anecdotal evidence presented by nonscientists (evidence like that offered by Dorothy Purley, quoted at the beginning of this chapter). In the case of the Grants uranium district, anecdotal statements from Native speakers may be in themselves incontestable—reports of increased cancers, for example—but they carry no weight in establishing a causal link between the reported illnesses and the existence of radioactive mine tailings or unreclaimed pits. Although anecdotal testimony has sometimes been accepted in court cases regarding other issues, the history of anecdotal statements in this region is one marked by what social scientists call *delegitimation.* Anecdotal statements about the health risks associated with unreclaimed uranium mines and tailings are gathered in preliminary studies or as testimony in open hearings and may be incorporated into draft environmental-impact statements but do not constitute scientific evidence. They are simply reported; any claim they may have on the truth can be—and in some cases has been—diminished by the overwhelming weight of contrary "scientific" evidence. The statements are, in effect, excluded from consideration, and the people who speak them are, by extension, excluded from any decision-making process bearing on their welfare.

Many "preliminary studies" suggested serious health risks to children in communities near abandoned uranium districts. One "preliminary" study showed "a twofold excess of miscarriages, infant deaths, congenital or genetic abnormalities, and learning disabilities among uranium-area families"[26] compared with Navajo families in nonuranium areas. Even after being informed of these and other findings, no federal or state agencies provided funding for further study. In fact, in 1983, one agency, the Indian Health Service (a division of the U.S. Department of Health and Social Services) had sent a report to Congress ("Health Hazards Related to Nuclear Resources Development on Indian Land," 1983) stating that there was "no evidence of adverse health effects in Indians in uranium development areas and that there is no need for additional studies or funding for such studies."[27] The one "official" scientific investigation of birth defects that was funded, primarily by the March of Dimes Birth Defects Foundation, was too "small" to render "significant" results. Its conclusion states: "It was unlikely that our small study population would have demonstrated a real effect in terms of statistical significance."[28] Since statistical significance in epidemiological studies generally requires large study populations, Indian communities are disadvantaged because they are usually quite small.

Thus, inadequate funding and the shortcomings of statistical analyses for small populations can result not only in a lack of "official" documentation to support the "preliminary" and "anecdotal" knowledge of health risks, but in the production of official documentation that is contrary to the preliminary studies. For the communities living in uranium districts, a little (underfunded) science is *not* better than no science at all. What gets circulated, and what has credibility, is the "official" report—even if that report is based on inadequate foundations.

Scientific knowledge in this contested terrain is deeply influenced by state and federal agencies, by funding, as well as many other nonscientific factors. Epidemiological studies are costly, as are the "experts" who administer them. Poor communities do what they can, but their findings have little purchase when it comes to lawsuits against state agencies or private companies. In the end, we must look seriously at the discrepancies between community-sponsored "preliminary" studies and federally funded "expert" accounts of health risks.

In the 1986 open hearings concerning the environmental and human impact of the unreclaimed Jackpile-Paguate mine, a radiation scientist representing Anaconda argued that individual lifetime risk of cancer in the most exposed individuals at Paguate (the village overlooking the 2,800-acre mine) under the no-action alternative (the proposal that Anaconda need not engage any reclamation of the massive mine) is far less than the lifetime risk of dying due to excess cosmic rays received by living in Denver, Colorado.[29] In his testimony, this specialist does not tell the audience how he arrives at this analogy, nor what the standards are for such a statement. He does not tell the audience that standards on the hazards of radiation exposure have changed drastically over time, such that smaller and smaller doses are recognized as sufficient to cause cancer. Since he is an "expert" in this field, his analysis overrides the anecdotal statements of the residents claiming to be adversely affected.

Public hearings for the environmental-impact draft statement for the Jackpile-Paguate mine's reclamation project began with no fewer than ten Ph.D.s and other "technical" experts in a variety of scientific disciplines, including a mining engineer, a plant ecologist, a radiation ecologist, an expert in biomedicine, and others. All testified in obfuscating technical language that America's largest uranium mine could be safely left unreclaimed. All were under contract with Anaconda.

Even if we ignore the fact that these testimonies are paid for by the uranium mining company, the discrepancy between these statements and earlier studies of the general area made by Los Alamos scientists and those made by the National Academy of Sciences (mentioned above), in which the uranium mining districts were called "national sacrifice areas" and zones in which human habitation should be forbidden, cannot be ignored. Since the Jackpile-Paguate mine was the largest in the area (and one of the largest in the world), it would be safe to assume that it was included in these assessments. In addition, scientists agree universally that uranium mining at this mine has caused cancer and death in miners (if not in nearby residents). Uranium ore and tailings, as well as the water used in the mining process, are known to be radioactive.

The role of the scientist providing "expert knowledge" and scientific validation for both corporations and the government in determining environmental and health standards for the production, processing, and disposal of radioactive materials and for mine reclamation demonstrates a persistent collaboration between some scientific knowledge producers and what can only be described as highly biased interests (in our example, the subsidiary of the Atlantic Richfield Corporation, Anaconda).[30] Of course, such collaborative relations do not include all scientists. Scientific "expert" knowledge is also marshaled *against* government and industry interests by antinuclear activists so that "objective" testimony ends up comprising multiple voices, demonstrating the malleability of scientific data and its interpretation. Even among partners, such as certain scientific communities and energy industries, disagreement exists. "Science" does not come as a hegemonic package of truth when its subject matter concerns politically charged and contested arenas such as land and the environment. Though the report from the Anaconda-hired scientists (claiming the uranium mine harmless) seems to contradict the LANL report (claiming the uranium district uninhabitable), the underlying message and the political ends appear to be the same: that the Indians, if not expendable, can be displaced. From the Indian perspective displacement may mean the same as expendability.[31]

Because scientific analysis is costly and requires specialized skills, open hearings more often than not consist of contestations between "expert" scientific knowledge and local "common-sense" anecdotal knowledge. Confronting the "experts" in formal public hearings, such as those held for the reclamation of the Jackpile-Paguate mine, often feels like an exercise in futility—especially when technoscientific discourse is marshaled in opposition to "simple" fears and commonsense knowledge—to those most affected, the local populace.

The discourses of science (and of the law) are formidable tools for legitimating dubious claims and delegitimating counterclaims. As became apparent in the hearings on reclamation mandates, Anaconda attempted to shield itself with scientific discourse that claims one of the world's largest uranium mines did not need to be reclaimed, that it could be left open with its tailings blowing in the wind, that it posed no risk to human or animal health. In response to the "experts," the Pueblo Indians of Laguna cited case after case of deaths caused by cancer. As Herman Garcia of the village of Paguate commented:

> [A]nd now I think the reason why the people in the Pueblo of Laguna are kind of concerned about this cancer illness is because like—and please don't compare it with the City of Albuquerque or New York. I come from a very small village, and I don't know how you'd figure that out; but, last year, in the Village at Paguate alone, we lost five people from cancer . . . these people that I'm talking about were nondrinkers and nonsmokers . . .
>
> That's why we're having such a hard time, and I think we've been as reasonable as we possibly could be, but how much longer do we have to wait to cover the land, the one we consider dangerous. I have to work because I can't really go by these studies, I'm no expert, and I think it would really make me feel good—like the ponds we consider hazardous, I'd like for some of these experts to go out there and swim in those ponds. Then when I see them swim, then maybe I feel more secure, and we might be able to swallow some of these studies that have been introduced here today.[32]

Beside presenting the oral accounts in open hearings, Anaconda substantiated its claims with voluminous scientific texts in the form of technical documentation produced by expert witnesses. In addition to the obscurity of the language, the sheer volume of documentation functions as a barrier to the uninitiated.

The dominance of text-based scientific and legal arguments and validation of the "facts" concerning Indian cultures by Euroamerican scientific experts is particularly problematic, because Indian peoples' heritage of knowledge is often based on oral traditions and organized around a very different set of legitimating strategies. Of course, increasing numbers of Indians wield the sword of legal and scientific discourse today with great skill and some notable success, but many Indians still do not use (and disdain to use) the master's tools to bring down the master's house.

Confronting scientific "truth" for many Indians, as well as non-Indians, in the nuclear landscape can be an extremely disempowering experience. Those not trained in the specialized discourse of radiation science confront an apparent discrepancy between what they experience in their bodies, such as cancer and its connection to the open uranium mine down the road, and what they are told is the "truth" about the risks from radiation exposure.

Objectivity and a Multicultural Voice

Increasingly, scientific and legal discourse is also being marshaled in support of the disenfranchised, the communities of color, and the poorer segments of society. In the uranium districts, important alternative studies have been initiated by the Southwest Research and Information Center, particularly the work of Chris Shuey and Paul Robinson. Investigating pollution surrounding Los Alamos, the Concerned Citizens for Nuclear Safety have produced scientific data of their own to support their claims of deliberate violations of environmental safety standards in disposing of radioactive waste. The same is true for other Indian and community groups throughout the country. The alternative technical data presented by these groups constitute one of the strongest weapons available to affected communities to force the state and private industry to act responsibly. However, lack of funding leaves many important studies left undone. And although important, scientific studies are useless in contending with the historical and political patterns of abuse that underlie much of the nuclear landscape. Nor can they contend with harm done culturally to communities. Not only does social and historical knowledge need to be part of environmental discourse, but so do non-Euroamerican forms of knowledge. True "objectivity" is rendered only within an inclusive field of knowledge, which is especially crucial in multicultural situations.

Open hearings in this contested domain far too often limit the field of objectivity, serving only as a staging ground upon which mechanisms of exclusion—achieved by the use of expert witnesses—are deployed. But some Indian voices from the margin, while humbled by these opposing technical discourses, assert themselves and a different kind of knowledge and experience, as exemplified by the testimony of Harold Lockwood of the Laguna tribe:

> Good Afternoon. My name is Mr. Lockwood. I'm a tribal member of the Laguna Tribe and I'm sorry I don't have any scientific credentials or any-thing. The only thing that I have that I can lay claim to, I'm an ex-Marine and Vietnam Veteran. Social responsibility. It seems some—while some of us were going to school, there was some of us still fighting in Vietnam for the rights of big companies to make profit . . .
>
> Religious meaning. The land is laying there open like a sore wound. My people believe in the land. We believe in our Indian ways. We believe in the heavens and stars. . .[33]

Scientific discourse may serve as a mechanism of exclusion in public hearings and in government documents at every stage of the nuclear cycle, but it hasn't entirely silenced the traditional Indian voice with its appeal to the heavens, the stars, and the earth. Although such public voices don't wield as much power as they should in the institutionalized process, they are still important. They exist in the public record as a vision of what the centers of power look like to those on its margins. Sometimes, the voice of the people is the only record we have of what is going on within the dark zones of the nuclear landscape.

But though these two opposing voices (scientific and traditional Indian) are clearly present, increasingly a mixed, multicultural voice that aligns scientific analysis with traditional indigenous knowledge is also heard. A discourse between scientists who support and respect traditional knowledge and Indians that make use of scientific knowledge from the

Euroamerican tradition comprise a discourse that emerges out of the multiracial and multicultural collaborations made necessary by far-reaching environmental problems such as nuclear landscapes.

The Story Isn't Over

In a 1995 speech in Albuquerque, New Mexico, before a grass-roots protest gathering for environmental and social justice for Indian peoples, Al Waconda of the Laguna Pueblo talked to uranium miners about the lack of redress:

> In 1990, a radiation Exposure Compensation Act was passed to provide compensation for underground miners who worked between 1947 and 1971. This compensation only addresses the workers in underground mining up to 1971. After 1971 and up to 1982, the uranium was in great demand and we in the open pit and surrounding areas were exposed to greater amounts of the radiation. We, as open pit miners, millers, and affected village members are left out completely. We have been contaminated for over 40 years up to now and still nothing is being done to help us . . .
>
> Even though our economic situation became better during the uranium boom, it is not right for us to be paying with our lives for generations to come.[34]

The sentiments of Indian people like Mr. Waconda and Dorothy Purley are shared by many Indians but not by all. Just as in contemporary Euroamerican culture, Indian culture is composed of people with an array of "positions" on all issues. As with issues like gambling and temporary storage of high-level nuclear waste, uranium mining on Indian land is not viewed uniformly by Indian people as a tragedy. A case in point is the reclamation of the Jackpile-Paguate mine by the tribal-owned Laguna Construction Industry. To ensure possible future economic mining development, the company "reclaimed" the mine—that is, reduced risk of contamination to surrounding inhabitants—while maintaining the capability to reopen the mine in the future for uranium mining development. This does not negate the very real tragedy of this region, but it does call attention to the complexity of the social situation and the powerful influence of economic development. After all, once a uranium mining wasteland is created, the options left for alternative development can be quite limited.

While uranium mining in the Southwest has slowed considerably and some attempts at land reclamation are in process or have been completed (including the Jackpile-Paguate mine), the extraction of uranium ore from the area continues today, as does the spread of pollution from uranium production. For instance, to the east of the Colorado Plateau, near the Grand Canyon in Arizona, the Havasupai tribe has been fighting Energy Fuels Nuclear Inc. to keep it from mining uranium just fifteen miles south of the Grand Canyon. Known as the guardians of the Grand Canyon, the Havasupai claim the right of religious access to what are, for them, sacred lands.[35]

According to researchers at the Southwest Research and Information Center, who have been monitoring uranium development in this region for many years, New Mexico is about to enter a new uranium development era. The corporations proposing development argue that new processing techniques pose less of a toxic threat and are less environmentally destructive than the practices of twenty years ago. Due to a complex combination of international trade restrictions, economic incentives, and new processing technologies, domestic uranium mining is once again a profitable venture. The market consists of U.S. domestic power plants that now need refueling to remain online. Thus, numerous mine sites—all bordering the Navajo reservation—are about to go into production for what promises to be a multibillion-dollar industry.[36]

Although the largest uranium reserves in the United States are found in the Grants Uranium Belt region, Indians outside that region were also affected, and their lands were used for processing and mining. For instance, Sequoyah Fuels Uranium Processing operated a uranium processing plant on Indian lands in Oklahoma for twenty-one years. The company "had been cited for more than 15,000 violations of federal and state law. . . . And there had been an estimated 124 cases of cancer and birth defects in families living adjacent to the plant."[37] The Indian grass-roots organization Native Americans for a Clean Environment (NACE) forced closure of the plant, but only after a six-year battle in which their financial resources were spent on legal expenses.

The Global Picture

By 1982 uranium production had been greatly curtailed in the Grants Uranium Belt, since even cheaper sources had been found outside the continental United States. The same transnational energy corporations that played so significant a role in the creation of the U.S. nuclear landscape are, of course, players in a larger global military economy in which uranium mining remains a requirement for the continuation of nuclear energy and weapons development. The extractive resources that fuel nuclear power are mined in many "Fourth World" lands, demonstrating further that nuclear colonialism follows a global pattern of exploitation. For example, as of 1980 "seventy percent of France's uranium [came] from Niger and Gabon in west Africa."[38] Transnational energy corporations have reaped maximum profits at the expense of many indigenous populations around the world. The uranium sacrifice zone has not been limited to the Grants Uranium Belt in the United States:

> Significantly, large proportions of the uranium production and reserves controlled within the five developed nations are located either within internal colonies of those nations, such as Indian reservations in the United States and aborigine reserves in Australia, or in colonies or neocolonies which remain controlled by developed nations. All of these are colonies whose resources and labor are being exploited considerably by energy resource corporations. In Australia, it is estimated that 80 percent of all uranium reserves lie on aboriginal lands. Aboriginal people in Australia, like American Indians, were pushed on to the least desirable lands within nations and have been virtually forced into accepting miserable agreements with energy corporations. The 1978 agreement between the aborigines and the companies (Ranger Uranium Agreement) gave the aborigines only 4.25 percent of the revenues of the uranium mine royalties.[39]

For many indigenous communities historically, as well as in many cases today, uranium mining is only a form of resource extraction for export. Because of this, native communities become "raw materials colonies" for the uranium companies and their home nation-states. The following list shows the aboriginal communities with the most significant uranium reserves:

1. *Australia*—particularly the Arnhem Land Area of the Northern Territory, home to a large existing aboriginal community;
2. *Canada*—particularly in a northern Saskatchewan area inhabited by Cree-Dene Native Americans;
3. *Southwest Africa (Namibia)* —under South African mining concessions in the "last colony in Africa";
4. *United States*—on Navajo, Laguna Pueblo, Havasupai, and Colville Confederated Tribal Lands, along with pre-1848 Hispanic Land Grants at Cebolleta and San Mateo Springs.[40] Also included are the Sioux lands in the Black Hills of Dakota, and the Spokane Reservation (30 miles upstream from the Yakima Reservation) in the state of Washington.

The uranium region forms the first layer of the map showing the transformation of land under nuclear colonialism. Its story spans forty-plus years of uranium booms and busts, concerns millions of acres, massive environmental pollution still left unreclaimed, and generations of Indians dying of cancer. Behind this landscape stand wealthy corporations, powerful federal agencies such as the Department of Energy (formerly the Atomic Energy Commission) and the Department of Defense, and scientific centers such as Los Alamos National Laboratory, Lawrence Livermore Laboratories, and Sandia National Laboratories in Albuquerque. But this particular part of the nuclear landscape does not exist in isolation. It is part of a larger terrain—part of a number of interconnected transformative processes that emerged in the postwar West and Southwest. Marking our entry into the nuclear age, the uranium zones of sacrifice were a fundamental part of the emergence of a new technological era that began in the 1940s. They are also the first sites in a constellation of toxic sites that are the product of a technological society unwilling to look closely at the human and environmental costs of its maintenance.

Without uranium there is no nuclear landscape, no nuclear weapons development, no nuclear energy industry. It underlies the creation of nuclear power centers hidden in the desert—centers of first-rate scientific research and development. After all, it all began in order to provide the scientists at Los Alamos with the material for making bombs.

Science Cities in the Desert

Outdoor Laboratories and Theaters of War

Viewed from space at night, the Southwest interdesert region appears as the darkest region in the United States. Only a few major cities show up as nebulae-clusters of light and industry. But studded throughout the darkest zones in this landscape are other, more isolated jewels, seemingly disconnected from the commercial centers, illuminating the dark ellipses on the landscape. Hard to place, these are also areas of high density, concentrations of energy, power, and a certain kind of intelligence. The dark zones are military reservations with their weapons testing ranges, and the bright spots mark concentrations of scientific intelligence for the research and development of weapons.

As William Thomas notes in *Scorched Earth*, "In the United States alone, the Department of Defense (DOD) and the nuclear weapons complex own or lease about 100,000 square kilometers of land. As much as half the airspace over the United States is restricted for use by the military."[1] Bases within the interdesert region make up a substantial percentage of this military acreage. Throughout the past five decades the desert lands of the Southwestern United States have been transformed into arguably the largest peacetime militarized zone on earth. They have become both the laboratories and testing fields for its most formidable weapons—nuclear and nonnuclear. Although it contains some of the world's largest military reservations, this landscape has been transformed with relatively little recognition by the general public, partly because of its low population density but also because the mechanisms of exclusion enumerated in the previous chapter work, in a somewhat altered form, to neutralize resistance to what, in essence, is a military occupation.

Whereas the last chapter focused on delineating the uranium mining zone and on how the uranium industry served the interests of the military in establishing the nuclear landscape, this chapter provides—in addition to mapping the spaces of military and nuclear concentration in the Southwest—a framework for seeing how science is enlisted in the service of the national security state that emerges after World War II. The effects of that alliance on the land and people of the American West have been incalculable. Each year uncovers some past misdeed for which few who are alive today can be held accountable. Accounts by veterans of atomic tests and reports of hapless, unwitting victims of nuclear experiments belie the ideal of an objective, pure science. Such science has been contaminated by the purely political goals of a highly militarized state. Seduced by the power of virtually unlimited research budgets and the highest of technologies, nuclear science as practiced in this region becomes tainted with the residue of its own experiments, conducted in the open-air and underground laboratories of the Southwest, often kept secret and virtually in isolation from anyone who might call its methods into question. Those who pay the price for a scientific "freedom" shorn of responsibility are of course the experimental subjects themselves—the marginalized poor, living alongside the research, devolopment, and training centers, and the backcountry farmers and ranchers located downwind from the testing fields whose families and livestock were contaminated by deadly fallout. This chapter identifies three forces—militarization, nuclearism, and concentrations of scientific power—that, together, combine to transform the Southwestern landscape and impose physical and cultural hardship on some of those who live there.

The military acquisition of Western land on a massive scale in the 1940s, 1950s, and 1980s must be seen as the consequence not only of military necessity but also of scientific research institutions initiated during World War II. One cannot examine the nuclear landscape without examining the role of science. The interdesert Southwest is not only a militarized landscape but also a scientific landscape—a collection of "outdoor" laboratories. With this view in mind, we can begin to question the direction, purpose, and end results of the system of knowledge production that leads to the designation of zones of sacrifice in the nuclear landscape.

Because of my personal history with this region, whenever I travel the backroads of the Southwest, I am keenly aware of the "signs" of power in the landscape. Such signs include high-wire fences, radar antennae, massive satellite communications dishes tilted up toward the stars, sonic booms, stealth aircraft, well-maintained roads in the middle of "nowhere" leading to various "installations," earth-shaking explosions, military trucks and personnel, unmarked trucks carrying "explosives," jet trails across the bright blue sky, guard towers, fencing and more fencing, and everywhere government signs that read "DO NOT ENTER." These forces composed of high technology, big science, and military occupation impose powerful boundaries upon the land itself, as well as the people who live near them.

Science and the Government's Agenda

The nuclear landscape in the Southwest is the result of a larger process of militarization and scientific advancement that was initiated when the United States entered the Second World War in 1941. The story of the Manhattan Project, Project Y, Los Alamos, and the Trinity tests is well-known. Less acknowledged are the millions of acres of land that were withdrawn for use by the military, as well as other secret scientific enclaves, known as "science cities," that were created during this time. A second wave of federal land withdrawals that occurred under the Reagan administration in the 1980s expanded these desert militarized zones.

The melding of basic science with military weapons development during World War II fundamentally and simultaneously transformed both the production of scientific knowledge and the Western landscape. The Office of Scientific Research and Development (the OSRD) and the National Defense Research Committee played particularly important roles in directing a growing concentration of scientific activity toward the Western United States during the war years:

The war speeded further specialization in many spheres of science, and this increased complexity hastened the involvement of the federal government. . . . [W]orld War II fostered teamwork [rather than fostering research by individuals] and large projects on a hitherto unprecedented scale, drawing the scientific community together in new interdependent relationships. That in turn fostered the need for expensive equipment and laboratories which only the federal government could provide. . . . Just as public work programs (such as road or railroad construction) in the West during the nineteenth century had been too vast for private enterprise to undertake unaided—leading to demands for government support—so by 1941 scientific projects were similarly engendering demands for public assistance.[2]

The OSRD and the National Defense Research Committee helped to bring science into an alliance with military demands and government funding sources such as the Department of Defense and the Department of Energy (which then was the Atomic Energy Commission) an alliance that the scientific community has, to this day, been unable and unwilling to dissolve.[3] Even as recently as 1994—a time when the nuclear weapons labs were supposed to be undergoing a conversion from military to peacetime commercial research—overall military expenditures at Los Alamos National Labs constituted 75 percent of the lab's total budget.[4]

Science Cities

Between 1939 and 1945 the West became home to important research laboratories and other scientific institutions, called "science cities," which depended fundamentally on government and defense money. Many of these science cities were created from scratch, so to speak, in remote places previously deemed "uninhabited." But the term "science city" can also apply (more loosely) to urban areas resuscitated by the influx of government money, intellectuals, and the growth of infrastructure and services that massive government projects require. In fact, the West saw three new kinds of scientific facilities established under the influence of the Second World War: university-centered labs such as Lawrence Radiation Laboratory at Berkeley, California, and the Jet Propulsion Laboratory at Pasadena, California; federal labs contracted out to universities or private companies like the Livermore and Albuquerque (Sandia) laboratories in

California and New Mexico, respectively; and the science cities, operated by universities or the government itself. The role of, in particular, the University of California but also institutions such as the University of Chicago or the University of Illinois at Champaign-Urbana, further point out the alliance of university-sponsored scientific research with the military. In return, universities received large research grants.

The so-called "science cities" were among the most dependent on federal and Department of Defense funding. Often secret and placed in remote locations, these were "complex communities," such as Los Alamos or Hanford, Washington, and China Lake, California, that were exclusively created to "undertake major federal scientific and military projects."[5] Although Hanford's mission as a plutonium production site has been essentially decommissioned (and parts of its surrounding lands determined to be some of the most polluted sites in the United States),[6] Los Alamos and China Lake have thrived and expanded through decades of Cold War politics. Also intact today are the great research laboratories of the early Cold War era Lawrence Livermore Laboratories, Los Alamos National Laboratory, Sandia Laboratories, the California Institute of Technology's Jet Propulsion Laboratory, and Michelson Laboratory and Lauritsen Laboratory at China Lake Naval Weapons Center in the Mojave. Thus, World War II and its aftermath saw the formation of the scientific-industrial-military complex that remains arguably one of the most powerful economic sectors in the United States.

If the Second World War was the catalyst that transformed *where* science was performed, the early Cold War period fundamentally altered *how* it was performed. The direction and the objectives of scientific research began to merge with the national security interests of the state, diverging radically from previous state-funded science projects such as civil engineering, fish and wildlife management, and agricultural research. State-sponsored science shifted its primary research and development interests from social and natural resources to weapons. The truly impressive concentration of intellectual power and economic resources that went into the creation of science cities such as China Lake and Los Alamos attest to this shift in the country's primary focus from economic development to national security.

Because it accumulates stockpiles of toxic materials and because it must test its products, militarized science has left—and continues to produce—a legacy of pollution extremely detrimental to human and nonhuman health. To many of those in the science cities and in the military testing ranges, desert lands were often little more than "land that could be safely blasted, pulverized and scorched by air-to-ground rockets."[7] The concept of the laboratory was extended outward to include the desert valleys, high pinion forests, and mountain ranges. In the words of one official publication of the China Lake Naval Weapons Center in the Mojave: The Navy's "indoor laboratories are complemented with *outdoor laboratories* where real combat conditions can be closely approximated for testing and evaluation."[8]

For the Native inhabitants of these places, military/scientific occupation meant, at best, low-paid jobs to help build, maintain, and clean the emerging cities.[9] At worst, Indians and other local populations were ignored completely—rendered invisible by a mixture of racism and a perception of desert lands as vast, uninhabitable wastelands. Worse than this, Indians and other local people may have been regarded as expendable subjects for radiation experiments—a gruesome possibility that has only recently been acknowledged with the release of previously confidential reports documenting the deliberate radiation releases from laboratories and undisclosed, secret nuclear tests, exposing downwind populations to fallout.[10] For example, recently released Department of Energy documents have revealed "tests" (by scientists in Los Alamos's early days) of radiation releases in the form of "simulated nuclear bombs" over New Mexico's Pajarito Plateau. Sources indicate that there may have been as many as 244 similar tests during this period. These tests, called the RaLa tests (for "radiolanthanum") exposed downwind communities to radiation. As noted in a report by the Advisory Committee on Human Radiation:

> The RaLa tests were conducted in Bayo Canyon, roughly three miles east of the town of Los Alamos, which grew up next to the lab. Although radioactive clouds due to the RaLa tests occasionally blew back toward the town, the prevailing winds usually blew those clouds over sparsely populated regions to the north and east. Aside from a small construction trailer park and a pumice quarry within three miles, the nearest population center was the San Ildefonso pueblo, roughly eight miles downwind of the test site in the Rio Grande valley. Several Pueblo Indian and Spanish-speaking communities lie within twelve miles of Los Alamos.[11]

Because of concerns for the safety of Los Alamos residents—where the scientists and their families lived—scientists began to conduct the RaLa tests only when the wind was blowing away from Los Alamos, toward the Native American and Spanish communities. This account is more than "anecdotal"; it is substantiated in the government-sponsored report on undisclosed radiation experiments.[12] As one area resident noted "Shots were fired when the wind was blowing to the northeast. At this point in time, that's where most of the population of this region lived. I mean, half of it is Spanish and half of it is Native American."[13] Additionally, the report notes: "Although many in Los Alamos—those who worked on bomb design—knew of the RaLa program and its potential hazards, there is no indication of any discussion with other workers or local communities. For example, from the mid-1940s to the mid-1950s, many Pueblo people who claim not to have been informed, and who the government admits "*may* not have been informed,*" worked at the lab as day laborers, domestics, and manufacturers of detonators."[14] It wasn't until 1963 that an official public statement revealed the radiation contamination of the Rio Grande Valley as a result of the tests. There are fifteen Pueblos in the Rio Grand Valley. Like the Moapa Paiute near the Nevada Test Site and the Pueblo and Navajo Indians in the uranium mining fields, the Indian people around Los Alamos supplemented their food supply from their surrounding environment more than Euroamericans, putting them at even greater risk from contaminated game, plants, and water.

The DOE has also revealed secret nuclear bomb tests conducted outside the Nevada Test Site—some of which are part of 204 "clandestine blasts" conducted in Nevada between 1963 and 1990.[15] In addition, significant nuclear tests were conducted outside of the Nevada Test Site for so-called peaceful uses of nuclear power, such as those that occurred in Alaska (Project Chariot), Colorado (Project Rio Blanco and Project Rulison), Mississippi (Project Salmon), central Nevada (Project Faultless and Project Shoal), and New Mexico (Project Gnome and Project Gasbuggy).

Deliberate releases of radiation occurred at Hanford, Washington. The "Green Run" experiment, for example, released cancer-causing iodine 131 in massive quantities over an unsuspecting population. In fact, between 1944 and 1947, more than 417,000 curies of iodine 131 were released at Hanford—an astounding figure when compared to the Three Mile Island accident, which released only fifteen curies of radioactive iodine. Although the health risks from exposure to radioactive iodine 131 were well known at this time, no standards for contending with these releases were established.[16] This doesn't mean that officials at Hanford were not aware of the health hazards. Employees for DuPont (contractor for the Hanford site at the time) were sent out into the surrounding area under cover to conduct tests of local grazing animals. The DuPont agents posed as researchers of animal husbandry for the Department of Agriculture. When farmers weren't looking, they surreptitiously sampled radioactive iodine levels in animal thyroids.[17] The farmers and local people were never told they were being exposed to, let alone monitored for, radiation. (Other releases of radioactive materials occurred at the AEC's Oak Ridge facility in Tennessee and at Dugway Proving Grounds in Utah.)

Whether the tests were conducted to track fallout patterns, check explosive viability, or understand the effects of accidental exposure, the result was that entire downwind animal and human populations became the experimental subjects.

Zones of Concentration on the Nuclear Landscape

While the range of the testing and experimentation covers many areas of the Western United States, the nuclear and militarized landscape of this study focuses on two major zones of concentration within the interdesert region. The first zone, on the eastern half of the interdesert region, includes a good portion of the state of New Mexico as well as parts of Colorado, Arizona, and Utah. This zone is home to Los Alamos National Laboratories (with its extensive toxic and nuclear waste repositories); Sandia Labs and Phillips Laboratory at Kirtland Air Force Base; Manzano Mountain (former site of the nation's largest nuclear weapons stockpile); White Sands Missile Range and the Trinity nuclear test site; Fort Bliss Military Reservation and Holloman Air Force Base (south of White Sands); Cannon Air Force Base; the Mescalero Apache proposed site for monitored retrievable nuclear waste storage; the Waste Isolation Pilot Project, or WIPP (the military's deep geologic nuclear waste repository); the Gnome and Gasbuggy nuclear test sites in New Mexico; the Rio Blanco and Rulison "peaceful use" test sites in Colorado; and the Grant's Uranium Belt region discussed in Chapter 2.

The second zone is composed of the land on the western half of the interdesert region. It includes the southeastern edge of California—the home of the China Lake Naval Weapons Center, Fort Irwin, and Edwards Air Force Base. Also in California, in the lower Mojave Desert and south of these military reservations, is Ward Valley—currently slated to be a significant dumping ground for "low-level" nuclear waste. Ward Valley is due east of another extensive military reservation, the Twenty-nine Palms Marine Corps Base, as well as the Chocolate Mountains Bombing Range, and, close by in Arizona, the Yuma Proving Grounds and the Luke Air Force Bombing and Gunnery Range. In addition to parts of California, Zone Two contains most of the state of Nevada, the most militarized zone of all—home to Nellis Air Force Base, Fallon Training Range Complex, the Tonopah Test Range, and other military reservations, as well as the Nevada Test Site (now also sited for a temporary storage facility for high-level nuclear waste, and currently storing so-called low-level nuclear waste within its boundaries). Zone Two also includes the high-level nuclear waste repository at Yucca Mountain, as well as the region most severely affected by downwind radiation from nuclear bomb testing. In addition, Zone Two contains two sites being considered for temporary high-level nuclear waste, one in southwestern Utah and the other at the border of Oregon and Nevada; an only recently closed low-level nuclear waste site outside Beatty, Nevada; the Utah Test and Training Range; and a major military installation for biological and chemical weapons (which also practices dangerous incineration of the chemical weapons stockpile) in Dugway, Utah. In Arizona, between Zone One and Two, there are more uranium mining and processing areas in the Grand Canyon, Tuba City, and Monument Valley regions.

Militarized Zones, Outdoor Laboratories, and Native Americans

Since scientific research centers and military installations with their "theaters of war" constitute a significant part of the nuclear landscape, they must be identified and added to the map on which we've placed the uranium mining regions identified in Chapter 2. Because scientific research makes possible the nuclear industry, including the nuclear weapons industry, it is not surprising that in each zone of concentration geographies of sacrifice have emerged around the most important scientific and military sites. The continued need for testing and development of ever more sophisticated weapons, fueled by the ideological conflict of the Cold War and its spiraling arms race, left behind it a landscape pockmarked with craters, littered with shell casings, dotted with inadequate, decomposing storage containers, crisscrossed with open trenches, and dusted with fallout. And use of the land as a testing field for high-tech weaponry is not a thing of the past. The Pentagon currently has plans for a 1 million-acre expansion of its 25 million acres of testing and training fields. The expansion is all in the West.[18]

But such concerns tell only half the story. All of these sites are surrounded by American Indians—some on reservations, others in small "colonies" (nonreservation Indian communities), and some in what, ironically, are called "squatter" communities by the United States government.[19] With every identification of a military reservation, testing range, or science city, a corresponding identification of Indian presence can usually be made. Whether the land in question is currently "occupied" by the Department of Defense, the Department of Energy, the University of California (contractor of Los Alamos), the Department of the Interior, AT&T (formerly Bell Labs and contractor for Sandia Labs), or Westinghouse (contractor for WIPP)—in all cases, Indian presence spreads out beneath and around the nuclear and militarized landscape of the Southwest. In the first zone are the Pueblo tribes, the Navajo, the Hopi, the Ute Mountain Ute, the Mescalero Apache, the Jicarilla Apache, and others. In the second zone are many different bands of the Western Shoshone, the Southern Paiute, the Owens Valley Paiute, as well as the Havasupai and the Fort Mojave, Chemehuevi, Colorado River, Quechan, and Cocopah tribes. Consequently, the sociological populations most severely affected by the pollution created by these installations, most disturbed by the blasting engines of fighter aircraft over their homes, most displaced by military land withdrawal and acquisition, and most endangered by the above- and below-ground testing of nuclear weapons over the past five decades are American Indians. This is not to say that non-Indians have not been at risk. Activities at nuclear and military laboratories and testing ranges have had severe effects upon all who live near them—including the scientists, the military personnel and their families, and others downwind. But Indians have traditionally gone unrepresented, bereft of power

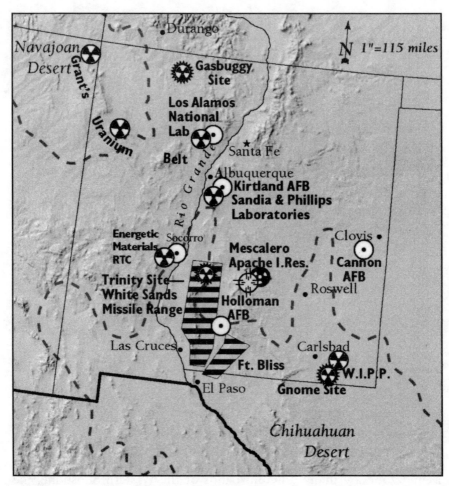

Figure 3.1 Zone One of the nuclear landscape
(Refer to the Legend of Map Symbols for identification of all symbols.)

Compiled by Valerie Kuletz; cartography production by Jared Dawson

bases from which to press their grievances. I highlight the plight of native peoples not only for these reasons but also because they have a unique and compelling historical and cultural claim to these lands, one that has been repressed for many centuries by their Euroamerican conquerors.

Zone One

Premiere Science City: Los Alamos Laboratory

The beautiful Pajarito Plateau upon which Los Alamos National Labs sits in Northern New Mexico is by no stretch of the imagination a wasteland.[20]

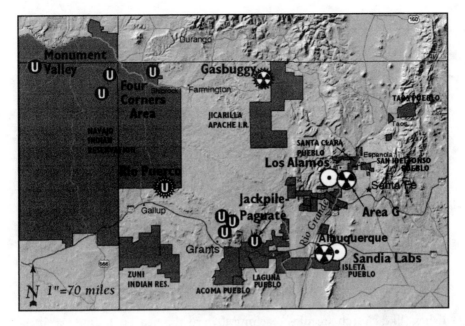

Figure 3.2 Northern half of Zone One

Indian reservations (identified by shaded areas) stand in close proximity to both the national nuclear weapons laboratories and the uranium mining district.

Compiled by Valerie Kuletz; cartography production by Jared Dawson

The area surrounding Los Alamos Labs contains evergreen and aspen forests, dramatic deep red canyons and high mesas where the great blue bowl of the sky reaches out in all directions. The plateau is covered with ancient Indian ruins (such as the extraordinary Bandelier ancient cliff dwellings in what is now the Bandelier National Monument), cultural artifacts of all kinds, and petroglyphs and sacred places that continue to be tended by the Indian people of the area. For instance, one can visit the Puye cliff dwellings that were settled by people of the ancient Anasazi culture, along with other prehistoric settlements including Tsankawi, Tyuonyi, Otowi, Shufinne, and Tshirege. Today, Los Alamos—best known of the science cities—is literally surrounded by Indian reservations and settlements that, of course, existed long before it came into being. To the north of Los Alamos lies the Santa Clara Pueblo, to the northeast the San Juan Pueblo and San Lorenzo Pueblo, to the east rest San Ildefonso and Nambe Pueblo, with Cochiti Pueblo and Santo Domingo Pueblo to the south and Tesuque Pueblo to the southeast. To the west and south lie the Jemez and the Zia Indian reservations. Farther north lies the Jicarilla Apache reservation.[21]

The siting of Los Alamos National Labs in this region seems oddly appropriate, since the area is a Mecca for those seeking to know the forces of power behind the divine, the emptiness, the chaos, the plan, the universe. Sacred sites are everywhere. In the nearby Jemez Mountains, it's possible to find a Christian monastery (the Paracletes), a convent (Handmaidens of the Precious Blood), and a Zen Buddhist monastery (Bodhi Mandala) all within a mile of each other. In such religious company, one can't help but associate the nuclear physicists at nearby Los Alamos with a priesthood—they are the high priests of our secular religion: science. A semiotic reading of the area turns up Christian crosses, Spanish missions, church bells, chanting Buddhists, sacred Indian shrines, ancient Indian ruins, and monumental satellite communications dishes (like church steeples reaching toward the heavens). One can literally read the presence of various "cultures" on the land—Christian, Spanish, Indian, scientific, even the "countercultural." The most prominent signs, though, are the artifacts from the Indian and the high-tech science cultures.

In Bandelier National Park near Los Alamos lies a sacred Indian site called the "Shrine of the Stone Lions," a wide circle of rocks stood on end around an inner circle of parched antlers. Inside the middle of the circle of antlers lie two large stones hewn in the rough shape of recumbent mountain lions, worn by weather. The shrine holds numerous offerings—feathers and constructions of cloth, stone, and grass whose meaning and purpose are indecipherable to the casual hiker passing by, but clearly represent recent offerings—suggesting that this spot is still considered a place of power. But while this is Indian territory, it is also, now, part of the nuclear landscape—an awareness that can come as a rude awakening. In 1992, as I sat resting beside this well-maintained shrine in the middle of a wilderness area, I twice felt the earth suddenly and violently shake beneath and around me and heard simultaneously two massive explosions. A visit from the lion gods? No such luck—it was a test explosion (of purpose unknown to me) conducted by the scientists at Los Alamos. At that moment, the two cultures could not have seemed more different, each inscribing, in its own way, a particular relationship with the earth. The striking difference between these two worlds as well as their close proximity throughout the nuclear landscape is at once tragic and strangely appropriate. Both recognize, albeit in different ways, the precarious relationship between human beings and the forces of power.

Nuclearism must be understood in terms of the impact it has not only on the physical bodies of those near its various centers, or on the land itself, but also on the cultural foundations of non-Euroamerican societies with traditions of commitment to, and identification with, particular regions, lands, and places considered by them to be sacred. Nuclearism contributes not only to physical and environmental harm but also, for many American Indians, cultural harm. For instance, the job opportunities that uranium mining or waste storage bring to impoverished reservations can serve as a wedge issue dividing traditionalists from progressives. Too often the choice is between economic and cultural survival, an all-too-familiar dilemma for Indians.

Not far from the Shrine of the Stone Lions, Los Alamos National Laboratory (LANL) spreads across 43 square miles of the high Pajarito Plateau of northern New Mexico. Well-known as the birthplace of the first nuclear bomb, Los Alamos National Laboratory harbors an estimated 2,400 pollution sites containing plutonium, uranium, strontium 90, tritium, lead, mercury, nitrates, cyanides, pesticides, "and other lethal leftovers from a half-century of weapons research and production."[22] These are the materials that for decades have been dumped into the beautiful nearby canyons on the Pajarito Plateau. As one reporter notes:

> Every day, the heartbreakingly beautiful canyons that slice through this mesatop town convey 250,000 gallons of industrial sewage toward the Rio Grande—itself contaminated with plutonium. Radioactive peach trees have been found growing downstream from the lab and traces of plutonium have been detected in chilies and in the catfish of Cochiti Lake. Honeybees in the canyons have tritium in their bodies.[23]

Los Alamos also has a history of illegally incinerating its radioactive waste, causing serious air pollution, a practice that only recently was stopped by lawsuits initiated by activists such as Jay Coghlin and others of the watchdog organization Concerned Citizens for Nuclear Safety. In 1991, after many years of illegal incineration, and after EPA audits proved LANL's violation of the Clean Air Act, the Environmental Protection Agency finally issued a Notice of Noncompliance (with the Clean Air Act) to the DOE and LANL. However, the EPA refused to impose the required penalties and commence shutdown procedures that should have legally resulted from noncompliance. According to Coghlin, the EPA's position was that it could not "sue DOE/LANL for penalties or shut down the incinerator because EPA and DOE are sister executive branch agencies and 'you can't sue yourself.'"[24] Although the controlled air incinerator (used to incinerate mixed and transuranic waste) has now been retired from service (because of CCNS pressure and legal action), the emergence of new incineration technologies at LANL may pose similar threats in the near future.[25] This recent victory for concerned citizens in the LANL region occurred in the nick of time because the incinerator had just undergone development studies in preparation for incinerating 1,236 cubic feet of plutonium-contaminated waste and 530 feet of mixed waste per year. After burning the backlog of wastes stored in barrels at LANL, it would have been ready to take waste from DOE weapons complexes around the nation.[26]

Residents of communities around LANL—including the Indians at San Ildefonso Pueblo—continue to insist on adequate monitoring of all the lab's activities because of the high incidence of thyroid cancer and other radiation-linked diseases.[27] But the secrecy surrounding the lab's activities (and their effects on the environment) has always proved an obstacle to access by the local population. In this regard little has changed since the detonations in the 1950s of "simulated nuclear devices" on and off lab property that exposed local communities to radiation contamination. (Forty years later, the strontium released during these tests can still be detected in Bayo Canyon.[28])

The lab's current radioactive materials dump—"Area G"—is at the border of Tshirege, the largest Anasazi ruin on the Pajarito Plateau. Area G began accepting radioactive waste in 1957. Since 1971, an estimated 381,000 cubic feet of LANL-generated transuranic (plutonium-contaminated) waste has been stored here; since existing records are inadequate no one knows how much went in before 1971. Wastes were simply interred without liners or caps, in bulldozed pits."[29] Today, post-Cold War Los Alamos

National Laboratory is poised to continue its role as a major center of weapons research and development, and to add to it the role of manufacturer of weapons for the nuclear stockpile for the twenty-first century. To maintain this position LANL's Area G not only stores so-called low-level radioactive waste and waste awaiting shipment to WIPP but has been scheduled for expansion. Although currently on hold, pending a sitewide environmental impact assessment, plans for expansion of Area G would, in terms of size, put it in a league with WIPP—the massive, deep geologic dump site in the southern part of the state for the nuclear complex's transuranic waste.[30] An expanded Area G would be able to contain 475,000 cubic yards of mixed waste in pits 2,000 feet long, divided into 25,000 cubic-yard segments. The dump is so huge that concerned citizens and Pueblo Indians strongly suspect that it will be used (as the incinerator would have been used) to receive waste from other DOE facilities. As New Mexico activist Mary Risely argues, the reconfiguration of the United States nuclear weapons complex (known first as Complex 21 and currently as Stockpile Stewardship) appears to be positioning LANL to "become a dumping ground and waste-treatment center for the entire nuclear weapons complex."[31] For example, the Calvin Commission, set up by the Department of Energy, recommended taking Lawrence Livermore Lab out of the nuclear weapons business and transferring all of its nuclear weapons assignments to Los Alamos National Labs.[32] In addition, LANL is currently being considered as a "pretreatment site" for the military's transuranic waste destined for the WIPP repository in southern New Mexico.

The Indian pueblos that all but surround the 43-square-mile campus of Los Alamos generally oppose the existing Area G facility as well as the new Area G development, and their concerns are not unfounded. Since the 1980s, physicians with the Santa Fe Indian Hospital have noticed a marked increase in the number of thyroid cancer cases at the Santa Clara Pueblo, just north of Los Alamos.[33] The San Ildefonso Pueblo is contesting the dumping of plutonium wastes near their water sources and traditional sacred burial grounds. One national news reporter writes that in 1992:

the Pueblos began to speak out in unprecedented ways. San Ildefonso Pueblo's Lieutenant Governor Gilbert held a press conference to oppose a 7 million-cubic-foot waste dump that leaks radiation into adjacent forestland.

The dump is slated for expansion. The people of Santa Clara Pueblo are [also] fighting plans by the Lab's Institute of Geophysics to detonate eight simultaneous underground TNT blasts, each of them at least a ton, in the sacred Jemez Mountains.[34]

Many nearby residents fear that Los Alamos's "Area G" will become a national center of concentration for plutonium-contaminated waste (transuranic waste) generated from weapons production, with the Pantex plant in Texas taking most of the plutonium from weapons disassembly. Many of the original plutonium production sites, such as Rocky Flats, Colorado, and Hanford, Washington, are now closed or closing. The reorganization of the United States nuclear weapons complex into fewer and more highly concentrated areas for the twenty-first century may lead not only to the expansion of Area G but to a new manufacturing mission at the labs, which in turn may well lead to the expansion of the nuclear landscape in Zone One. New Mexico, the third-poorest state in the United States, looks more and more like a sacrificial lamb every day.

Sandia National Laboratories and White Sands Missile Range

Radiation pollution problems similar to Los Alamos have also occurred to the south of Los Alamos at the Sandia Laboratories, endangering the people of Albuquerque, nearby Indian reservations, and the communities downstream on the Rio Grande.

One of the three major United States nuclear weapons labs (the other two being Los Alamos and Lawrence Livermore laboratories), Sandia National Laboratories headquarters is south of Los Alamos on 2,842 acres on the Kirtland Air Force Base near Albuquerque. The DOE has an additional 15,003 acres granted by Kirtland Air Force Base, the state of New Mexico, and the Isleta Pueblo.[35] As noted by Debra Rosenthal, the civilian scientists, engineers, and technicians at Sandia are mostly responsible for the "weaponization" of nuclear bombs, which means they "design all the 'peripheral parts and components' that detonate a warhead, and they figure out how to put the guts into 'delivery packages'—bodies that can be dropped, shot through water, or whatever the military orders."[36] Sandia Labs is surrounded by a highwire fence within the Kirtland Air Force Base. Also fenced off within Kirtland is Manzano Mountain, a military "base

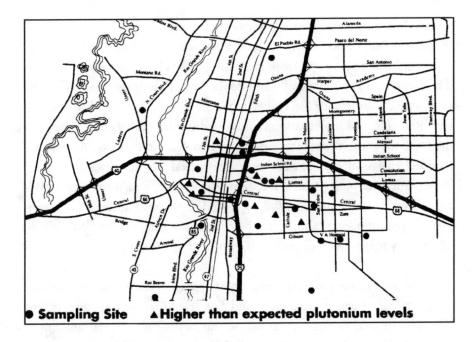

● Sampling Site   ▲ Higher than expected plutonium levels

Figure 3.3 Activist map of Albuquerque, New Mexico

From: All People's Coalition, *Enchanted Times*

within a base"—until recently, the largest single nuclear weapons holding station in the world.[37] This facility has been the home of 1,000 bombs that activists claim lacked modern safety features designed to prevent accidental nuclear blasts. (Weapons have since been moved out of the base to other areas in the region. Their exact location is not clear.)

Although (according to DOE) no official epidemiological studies have been conducted to examine the impact of SNL on the health of the surrounding communities, residents of Albuquerque (comprising about one-third of all people in the state of New Mexico) have compiled their own maps of radiation pollution in the state, with Albuquerque, Kirtland Air Force Base, and Sandia Labs at the center. They claim that the labs and the base have produced serious pollution of the nearby Rio Grande and that plutonium has been found in soil in the city.

In 1991 Sandia National Labs requested that the city of Albuquerque allow it to increase "amounts" and "types" of radioactive materials to be dumped into the sewer system and the Rio Grande. Sandia's proposal was defeated as a result of public opposition, including opposition from the Indians of Isleta Pueblo, who use the river water for drinking and irrigation.[38] Although prevented from increasing its level of contamination, Sandia continues to systematically and deliberately pollute Albuquerque with radioactive isotopes. In December 1996, the Isleta Pueblo and the Southwest Research and Information Center filed suit in federal court to require the DOE to issue an environmental impact statement that would provide a comprehensive analysis of existing and potential new activities at Sandia.

According to activists, the Department of Energy facilities that dominate this zone in the nuclear landscape abide by health standards and compliance requirements tailored to their own interests, not the public's. In effect, they live under a different set of rules. For instance:

> Unlike [commercial] NRC-regulated industries, DOE facilities are not subject to a 7-Curie per year maximum discharge of radioactive wastes to sewers. In fact, DOE's regulations set no limits on the total amount of radioactivity that can be disposed of in a year's time. By simply increasing the amount of water—and thus reducing the amount [concentration] of radioactive materials—DOE facilities can dump substantial quantities of radioactive materials into sewers.[39]

Multicultural Alliances—Resistance from the Margins

Because of this double standard for government and the secrecy of federal agencies, local activists provide the only information available about pollution. Community activists in the state of New Mexico—including some of the Indian communities—are among the most energetic and committed in the country. Their knowledge and technical expertise is extremely sophisticated, and they work to create interracial alliances to combat common problems. Despite serious racial tensions within the state, the struggle against nuclear waste in these often impoverished communities binds together people from different communities, cultures, and classes. Leaders with the San Ildefonso and the San Juan pueblos meet with members of the All People's Coalition, Concerned Citizens for Nuclear Safety, and the Los Alamos Study Group to share information and develop strategies concerning the Area G repository at Los Alamos. Activists in Albuquerque,

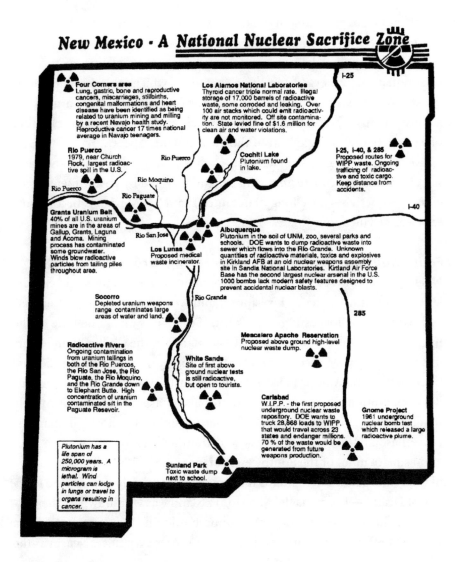

Figure 3.4 Activist map of New Mexico

From: All People's Coalition, Albuquerque

Santa Fe, and in smaller towns and cities throughout New Mexico, as well as in the different Indian reservations (including some of those in the uranium-mining districts) often work together to combat WIPP. Within Zone One of the nuclear landscape, knowledge about nuclear pollution and its hazards inevitably comes out of the combined efforts of those most at risk, not from government documents directly. Although not highly visible to the rest of the country, these unofficial studies cannot be excluded as easily from policy deliberations as uranium miners' claims for the very reason that they emerge from these coalitions, which include white, middle-class activists.[40] Still, it is often only through local documents—activists' maps of radiation pollution (such as those shown here)—that one can actually *see* the extent of the nuclear landscape.

Local activists' maps make visible what is so often denied and kept secret by industry contractors with the military and by government agencies. These activists have long maintained that New Mexico is becoming a "nuclear sacrifice zone."

Four Thousand Square Miles of Proving Grounds

Nuclear weapons research and development at Los Alamos and Sandia labs (along with Lawrence Livermore) and weapons development in general require land for testing—lots of it. (See Figure 3.1, "Zone One of the nuclear landscape.") White Sands Missile Range in the Chihuahuan Desert in southern New Mexico was created for this purpose. Claiming the distinction of being America's largest military installation (a claim other military reservations in Zones One and Two also make), White Sands Missile Range spans 4,000 square miles of desert. Combined with Holloman Air Force Base and Fort Bliss the test and training region covers more than 7,000 square miles of the Southwestern landscape. Within this vast reserve of the White Sands range stands the region appropriately named "the Journey of Death"—Journada del Muerto. The land was withdrawn by the government in 1945 to test the first atomic bomb and has been used for a variety of military war game and testing purposes ever since. Nearby is the Mescalero Apache Reservation.

Today's high-tech weapons are so powerful that they are literally outgrowing even test ranges as big as White Sands, which means that surrounding areas are at greater risk. White Sands is used for everything from full-scale battle practice, with jet planes and missiles powered by remote control from the basement of the "Range Control Center," to the development and testing of top-secret lasers like Miracl (Mid-Infrared Advanced Chemical Laser) which is capable of targeting satellites. Two researchers wrote in 1991, "White Sands averages more than twenty 'missions' a day and more than two 'hot firings' each day. In a hot firing, a missile or other weapon, is actually launched."[41] Between 1945 and 1993, 43,631 missile firings have taken place. An aviation publication reported in 1994, "Additionally, 1,000 training missions, hundreds of laboratory environmental and captive flight tests, and more than 3,000 nuclear effects tests occur here each year."[42] Electronic warfare is played there, and the Patriot Missile was tested there, as well as "conventional" explosives that can simulate the blast of a nuclear explosion. According to the 1991 report:

> In fact, the Army can just about produce the power of a small nuclear explosion in the battlefield now with conventional arms, such as a bomb that sprays a fine mist of fuel for miles, then erupts in a conflagration that literally sucks molecules out of soldiers. The Army's Nuclear Effects Directorate has a solar furnace forty-five feet high and one hundred feet long in the southwest corner of White Sands that can create thermal radiation bursts similar to a nuclear explosion.[43]

Indeed, great demands are placed on today's testing ranges. For instance, not only large "strategic" nuclear bombs require testing but also smaller "theater" nuclear artillery munitions, which typically are fired only across the width of a battlefield (and, say defense officials, are much more likely to be used on the post-Cold War battlefield).[44]

Zone One, then, takes shape as a layer of nuclearism and militarization superimposed upon a landscape that has been historically imprinted with more Indian and Hispanic presence than any other region in the United States. To the uranium mining fields can now be added the 43-square mile-campus of Los Alamos, Sandia Labs with its massive weapons arsenal, Kirtland Air Force base encircling Manzano Mountain, and the 4,000 square miles of desert that is White Sands Missile Range, with the Fort Bliss Military Reservation, as well as other military reserves, extending the militarized zone all the way into Texas. Because of the nature of radiation and toxic chemicals, all these installations reach far beyond their borders in influence. Their toxic residues move through water, air, soil, and the genetic structure of living bodies. In Chapter 4, "Nuclear Wasteland," we will add WIPP, the deep geologic burial installation for plutonium-contaminated waste and the above-ground monitored retrievable

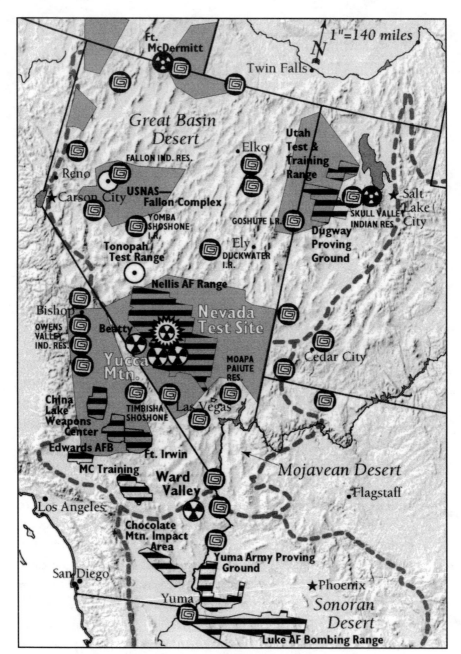

Figure 3.5 Zone Two of the nuclear landscape
Shaded areas here designate military air space and military operations areas. Such areas extend the zone of military occupation far beyond land holdings. (Refer to Legend of Map Symbols for identification of other symbols.)

Compiled by Valerie Kuletz; cartography production by Jared Dawson storage facility at one time proposed for the nearby Mescalero Apache reservation, to the map of Zone One.

Zone Two
The Mojave Desert

Walking among the hills of the Indian Wells Valley, home of the largest naval weapons research, development, and testing installation in the world, I gain enough altitude to look out over the sparse but sprawling human developments in what is an otherwise stunningly beautiful and stark desert valley surrounded by mountain ranges in hues of blue and purple. On some days the place appears severe and desolate because of the relative scarcity of trees and brush. But on this late October morning the valley rests beneath the moving shadows of great rolling cumulus clouds tumbling over the High Sierra Nevada to its west. Some of the highest mountain peaks in the continental United States loom spectacularly out of the monumental jagged backbone of the mountain range. Standing near the El Paso Mountains and the mountain the locals call Black Mountain— sacred to the Shoshone and Paiute and strewn with ancient petroglyphs— I look across the valley to another sacred area, the Coso Range. Suddenly, and without warning, I am buzzed by one of two fighter jets that seem to jump out from behind a hill as if from nowhere. The sound is deafening, and their proximity and menacing power prompt me to duck and cover beneath a creosote bush. The wasplike jets (there are always more than one) circle relentlessly, dipping and gliding among the hills, down valleys, over mountains, and off toward adjacent Panamint Valley. When they're gone, I move on to a larger hill for a better view of the area and am stopped dead in my tracks by the sound of a huge explosion—a significant test— coming from the other side of the valley in the area of the Coso Range. A large white and gray cloud of smoke billows ominously out of the distant range. It's just another day in my old hometown.

The nuclear landscape must be understood as part of the larger militarized "zone of occupation" (with science cities, theaters of war, and military testing fields) that overlaps and is superimposed on the Indian landscape of the region. Even when the military purports to develop and test only "conventional" weapons, it still shares a history and interests with nuclear research centers and ranges. China Lake Naval Weapons

Center, for instance, while not now considered "nuclear," was, in fact, initiated in the same period as Los Alamos and was part of Project Y (the Manhattan Project) in its early days. Scientists move easily from one institution to another, from one secret project to another. And different centers specialize in different "parts" or aspects of the same weapon or delivery system. Expertise is specialized, as are research facilities, but scientific knowledge of the kind required for weapons development travels—it circulates—through the interwoven and fused networks of the Department of Energy and the Department of Defense. Many of the workers—military and civilian—share a perception of the land as an outdoor laboratory.[45] The landscape itself acts as a "testbed," a "proving ground," for scientific research, whether for conventional or unconventional weapons. The region is constructed into a scientific landscape, a literal extension of the laboratory into the desert terrain. In this way, the interdesert region is used as a military zone, a scientific laboratory, and a dumping ground at one and the same time. Like our national forests, the desert becomes "a land of many uses."

China Lake is the Navy's largest research, development, test, and evaluation facility. Also known as NWC (Naval Weapons Center) and more recently NAWS (Naval Air Weapons Station), China Lake Naval Weapons Center is located in the Indian Wells Valley of the Mojave Desert (at the south end of the Great Basin Desert) in California, with the Sierra Nevada to its west, Death Valley to its east, and the desiccated Owens Valley to its north. Established in November 1943, by 1968 China Lake had developed in the Navy's own words "over 75% of the airborne weapons of the free world [and] 40% of the world's conventional weapons."[46] There are 1,100 buildings at China Lake, more than 1 million acres of land, and 20,000 square miles of controlled airspace. China Lake represents 38 percent of the Navy's entire land holdings. Near it are two other "military reservations," Fort Irwin, which comprises more than a half-million acres, and Edwards Air Force Base, which is roughly half the size of Fort Irwin. Together, these military installations form a significant militarized zone in the upper Mojave Desert.

Unlike the other armed services in the United States, the Navy is the only one with its own navy, air force, and army. The navy has pursued land and airspace withdrawals aggressively.[47] Its strength is evident in many areas of the West, but especially in Nevada and California. With a yearly budget of close to $1 billion, China Lake Naval Weapons Center employs more than 5,000 civilians and nearly 1,000 military personnel. As an institution the Navy moves slowly and is not known for its willingness to include the public and outside parties in its activities and decisions. However, a handful of laws have forced the Navy both to recognize the rights of Indians in a very limited capacity and to develop at least some standards for limiting environmental damage. (These laws are NAGPRA—Native American Graves Protection and Repatriation Act, NEPA—National Environmental Policy Act, and AIRFA—American Indian Religious Freedom Act.)

Because of the public concerns for environmental and cultural resources, the China Lake Naval Weapons Center now dons a cloak of concern and claims to have assumed a "stewardship" role over the land, protecting endangered species, Indian petroglyph rock carvings,[48] and sites of religious significance to contemporary Paiute tribes of the Owens Valley and Western Shoshone Indians (specifically the Timbisha Shoshone) who live in the area. In an official 50-year commemorative publication about China Lake, at a time when the Navy was virtually (and conveniently) writing the Indians out of existence, one writer glowingly wrote of the Navy's reverence for the Indian rock art:

> By the time the United States Navy chose the ancient valley as a rocket laboratory 50 years ago, most of the Valley Shoshone were diluted into the white men's lifestyles. Yet it was the United States Navy that preserved the haunting rock art—petroglyphs—that, at the end of 1993, no living Shoshone has been able to decipher. They are kept as a guarded shrine deep inside the Navy's 1.3 million acres.[49]

A very different story about guarding this "shrine" is told by the Paiute and Shoshone of the area who see the Navy as intruders on, and destroyers of, their sacred land:

> But now it looks like they've done bombing out there too [referring to Coso, site of high concentration of petroglyphs] because the shells are out there still. We didn't get to go see the petroglyphs [on a recent visit] but

they say that from the bombing that the rocks with the petroglyphs are breaking down.[50]

Navy claims of stewardship, such as the one quoted here, are inevitably compromised by NWC's use of the land as a testing range for the weapons of war. The Coso Range—a traditional and contemporary sacred Indian site—is, as the Navy states, "officially called the Military Target Range, [and] constitutes some 70 square miles of mountainous area in the northern part of NWC, with various targets—bridges, tunnels, vehicles, SAM sites—emplaced in a natural forested environment for tactics development and pilot training under realistic conditions."[51] This use of the land hardly constitutes stewardship or reverence. The rhetoric of environmental and cultural concerns is at odds with the military's environmental record. As Thomas notes, "The Government Accounting Office (GAO) reports that the United States Department of Defense currently generates 500,000 tons of toxics annually—more than the top five chemical companies combined."[52] If China Lake is the largest naval installation in the world, it must be reckoned as one of the most significant contributors to this annual tonnage of toxins. (Actual statistics of NWC's waste stream is not public knowledge.)

Although the presence of Indian populations that have traditional claims to this land is not immediately apparent (at least not to many Euroamericans), it is not because they have all been assimilated or "diluted into the white men's lifestyles." The Indians of California and Nevada learned to become "invisible" for reasons of survival—a lesson they carry with them today. This secretiveness has been particularly true for the small bands of the Western Shoshone and Paiute of this high desert area. Although they once migrated over a large area, today they are clustered outside the militarized domain in the Owens Valley, Tehachapi Mountains, Lake Isabella area, and Death Valley. Indeed, one can drive through Death Valley National Park and not know that a "squatter" community (the Timbisha Shoshone) lives a mile away from the visitor center.

As nations, the Western Shoshone and Southern Paiute cover extensive territories and are divided up into fairly distinct tribes and bands. These contemporary local bands trace their ancestry in the China Lake area and surrounding region back thousands of years. Archaeologists find evidence of Shoshone and Paiute habitation reaching back at least 12,000 years. Consequently, like the Pajarito Plateau in New Mexico, this land contains important burial and ceremonial sites. In this extremely arid environment exist countless artifacts—etched on canyon walls, buried among the rock and in the sand, in the high pinyon forests, and scattered across the hills, valleys, and shallow washes—marking historical Indian presence. Besides serving as home to the largest petroglyph rock carving areas in North America, the Coso Range (now under the control of the Naval Weapons Center), particularly the hot springs there, serve as a traditional holy ground that is used for healing ceremonies by the Paiute and Shoshone, forming a geocultural link to their ancestral past and serving as a testament to their presence on the land. The Coso Range is now also a site of contestation between these Indian groups and the Navy, who, as noted earlier, refer to it as a "Military Target Range" and as an "outside laboratory" with "propulsion, warhead, and environmental test facilities."

The China Lake area of the Mojave is separated from Yucca Mountain in the Amargosa Valley only by Panamint Valley (now dubiously protected by the Desert Protection Act) and Death Valley, and the desert mountain ranges in between. Traditional Indian use of this land mass has nothing to do with recent white Euroamerican geopolitical state boundaries. The Indians from the Owens Valley and from Death Valley migrated seasonally to the Nevada Test Site area and to Yucca Mountain, which they consider a holy mountain.[53] The Owens Valley Indian groups and the Death Valley Timbisha Shoshone are therefore included in the Yucca Mountain case study discussed in the second half of this book. Interviews with representatives of these tribes reveal the complexities of their relationship with the massive naval weapons center.

Like other areas in the Southwest, large parts of the Mojave have been reserved for—or rather sacrificed to—weapons testing and development. Like Los Alamos, China Lake is composed of one of the largest concentrations of scientists, engineers, and technicians in the country. The work that goes on in this "secret science city in the desert" is strictly classified. Its lands remain inaccessible to unauthorized personnel. That this sea of creosote, with its mountain ranges, its canyons, pinyon forests, and valleys, can be called a wasteland and set aside as an experimental test range sacrificed to "national security" is indeed ironic when directly next to it is Death Valley National Park, an area preserved as a "national treasure." The signification of these areas as wasteland or national treasure demonstrates the arbitrary nature of the signifier, but it also shows how such designations can be precise and strategically used for political ends.

Like the upper Mojave, the lower Mojave and the upper Sonoran deserts are used extensively as a militarized zone—in particular, as a gunnery range and as a war games theater (and in the near future most likely as a radioactive waste dump site at Ward Valley). Fort Irwin, Twenty-nine Palms Marine Corps Base, the Chocolate Mountain Bombing Range, and the Yuma Proving Grounds complete a highly militarized sacrificial landscape in the Southwest.

Nevada's Military Reservations

Last but not least, between the two desert militarized zones of Eastern California and New Mexico, and completing Zone Two of the nuclear landscape, lies the most militarized zone of all—the Great Basin Desert of Nevada. Moving east and slightly north from China Lake—over Panamint Valley, Death Valley, and the mountain ranges that divide them—we come to the Amargosa Valley at the western edge of the Nevada Test Site and Nellis Air Force Base (where Yucca Mountain and a proposed interim waste storage site reside). If Los Alamos is the brains of the nuclear landscape, the Nevada Test Site is its heart. This is ground zero.

Like other military reservations, laboratories, and weapons research enclaves considered thus far, the militarized Nevada interior and Great Basin Desert region began with the emerging new technological paradigm in the 1940s and expanded in the 1950s and 1980s as the Cold War's demand for high-tech weaponry escalated.

The Nellis Range and the adjoining ranges of the Nevada Test Site and the Groom Range together have the distinction of being the largest single piece of militarized land in Nevada and perhaps the United States. As David Loomis notes in *Combat Zoning*:

> On October 29, 1940, President Roosevelt established the Las Vegas Bombing and Gunnery Range. Now called the Nellis Range it is the largest military

range in the Western world. Executive order 8578 established the range under an obscure legal authority granted by the Army Appropriations Act of July 9, 1918. It provided for allowing the president to reserve unappropriated public domain lands for aviation fields for testing and experimental work. . . . The original executive order reserved 3.5 million acres of the range.[54]

Loomis also notes the criteria for selection of the site—criteria (similar to those used for China Lake and White Sands Missile Range) contributing to a common perception of desert lands as expendable:

> The weather is excellent for flying and there was plenty of government land available for a dollar an acre. The land was cheap because *it really wasn't much good for anything but gunnery practice—you could bomb it into oblivion and never notice the difference.* [My italics.][55]

Evidential Politics of Presence

Not mentioned in the quote above are the indigenous inhabitants of this land—the scattered colonies and surrounding tribes of Western Shoshone and Southern Paiute Indians—nor the land's cultural use and significance. The contemporary Indian communities that border the combined land mass of Nellis Air Force Base and the Nevada Test Site include the Moapa Reservation to its southeast, the Pahrump Paiute Tribe and the Las Vegas Paiute Colony to its south, the Duckwater Shoshone and Yomba Shoshone reservations to its northwest, the Timbisha Shoshone to its west, and the Goshute reservation to its northeast. Like Los Alamos, the Nevada Test Site is surrounded by Indians. But this list doesn't begin to indicate the true cultural and historical use of the area by many more bands of Mojave and Great Basin Indians in more remote outlying areas. According to the Western Shoshone, the Nellis air base and the Nevada Test Site are at the lower end of "Newe Segobia," Western Shoshone aboriginal homeland:

> The Western Shoshone people of the Inter-mountain West called themselves the Newe (people). They occupied a large area in the Great Basin region, from southern Idaho (north) to Death Valley, California (south),

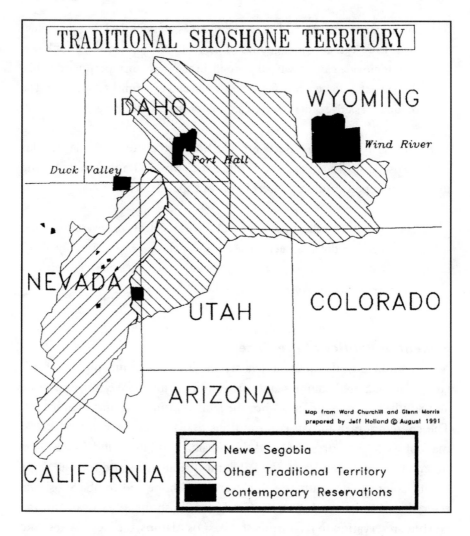

Figure 3.6 Newe Segobia and traditional Shoshone territories (already in image)

From: Churchill, *Struggle for the Land* (Compiled by Ward Churchill and produced by Jeff Holland)

and from the Smith Creek Mountains in central Nevada (west) to the area around present-day Ely, Nevada (east). The Newe called their homeland Pia Sokopia (Earth Mother). They developed a distinctive way of life before white contact, one that continued to exist even after white people entered the Great Basin.[56]

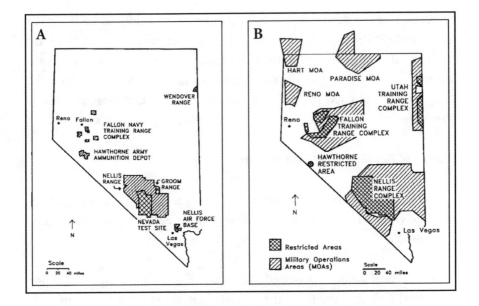

Figure 3.7 Nevada military (A) land withdrawals and (B) controlled air space

From: Loomis, *Combat Zoning*

The 1983 Treaty of Ruby Valley demonstrates the Western Shoshone's *legal* claim to the Nevada Test Site and the Nellis Range (and much more). They have for years actively resisted further encroachment or interference by United States authorities, as evidenced by the celebrated Dann Ranch case.[57] Since 1984, demonstrations led by Western Shoshone elders outside the Nevada Test Site have become a regular event where protesters who cross the cattle guard onto the NTS domain ceremoniously show their Western Shoshone visas to the guards arresting them.

Although they lack a separate treaty, the Southern Paiute also rightfully claim this region as their aboriginal lands. The two Indian nations share a long history of mutual use of much of what is now the state of Nevada, as well as parts of California, Arizona, and Utah. This history has been substantiated in Euroamerican terms by abundant archaeological evidence, as well as by ethnohistorical evidence.[58]

Today, in the state of Nevada, in addition to Nellis Air Force Base and the Nevada Test Site, we can add the following military reservations: Fallon Navy Training Range Complex, with its airspace; the Hawthorne Army Ammunition Depot, with its restricted airspace; the Reno Military

Operations Area Airspace; the Hart Military Operations Area Airspace; the Paradise Military Operations Area Airspace; and parts of the Utah Training Range Complex, with its airspace.[59] Military ranges in Nevada alone amount to four million acres. Approximately 40 percent of Nevada's airspace is designated for military use. All of these facilities are close to Paiute and Shoshone reservations and colonies.

Nuclear Testing and Downwind Victims

> The greatest irony of our atmospheric nuclear testing program is that the only victims of United States nuclear arms since WWII have been our own people.[60]

The most profoundly devastated area of the nuclear landscape—and perhaps of the earth—exists on the Nevada Test Site. Groundwater in some aquifers on the Nevada Test Site is contaminated by tritium 3,000 times in excess of safe drinking water standards, as well as by plutonium and other radioactive isotopes. Since 1951, radioactive releases from the Nevada Test Site have emitted more than 12 billion curies into the atmosphere, and in high fallout areas near the Nevada Test Site, childhood leukemia rates are 2.5 times the national average. Wildlife (such as deer) have access to radioactively contaminated water on the Nevada Test Site and have been found off-site with extremely high levels of tritium in their blood.[61]

Although the Nevada Test Site story has been told less than the story of Los Alamos, it is not an unfamiliar tale to modern readers or moviegoers. (In films such as *Hair*, *Blue Sky*, and *Desert Bloom*, the Nevada Test Site becomes the stage for nuclear fears in the popular culture.) This piece of land is the symbol of the power and especially the peril of the nuclear age; and because of this, the Nevada Test Site unfailingly conjures up images of dis-ease, fear, and apprehension. Interestingly, the Los Alamos story can be, and is often, told without eliciting such negative emotions. Because the Los Alamos narrative is one of scientific mastery, achievement, success, and advancement, it constructs Western knowledge as that which has made it possible to "harness" the infinite energies embedded within the core of the material world itself. The Nevada Test Site, on the other hand, enjoys no such tale of triumph. It is the darkest zone on the nuclear land-

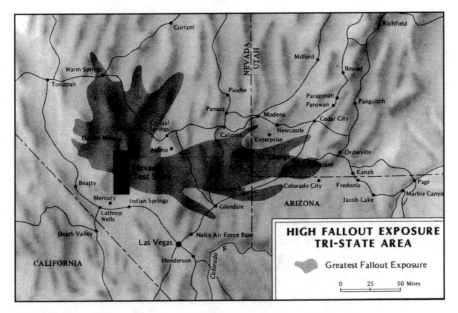

Figure 3.8 Downwind exposure areas from the Nevada Test Site

From: Ball, *Justice Downwind* (Tom Patterson, cartographer)

scape, the proving grounds for this mastery of energy. The image of the brilliant scientist drops out of the picture at this stage, supplanted by the mere technician. The mushroom cloud—the Nevada Test Site's potent symbol—looms large against the backdrop of an "unpopulated" Nevada desert. The cloud reminds us that radiation is real, and we fear that we haven't "harnessed" this energy at all. But the cloud dissipates, leaving no *visible* reminder of its deadly byproduct of radiation—until it's too late.

"Nutmeg" was the code name for the secret 1950s project to find an on-continent testing range for nuclear explosives. Like "Project Y" and the "Manhattan Project," secret names are necessary for activities in the nuclear landscape. In 1951 "Nutmeg" chose the Great Basin Desert as a replacement for the Marshall Islands, the United States's previous nuclear testing location. The Nevada Nuclear Test Site was thus carved out of 435,000 acres of the Nellis land domain, and "legally" transferred from the Air Force to the Atomic Energy Commission (now the Department of Energy) in 1952. In 1961, 318,000 acres were added, making the Nevada Test Site 753,000 acres.[62] And yet later it was expanded to 867,000 acres.[63] Since 1952, 928 above-and below-ground nuclear bombs have been detonated.

Here is the heart of the nuclear landscape—the epicenter of the geography of sacrifice where each atmospheric test contained as much radiation as the Chernobyl disaster, where underground tests leak radiation, and where purposeful "vents" allowed radioactive emissions into the air. Moving outward from this knot of imploding atoms are the winds of death: death for the downwinders in Utah, Nevada, Arizona, and others farther afield, including the Indians (the lowest "low-use segment of the population") who were largely invisible to the technicians playing with power in the desert.[64] As Howard Ball has stated:

> The deadly atomic sunburst over Hiroshima, in 1945, produced 13 kilotons of murderous heat and radioactive fallout. At least 27 of the 96 above ground bombs detonated between 1951 and 1958 at the Nevada Test Site produced a total of over 620 kilotons of radioactive debris that fell on the down winders. The radioactive isotopes mixed with the scooped-up rocks and earth of the southwestern desert lands and "lay down a swath of radioactive fallout" over Utah, Arizona, and Nevada. In light of the fact that scientific research has now confirmed that any radiation exposure is dangerous, the "virtual uninhabitants" (over 100,000 people) residing in the small towns east and south of the test site were placed in potential medical jeopardy by the AEC atomic test program.[65]

Western Shoshone Chief Raymond Yowell offers the Indian perspective on the hazards of living in the shadow of these tests:

> We are now the most bombed nation in the world. . . . [T]he radiation has caused Shoshone, Ute, Navajo, Hopi, Paiute, Havasupai, Hualapai and other downwind communities to suffer from cancer, thyroid diseases and birth defects.[66]

Although, in some cases and wholly inadequately, the Department of Energy has admitted responsibility for health damages, it remains totally deaf to the land claims made by Indians of the area. The land mass we know as the Nevada Test Site has, like all of these landscapes, another name, or names, and another narrative seldom told. This region is made up of three cultural "districts:" the Ogwe'pi (Oasis Valley) district, the Eso (White Rock Spring) district, and the Ash Meadows district, which together form part of the traditional home of the Southern Paiute and the Western Shoshone. The area we now call the Nevada Test Site served as a region of wild resource harvesting and game hunting for Indians well into the twentieth century, indeed right up to the time the land was withdrawn by the military and Department of Energy. As noted by Richard Stoffle, an anthropologist conducting studies of the Yucca Mountain and Nevada Test Site areas:

> The southern Great Basin is arid on the whole, but there are important oasis areas around the springs and along the watercourses, most of which are ephemeral. Paiute and Shoshone people in the area developed a "transhumant adaptive strategy" that involved the harvesting of a great diversity of plants and animals over the course of a complex annual cycle that involved period[ic] travels throughout an extensive territory.[67]

Indians have always lived, and still live, around the Nevada Test Site area in such places as Oasis Valley, Ash Meadows, and Pahrump Valley. And although in smaller numbers, Indians lived at numerous places within the Nevada Test Site itself.

Claims Made by Downwinders

At various times since 1956, victims of downwind radiation pressed their claims against the government. In a 1956 trial, atomic scientists successfully testified in support of the government's claim not to have endangered the populations downwind from the test site. Both scientists and government officials were later exposed as having lied to the court, as well as having suppressed Atomic Energy Commission reports that proved the government's knowledge of health dangers from the nuclear tests. (At the Hanford Nuclear Reservation between 1951 and 1954, the AEC purposefully exposed their own experimental sheep to radiation specifically comparable to fallout levels on Utah and Nevada from the atmospheric testing, with resulting death and sickness.)[68] In the early 1980s, more than a thousand residents of southern Utah attempted to sue the government for being used as unwitting guinea pigs of a government experiment without adequate warnings of the dangers. Hundreds of people, it was charged, had died of cancer as a result of exposure to fallout from the tests.[69] But once again, mechanisms of exclusion were at work to undercut claims of a *causal* link between illness and testing. As in the case of the Navajo and Pueblo uranium miners, only a handful of deaths were ruled to be the result of radiation-related sickness. In the 1984 ruling on this collective lawsuit, only ten people were acknowledged to have suffered cancer caused by fallout. Only those few were entitled to damages. Even this partial acknowledgment of guilt was reversed by a 1987 Tenth Circuit Court of Appeals in Denver on the basis of the Federal Tort Claims Act of 1946, which gives the federal government the right to engage in activities that are vital to national security even if they cause injuries. Not until a 1989 ruling in favor of the residents of Fernald, Ohio (whose property was contaminated by radioactive materials), did the courts begin to shift position. This decision came on the heels of a 1988 directive from Congress to recognize and compensate atomic veterans—those soldiers placed directly in harm's way during atomic tests. Finally, in 1990, the Radiation Exposure Act became law, offering a formal apology and some (although not adequate) payment for damages. More than 800 claims have been paid since 1990, although these, still, in the opinion of the downwinders, have been woefully inadequate in the face of radiation-induced suffering, illness, and death.

Few, if any, of those compensated in the downwind areas are American Indians, but many Indians experienced the above-ground testing first-hand. Timbisha Shoshone elder Pauline Esteves (living in Death Valley near the Nevada Test Site) recounted for me the first time she felt a nuclear explosion and saw the colorful mushroom cloud:

> It was too warm in the house so we were laying [sleeping] outside. We always had beds outside. And my mother woke us up, and she says, "Get up! Get up! Something's going on!" Then we heard the weird sound, you know, and then the feeling of the shaking. And she says, "An earthquake," but finally she says, "Earthquakes don't have light." You know, they don't have light. And she pointed over in the direction from where it came. And we got

shook up real good, and other people were woke up also. Then my mother says "That's smoke! That's a fire! Maybe Las Vegas is on fire. . . . That's where the light was, and there's the smoke." But then she looked and said, "But that's not smoke we're seeing. Look at the colors of it. She says no smoke makes those colors. Something's going on. And then I told her, "Well, maybe it's them soldiers out there." . . . Nobody told us, you know, what was going on over there. Then we started to find out.[70]

Today, a number of Indian communities are in the midst of the arduous task of gathering epidemiological information to present formal claims. Yet again demonstrating the "scientific" mechanisms of exclusion to which Native Americans are subject, the few epidemiological studies covering people in the Test Site's surrounding region do not take into account Indian lifestyles.[71] Indians in the area have, over the past 40 years, relied more heavily than their Euroamerican neighbors on wild natural resources like pinyon nuts, deer, and rabbits. They use more of the animal, waste less, and thus probably come into contact with more contaminated material than Euroamericans (such as those living in nearby urban environments like Las Vegas).[72]

Like New Mexicans, many concerned residents of Nevada have become activists and watchdogs of the government's use of Nevada lands. White activists have also formed alliances with some Native communities. The government-watch organization Citizen Alert is aligned with Citizen Alert Native American Program. Citizen Alert Native American Program, in conjunction with Nevada's Western Shoshone Indian Tribes (and also some Southern Paiute tribes), began an epidemiological analysis for Indian communities in the mid-1990s. Diane Quigley, director of the Massachusetts-based Childhood Cancer Research Institute and director of the study, has publicly questioned why the government spent millions of dollars at other nuclear weapons sites to determine the health risks to local populations but ignored Nevada, especially Nevada Indians.[73] Though current attempts at epidemiological studies for Indian communities are important, it remains difficult to produce conclusive evidence within the limited scope of scientific statistical studies. As in the uranium-mining communities, Indian communities in fallout paths constitute too small a population to produce the "conclusive results" required by government agencies responsible for redressing past transgressions. Native Americans whose homelands have been subjected to these large-scale experiments in nature have been excluded from any due process that questions the ethics, legality, or validity of such tests.

The actual extent of the Nevada Test Site's impact on the interdesert region, its downwind "outback," and western territories farther afield has only begun to be revealed. For instance, a recent study released in 1997 by the National Cancer Institute has identified serious risk of thyroid cancer caused by downwind radiation exposure, specifically iodine 131, due to tests conducted during the period of above-ground nuclear testing. The 100,000-page study documents that American citizens extending across the entire United States were put at risk, with the highest risk attributed to those living in Western states north and east of the Nevada Test Site.[74]

What has taken place out in this "barren" isolated and "expendable" landscape has made itself visible in the form of sickness, cancer, and deformities in adults, children, and nonhuman life. And it will continue to express itself in future generations. While Atomic Vets, Utah Mormons, and the Indians of the Great Basin and Mojave deserts are not usually outspoken critics of the federal government, their stories make visible the secret nuclear landscape and the power relations that have created it. Collectively their bodies map the nuclear landscape, and their scars reveal the hidden costs of nuclear technology, military secrecy, and national sacrifice.

Other Test Sites and Stockpiles

While the Nevada Test Site is the central location for most downwind radiation, other tests have also been reported in the Great Basin Desert area. *The Milwaukee Journal* printed in 1993:

> The USAF deliberately staged at least eight nuclear reactor *meltdowns* in the Utah desert in 1959. Salt Lake City's *Desert News* reported that the total radiation released was 14 times more than that dispersed by the 1979 Three Mile Island disaster. At least two towns were in the fallout path of radiation clouds that spread from the Dugway Proving Grounds where the meltdowns

were set off. The 'tests' were Air Force attempts to assess the hazards of a reactor meltdown aboard an experimental nuclear-powered aircraft that was never developed.[75]

Secret tests were also conducted in Idaho, New Mexico, Utah, and California.

The largest nuclear test in the United States was not detonated on the continental United States but in the Aleutian Chain off the coast of Alaska on Amchitka Island. Like so many secret activities during the Cold War, the Amchitka blasts (named Long Shot, Milrow, and Cannikan) were made public only recently by the Department of Energy. As in Nevada the Natives and the environmentalists, along with (unique to Alaska) the fishing communities, are demanding more information about the effects of the tests.[76] The Amchitka tests were actually meant for the Nevada Test Site, but they were so huge that scientists thought they might damage buildings in Las Vegas. Thus, Amchitka Island joined the growing list of geographies of sacrifice.[77] In late 1996, scientists working for Greenpeace reported the presence of radioactive contamination on the island and in its vicinity and called on the DOE to take active measures in assessing and restoring the health and safety of the surrounding environment.

The silent presence of plutonium stockpiles must be included in any account of these domestic theaters of war. They, too, are part of the geography of sacrifice and, at least in the United States, are found primarily in the West. Like revelations of previously undisclosed tests, information about the plutonium stockpile has only recently surfaced. From 1945 through 1988 the United States produced 90 tons of weapons-grade plutonium. At least 32.5 metric tons are still being stored at sites around the country. By far, the biggest stockpiles are in the Western United States and may be destined for sites specifically within the zones of sacrifice outlined here as the United States moves to consolidate its weapons development facilities.

North Americans tend to think that military spending has significantly decreased since the breakup of the Soviet Empire and the resulting evaporation of the Cold War arms buildup. To some extent and in some areas this is true. But the military and scientific complex is now so central to the economic and cultural structure of the United States that it has become exceedingly difficult to imagine its dissolution. As a 1994 article in *Scientific American* notes:

> [Military] budgets are down 35% in real terms from their peak in 1985, and the administration's proposed defense budget for 1995, at $263.7 billion, continues that trend. *But the research and development component, at $39.5 billion represents a 4% increase.* Basic research, which amounts to 1.23 billion within that total, is also slated for a small increase. [78] [My italics.]

Despite the so-called end of the Cold War, it is doubtful we will see the lands withdrawn over the last forty to fifty years given back to the "public domain," let alone to the Indian tribes that claim them. Nor will we see the dissolution of the laboratories and scientific cities in the desert. In fact, a reconfiguration of the nuclear weapons complex is currently under way. Essentially, this reconfiguration concentrates more nuclear weapons activities in fewer places. As of this writing, the question remains whether the refurbished weapons complex will be placed firmly in the Southwest with primary centers at the Nevada Test Site and/or at Los Alamos.[79] But it is highly likely that, given the concentration of DOE and DOD facilities in the region, the Southwest will see a new generation of nuclear development.

In addition to the Complex 21/Stockpile Stewardship agenda, the militarization of the Southwest moves forward by the strategic linkages currently proposed for all test and training ranges in the interdesert region. With China Lake Naval Weapons Center and Nellis Air Force Base at its center, these links form "an integrated test and evaluation range structure." In the words of General Colin Powell in 1993: "An integrated test and evaluation range structure linking existing ranges across six Western states and supersonic areas off the California coast would provide a land, airspace, sea area to accommodate a large portion of our joint training, test and evaluation needs well into the next century."[80] Thus, not only is the West further constructed into a militarized zone, but these militarized zones are consolidated into a vast experimental theater where weapons scientists and military planners can design, develop, and test new generations of weapons with too little regard to the effects their activities have on the

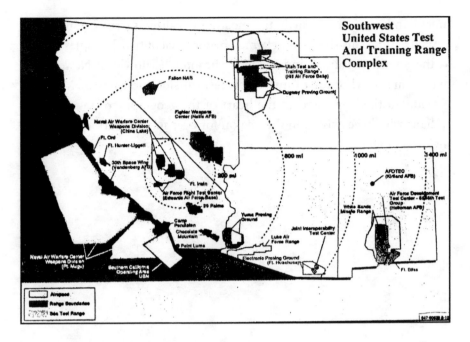

Figure 3.9 Southwest United States Test and Training Range Complex
Department of Defense

people of the region, including that segment of the population powerless to oppose them on anything but moral ground—their land, their birthright.[81]

Our map of the nuclear and militarized landscape of the interdesert region is nearly complete. On it we can see the geography of sacrifice beginning with uranium mining, an activity that extended throughout the Cold War period and one that has left an unrehabilitated toxic wasteland on the Hopi, Navajo, Pueblo, Havasupai, and Ute Mountain Ute reservations. In Zone One and Zone Two we have seen the creation of scientific centers of nuclear and conventional weapons that emerged as "secret science cities in the desert," and the pollution that accompanies them, which is inevitable given their production and research mandates. And we have seen the massive withdrawal of millions of acres of desert land and air space for the testing of the weapons of war. Finally, we have included the Nevada Test Site—the most severe nuclear testing region on the globe, the most bombed place on earth, the most fully realized sacrifice zone in the United States. This site is also claimed by the ancient tribal peoples known as the Southern Paiutes and Western Shoshone (who call it Newe Sego-bia), some of whom continue to protest outside the gates of Mercury, Nevada, to this day. Here, at the heart of the geography of sacrifice, the Indians who have existed in this region for over 10,000 years are the most invisible of all.

· 4 ·

Nuclear Wasteland

> As we allow ourselves to feel our pain for the world, we
> find our connection with each other.
> —JOANNA MACY, *Despair and Personal Power
> in the Nuclear Age*[1]

We are in the midst of a nuclear-waste crisis. Nuclear power plants worldwide are running out of room to store the waste they have generated, and
safe repositories have not been found. Continued production of nuclear
power now depends upon the ability to safely dispose of toxins with a
240,000-year lethality. Nuclear waste is a silent challenge, a silent threat.
This chapter reveals the scope of this quiet crisis. By illuminating the volume of deadly waste that has accumulated and describing what radioactive
waste does to human bodies, we can begin to understand what has been
done in our name and, therefore, what needs to be done to protect life for
future generations. Any accounting of nuclear waste requires that those
primarily responsible for its accumulation be identified, as well as the ways
in which policy makers have failed to contend with the threat to human
health and safety posed by nuclear waste. The current nuclear-waste crisis
cannot be remedied by technoscientific solutions alone but must also be
part of new social policies that examine the role of industry, the military,
and the scientific research institutions that promote nuclearism. This
chapter identifies the target sites for nuclear waste in Zone One and Zone

Two of the nuclear landscape and attempts to explain why Indian communities have been selectively chosen as "guardians" of postindustrial society's most lethal waste product.

The nuclear-waste crisis, unlike what we found in Chapters 2 and 3, is not so much driven by the military as it is by the commercial nuclear industry—the nuclear weapons complex's offspring. Ironically, the U.S. government, having emerged "victorious" in its ideological struggle with communism, must now contend with the mess created by this sorcerer's apprentice (the commercial sector), which, in the name of efficiency, churned out ten times the amount of waste as its master (the military sector).

The Nuclear Legacy

With a lethal longevity of 240,000 years, plutonium is one of the most deadly elements created by the splitting of the atom in nuclear reactors. It takes "only 10 micrograms of plutonium to induce cancer, and several grams of plutonium, dispersed in a ventilation system, can cause thousands of deaths."[2] In light of this, global figures on the amount of plutonium we have generated since the 1940s are arresting and terrifying. By 1995, military weapons-grade plutonium, in the form of active and dismantled bombs, amounted to 270 metric tons. The commercial stockpile of plutonium in nuclear-reactor waste and isolates from spent fuel amounts to approximately 930 metric tons and will more than double, increasing to 2,130 tons, by 2005, only eight years from now. As the nuclear physicist Makhijani notes "every four or five years we're making about as much plutonium in the civil sector as we did during the whole Cold War."[3] This figure does not include the waste from eighty radionuclides that are capable of releasing "ionizing radiation," which causes harm to humans and animals in the form of genetic mutations, cancer, and birth defects.[4]

By the celebrated end of the Cold War in 1989, the United States alone had generated 21,000 nuclear weapons. The planned reduction of nuclear warheads from 21,000 to 3,500 by the year 2003 will require the disassembly of 2,000 weapons a year for thirteen years. Even if this task can be accomplished without accidents, disassembly will still produce a great deal of nuclear waste. Added to the tons of nuclear waste generated by power plants in the past, present, and future, and the 132 sites in thirty states where nuclear arms production has left an environmental cleanup bill

Figure 4.1 Burial of solid radioactive waste, in unlined trenches
Example of one type of disposal procedure for the burial of radioactive solid
waste. Savannah River Site, South Carolina.

Photo by Robert Del Tredici

estimated at more than $500 billion,[5] it is not an overreaction to say that we
are in the midst of a national and global crisis. Indeed, the multibillion-
dollar cleanup bill is itself misleading—not all sites *can* be cleaned up.
Today, we do not have the technology to correct serious contamination
areas such as (in the words of the DOE) "large contaminated river systems
like the Columbia, Clinch, and Savannah rivers, most ground water,
nuclear explosion test areas on the Nevada Test Site," and "plutonium not
now identified as surplus."[6]

Management—or the lack thereof—of the radioactive waste generated
by the U.S. nuclear complex over the past fifty years has been nothing less
than scandalous, with careless dumping of radioactive waste in pits and
unlined trenches, as well as burials of the waste in cardboard boxes and
even intentional injection of it into deep wells. The contamination of U.S.
nuclear complex facilities and their surrounding areas such as those at
Rocky Flats, Colorado, Hanford, Washington, and Savannah River, South

Carolina, has been well-documented. Contamination of the soil and water at the Hanford facility indicates the severity of the problem, and Hanford is only one of ten such Department of Energy facilities. As noted by one nuclear weapons complex watchdog group:

> Hanford stores 8,200,000 cubic feet of high-level waste and 500,000 cubic feet of transuranic [plutonium-contaminated] waste. Hanford buried 18,000,000 cubic feet of "low-level" waste and 3,900,000 cubic feet of transuranic waste. By 1984 their reprocessing facility had discharged 210,000,000,000 gallons of radioactive waste into the ground water (yes, that's the right number of zeros). The N-reactor [the plutonium production reactor] also discharged 1 billion gallons to the soil annually.
>
> Over 500,000 gallons of *high-level* radioactive waste have leaked from storage tanks. Other wastes were intentionally released into the Columbia River, which flows through the site.[7]

The Effects of Radioactive Elements on the Human Body

To properly understand the scope of the problem it is necessary to take into account the detrimental health effects of these materials. As I suggested in Chapter 3, the human body must be included in any map of the nuclear landscape. If we take seriously Foucault's thesis that power is exercised at the margins, that it is made visible in the docile bodies of those subject to it, and that power is enforced through knowledge regimes (literally, disciplines) and practices, we must look for the signs of nuclear colonization on the bodies of those colonized by nuclear power. Though we are all subject to nuclear power and are all the subjects of nuclear tests, those marginalized people inhabiting lands already marginalized as arid wastelands remain subject to the ongoing nuclear experiment whose latest phase represents a 10,000-year "live" test of waste-storage facilities. As Foucault said, "Where religions once demanded the sacrifice of bodies, knowledge now calls for experimentation on ourselves, calls us to the sacrifice of the subject of knowledge."[8]

Perhaps the lack of public concern and consciousness about the problem can be attributed in part to the fear produced by the "unthinkable" longevity and lethality of radionuclides. Perhaps the fear produces collective denial. As Lewis Mumford wrote in 1959: "In acquiescing to nuclear weapons, we have deliberately anesthetized the normal feelings, emotions, anxieties and hopes that alone could bring us to our senses."[9]

On the scale of human history, many isotopes remain radioactive virtually forever. Elements such as plutonium are, for humans and other living creatures, the most toxic substances on earth. These isotopes don't just make people sick; they alter genetic structure and our cellular behavior. According to recent studies, small doses of radiation over long periods of time are no less severe than massive one-time doses. "Short-term effects of chronic exposure to radiation are radiation sickness—nausea, vomiting, dizziness, headache, and so on. Long-term effects of chronic exposure to radiation are cancer, reproductive failure, birth defects, genetic defects, and death."[10] Because ionizing radiation can affect our genetic structure, its effects can be passed on from generation to generation, so that damage is rendered *intergenerationally*. We have tragic proof of the human effects of radiation exposure intergenerationally and otherwise. Children of northern Ukraine born *after* the 1986 Chernobyl accident show far greater incidence of birth defects than those born at the time of the accident, as did children born after the nuclear attacks on Hiroshima and Nagasaki.

The U.S. Department of Energy itself estimates that as little as 10 millionths of a curie of plutonium, if inhaled, can cause cancer. According to the latest accounts, the Chernobyl explosion released "more than 185 million curies of radioactive material, and possibly as much as 250 million curies during the first 10 days after the accident."[11] The first 27 victims of the Chernobyl accident were buried in lead coffins because they had become sources of contamination. Nine years after the Chernobyl accident an estimated 125,000 people have died. But not until the second decade *after* the disaster do doctors expect the number of cancer cases to peak.[7]

It is necessary for people to face these grim and tragic statistics in order to understand what is at stake in the nuclear waste crisis. Such statements are not meant to sensationalize the issue but to help the reader recognize the gravity of the threat that nuclear waste poses. Geographies of sacrifice are about *bodies* of land, human bodies, and the "body politic"—now, and in the future.

Many other examples of the risks posed by radiation exist close to home—for instance, the cancer clusters near Rocky Flats, Colorado, where plutonium was made into nuclear bomb "triggers" for hydrogen bombs.[13] As Bartimus and McCartney note: "[Dr. Carl] Johnson [the county health director who studied cancer rates in the area] said most of the excess cases, such as leukemia and cancers of the lymph, lung, thyroid, testes, and breast, paralleled those of Hiroshima and Nagasaki survivors."[14] Run by Rockwell International for the Department of Energy, the Rocky Flats plant had produced so much pollution and had been so seriously mismanaged that in 1989 both the FBI and the Environmental Protection Agency "raided" the plant (a raid they codenamed "Desert Glow"): "The FBI said in an affidavit that it even had infrared aerial photographs that showed illegal waste incineration at night in a building previously ordered shut down for safety reasons."[15]

Similar examples of health problems associated with the nuclear industry can be found at the Hanford Site, the Pantex plant, the Savannah River site, and others. Interviews with Native American communities around the Nevada Test Site and documentation on other downwinders near NTS also reveal the detrimental health effects of nuclear activities. As noted in Chapter 3, studies of the pueblos around Los Alamos have turned up elevated cancer rates, which may be linked to suspected contamination by radioactive wastes leaking into nearby water sources. Mounting evidence, both statistical and anecdotal, indicates that living near nuclear power plants and weapons facilities (that develop and store radioactive materials) and nuclear weapons testing ranges is detrimental to human health.

If 10 millionths of a curie of inhaled plutonium can cause death, how can one come to grips with the fact that atmospheric nuclear testing from 1945 to 1963 discharged 5 tons of plutonium into the atmosphere? How do we contend with the fact that by 2005 the global community will have produced and stockpiled 2,130 tons of plutonium? What effects has this had on our bodies and the biosphere? Aside from important early studies on health risks related to specific radiation contamination sites, no one has as yet come up with a way to verify in a *comprehensive* way the impact such a toxic environment has on the body.[16] The Department of Energy says radiation from the activities of the nuclear industry has had no significant effect on our health and safety. But why does one in three Americans get cancer, and about 20 percent of us die of it? Why since the 1970s has cancer risen in the United States 18.6 percent for men and 12.4 percent for women?

Ironically, because of their horrifying implications, the general public appears to find such statistics easier to ignore. Even so, images surface in popular culture where toxic wastes and lethal pollutions have captured the collective U.S. imagination. In the "entertaining" realm of popular culture as portrayed in movies, books, and on television are found images of a future underclass forced to live in "toxic colonies," of mutant cartoon characters, of zones of toxic wastes. At some level, humans know that the toxic threat is out there—whether it's nuclear, chemical, or biological. We suspect it's connected to war, industrialization, and to science that has gotten "out of control." And we fear that it's affecting us, as cancer and immunological diseases reach epidemic proportions. But we can't seem to fully face this invisible threat, and we certainly aren't encouraged to investigate it (not when the DOE continually argues that "background radiation" is higher than any nuclear waste we're likely to come in contact with).

Doctors are ridiculed if they suggest that soaring cancer rates might be associated with a toxic environment. Pressure to "individualize" the problem is great. Women are told to cut down on consumption of dairy products to prevent breast cancer. But this attempt to lay the blame on individuals appears trivial when every three minutes in the United States a woman is diagnosed with breast cancer, when one in eight women in America can expect to contract breast cancer. No one knows what is causing the epidemic.[17] Women resort to individualized, "lifestyle" adjustments to lessen the risk, yet the epidemic continues.

Efforts to individualize the nuclear problem effectively mask the real social nature of nuclearism and constitute a mechanism of exclusion on a mass scale, in effect saying "radiation doesn't cause cancer, (individual) people do." If citizens are to alter the health risks associated with a toxic environment, they must contend with a powerful nuclear industry, a political and economic system that has grown to depend on nuclearism, and entrenched government agencies that keep its legacy silent. *Seeing* the nuclear wasteland, then, is a political act because it leads to the beginning of action that is not limited simply to lifestyle changes—such as not smoking, for instance—but extends to taking collective action to stop the drift toward environmental disaster.

The nuclear-waste crisis cannot be regarded merely as a "crisis of perception and fear," as the DOE and certain mainstream science writers would have it.[18] If people's fears about threats to health and safety, concerns substantiated by a verifiable history of neglect and irresponsibility on the part of the Department of Energy and the nuclear industry, are to be quelled, they need to be addressed by these very institutions and not dismissed as hysterical paranoia.

Confusion in the Field:
Problems with the Nuclear Industry and Its Regulation

Seeing the nuclear wasteland can be difficult when it is obscured by faulty classification systems for identifying the waste itself and by an inadequate national policy to deal with it. In this case, it is not so much denial produced by fear that keeps people from becoming aware of the crisis but confusion promulgated by those responsible for producing and regulating nuclear materials—the exclusionary principle at work through a public relations effort masked as science. The faulty classification system with its attendant obfuscating technoscientific jargon is the product of a Nuclear Waste Policy Act[19] that was written primarily for the benefit of the nuclear power industry, not the public.

Much has been written about the nuclear industry, pro and con, but not a great deal has been published concerning the issue of waste and how it has been legislated and classified.[20] Nuclear waste is categorized in United States waste regulatory policy primarily according to the processes that produce it, not according to the threat it may pose to health nor its longevity as a hazardous material in the environment. The following is the current Department of Energy's classification system for nuclear waste:

- *High-Level Waste*: Spent fuel from nuclear power plants and first-cycle reprocessing wastes from plutonium and uranium extraction. (Most high-level waste is derived from commercial power plants used to generate electricity. Proposed site for such wastes is Nevada's Yucca Mountain.)
- *Monitored Retrievable Storage (MRS) Facilities* are for the temporary storage (approximately 50 years) of high-level nuclear waste (specifically, spent

fuel rods from commercial power plants) until a national permanent deep-geologic repository is ready to accept waste (probably not until 2010 at the earliest).

- *Transuranic Waste (TRU)*: Primary radioactive contaminants are transuranic elements (mainly plutonium, neptunium, americium) at levels above 100 nanocuries per gram. (Most waste belonging to this category derives from nuclear weapons production. Site for disposal of such wastes is New Mexico's Waste Isolation Pilot Plant, or WIPP, constructed out of the Carlsbad Salt Caverns.)
- *Uranium Mill Tailings*: Composed of discharges from the production of yellow-cake (U_3O_8) at uranium mills. Their main radioactivity content is due to radium 226 (half-life 1,600 years) and thorium 230 (half-life about 80,000 years). Mill tailings constitute well over 90 percent of the volume of all radioactive waste and are regulated by the Uranium Mill Tailings Remediation Act.
- *"Low-Level" Waste*: Includes everything from highly radioactive reactor internals to slightly contaminated booties and gloves. There are three classes of "low-level" waste, A, B, and C. The responsibility for disposing of "low-level" wastes was transferred to the states by Congress in 1985.
- *Greater-than-Class-C (GTCC) Waste*: Some reactor wastes are hotter than allowed under Class C wastes, yet do not belong in any of the waste categories. According to the Nuclear Regulatory Commission, greater-than-Class-C waste should be treated as high-level waste and disposed of in a repository. However, the Department of Energy has made no provision for repository of disposal of greater-than-Class-C waste.
- *Naturally Occurring and Accelerator Produced Radioactive Materials (NARM)*: This includes some wastes not included in the catchall category of "low-level" waste but which may pose quite significant risks in many areas of the country.[21]

This classificatory approach (unaided by the above descriptions) produces public confusion and, according to critics, contributes to mismanagement of nuclear waste by the government bodies responsible for it: the Department of Energy, the Nuclear Regulatory Commission, and DOE's Office of Civilian Radioactive Waste Management (OCRWM). One of the problems with this scheme of classification is that it misrepresents the toxicity of the waste. For instance, as Makhijani and Saleska state:

> [D]espite what is implied by their names, the two categories of waste named "high-level waste" and "low-level waste," are defined without systematic reference to their actual radioactivity levels. Instead, they are defined solely by the process which produced them. "High-level waste" is defined as spent reactor fuel, or those wastes resulting from the reprocessing of spent reactor fuel. "Low-level waste" is actually a catch-all category that is defined simply to include all radioactive waste that is not high-level waste, transuranic wastes, or uranium mill tailings.
>
> *Thus, the current radioactive waste categorization is in the untenable situation of sometimes labeling as "low-level" radioactive wastes which are actually several times more radioactive than other streams of radioactive waste which the current system labels "high-level." [M]any of the longer-lived and more dangerous categories of low-level waste, which is disposed of in shallow land burial, is also more radioactive than transuranic waste, which has been designated for disposal in a deep geologic repository.*[22] [My italics.]

In addition, the present classificatory scheme does not refer to the waste's longevity, or length of toxicity. Again, Makhijani and Saleska clarify the situation by stating: "Both high-level and low-level wastes as currently defined can contain significant quantities of both long and short-lived radionuclides."[23] For example, the "low-level" nuclear waste dump sited for Ward Valley in California's Mojave Desert would contain some of the most toxic and longest-lasting radioactive wastes, including strontium, cesium, and plutonium, in shallow, unlined trenches above an aquifer and just 18 miles from the Colorado River. So on top of the principle of exclusion, local knowledge that is delegitimated—rests a strategy of confusion—knowledge that science legitimates but chooses to represent in ways that further political ends.

The 1982 Nuclear Waste Policy Act

Because the Nuclear Waste Policy Act of 1982 is based upon this problematic classificatory scheme, and for other reasons, it is inadequate for contending with the nuclear-waste crisis. Although the NWPA is currently undergoing revision, this is not to correct the faulty classification scheme for radioactive wastes. In the same way that different kinds of waste are not classified in accordance with the threat they pose for human health or the environment, the Nuclear Waste Policy Act of 1982 does not make public health and safety its number one goal. Though safety is a consideration, of primary concern is the timely implementation of burial site construction.[24] In this way, the NWPA protects the capital investments of the nuclear industry, first and foremost by relieving it of the burden of waste storage.

Responsibility for oversight of the nuclear waste siting and site characterization processes rests mainly with the Department of Energy; neither the Nuclear Regulatory Commission (NRC) nor the Environmental Protection Agency (EPA) have powers sufficient to oversee the DOE. For instance, as noted by Jacob, "a complete review of environmental impacts [of a waste site] under NEPA standards would not occur until billions of dollars had already been spent for characterizing three sites and after DOE had selected one of those sites for the repository."[25] In addition, because safe containment of materials that last for 240,000 years is impossible to fully assess, the NWPA text refers only to "potential risks" posed by nuclear waste, not to actual risks; it offers only a "reasonable assurance" of safety and only "adequate protection" to the public. But what do potential risk, reasonable assurance, and adequate protection really mean?[26] If safety of lethal materials that last for 240,000 years is impossible to assess, why doesn't the NWPA include in its evaluation of a solution the possibility of stopping production of said waste? Here we see the pattern of exclusion continued: All discussion of solutions for the alleviation of high-level nuclear waste are forced to remain within strict boundaries (set by the DOE) that disallow any discussion of production.

Faced with setbacks at Yucca Mountain and in an attempt to find interim solutions to the nuclear-waste crisis, legislators amended the Nuclear Waste Policy Act in 1987 to give more power to the states and Indian tribes to both accept and help regulate waste containment but not enough power to fully contest the DOE's mandates to establish a permanent national repository. Although forced to offer more public information hearings and community "open hearings" to solicit the complaints and concerns of the host state, the DOE did not have to alter its path as a result of such concerns—just take them into consideration. The 1987 amendment also restricted all site characterization research to Yucca Mountain—making it the only site possible for permanently storing high-level nuclear waste.

The Nuclear Waste Policy Act of 1982 purportedly established a national policy for "safely storing, transporting, and disposing of spent nuclear fuel and high-level waste."[27] That it took thirty-seven years to recognize that a national policy was needed is itself indicative of how insensitive federal agencies had been to the problem. Nor does the act cover military wastes. Furthermore, by focusing on a technical, deep-geologic solution to waste buildup, the NWPA ignores completely the fact that the continued use of nuclear power only adds to the problem. What could have been a far-reaching and innovative piece of legislation was derailed by efforts to find an expedient solution. Rather, the NWPA keeps U.S. nuclear waste policy focused on how best to serve the continuation of the nuclear utilities, and the states and regions serviced by them.

At the time of this writing (in 1997), the Nuclear Waste Policy Act is once again undergoing revision in Congress. A variety of bills concerning nuclear waste and energy have come before the House and the Senate. Of the different bills presented to amend the NWPA, some certainly reflect its original mandate for a quick solution, that is, to expedite the nuclear waste disposal process at any expense (including that of public health and safety). What the final revised act will look like remains to be seen. Bills that have passed the House and Senate allow for interim storage with a 100-year renewable license at the Yucca Mountain site (further committing the site before it has been deemed safe). However, President Clinton has promised to veto these bills. The new act may also relax requirements under the Safe Drinking Water Act and—under certain conditions pertaining to the costliness of compliance—would direct the president to exempt the DOE from some federal, state, and local laws.

With a problem as great as nuclear waste the above inadequacies in legislation and in technical classification pose serious doubts about the government's ability to manage nuclear power. The Department of Energy's past record for safety and openness has not won public confidence. Resistance by local communities to storage of nuclear waste is high. But for many years the Department of Energy, along with other powerful social groups and institutions, moved forward along the nuclear path with very few obstacles. Indeed, until it was disbanded in 1973, the Atomic Energy Commission (AEC) held two incompatible mandates: both to promote and to regulate nuclear power. (The AEC was subsequently separated into the Nuclear Regulatory Commission and the Department of Energy.) Recognizing that the nuclear industry has always been something of a self-regulating industry aids in understanding the state of affairs today.

Nowhere to Put It

The Department of Energy and its predecessor, the AEC, have sought for more than three decades to find a solution to the nuclear-waste problem, belying a blind faith in technology to provide an answer. In the summer of 1994, as I flew into Las Vegas to attend a tour of Yucca Mountain, the headline of the *Las Vegas Sun* read: "Nuke deadline looms: 20 states press DOE to take waste by '98."[28] In effect, twenty states filed suit against the federal government because it could not fulfill its mandate to find a permanent repository for the nation's high-level commercial nuclear waste by the year 1998. All twenty states have "nuclear power reactors that are storing spent radioactive fuel rods underwater or in dry casks awaiting permanent disposal elsewhere." As Daniel A. Dreyfus, director of the Office of Civilian Radioactive Waste Management, explained:

> [W]e now do have utilities that are approaching the limit of their pool storage and are going to dry storage out of necessity as opposed to choice.
>
> We also have reactors which are shut down which will have a problem, high-cost maintenance, to maintain a pool if they continue their storage as pool storage for a very long period of time because the pool and the hot cells and the ability to transfer fuel is an expensive upkeep problem of some consequence.[29]

Storage ponds at nuclear facilities are full, and some are leaking, contaminating surrounding areas. Facilities have run out of room for the spent radioactive fuel rods usually stored underwater or in dry casks. Either nuclear facilities must shut down, or, to continue production, they must find a place to store the lethal materials. Yucca Mountain, the only site undergoing the required feasibility studies, has yet to move beyond the safety analysis stage. As one congressman put it in reference to Yucca

Mountain: "We have poured a lot of money into that empty hole, and we have got to make some progress now."[30]

But the kind of "progress" the Florida congressman wants to see is not necessarily in the best interests of current or future generations. Deep-geologic containment is like, as one author put it, "burying uncertainty."[31] Though putting all this waste in the interdesert region may seem a reasonable solution from a certain scientific, practical, and even political point of view, this "viewpoint" is based on an ideological foundation that has its roots in the Western scientific technological paradigm, with its ties to a culture of ecological plunder and racial conquest. The "deserts as dumps treatise" proclaims that deserts are the best "ecosystem" for nuclear waste.[32] The irony is that the interdesert region is the one area in the United States that uses the least amount of nuclear power. (Only Arizona and Texas have nuclear-generated power.) The interdesert land mass is also the "darkest" area within the continental United States—that is, the area with the least electric power consumption. Put another way, the nuclear landscape is largely made up of nonnuclear-power territories.

Nuclear Waste and Indigenous Communities

Geographies of sacrifice are socially constructed spaces, and they hold different consequences for groups that are situated differently within late modern societies. Though everyone potentially feels the impact of the nuclear legacy, some gain wealth from it, and some suffer its immediate consequences. Some have more power than others in their attempts to keep it at bay, or at least to get recognition of their struggle—for example, the white, middle-class property owners of Concord Naval Port in California. Confronted with the possibility of becoming a port for nuclear waste imported from twenty-eight other countries, San Francisco Bay Area residents voiced their outrage during a DOE open hearing, which received television, radio, and newspaper coverage. Social protest of this kind does not garner such publicity in more impoverished rural areas inhabited by less privileged people, although protest does certainly occur in these areas. For instance, the plight of the uranium miners in New Mexico is rarely, if ever, heard outside local New Mexican and Indian newspapers. My own investigation into the claim of nuclear colonialism required familiarity with newspapers from Indian communities where the issue was not only identified but discussed on a regular basis. But other than in the Indian press and a handful of antinuclear publications, the idea of "nuclear colonialism" never comes up.

When people say that nuclearism is the "price we pay for freedom," they usually omit the fact that this price is paid by those with disproportionately less power. Though poor communities often pay the highest price, more privileged Americans are not exempt from some kind of "payment." Indeed, given that we are contemplating materials that transgress the social demarcations of borders and boundaries, it sometimes seems superfluous to talk about maps at all. Admittedly, there is irony in mapping a nuclear sacrifice zone when nuclear pollution tends to make boundaries obsolete. Even so, as we have seen with the uranium mining district, as well as the nuclear testing ranges, identifiable zones of *concentration* of nuclear activity exist that are substantively different from other regions. Likewise, some regions and people are actively targeted for nuclear waste disposal. As Grace Thorpe, tribal judge and health commissioner for the Sauk and Fox Nation of Oklahoma, put it:

> The U.S. government targeted Native Americans [for nuclear waste disposal] for several reasons: their lands are some of the most isolated in North America, they are some of the most impoverished and, consequently, most politically vulnerable and, perhaps most important, tribal sovereignty can be used to bypass state environmental laws.
>
> How ironic that, after centuries attempting to destroy it, the U.S. government is suddenly interested in promoting Native American sovereignty— just to dump its lethal garbage . . . [and] serve as hosts for the nation's nuclear garbage dump.[33]

The only two potential national, deep-geologic, high-level, and military waste sites in the United States are on or near traditional Indian lands; all recent proposals for temporary nuclear waste storage sites are for Indian reservations; and the nation's new premiere "low-level" nuclear dump site also borders native communities on traditional native lands. The U.S. government has offered (through the office of the U.S. Nuclear Negotiator) often destitute Native communities substantial sums of money just to consider waste-storage possibilities. As noted by Indian environmental activist Winona LaDuke:

> Indian reservations, which constitute [only] four percent of US lands, hold vast supplies of uranium, coal and timber. These vast, isolated lands are also attractive to industries searching for disposal sites for nuclear waste. In the past four years, more than 100 separate proposals have been made by government and industry to dump waste on Indian lands. To date, Indians have received 16 of the 18 "nuclear waste research grants" issued by the US Department of Energy. . . . [I]n 1987, CERT (Council of Energy Resource Tribes) received $2.5 million from federal nuclear waste contracts—more than half the organization's total income. In 1992, CERT received $1.2 million in federal grants for nuclear waste programs—80 percent of the group's federal grants.[34]

The 1982 Nuclear Waste Policy Act, although recognizing Native American sovereignty rights and granting tribes power equal to that of states, contains the very seed that allows Indian tribal land to be targeted as potential waste dumps. Granting sovereignty makes it easier for the government (or industry) to bypass state regulation—if the tribes can be convinced to take the waste. Sovereignty is granted when it benefits the granter. U.S. colonization practices "go nuclear" when American Indian tribes become the keepers of the zones of sacrifice in the "new world order." In an extraordinary display of double-speak, David LeRoy, the U.S. Nuclear Negotiator, argued that Native Americans are the best qualified to host temporary nuclear-waste facilities. Referring to traditional Indian values regarding land use, he said:

> The heritage which reveres the environment often can perceive, in very subtle and very significant ways, how necessary and how appropriate, and how environmental the call for the safe storage of spent fuel [is] for many generations of Americans yet unborn—native and non-natives. [T]hat environmental sensitivity [i]s a great asset because we are asking to create an environmentally sensitive facility for an environmentally sensitive mission.[35]

For the U.S. Nuclear Negotiator, the Indian "heritage" of "environmental sensitivity" is what ultimately "legitimates" a U.S. environmental policy that many have called racist. Grace Thorpe (of the Sauk and Fox Nation) sees her heritage differently:

> The Great Spirit has instructed us that we have a sacred bond with our Mother Earth and an obligation to the creatures who live upon it. This is why it is disturbing that the federal government and the nuclear power industry seem determined to ruin forever some of the few lands we have left.[36]

Deep-Geologic Repositories:
The Yucca Mountain Project and WIPP

The two deep-geologic nuclear-waste repositories in the United States are the military's Waste Isolation Pilot Project, known as WIPP, which is ready and waiting to receive transuranic (plutonium-contaminated) wastes, and the proposed Yucca Mountain site, which is not yet (but is likely to be) designated as the country's site for (mostly) commercial nuclear waste. WIPP is in Zone One of the nuclear landscape, in the Chihuahuan Desert in southeastern New Mexico. Yucca Mountain is in Zone Two of the nuclear landscape, in the Great Basin Desert in southern Nevada. [See Chapter 3, maps of Zones One and Two.] Each site has been the subject of intense political debate as well as significant scientific controversy. Each site is also the first of its kind, since deep-geologic burial of nuclear waste has never been attempted anywhere else on earth (a deep-geologic burial facility is here understood as different from "dump-and-cover" nuclear waste disposal practices, which have occurred in many places around the globe). Given the enormity of the nuclear-waste crisis, and the longevity and lethality of nuclear materials, development of these sites can be understood as world-historical events, and as monumental experiments in civil engineering. They promise a permanent solution to a seemingly intractable problem.

These two repositories serve as parallel centers of nuclear activity within each of the nuclear zones I've described. Radiating outward from both of these "ground zeros" spread the webs of nuclearism found in the U.S. Southwest. Although these massive repositories remain relatively hidden in desert lands, nuclear waste itself will become much more visible as it becomes mobile, passing through everybody's backyard in transit to these sites. When the transportation of waste begins, nuclear materials from across the country and from abroad will be drawn into each dark center. By rail and by highway, nuclear waste will converge on WIPP in New Mexico and on Yucca Mountain in Nevada.

WIPP—Zone One: Back to the Salt Mines

Scheduled to open in 1998,[37] the Waste Isolation Pilot Project (WIPP) near Carlsbad, New Mexico, will be the nation's first permanent repository for plutonium-contaminated (or "transuranic") radioactive waste created from nuclear weapons production. (For WIPP's location in Zone One refer to Figure 3.1.) The disposal area will exceed 100 acres, although the site's surface area covers more than 10,000 acres. The WIPP "mine" sits 2,150 feet below ground in salt beds. The repository's design calls for "creeping" salt to seal in the waste—a process that is supposed to isolate waste for tens of thousands of years. Controversy over WIPP focuses on potential groundwater contamination, gases that would be generated by the decomposing wastes, and the hazards posed by transporting the approximately 30,000 truckloads of waste to the site.[38]

Although lawsuits and public opposition have kept WIPP from opening so far, it is scheduled to be opened in 1998.[39] Because opponents claim the site is unsafe for the disposal of nuclear waste and because many of New Mexico's residents resist the importation of more nuclear materials into their already saturated state,[40] WIPP's siting in southeastern New Mexico has galvanized intense grass-roots political resistance since the late 1970s. Scientists have taken up positions on both sides of the salt-tomb debate. Recent evidence, however, indicates that the salt beds are not dry as theorized in 1957 when the National Academy of Science determined salt mines to be the best solution for nuclear waste.[41] Rather, these salt caverns show water moving through them, water that could contaminate the Rustler Aquifer that lies above the WIPP mine. This aquifer feeds rivers that serve as major sources of water in southeastern New Mexico.[42] The water could also mix with the salt and begin to corrode the canisters full of radioactive waste. In addition, the buildup of gases generated from decaying matter could conceivably mix with the brine seeping into the waste rooms and create enough pressure to force the "radioactive slurry" through fractures in the rock.[43] Indeed, it is the mobility and transformative powers of matter itself that threaten to defy absolute control and containment of this deadly waste.

Like Yucca Mountain, WIPP was chosen not just for scientific reasons but for political ones. Even with serious cause for concern about the safety of the repository, the Department of Energy (and its contractor, Westinghouse) are adamant about its use as a military waste dump and are pushing hard for an early opening date. Southeastern New Mexico is a severely economically depressed region. Its potash mining industry collapsed in 1968, and WIPP promises new jobs. In fact, as Reith and Thomson note in *Deserts as Dumps?*, "a potash company near Carlsbad wrote the Atomic Energy Commission (AEC) to suggest the use of former potash mines for waste emplacement."[44] Waste promises to be a moneymaking proposition for some locals. On the other side, the Department of Energy is caught in a nuclear-waste and contamination crisis resulting from fifty years of irresponsible dumping and storage of radioactive waste within its nuclear weapons complex. Together, the local and national crises push (like creeping salt) toward an expedient solution to their problems that may not, however, prove to be a safe one.

Destined for WIPP is waste generated by the nuclear weapons complex—but only waste generated after 1970. As Debra Rosenthal notes:

> Most of the 250,000 cubic meters of radioactive waste accumulated since the beginning of the Manhattan Project is buried in shallow trenches. It is difficult to retrieve because the soil surrounding it has also become radioactive. It will stay put for the foreseeable future, unlike the 57,359 cubic meters of transuranic [plutonium-contaminated] waste stored in warehouses in Los Alamos and nine other DOE facilities around the country since 1970.[45]

Therefore, even if WIPP were totally safe, it is only a partial solution to the current problem. It is being built primarily as a repository for the nuclear weapons complex of the twenty-first century. Seventy percent of its capacity is reserved for radioactive waste from the production of nuclear weapons over the next twenty years. Rather than simply store existing waste, WIPP is meant to prolong the production of nuclear weapons.

Since WIPP was not originally supposed to receive commercial high-level waste, but only defense transuranic waste, and because it is defined as a "research and development facility" to "demonstrate" safe disposal of defense waste, it is not subject to oversight by the Nuclear Regulatory Commission (NRC), nor does it need licensing by the NRC. However, because WIPP contains mixed waste—radioactive and hazardous chemical—and because the Environmental Protection Agency (EPA) does have radiation protection standards, it must comply with certain safety standards set by the EPA. Many concerned citizens are currently attempting to get the EPA to tighten its safety standards concerning WIPP. They want the DOE to demonstrate a *convincing* capability to comply with EPA standards. Susan Hirschberg, former waste and contamination director for Concerned Citizens for Nuclear Safety in New Mexico, notes:

> The Department of Energy [currently] doesn't need to provide hard data to prove it can comply with EPA regulations. When you're trying to predict what's going to happen for 10,000 years, it seems like [hard data or proof] is a reasonable thing to require. And in fact there are a couple of experiments in process right now which would be done in a couple of years that could provide some very important information. But these won't be included in what's called the "certification application" that the DOE submits to the EPA.[46]

This sidestepping of due process is typical of the mechanisms of exclusion that we have seen in so many instances—evidence useful to antinuclear activists or Native Americans (as well as all citizens of the state) is discounted if it does not meet a requirement (in this case, a timetable) that has been dictated by political objectives.

In May 1995 Don Hancock and others of the Southwest Research and Information Center, along with New Mexico Attorney General Tom Udall, filed lawsuits in the D.C. Circuit Court of Appeals against the Environmental Protection Agency to force it to issue its "final compliance criteria" in a timely manner. The compliance criteria are basically the radiation protection standards that the DOE will have to prove it can meet *before* opening WIPP for operation. The lawsuit also attempted to force the EPA to keep the standard-setting process within the public arena. According to Hancock, the EPA has bypassed the open public review of safety standards by operating through the nonpublic Office of Management and Budget (OMB). Once again, New Mexicans are forced to go to great lengths to keep the government regulation process fair and open. The legal and technical expertise to press for compliance is beyond the scope of the average citizen. But after twenty years of experience, organizations such as CCNS and the Southwest Research and Information Center have become experts in their own right. However, in the spring of 1997 the EPA won the lawsuit filed against it by those seeking to keep WIPP from opening.[47] But as noted by Hancock, DOE still has many hurdles to pass before being able to officially open its cavernous chambers to truckloads of transuranic waste. More lawsuits are on the horizon concerning WIPP's ability to comply with current radiation standards, more contention among scientists over technical reviews is flaring up, and more open hearings and public debates are scheduled before WIPP can be issued a permit to accept the waste.

Antinuclear activists and analysts recognize the urgency of the current waste crisis but contend that building a deep-geologic permanent repository (that will not allow waste to be exhumed, in the event of an emergency) could turn into a serious disaster if it proves to be unsafe. They also fear that current congressional budget cuts to environmental restoration and waste management programs will only hasten the opening of the controversial repository. If WIPP proves not to be safe, residents of New Mexico and Texas will pay the highest price.

It is important to note that, along with other white and Hispanic local populations, the Mescalero Apache Reservation is in the greater WIPP region. WIPP is one of the reasons some of the Mescalero Apache opted to store nuclear waste in an MRS, an above-ground, temporary facility.[48] The logic is tragically sound: Because the reservation residents already have a massive deep-geologic nuclear-waste repository going in virtually next door (WIPP is some sixty miles distant as the crow flies), they may as well make some money on storing nuclear waste themselves. As one Apache put it when asked why the Mescalero Apaches would even consider storing the waste: "Their reasoning is that since they are getting impacted by nuclear waste [anyway] they should have a chance to benefit economically and be in the driver's seat."[49] Unfortunately, this driver's seat is on a metaphoric nuclear waste-bearing truck moving down the cracked roadway known as New Mexico's "nuclear highway."

Yucca Mountain—Zone Two

West and north of WIPP, across the state of Arizona, is the other deep-geo-logic repository site destined to serve the nation's nuclear-waste-storage needs: Yucca Mountain. This small mountain stands at the intersection of the Great Basin and Mojave Deserts. Two-thirds of the mountain also stands within the Nevada Test Site.

Like WIPP, Yucca Mountain is surrounded by controversy and debate. And like WIPP, the siting is generally accepted to be politically expedient rather than based solely on technical qualifications. As noted by Gerald Jacob in *Site Unseen*: "[Y]ucca Mountain, Nevada [w]as an indefensible choice if one viewed it as the best site selected from an inventory of all geologically suitable sites. Potentially acceptable sites had all been identi-fied long before the development of the site selection criteria required by the NWPA."[50]

Unlike WIPP, Yucca Mountain is not much of a solution for future gen-erations of nuclear waste. As one scientist with the Yucca Mountain Project told me: "By the time Yucca Mountain is finished, it will be filled, and another repository will be needed." The projected capacity of Yucca Mountain on completion is 70,000 tons of high-level radioactive waste (approximately 90% from commercial sources and 10% from military sources). There are 112 commercial power plants in the United States today (and more in 28 countries abroad) that are anxiously awaiting the opening of the long-promised "permanent" repository. But after eight years of fea-sibility studies that have cost $1.7 billion, Yucca Mountain has yet to be determined safe for high-level nuclear waste. The cost is quite impressive. Feasibility studies in 1995 alone cost $1.46 million *per day*.[51] Total cost of construction of the repository is estimated at $15 billion.[52] But the mone-tary costs are the least alarming ones. Thirty-two earthquake fault lines lie in the vicinity of the mountain; there is evidence of recent volcanic activity in the area; and scientists have raised the possibility that all that waste, when buried together in one place, might "go critical," erupting "in a nuclear explosion, scattering radioactivity to the winds or into ground water or both."[53] For once, the state of Nevada and the Indian tribes of the area agree: They're both against it.

In the second half of this book I explore the complex issues surrounding the Yucca Mountain proposal, as well as its perceived impact on the Native people of the area and what they have to say about it. For now it is sufficient that Yucca Mountain be made visible as a central node in the web of sitings in Zones One and Two of the nuclear wasteland. Although in many respects it is a world-historical event, the siting of a nuclear waste repository at Yucca Mountain is shrouded in the darkness of the Nevada Test Site—one of the darkest and most invisible zones in the nuclear landscape.

Because of its destined role as the home of waste that remains lethal for 240,000 years, Yucca Mountain is also the most scientifically studied piece of land in the world. That fact alone should indicate its position as one of the premier symbols and manifestations of the nuclear wasteland. But it is also considered holy land by the Western Shoshone and Southern Paiute, whose visions warn of a great snake within the mountain, which, if disturbed, will move with perilous consequences. I have been told by Southern Paiutes that the mountain is also a place of transition from this world to the afterlife, that it is over this mountain that the Paiute Indians are said to pass on their journey through and beyond death. In fact, on and around Yucca Mountain, including the larger Nevada Test Site region, archaeologists have found significant numbers of artifacts, cultural resource sites, and even burial sites—so much so that the Department of Energy is required to contract with archaeologists and anthropologists to work with Indian groups to identify and sometimes remove important burial remains and cultural artifacts. This so-called wasteland is actually a culturally complex area where three major Indian nations historically converge: the Southern Paiute, the Western Shoshone, and the Owens Valley Paiute. Contrary to popular misconception, Indians *were* removed from the Nevada Test Site when it was expropriated by the Department of Defense in the 1950s. The Western Shoshone continue to claim the land and call themselves the "most bombed nation on earth." Indian people of the area do not speak with one voice of protest against the Department of Energy's activities in the region. They have different concerns and opinions about the area (and even different opinions about which tribes have authentic traditional rights to the mountain). But not one with whom I spoke accepts its designation as a nuclear-waste dump, nor is any looking forward to the thousands of truckloads and railroad cars of nuclear waste expected to move through the area.[54]

Because no sites other than Yucca Mountain are being evaluated as a potential repository for the country's most lethal wastes (indeed such evaluations would be too expensive), the Department of Energy effectively has placed all its eggs in one basket. This fact alone should call the scientific basis of its selection into question. In addition to earthquake faults and a history of volcanic activity,[55] tritium pollution has been discovered in the Yucca Mountain region. I found out about this in 1994 while on a private tour of the mountain. At that time one scientist I spoke with conjectured that tritium particles had moved down via water flow from Paiute Mesa, a region of the Nevada Test Site contaminated by nuclear explosions. Current speculation by scientists studying the mountain holds that rain contaminated by worldwide atmospheric testing seeped into the ground water.[56] One also has to wonder about the impact the underground nuclear tests have had on the integrity of the geology of the Nevada Test Site land base on which Yucca Mountain stands.

Such problems don't get the media attention they deserve largely because Yucca Mountain is invisible to a public that refuses to concern itself with what's not in its backyard. To contend with technical problems raised by the site characterization studies, the new Nuclear Waste Policy Act is expected to relax safety stipulations. If the mountain cannot be verified as safe by scientific experts, the policy makers will bend science to its will, making it safe by changing the criteria for safety, by changing the radiation levels considered safe for human beings. Such legislation constitutes a very clear example of the way some scientific "facts" get constructed—not by objective assessment but by reconstructing the original set of standards (to suit political ends). By altering the requirements scientific experts are able to put their seal of approval on the project.[57] Thus, scientific facts, when used as mechanisms of exclusion, are purposefully malleable to suit particular needs at particular times. What constitutes the truth one day may change the next.[58]

Monitored Retrievable Storage Sites

Delays in building a deep-geologic, permanent nuclear-waste storage facility such as Yucca Mountain and a lack of storage space at nuclear power plants and at nuclear weapons facilities have created a need for a temporary monitored retrievable storage site (MRS). The creation of an MRS is part of the Department of Energy's mandate under the Nuclear Waste Policy Act to off-load commercial waste from nuclear power plants on a timely basis.[59] Temporary here means approximately forty to fifty years, enough time to allow for the development of a permanent repository such as Yucca Mountain. Paradoxically, one problem with the notion of a temporary solution lies in the search for a safe permanent burial site. If a permanent site cannot be found—that is, if scientists cannot ensure safety for 10,000 years (let alone for 240,000 years) then a deep-geologic repository will not be constructed, and any "temporary" solution to the storage problem at existing reactor sites and elsewhere may turn into a permanent storage site by default. Native Americans who oppose MRS development on their lands are afraid of just such a contingency arising. Because Native communities are most commonly considered for MRS sites (with the recent exception of the Nevada Test Site), the issue of a temporary solution to nuclear-waste storage becomes by default a Native American issue. The reasons only Native communities are considering the MRS option are complex but can be explained to a considerable extent by poverty, as well as by the fact that they have been aggressively propositioned by government agencies.

Temporary housing for 23,000 metric tons of highly radioactive nuclear waste that has been accumulating since the 1940s (and that promises to accumulate into the future) is very hard to find—even for the short term. In 1987 Congress authorized the Department of Energy to build an MRS facility. Ultimately, no state, county, or municipality was or is willing to even consider harboring the most toxic substances on earth.[60] The Office of the Nuclear Negotiator—the DOE office responsible for finding a home for the waste—"found" only Indian tribes willing to consider the possibility. In fact, the Office of the Nuclear Negotiator has been accused of "targeting" Native lands. Some tribal leaders have called the lucrative "grants" the DOE offers just to consider taking the waste a form of "economic blackmail:"[61]

> Sixteen tribes initially applied for $100,000 grants from DOE to study the MRS option on Native lands. The lucrative DOE offer included up to $3 million to actually identify a site for an MRS and as much as $5 million per year for any tribe to accept the deal. *The government also offered to build roads, hospitals, schools, railroads, airports and recreation facilities.* [My italics.][62]

The $100,000 grant to consider the waste storage option was also promised (by the U.S. Nuclear Negotiator, David Leroy) to participants of a 1992 conference of the National Congress of American Indians (which had convened to address the Department of Energy's new strategy for management of commercial spent nuclear fuel). The promise was made to "each and every willing tribe."[63]

Today, at the time of this writing, it is unclear which, if any, tribes will accept an MRS facility, but during the mid-1990s those that were actively considering such a proposition were the Mescalero Apache in Southeastern New Mexico, the Skull Valley Goshute in northwestern Utah, and the Fort McDermott Paiute-Shoshone Tribe of northern Nevada—all lands within our designated "nuclear landscape."

There are various reasons that state and other local government bodies refuse to consider an MRS. Foremost among them is the fact that their voting citizens include a wider array of positions along the economic spectrum. In other words, "development" opportunities safer than hosting nuclear waste exist for a greater number of constituents. Also, scientists disagree about the safety of above-ground nuclear waste storage—just as scientists disagree about all nuclear-waste-storage proposals. Some scientists argue that above-ground storage is far more hazardous than deep-geologic containment because it is more vulnerable to the elements and to surface movement of the earth should there be an earthquake.[64] MRS storage also requires packaging of the waste by manipulating the hot fuel rods for tighter storage, which means additional handling and subsequent increase in risk. The DOE has raised the possibility that an MRS could serve as a possible terrorist target. And then there is the problem of transportation. A state that hosts the only MRS in the country would see a lot of high-level nuclear-waste shipments on its highways, railroads, and byways.

The larger the community body, the less likely it is to consider a repository—there's just too much opposition. Though some counties may be impoverished enough to consider an MRS, they quickly find their desire thwarted by opposition at the state level. Indian reservations, on the other hand, are both small and "sovereign"—outside the immediate control of the state in which they reside. They are also outside the jurisdiction of federal agencies such as the Environmental Protection Agency and not subject to the same regulatory agencies as the state. Because tribal communities are relatively small in population, they do not require extensive public relations campaigns to persuade them (as does a large territorial body like a state). In addition, because they are often extremely impoverished, they are vulnerable to bribes. If we add to this the fact that many of these tribes are already near nuclear facilities and military weapons testing ranges in the nuclear landscape, then they begin to look like ideal sites to the OCRWM and toxic waste industries. The Mescalero Apache, on many counts, fit the bill, as do (most certainly) the Skull Valley Goshutes and the Fort McDermitt Paiute-Shoshone.

The Mescalero Apache Tribe—Zone One of the Nuclear Landscape

Located between the White Sands Missile Range and WIPP, the military's deep-geologic nuclear waste repository, and neighboring the Fort Bliss military reservation stands the Mescalero Apache Reservation.

In the mid-1990s the Mescalero Apache were the furthest along in the MRS waste-acceptance process. Relatively speaking, the Mescalero Apache are not an economically impoverished people—if you base your economic analysis on the existence of successful industry. The tribe's cattle company has 7,000 head, its ski resort draws 250,000 visitors annually, and its lumber company puts out 16 million board-feet per year.[65] Wendell Chino, president of the tribal council, promoted acceptance of the waste and boasted, "The Navajos make rugs, the Pueblos make pottery, and the Mescaleros make money." Others, however, contend that many Mescalero Apache live in dire conditions.[66] One Apache woman suggested as much when she said: "The federal government has forced us to choose between being environmentally conscientious or keep from starving."[67] Like this reservation member, many tribal members are adamantly opposed to the use of their land as a radioactive waste dump and have been engaged in a bitter internal struggle over the decision.

The tribe split along two factions: the prodevelopment tribal council and its supporters and the traditionalists who oppose acceptance of the waste. Like some other toxic-waste struggles, this one produced a noteworthy woman activist. Rufina Laws, a Mescalero Apache woman of remarkable dedication, vision, and persistence, almost single-handedly led the effort to oppose the powerful tribal council and to educate tribal members about the hazards of nuclear waste. Her efforts resulted in a no-acceptance vote by the tribe in the winter of 1995. The no vote was contrary to all previous indications, and news of it was picked up by the world press and acclaimed by environmentalists and indigenous communities throughout the United States. However, by early spring of 1995 tribal council members had gathered enough petition signatures to force another referendum and succeeded in securing a slim victory to accept the MRS proposition.

Laws also claims to have received death threats and public condemnation for opposing the MRS development. Here, as in other tribal communities, the nuclear-waste option turned tribal members against one another and revealed corruption within tribal governments.

For now the Mescalero Apache appear to have once again decided against accepting the waste. Though the tribe's reasons aren't entirely clear, it did encounter opposition not only from within but also from without its reservation boundaries. The state of New Mexico opposed the tribe's right to accept the waste and seriously questioned the tribe's sovereignty on this issue. The state threatened to block the transport of radioactive shipments on its highways, which are, of course, controlled by the state, not the tribe. Under pressure from the state, Congress cut off funding for the Office of the Nuclear Negotiator, effectively eliminating the tribe's source of federal grant money. Because of this, the Mescalero tribal leaders decided to bypass the federal government altogether by going straight to the private source itself—the nuclear-power companies. At one time they even began drafting a nonfederal, independent business agreement to accept the waste. Ms. Laws noted that the deal was made between the tribal council and CEOs from twenty-four nuclear power companies.[68] For now the Mescalero have backed off from such business agreements. But even if at some point they decide to move forward, it remains unclear whether the federal government would bless such a deal and whether the Nuclear Regulatory Commission would actually license such a facility. At the time of this writing, rather than the Mescalero, the Skull Valley Goshutes in Utah have now moved onto center stage for an MRS site.

Who controls and transports nuclear waste promises to be a highly contentious issue as state, federal, and tribal powers struggle against one another for jurisdiction. The federal government controls the interstate highways, the state controls all other highways, but the tribes have jurisdiction over their territories. The power plays involved overlap at times with another contentious issue involving tribal sovereignty—gambling. In 1994 in northern New Mexico, close to Santa Fe, the Pojoaque Pueblo applied for a license to build a gambling casino, but because the state is antigambling, licensing was stalled. As Masco notes, to get the licensing process moving, "pueblo leaders announced that they were interested in storing high-level nuclear waste (i.e., plutonium contaminated waste) from dismantled U.S. nuclear weapons."[69] In the end, the pueblo got the gambling rights they wanted. Thus, nuclear waste has become a bargaining chip in contestations between private enterprise, state, federal, and tribal governments, further complicating an already unmanageable problem.

The Fort McDermitt Paiute-Shoshone and the Skull Valley Goshutes

Zone Two of the nuclear landscape is home to the other two tribal communities that are currently (or were recently) considering hosting an MRS: the Fort McDermitt Paiute-Shoshone and the Skull Valley Goshutes.

Straddling the tip of Zone Two, at the border of Nevada and Oregon, the Fort McDermitt tribe only recently considered an MRS storage facility on the Oregon side of their reservation. Like the Mescalero Apache, the Fort McDermitt tribe is divided on hosting such a facility. Other tribes in the region have attempted to convince them of the danger of such development. As in the case of the Mescalero Apache, the tribe divided between progressivists who see waste storage as a form of economic development, leading to jobs and a relief from poverty, and traditionalists who claim that the environmental risks are too great and that housing waste would be contrary to Indian spiritual and cultural values. In the Fort McDermitt case, even a pronuclear Department of Energy contractor suggested that making an offer to such an impoverished tribe was tantamount to environmental racism.[70] For now it appears that the tribe has declined the offer, but only after a great deal of effort on the part of Native environmentalists who converged on the tribe with an impressive antinuclear information campaign.

To the east and also near the border of Nevada, in western Utah (at the edge of the Great Salt Lake Desert), the Skull Valley Goshute tribe is seriously considering the MRS proposition. Like the Fort McDermitt tribe, the Goshutes are impoverished. But that is not all. This small tribal community is literally surrounded by an environment made toxic by both state-run and independent waste-management industries, as well as by military biochemical facilities, including the Army's chemical weapons incinerator. The Goshute land proposed for the MRS now serves as a testing ground for corporations involved in rocket manufacture. This lease brings in 90% of tribal income and will soon expire. When Goshutes are asked why they are considering hosting an MRS, they talk about the difficulties of getting safer industries to come to their area. As tribal member Leon Bear says:

> People need to understand that this whole area has already been deemed a waste zone by the federal government, the state of Utah, and the county. . . . Tooele Depot, a military site, stores 40% of the nation's nerve gas and other hazardous gas only 40 miles away from us. Dugway Proving Grounds, an experimental life sciences center, is only 14 miles away, and it experiments with viruses like the plague and tuberculosis. Within a 40-mile radius there are three hazardous waste dumps and a "low-level" radioactive waste dump. From all directions, north, south, east, and west, we're surrounded by the waste of Tooele County, the state of Utah, and U.S. society. Over 30% of the tribe is children, so yes, we're very concerned about all this.
>
> So that's why it's so hard to talk with businesses or anybody else about economic development. They're all scared to come out here, much less develop things here. But I live here. I like it here. I'm not going to move.[71]

Many Indians are attempting to educate those enticed by the money about the risks of housing high-level nuclear waste. Even though most communities are desperately poor, they are becoming less willing to consider an MRS facility.[72]

The environmental justice movement has emerged to combat the inequitable burden of environmental degradation placed on poor communities and communities of color.[73] The targeting of Native American lands for temporary nuclear waste storage can be seen as a form of environmental racism and what Indian people themselves call nuclear colonialism. Offers of large sums of money, schools, hospitals, and other vital needs in exchange for housing nuclear waste only lends credence to the charge that the U.S. government engages in nuclear colonialism and environmental racism.

Low-Level Nuclear Waste:
Ward Valley and the Mojave's Indigenous Peoples

> The Creator designed that area for the tortoise. You don't have to look for them; they are there. The tortoise is our tie to the land. If they go, we will go. What is at stake is the survival of our people.
> —WELDON JOHNSON, Mojave tribe

"Low-level" nuclear waste is disposed of in shallow earth excavations that average about 15 meters wide by 15 meters deep by 200 meters long. Low-level nuclear waste has been "disposed of" for more than forty years in such shallow trenches on land and in the ocean. Originally, six commercial low-level radioactive waste sites were opened in the United States. The number was reduced to three because of "unanticipated problems with the integrity of the burial sites." Indeed, proponents and waste-management experts themselves note that "virtually none of the six commercial and six DOE sites has proven 100 percent effective."[74] The three longest-lived low-level commercial burial sites include Barnwell, South Carolina (in the state hosting the Savannah River DOE facilities); Richland, Washington (in the state hosting the Hanford plutonium production DOE facilities); and Beatty, Nevada (in the state hosting the Nevada Test Site). However, these sites are all closed or closing because of public opposition, lawsuits against the companies running the sites, the lack of site integrity (meaning that some burial sites are leaking), and lack of space. Consequently, there is a race to find replacements. Major nuclear weapons facilities, such as laboratories, testing ranges, and production plants (for instance Los Alamos and the Nevada Test Site) host their own "private" low-level nuclear waste sites. Information about these sites is far more difficult to obtain. For instance, only through archaeological maps of the Nevada Test Site did I become aware of such burial sites in that highly secretive location.[75]

This state of affairs in the low-level radioactive waste industry has resulted in a proposal to open a site in Ward Valley in California's Mojave

Desert. It would be the first nuclear waste site to open in the nation in more than twenty-five years. Opponents of the proposed dump at Ward Valley fear that it may end up becoming a national (and only temporary) solution to the low-level radioactive waste crisis. The Low-Level Radioactive Waste Policy Act of 1980 makes states responsible for the disposal of waste generated within their own state boundaries. But, since every state may not be able to afford its own dump, states have the option of forming regional compacts and taking turns hosting a low-level radioactive dump. But things aren't proceeding as envisioned by the act. As one opponent of the Ward Valley dump explains:

> California is in the Southwestern Compact with Arizona, South Dakota, and North Dakota. Radioactive dumps in Illinois, Kentucky, and New York have been closed. The nation's two remaining low-level radioactive waste dumps, at Richland, Washington and Barnwell, South Carolina, are closing, and no other state has agreed to open its doors to nuclear waste.
>
> The Nuclear Regulatory Commission has unilateral "emergency access provisions" to direct nuclear wastes from anywhere in the country to any open dump. *Last year the Southwestern Compact Commission, appointed by the governors of the four far-flung states, decided to keep the option of accepting out-of-compact waste at Ward Valley.* Dump opponents fear that Ward Valley would become the nation's dumping grounds for over 112 commercial nuclear reactors.[76] [My italics.]

Nor is the waste just "hospital gowns and booties":

> The sophisticated public relations campaign by the nuclear industry would have the public believe that Ward Valley will be home to hospital gowns and booties and an occasional X-ray machine. US Department of Energy records, however, show that the dump would receive some of the longest-lived and most dangerous wastes—including cesium, strontium, and plutonium—from nuclear power reactors.[77]

Ward Valley is in Zone Two of the nuclear landscape at the southern end of the Mojave Desert, below the militarized zones of China Lake Naval Weapons Center, Edwards Air Force Base, and Fort Irwin mentioned in

Chapter 3. It is just west of the town of Needles, and it's just east of a massive Marine Corps Training Center, so it has its own militarized zone—reinforcing the argument that (when we don't designate them national treasures) we tend to turn our desert regions into wastelands fit only for war games and radioactive/toxic waste dumps. The recently approved Ward Valley facility will include five unlined trenches the size of football fields. The dump will be only eighteen miles from the Colorado River, and it will sit above an aquifer.

But place-names in the Ward Valley region tell another story. Maps of the area show the Chemehuevi Mountains, the Piute Mountains, and the Chemehuevi Valley. Ward Valley is bordered by the Fort Mojave Indian Reservation, the Chemehuevi Indian Reservation, and the Colorado River Indian Tribes Reservation. Although offered money and the prospect of jobs, many Indian residents have actively opposed the dump. Formerly known as Nuclear Engineering Corporation, U.S. Ecology (which does not enjoy a stellar reputation in the management of other low-level waste dumps, such as the one recently forced to close near Beatty, Nevada) stands to reap large profits from the Ward Valley venture. Thus, it offers not only jobs to the locals of the small nearby town of Needles, but it will also pay the town $1 million a year for thirty years of operation. U.S. Ecology has bought the local high school science textbooks and has set up a school scholarship program. It has also offered to build the Fort Mojave Indians a museum (there are countless artifacts and petroglyphs in the area), as well as a cultural center. But the unlined shallow trenches may contain as much as 100 pounds of plutonium, a lethal price for a museum—indeed, a museum may be the only appropriate structure to build for the Indians if the project goes forward. Though Indian communities in the area have formed intertribal alliances and work in coalitions with environmentalists, their interests have tended to be unacknowledged by the state. As one member of the Fort Mojave tribe notes:

> They intend to transport nuclear waste through our reservation and through the town of Needles. They have never asked our permission or held a hearing on this issue. There is no provision to train our people should there be an accident, no plans to deal with the terrible dangers of a nuclear waste transport accident.

We will be needing water to grow. There is much water beneath Ward Valley and it will eventually become contaminated. This is a terrible crime. Our poor desert tortoise never even had a chance. Both the tortoise and the land are sacred to us. We have used this land for thousands of years. We use the plants here to heal ourselves. Now it will all be destroyed. It's wrong all the way around.[78]

A clear pattern emerges from consideration of the Owens Valley Paiute, Southern Paiute, and Western Shoshone near the Yucca Mountain site, the Mescalero Apache close to the WIPP site, and the other tribal communities targeted for MRS sites, as well as the Indian presence near the low-level radioactive waste site at Ward Valley. Nuclear-waste sitings in the inter-desert region are nearly always juxtaposed with Indian presence. Each type of containment facility—deep-geologic disposal, above-ground temporary disposal, or shallow disposal—is sited for lands that are contested. These lands are either Indian aboriginal homelands (for the Shoshone, Paiute, and Chemehuevi) or lands where Indians were relocated during the many "trails of tears" that constitute the history of Euroamerican-Indian relations. If Indian people weren't in these desert regions to begin with, then they were driven here by the U.S. government and by white settlers. Now that mostly non-Indians want these desert lands for what can only be seen as a kind of inverse form of "development" (burial of nuclear waste), the United States once again asserts its "God-given right" (its manifest destiny) to territories formerly designated "wilderness" or "Indian Country" on early maps of the region. It is ironic that the "wasteland" white people thought they would never want begins to look—fifty years into the nuclear age—like a lucrative investment. Meanwhile, such companies as U.S. Ecology (with its scandalous history of safety violations) stand to benefit from a probusiness Congress determined to slash funding for health, safety, and environmental protection, and indeed, to weaken the regulations themselves.

The struggles going on in these out-of-the-way places, struggles that the mainstream media ignore more often than not, are quite familiar to the Indian people who inhabit them. My interviews with Indian people in the interdesert region have revealed that many feel these struggles to be reminiscent of an older relationship between white people and Indians, only

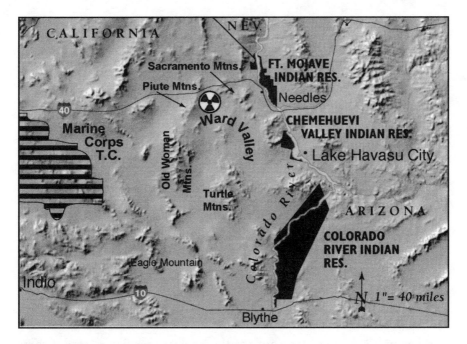

Figure 4.2 Ward Valley and surrounding Indian tribes

Compiled by Valerie Kuletz; cartography production by Jared Dawson

now the terms of the argument have changed, and the doublespeak is slicker. Many Indian people have expressed to me that they see the nuclear wasteland as a form of twentieth-century genocide. This, in conjunction with the strong military presence in the interdesert region, gives them the feeling that history is once again repeating itself, that the nuclear landscape is a contemporary form of the colonialism that won the West.

The Nuclear Waste Crisis in Context

Why has the "nuclear crisis" become old news? Perhaps because the collective fear engendered by the alarming arms escalation at the height of the Cold War in the Reagan era has dissipated. Mutual assured destruction is held momentarily at bay. The nuclear era is not yet over, however, and in some ways it has just begun. Today, a new nuclear geopolitical era is swiftly coming into focus as Russians and China peddle nuclear technology to Iran and Pakistan, as France concludes nuclear tests in its South Pacific territories (to the anger of both indigenous and nonindigenous people there), as North Korea balks at U.S. inspection of its nuclear facilities, and as pounds of weapons-grade plutonium are smuggled across European borders. With thousands of tons of nuclear waste, and lots of confusion about what to do with it, the full extent of the nuclear-waste problem remains hidden behind layers of bureaucracy. By ignoring the emergence of a nuclear wasteland, people miss an opportunity to contend intelligently with the problem, not only on a scientific basis, but also on a social and ethical basis. By not *seeing* the emerging nuclear wasteland and by allowing the waste to be buried and "forgotten," people lock future generations into an even more untenable situation than exists today. "Total containment" of nuclear waste represents, if not a technoscientific fantasy, at least one of the largest and most crucial "experiments" that modern science has conducted, second perhaps only to the atomic bomb itself. Solutions to both require political will as well as scientific expertise.

Coming to a Town Near You

Perhaps public recognition (outside the nuclear sacrifice zones) of these massive repositories, and of the nuclear-waste crisis in general, will appear when shipping the rods in casks on public transportation routes around the country begins in earnest. The logistics of transport, for either a temporary or a permanent storage repository, is daunting. In either case, thousands of tons of commercial and military nuclear waste will soon be moving around the country by rail and by truck, in much greater quantities than military waste has moved between sites for the past five decades. In addition to any other problems or presumed benefits, an MRS or a single deep-geologic repository will require movement of high-level nuclear waste on an unprecedented scale. The shipment of high-level nuclear waste may well become the biggest obstacle to the implementation of plans made by the Office of Civilian Radioactive Waste Management. Because the shipping has the potential to affect millions of Americans, and not just those in New Mexico or Nevada, the nuclear-waste crisis may finally become visible. The next "national sacrifice area" may well be a stretch of local highway.

More than 15,000 truck and rail shipments through forty-three states over a period of thirty years will be required to move the nation's waste from nuclear power plants to Yucca Mountain (should Yucca Mountain become the national repository).

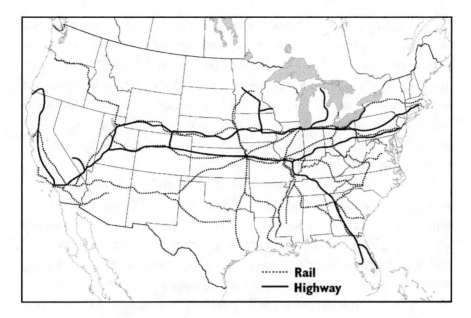

Figure 4.3 Nuclear waste shipment routes
Produced by Jared Dawson; based on Department of Energy map

Large amounts will enter U.S. ports from twenty-eight countries abroad. Some comparative "facts" reveal the inequity of the nuclear burden in the transportation scenario: According to a study by the state of Nevada, the total number of shipments from sites within the United States amounts to 9,421 casks by rail and 6,217 casks by truck, all of which will move through Nevada. The number of nuclear power plants in Nevada is zero. The state *not* using nuclear power through which the largest number of shipments will pass (other than Nevada) is Utah (8,179 rail casks and 6,173 truck casks). In fact, waste shipments will pass through ten states that do not have nuclear power. On the other hand, Vermont, the state with the highest dependence on nuclear energy, will have only 584 shipments by truck and no rail shipments at all.[79]

Importing Nuclear Waste—The World's Nuclear Waste on U.S. Highways

Importation of high-level nuclear waste provides a perfect example of how nuclearism cannot be separated from militarism, even when nuclear power is used for "peaceful" purposes. During the "Atoms for Peace Program" of the 1950s and 1960s, the United States encouraged development of atomic energy in exchange for promises by developing and developed nations not to create nuclear weapons. The United States thought it could have its cake and eat it too: It could support a nonproliferation policy while continuing to encourage the use of nuclear power. That policy proved to be the devil's bargain: nuclear power for a promise to renounce nuclear weapons. Even today, U.S. policy encourages nations to continue operating nuclear power plants rather than decommission them.

Before 1964 the United States "leased" uranium fuel in bilateral agreements. After 1964 the United States sold nuclear fuel. In order to control all aspects of the nuclear cycle in the global arena, the United States developed an "Off-Site Fuel Policy" from 1964 to 1987 that encouraged the return of highly enriched uranium to discourage foreign countries from stockpiling spent fuel (which can be used for making nuclear weapons). Thus, spent fuel (high-level nuclear waste) will be returning to the United States from at least 28 countries, through as many as ten ports of entry—for example, through the Concord Naval Weapons Station port in California's San Francisco Bay Area, one of the most densely populated regions in the country.[80]

Power at the Margins

With the inclusion of the nuclear wasteland our map of the nuclear landscape is complete—spatially and temporally—as it reaches into the future with the proposed siting of radioactive waste repositories in the interdesert region. This era—the nuclear era—is only fifty years old, but it presents a problem so immense that it will require far more than a mere technological fix to remedy. We will have to imagine how we are going to go about the project of protecting life (as we now know it) for at least 240,000 years.

Though it has manifested itself all across the United States, nuclearism has settled into the interdesert region for the long term, or so it promises. The last fifty years have given this region uranium booms and busts and left their tragic scars on the land's face and beneath its surface, as well as in the bodies of the miners and within their communities. Nuclearism has given this region science cities in the desert, and here forged bonds between scientific knowledge production and military mandates for the development and testing of the weapons of war. This bonding created "outdoor laboratories" of immense size used to test strategic and "theater" nuclear bombs, as well as powerful "conventional" weapons. On-continent testing of nuclear weapons has left a legacy of sickness and death in downwind communities and an as-yet-undetermined contribution to cancer and other lethal epidemics in our society. Finally, this region is positioned not only for the concentration of facilities for the nuclear weapons complex for the twenty-first century but also for the burial and containment of all types of nuclear waste—from both the continental United States and from many other nations for whom the United States has guaranteed storage. These activities have taken up millions and millions of acres, thousands of square miles of land and airspace and affected many of the longtime inhabitants of this region. The social and environmental transformations brought about by these forces have only just begun to be explored—as it is only now that the geographies of sacrifice that make up much of this landscape have become evident.

The narrative map that I have drawn insists that people recognize, become conscious of, Indian presence within the nuclear landscape. Or perhaps I should say nuclear presence within the Indian landscape. The two landscapes—Indian and nuclear—exist in the same place. While this may seem a very straightforward statement, it is remarkably hard to actually see, which is why the map is necessary.

This narrative map is not meant to suggest that all Indians oppose nuclearism in Indian country. They do not agree on whether waste disposal, as a form of development, will bring jobs, immediate sustenance, or relief from poverty. The map is not about the variety of positions taken on any of these subjects—that will be addressed in the second part of this book. The map attests that (1) nuclearism and militarism have had a transformative influence on the Southwest interdesert region, that (2) this transformation has, in turn, exerted a profound influence on the Indian inhabitants of the region, and that (3) taken together, the various stages of transformation I have described—from uranium mining to the establishment of weapons research facilities and from the establishment of massive testing ranges for nuclear and nonnuclear weapons and technology to the burial of the waste from all forms of nuclear production—have occurred on or near Indian communities. Consequently, those who benefit least from nuclear developments end up paying the highest price for the excesses of our nuclear culture.

This map also begins to make visible the centers of power that have made this landscape a reality, that is, particular industries, particular scientific communities (blind to the consequences of their work), certain government agencies, and the military establishment. Yet it is only by focusing on and listening to those who live at the margins of this power configuration that we can come to know and see the power at work behind the transformation of the land.

The fact that an Indian map beneath the nuclear map exists may seem simple, but until it's made clear—made visible—we can't begin to ask deeper questions about the mechanisms of power and exclusion, of visibility and invisibility, of knowledge, power, and marginalization, and of postcolonial racism that arise within this landscape. In this map of marginalized land and marginalized people resides profound power—the power of war and of energy. On this landscape resides the state's raw apparatus for maintaining power. It is, after all, a militarized zone. Mapping it reveals the invisible center of power, which may only be possible with the view from the edge, from the center's periphery, by those living uneasily on its side—along the borders of the installations, the testing fields, and the dumping grounds of their lethal waste.

·PART TWO·

Power, Representation, and Cultural Politics at Yucca Mountain

Yucca Mountain, Nevada
From the U.S. Department of Energy/Yucca Mountain Project

· 5 ·

The View
from Yucca Mountain

Perspectives and Boundaries

Mapping the nuclear landscape is a political practice of *seeing* because it makes visible the unseen inhabitants of deterritorialized—that is, sacrificed—geographies as well as the landscape itself. Part One of this book used spatial coordinates (official and alternative maps and zones of concentrated nuclear activity), and historical and contemporary narratives to foreground the emergent nuclear landscape. Part Two uses similar mapping, spatial, and narrative strategies to illuminate some of the ways different groups in this region view, experience, construct, and organize the Yucca Mountain landscape. Because of the existence in this local region of inequitable positions of power between its different inhabitants, the second half of this book also concerns power relations and how such power relations are developed through cultural narratives about people and place, where different groups with their different knowledge systems meet and vie for legitimacy.

This chapter also introduces the reader to the many perspectives and uses of the Yucca Mountain region—a region organized around and extending outward from the center point of Yucca Mountain. One can

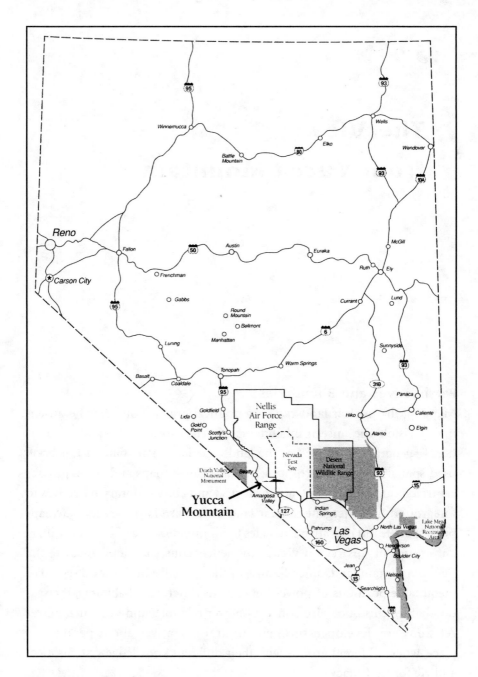

Figure 5.1 Yucca Mountain and Nevada

From: The U. S. Department of Energy, DOE's *Yucca Mountain Studies*

travel this area along different narrative and geographic pathways, through both space and time. For instance, traveling from Las Vegas in a northerly direction in a Yucca Mountain Project tour bus, the land can be viewed through the lens of the DOE's public relations campaign. Or, gathering like gypsy moths around the flame of protest, people can view the land through the lens of antinuclear and Western Shoshone land-rights activists at Cactus Springs or Peace Camp outside the gates of the Nevada Test Site. These protests—which are very near Yucca Mountain—can be reached by car from different directions: from the town of Beatty to the north, from Death Valley to the west, from Pahrump and Las Vegas from the southeast. (You can't reach the gathering place directly from the east because passage across the Nevada Test Site and Nellis Air Force Range is prohibited.)

The more discerning observer can peel away the contemporary asphalt-paved roads and recognize that many of these paths preexisted white occupation. Many of the roads follow old Indian passageways that intersected and stretch out across Yucca Mountain. Western Shoshone and Southern Paiute Indians moved across this area from all directions and lived in encampments at different places around the mountain. For instance, just north of present-day Beatty and northwest of Yucca Mountain, Western Shoshone lived in the permanent spring area of Oasis Valley, called the Ogwe'pi district. To the south lay the Western Shoshone and Southern Paiute spring area called the Ash Meadows district. In lower Amargosa Valley, Southern Paiute lived near springs at Pahrump ("Pa" meaning water) and at the Indian Springs/Cane Springs district. The paths that crossed Yucca Mountain itself lead northeast of the mountain to another camping/spring region, in the Belted Range, deep into what is now the Nevada Test Site. This region was called the Eso district and was then inhabited by Western Shoshone.[1]

Although this is a very dry landscape, clearly it is not, and was not, without water, as the place names of Oasis Valley, Indian Springs, Cane Springs, Ash Meadows, and Pahrump suggest.

This older history of land use is not evident to the average motorist traveling down U.S. 95 en route to Las Vegas. Nor is it generally recognized by the physical and biological scientists studying Yucca Mountain as a possible high-level nuclear waste dump. Nor is it recognized by politicians

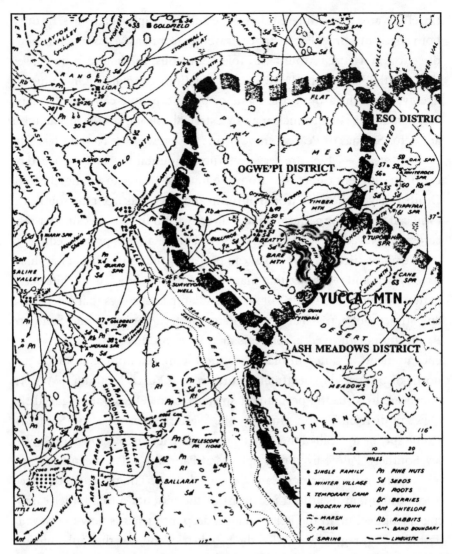

Figure 5.2 Native American use patterns in the Nevada Test Site and Yucca Mountain area

Adapted from: Stoffle et al., *Native American Cultural Resource Studies at Yucca Mountain, Nevada* (according to Steward 1938)

who need to find a permanent nuclear waste disposal facility outside their home states. The ancient Indian pathways that converge at Yucca Mountain and that organize the space of this region by way of Indian occupation and movement lie beneath the surface of other constructions of space. For the Indians, space here is organized according to these passageways, springs, valleys, and mountain peaks. Yucca Mountain rests between Bare Mountain, Little Skull Mountain, Timber Mountain, Shoshone Mountain, the Belted Range, and Paiute Mesa. From its crest one sees the important spiritual peaks of Mt. Charleston and Telescope Peak—peaks that preside over this terrain like monuments from another time. It rises gently out of the Amargosa Desert to separate Crater Flat from Jackass Flats where rabbit drives were held. Although often dry, the region provides animals for food, wild plants and seeds for seasonal harvests, and many medicinal plants. There is extensive rock art in Fortymile Canyon, as well as camp sites near springs and tinajas. There are also "power rocks" and places where Annual Mourning and other ceremonies were held (such as White Rock Spring, Ammonia Tanks, the Prow Pass). It is a terrain carved out of the earth from "the time when animals were people," those "beautiful progenitors of present day species"[2]—when giant snakes moved across the land creating monumental desert washes and coiled up to form mountains. Here, Coyote roamed mischievously across the desert, defining and creating whole ecosystems in his wake.

Euroamerican space, on the other hand, is here organized according to a series of highly rationalized, straight, gridlike boundaries imposed from above. For the Department of Energy, Yucca Mountain rests in a square space identified as "Area 25" within a checkerboard of squared-off regions mapped onto the land at the Nevada Test Site. It is the space of the modern industrial state, the organization of what amounts to a periphery inside the core power itself. Military power here blankets the local landscape, disciplining that landscape into a geometry of testing fields. Close examination of archaeological maps dramatically illustrates the layered aspect of cultural occupation, as well as the violence imposed on this landscape by the Department of Energy, in which it identifies numerous radioactive waste dumps scattered across a region that also contains springs held sacred by the Shoshone and Paiute Indians (see figure 5.3). The juxtaposition of military and Indian occupation is made clear when the grid of the Nevada Test Site is superimposed on the map of the shelters, springs, camps, and burial sites of the preexisting Indian population (see figure 5.4).

This highly militarized zone in which Yucca Mountain sits is also a zone of intense scientific study—an outdoor laboratory for different kinds of

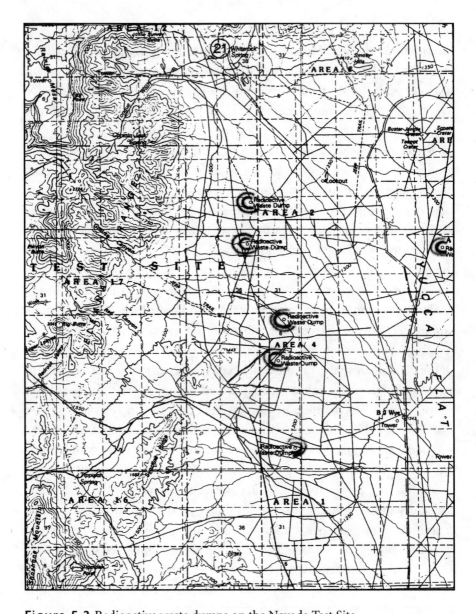

Figure 5.3 Radioactive waste dumps on the Nevada Test Site

Adapted from: Stoffle et al., *Native American Resource Studies at Yucca Mountain, Nevada*

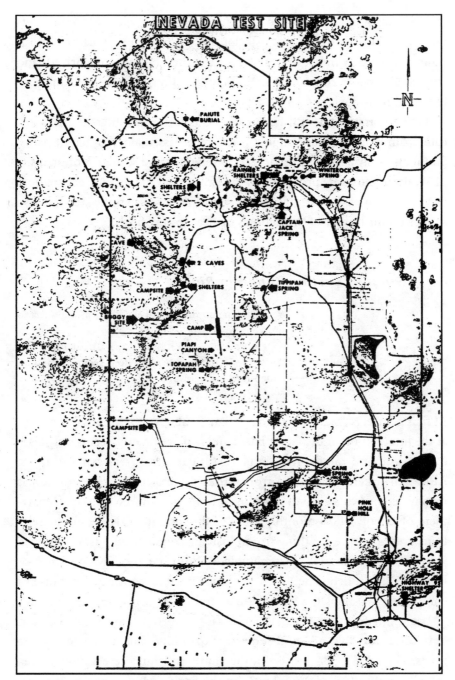

Figure 5.4 Springs, shelters, and burial grounds used by Indians at the Nevada Test Site

Adapted from: Stoffle et al., *Native American Resource Studies at Yucca Mountain, Nevada* (From F.C.V. Worman 1969)

scientific analysis. Through the scientific perspective, Yucca Mountain gets mapped from the inside out as scientists with the project bore into it removing long cylindrical "cores" that are then tagged, categorized, and studied in order to construct a map, a cross section, of the mountain's geologic and hydrologic properties.

Thus the mountain and its surrounding region can be seen prismatically from many different angles. It can be accessed along different paths. Simultaneously a site of Euroamerican religious and secular protest, a site of Western Shoshone protest, a zone of historical indigenous occupation, travel, ceremony, and origins, and a site of intense scientific study, it also resides on the border of the nation's nuclear testing fields.

From Ground Level to Mountain Ridge

> We're banking on the natural environment to protect us for 10,000 years!
> —DEPARTMENT OF ENERGY TOUR GUIDE explaining why the DOE wants to use a deep-geologic tomb for high-level nuclear waste

At first glance, Nevada's Amargosa Valley (where Yucca Mountain resides) at the intersection of the Great Basin and Mojave deserts, seems only a sea of creosote and range after range of (apparently) treeless mountains. Although it can be reached from other directions, Yucca Mountain is mostly reached by a road that begins in Las Vegas, from which the Department of Energy offers monthly tours of the mountain. These public relations events sport everything from plush air-conditioned buses, equipped with television monitors playing videos about the Yucca Mountain Project, to a free lunch. The lunch has since been discontinued because of complaints that the DOE was trying to unduly influence public opinion.

Beginning from Las Vegas, the tour moves north toward the mountains as the city fades into new and endlessly expanding pink and beige housing tracts. The DOE guide points out the Southern Paiute Reservation, sacred Mt. Charleston (called *Nuvagantu*) in the Spring Mountains (mythological site of Southern Paiute origins), Indian Springs with its government gunnery range, then the boundary to the Nevada Test Site, and even "Cherry Patch Ranch," the brothel servicing the surrounding (mostly military) community. When the tour bus finally turns off the highway and moves northeast toward Yucca Mountain, the feeling of desolation increases as the bus passes through check points where fatigue-clad military personnel board the bus to check for forbidden cameras, recording devices, and weapons. Radiation-monitoring tags clipped onto shirts serve as an additional reminder of the tight security at the Nevada Test Site. A guide informs tourists that they can write to the Department of Energy "in a month or so" to find out if they've actually been irradiated.

The expanse of heat-pounded scrub and hot barren sand is interrupted by signs of abandoned MX Missile construction sites (an attempt to make this region the sacrificial target for Soviet nuclear missiles) and buildings of a disbanded nuclear powered rocket program.[3] But the surrounding desert mountains possess the ability to transform space, or one's experience of space. The top of Yucca Mountain alters ones perception of the desert region from what it was on the road leading up to it. Stretched out below the crest of the mountain lies an immense desert floor fanning out in all directions. Yucca Mountain is part of many other mountains—multiple ranges of different colors that form a terrane geography of arcs, circles, and lines that at once define and emerge from the earth's softer plane of intersecting valleys. Gentle hues of pink, blue, violet, gray, sandy brown, and vermilion blend almost imperceptibly beneath an all-encompassing vaulted dome of blue sky. Ancient red volcanic cones rise up and out from the desert floor like prehistoric anthills. The wind is strong, and everywhere there is the monumental presence of rock.

Puha (Power) and Prometheus

Yucca Mountain may be comparatively small, but it is a powerful place nonetheless. The Western Shoshone and Southern Paiute Indians call the power such places possess *Puha* because the mountain, like all things Euroamericans call "inanimate," possesses energy, vitality, life force.[4] Space, and the different elements within it, are articulated by *Puha*, which resides dispersed throughout the landscape. For the Western Shoshone, Yucca

Mountain also forms part of the large expanse of desert, valleys, and mountains called *Newe Sogobia*, "Mother Earth," land of their origins. The Southern Paiute see the mountain as a place of power in another way as well. According to Richard Arnold (the Indian representative for the Yucca Mountain Project), Southern Paiutes cross over Yucca Mountain at death in their journey to the afterlife.[5] Indeed mountain peaks for both the Shoshone and Paiute are "sites of human creation, the points from which humans emerged [out of the womblike regenerative earth] and were dispersed."[6] Separating the northern and southern portions of Yucca Mountain is the Prow formation (so called because it resembles the prow of a ship), historically used for religious ceremonies and Indian gatherings, and recognized by archaeologists with Native guidance as a very powerful and important site.

The mountain has power also because it is high—a point of intersection between earth and sky. Along its back you feel wind energy and the sun. Although it's not as high as some of the surrounding peaks, it cleaves in upon itself in a series of washes—Fortymile Wash, Dune Wash, and others—which previous generations of Indians used to hunt game, gather edible and medicinal plants, and used as passageways to important springs. Partly because of the severity of this landscape, access to food and water is vital, taking on spiritual significance. Thus, Yucca Mountain was an important passage way on many levels. For the present-day observer, as with the Indians of the past, the mountaintop vantage point offers a "superhuman" view of space from which other significant sites from all directions in the landscape can be viewed.

Yucca Mountain is also powerful because it is the site of so much activity. At the foot of the mountain—out of sight from the summit—hundreds of men scurry about a monumental hole drilled into its side. Reduced to miniature proportions by the size of the tunnel, from a distance they look like ants. The hole in the mountain will hold the most toxic, lethal waste known to humanity. Watching this scene, one can't help but contemplate the compulsion to produce more and more power, the splitting of the atom, the transformation of *Puha* into "energy." The mountain seems to be all about power: the power of place, political power, military and economic power, and nuclear power.

The titanic scale of the tunnel and the reason for its existence also bring to mind the myth of Prometheus—only this time it's nuclear power that is the (unnatural) fire stolen from the gods. In the myth, Prometheus's punishment for stealing the fire is, of course, to endure having his liver—that toxin-cleansing organ—forever devoured by birds of prey. Just as Prometheus endures this ravaging virtually forever, so too does the specter of nuclear waste haunt the future. Prometheus and *Puha* each, in their way, offer radically different perceptions of power: *Puha* as life force, intrinsic and dispersed throughout the natural world; Prometheus's power, external, stolen, and ultimately self-destructive.

Compared to the view of nuclear landscapes through time and space in Part One of this book, the view from Yucca Mountain seems small. But because of its centrality in the nuclear-waste crisis, because of its prominence as an object of scientific study, and because of its location within both a sacred landscape and a sacrificial landscape (the Nevada Test Site), it is an important site within the nuclear landscape upon which to dwell. A lot of hopes and fears rest on this small mountain, too. The many people—mostly Indians, scientists, activists, and concerned Nevadans—who have converged on this site, sometimes pursuing conflicting interests, add to a sense of the mountain's power and make it a fit subject for a case study of how the nuclear landscape is defined and by whom.

The Yucca Mountain region is spatially organized by geographic boundaries, political boundaries, and cultural boundaries. It is also conceptually organized by Euroamericans within a hierarchy of disciplinary boundaries (which affect how the mountain gets identified and therefore designated for use as a waste dump). For Native Americans it is organized by a geography of past and contemporary use, as well as within a web of cosmological boundaries articulated in historical and mythological stories. Differently situated people see things differently and move through this region in different ways, as the example of *Puha* demonstrates. To ignore the culturally layered nature of this geographic region is to miss a great deal of its richness as a place of power.

From a geopolitical perspective, Yucca Mountain exists within a militarized, federally managed frame of reference, partly within land controlled by the Bureau of Land Management, partly on land controlled by the

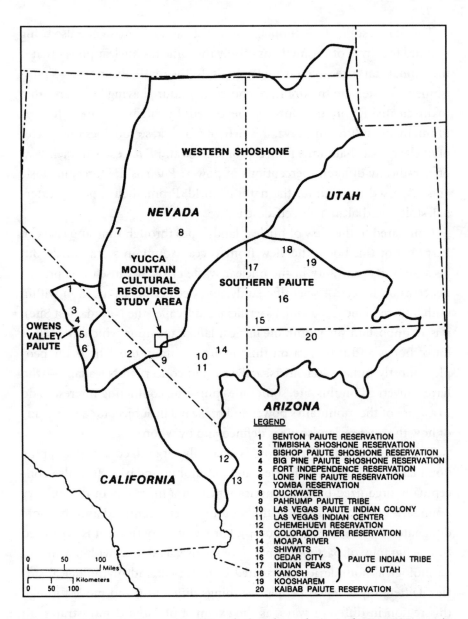

Figure 5.5 Indian tribes and traditional ethnic boundaries in the Yucca Mountain study region

From: Stoffle et al., *Native American Resource Studies at Yucca Mountain, Nevada* (adapted from D'Azevedo, 1986)

Department of Energy on the Nevada Test Site, and partly on land controlled by the Department of Defense—Nellis Air Force Range. The presence of these charged political boundaries mark it as a highly political site with a particular military and economic history. From a cultural perspective, the mountain exists within an extensive region traditionally co-inhabited and used by three major Indian ethnic groups—the Western Shoshone, the Southern Paiute, and the Owens Valley Paiute.

Contemporary political boundaries, like those at Yucca Mountain, always have an impact on vision: They make certain aspects of the landscape visible. At the same time, they render certain places and people invisible. A contemporary map of the Nevada Test Site, or of the state of Nevada, for instance, is a set of visual boundaries that organizes our field of perception of Yucca Mountain. Such maps don't show us the Western Shoshone and Southern Paiute territories, just entities such as state boundaries, military ranges, modern townships, and wildlife preservation areas. Seeing the traditional Indian domain takes more work because it resides on a historically deeper level in the landscape, which has been paved over by Nevada's contemporary institutional powers. Underlying these mapped and bounded organizations of space are narrative constructions of the land. In the case of Yucca Mountain, we find different narrative constructions depending on what maps and boundaries we investigate. Because all maps and narratives are cultural tools that define the world, we can see and briefly inhabit different worlds by looking at different visual and narrative representations of space.

I started this project thinking my case study would focus only on Yucca Mountain as the site of the U.S. high-level nuclear-waste storage repository. That is, I saw only the first layers of the landscape in this multitiered region. My view was organized by state, political, and scientific boundaries. But to view the mountain in this way, ignoring its larger cultural domain, is to privilege a particular Euroamerican practice and logic of isolating phenomena in order to study them. But I soon realized that to understand the Indian view of the mountain meant that I would have to widen the angle of my cultural lens. Doing so meant including many other sites of contestation between Indian people of the area and government institutions. The more I looked at maps of the area, hiked it, drove around in it, read about it, and especially talked with people in the region, the more difficult it became to identify the area of study. The region of study kept expanding. In the end, this narrative was informed by interviews with Indian people and by preexisting anthropological studies of the region regarded as the traditional domain of the Western Shoshone, Southern Paiute, and Owens Valley Paiute.

Historically, the Euroamerican creation of state territorial boundaries greatly affected the integrity of the Indian ethnic groups in the region. As Richard Stoffle notes:

> In the nineteenth century, Euroamericans established state territorial boundaries and jurisdictions that divided Western Shoshone lands between two states, Nevada and California, and divided Southern Paiute lands between four states, Nevada, Utah, Arizona, and California. These developments contributed to an undercutting of the national functions and integration of these ethnic groups. In the twentieth century the federal government began to set aside portions of traditional territory as reservation lands for Western Shoshone, Southern Paiute, and Owens Valley Paiute people. In doing so, the federal government began to treat local labor camp populations as tribes and their leaders as chiefs. This political fiction recognized legitimate local leadership and control over local resources, but ignored the traditional cultural rights and obligations of the larger nations to use and manage the natural resources throughout their ethnic group territory. For each of these nations, their territory had been conceived as their Holy Land and their responsibilities toward the natural resources had been understood as responsibilities toward a Holy Land.[7]

Stoffle goes on to note that today, "Southern Paiute, Western Shoshone, and Owens Valley Paiute people continue to weave themselves back together through kinship ties [into the three separate groups] in an effort to compensate for state and federal administrative decisions that force separation of the ethnic group."[8] Western Shoshone have also constituted themselves politically through the Western Shoshone National Council, a political body that has inclusive representation of the various local Western Shoshone bands. Similarly, the Southern Paiute have recently instigated "intra-tribal dialogue on matters of mutual interest, such as the Yucca Mountain waste facility, the Nevada Test Site . . . [and] other projects potentially affecting tribal lands."[9] Significantly, the area surrounding Yucca Mountain, including the Nevada Test Site, was also traditionally used as a seasonal "commons" for the Southern Paiute and the Western Shoshone until as recently as the 1940s, when it was appropriated by the Department of Defense.

At least seventeen tribes with traditional claims to the site have been identified by the Yucca Mountain anthropologists.[10] These tribes extend from as far away as the Owens Valley in California to the Western Shoshone Duckwater reservation in central Nevada, to the Southern Paiute Kaibab tribe in Arizona near Utah. Some are as near to Yucca Mountain as the Timbisha Shoshone tribe in Death Valley, or the Indian colonies near Beatty and Pahrump, Nevada. Thus, seeing the Indian perspective or logic of the mountain—the Indian organization of space— requires a wide-angle lens. Using an indigenous lens not only makes the Indians of the region visible; it also helps us to understand the web of meanings that traditionally make up this region.

If we see the Indian inhabitants of the region from within this zone of indigenous occupation—in other words, from within a cultural perspective—we become aware that these same Indian groups that are involved in the Yucca Mountain politics are also engaged in many other struggles. The struggle over Yucca Mountain emerges as part of a larger pattern of contestation over land use. For instance, different bands of the same three ethnic groups that have taken part in the DOE-sponsored Yucca Mountain Study Project also contest the U.S. Navy's use of sacred Coso Hot Springs for geothermal energy in the Mojave Desert in California, the National Park Service's management of Death Valley, the Ward Valley low-level nuclear waste dump in Southern California, the expansion of Air Force military training areas in central and upper Nevada, the nuclear testing on the Nevada Test Site, and the extensive militarization of this entire interdesert region. Using wide cultural parameters, one sees the Indian populations more clearly, and a pattern of contestation emerges in a landscape punctuated by land-use struggles. Consequently, Indian protests over the use of Yucca Mountain as a high-level nuclear-waste dump cannot be seen as an anomaly. Rather, they are part of a persistent pattern of resistance to military occupation and nuclear activity. Such patterns allow us to talk about nuclear colonialism and environmental racism. One Western

Shoshone man described the numerous land-use struggles faced by his people in the following way:

> You know, if we had all of our resources and all of our lands made available to us, I'm certain we'd be able to teach our people to be good Shoshone Indians, and be good Shoshone citizens. But we're not given that opportunity. It's been stolen from us. Our birthright has been stolen from us—when they do nuclear testing, when they withdraw lands for a bombing and gunnery range, when they withdraw lands for supersonic operations areas, when they withdraw lands for a high-level nuclear-waste repository, when they withdraw lands for transportation corridors for nuclear waste, or for gold mines, and on and on.[11]

He could have added to his list of assaults on the land and his people electronic warfare experiments, toxic waste dumps, low-level nuclear-waste dumps, chemical warfare operations, the incineration of toxic warfare chemicals, and military war-game theaters.

Widening the lens to capture the area surrounding Yucca Mountain reveals a history of Indian presence, including a history of painful relations with Euroamericans, whether they be the U.S. Cavalry, the pioneers, the prospectors, the U.S. military, or nuclear scientists. For the Indians in the region (precontact and postcontact), Yucca Mountain was socially organized according to survival needs and ceremonial and sacred uses.

Not only do different stories told by different cultures exist in this landscape, but multiple dimensions of meaning and signifying practices emerge in their telling. Comparing the ways two different cultures perceive the mountain or spatially organize this region is a way of making the *social* construction of place more visible.[12] Such comparisons also make it possible to see alternatives to the wasteland discourse—a discourse too readily used to legitimate the burial of nuclear and toxic waste, serve as an easy solution to an intractable problem, and ignore the problems inherent in the continuation of nuclear power.

One need not even compare different cultures, however, to see that contradictory signifying practices and conflicting narratives exist concerning Yucca Mountain. In addition to capturing an Indian landscape, a wider focus also reveals how very similar lands are used for different cultural purposes, sometimes contradictory ones, even within the same culture. For instance, Euroamericans place nuclear-waste dumps, nuclear weapons-testing fields, gunnery ranges, and other war-game theaters directly adjacent to national parks, desert protection areas, and wildlife refuges.[13] As Solnit notes, "The right hand of federal government does not know what the left hand is doing . . . [a] good map reveals [that] Nellis [Air Force Range] overlaps more than fifty percent of the National Desert Wildlife Refuge."[14]

Land that is signified as a zone of preservation or as a national treasure (sacred in a secular sense) is often also signified as a zone of sacrifice. The juxtaposition reveals both the arbitrary nature of the sign (exemplified by contradictory signification strategies) and the purposeful nature of political boundaries. It also reveals the contradictions present in Euroamerican culture, where wilderness and "empty" space are both sacred *and* expendable.[15] Death Valley, for instance, is sacred to Americans because empty wilderness in the Euroamerican cultural tradition is often where holiness is (when it's not viewed as a living hell). But the "national treasure" of Death Valley is also placed between the China Lake Naval Weapons Center and the Nevada Nuclear Testing Site.

Perceptions of Nature and Their Material Consequences

Yucca Mountain calls forth not only issues concerning power in its many forms but also questions about our "current estrangement from the animate earth."[16] Understanding this estrangement requires looking at how we perceive the earth and how we represent it. Stories about nature are articulations of perceptions, and they legitimate and instigate actions that have an impact on the earth. For instance, if one sees Yucca Mountain as having *Puha*, it becomes problematic to designate it as a burial tomb for toxic waste. If one sees Yucca Mountain as a mass of inanimate material, such as "welded tuft," with characteristics that discourage water permeability—a mountain having a deep water table and a significant unsaturated zone—then one might more easily consider its use as a toxic waste dump. More abstractly, if one perceives the mountain within a space that is epistemologically organized by the *relationship* between its constitutive elements, including human beings, as in the traditional Indian way of understanding the mountain, then we may be less inclined to relegate it to a waste dump. On the other hand, perceiving the mountain within a space epistemologically organized by the *separation* between its constitutive elements—an organization that splits subject from object and separates us from the mountain—makes it more likely that it will be designated as expendable.

The stories or "facts" we tell about the world inform the ways we interact with it and, thus, the world we eventually create. Some perceptions, stories, representations, and epistemologies may be less dangerous, and perhaps—in the long run—better for humans and the nonhuman world than others. At the very least, we should open our field of perception and begin to consider the multiple dimensions of meaning (layered and folded into one another) that different people and different cultures bring to the material or natural world—especially at sites such as Yucca Mountain that are highly political, contested, and promise to have a profound influence on future generations. Some of the Euroamerican cultural influences that help to establish the unseen geographies of sacrifice in these desert regions may well benefit from alternative indigenous perspectives.

Investigating the complex cultural influences that help to establish geographies of sacrifice by way of legitimating them (even when some cultural influences exist in clear contradiction with others) requires not only an awareness of the signifying contradictions within our landscapes but also a critical examination of scientific narratives about nature, and the cultural and political contexts from which they emerge. The Yucca Mountain Project is an extremely large and complex set of scientific studies within which different scientific and technical narratives about the mountain are constructed. Because of the nuclear-waste crisis, it is important that we understand all aspects of how nuclear waste might be contained. But such studies do not occur outside of political or cultural contexts, and the narratives they create are not the only truths about the mountain and the region. Chapter 9 will examine some of the scientific narratives about nature at Yucca Mountain. By so doing, I view Western scientific narratives through an ethnoecological lens just as one might view Native American representations of nature as an indigenous ecology. In this way, Western science is understood as an ethnic knowledge production with its own ethnically based representational forms.

In addition to cultural and geopolitical boundaries the place called Yucca Mountain exists within (and has meaning because of) other parameters determined by various knowledge disciplines. For instance, ecologists working on the environmental compliance aspect of the Yucca Mountain Project see the region as part of the lower Great Basin Desert ecosystem within the Amargosa Valley trailing off into the Mojave Desert ecosystem (also seen as an extension of the Great Basin Desert). Their boundaries are drawn up, in part, by the flora and fauna—for instance, by the habitat of the endangered desert tortoise whom they must tag and trace in the landscape. For the earth scientists, the mountain is an entity described by the scientific language of volcanology, hydrology, and geology. Their boundaries are marked by ground-water tables, fault lines, and rock formations, the presence of volcanic activity. A geologist's historical boundaries are recorded in the rocks themselves, not in human occupation of the terrain.

Alternatives to the scientific perspective appear in the marginalized world view of the Indian people of the area and will be the subject of Chapter 8.[17] Both world views express a *cultural* representation of nature, and neither is without its complications and contradictions. Also, these "opposing" views are not entirely separate entities. They blend into and inform one another at various times, one view becoming more dominant than the other, depending on whom you talk to.

In addition to examining the Western scientific and Indian narratives about nature, a third, unanticipated issue emerged out of this study concerning the Indian people who inhabit this land. Indians have been the object of study for many years.[18] As with "nature," we have many ways of seeing the Indian inhabitants here (as well as many ways of *not* seeing them). Powerful political issues are being played out not only in the social construction of nature but also in the social construction of Indian identity. In the current complex phase of postcoloniality, Indian cultures, particularly in this general region, are undergoing something of a renaissance or reemergence. A handful of laws concerning cultural resources, sacred sites, religious ceremonial sites, human remains, and historic preservation have given Indians the leverage to begin long-overdue, but sometimes disturbing, dialogues with the institutional powers of the region, and this has an effect on cultural identity.

Cultural identity often gets constructed and cultural change often initiated at the borders between different ideological systems—on the borderlands between, for instance, Indian people and non-Indian scientists, where opposition requires cultural identification. On the other hand, borders are never static or absolute, and are always permeable at highly contested sites such as Yucca Mountain, opening the way for cultural change through confrontation and interaction. One way of seeing the political dynamics behind this kind of interaction is to examine Indian reactions to the Yucca Mountain cultural resource studies and related documents, which is the subject of Chapter 6. Here, cultural resource documents illuminate the political currents that lie just beneath the surface of DOE-Indian interaction in this area; they also show how political influence is exerted through narrative accounts of Indian people. For instance, if certain oppositional Indian voices are narratively suppressed in official documents, then Indian opposition to using Yucca Mountain as a nuclear waste repository remains muted.

Understanding the politics of presence and invisibility in these contested landscapes also shows how some cultural representations—stories, assertions—of place and nature get lost or buried. For example, if elder Indians who see and talk about *Puha* aren't taken seriously, then how can *Puha* exist as a viable description of the natural world? The question is particularly important because Indian elders are dying, and with them their knowledge about nature. As one Western Shoshone elder put it: "You know we're all going up in years! And that's why we say we have got to get this thing going, get it off the road, get it off the ground! Everyone is getting old. The memory of the old people is getting lost!"[19] That knowledge does not merely concern as-yet undiscovered miracle drugs. One cannot easily dismiss collective knowledge of a region's natural history by a people who have continuously inhabited the region for ten thousand years. Dismissing such a knowledge base simply because it is transmitted orally is a form of "graphocentrism." No Euroamerican people possess such a long memory of a region.

Yucca Mountain exists within vastly different worlds simultaneously. These different worlds have different positions of power as narratives. And all of them are influenced by political events. Within this highly political context these different narratives overlap and intersect. Yucca Mountain is a point of intersection, not only between the Great Basin and the Mojave Deserts, or between different Indian ethnic groups, but also between different political entities, and between indigenous and Western narratives about nature and epistemological organizations of space.

In accordance with the theme of boundaries and perspectives, and the intersection between different worlds and systems for organizing space, one must finally acknowledge the fact that Yucca Mountain exists within the late capitalist economic system. Indeed, the global capitalist economy is the reason for its existence as a proposed repository. Historically, contact with Euroamericans drastically altered and transformed the local subsistence economy of the Indian people of the area. Today, extending that transformation, the existence of the nuclear landscape continues to link indigenous groups in the area to the global economy. Yucca Mountain is nothing less than the sink hole outside the urban world market (which includes the sale of weapons and nuclear technology). It is a place where capitalism (or late industrialism) self-destructs. Thus, unseen economic and political boundaries expand outward dramatically. In fact, all geographies of sacrifice in this book must be seen as the creations a world economy that requires for its existence continual expansion, an ever-increasing consumption of natural resources, including all forms of power, and eventual zones of sacrifice for its waste byproducts. The importation of nuclear waste from outside the United States provides just one example of how Yucca Mountain serves this economy. Here, links between national security, national competitiveness, multinational nuclear corporations, and the continuation of global economic expansion become apparent. On a different scale altogether from the roads moving through Beatty or Pahrump, *this* network of pathways connects Yucca Mountain to distant points on the globe.[20]

Other Actors and Institutions

All of these boundaries and perspectives imply a multitude of players, each with a different interpretation of the significance of Yucca Mountain. The Yucca Mountain Project consists of two different "processes:" the site characterization and the environmental impact statement. Site characterization is conducted to "determine the suitability of the site for a spent nuclear fuel and high-level radioactive waste repository." Scientists study the "structural, mechanical, chemical, and hydrological characteristics of Yucca Mountain." The mountain is assessed on the surface, underground, in laboratories, and from computer modeling. Of interest to researchers are underground water movement, earthquakes, volcanoes, and climate changes. The other "process," the environmental impact statement, is a legal process based on the National Environmental Policy Act. It seeks to determine environmental effects that might occur if a repository were "constructed, operated, and eventually closed at Yucca Mountain."[21] The Environmental Impact Statement uses knowledge of the mountain gained from the site characterization study in addition to its own studies. Both scientific processes are conducted by reputable, well-trained scientists.

The state is, of course, present at every turn and at every level. On the federal level, the Department of Energy is the central governmental agency overseeing the Yucca Mountain Project, but it also employs numerous outside agencies to conduct exploratory studies and programs. The arm of the Department of Energy that handles nuclear waste is the Office of Civilian Radioactive Waste Management, and all funding for the program comes from the Nuclear Waste Policy Fund. In addition, DOE contracts outside companies to conduct environmental impact studies. Science Applications International Corporation (which has a contract with DOE via TRW Corporation) is the central contractor for all things "environmental." Under its auspices fall cultural resource studies (archaeology and anthropology) and the Native American Program (basically sociology, but a sociologist isn't employed to conduct this program). Science Applications' studies are broken into two broad categories: "field programs" and "environmental regulatory compliance." Field programs monitor air and water quality and water resources, as well as radioactivity and meteorology, and studies of terrestrial ecosystems and reclamation. Archaeological studies are part of the field program but are conducted by another contractor, Desert Research Institute. Some of the biological studies are conducted by the outside contractor EG&E Measurements. Science Applications' Environmental Regulatory Compliance branch uses data from the field program in an effort to comply with state and federal regulations that include archaeological protection and historic preservation laws.

Administering an environmental program as big as that at Yucca Mountain is a difficult task, since the Yucca Mountain Project's organization is labyrinthine. (In 1995 the Yucca Mountain Project employed approximately 1,500 people.) The "site characterization" of Yucca Mountain currently under way is a project defined by both the political climate of the time and the structure of the DOE bureaucracy, which is, itself, massive. Science Applications maintains its contract with the DOE through TRW, the Yucca Mountain Project's management and operator contractor, which harbors under its wings ten other independent companies (subcontractors) and many research institutions.[22]

On top of this structure rests the federal oversight committees—the Nuclear Regulatory Commission and the Nuclear Waste Technical Review Board (a congressionally mandated board reviewing the technical adequacy of DOE's programs), as well as a local oversight committee for the state of Nevada, which employs analysts and on-site monitors of the studies conducted on the mountain (and which adamantly opposes the importation of nuclear waste into Nevada). The large number of institutional, business, and cultural entities results in a diverse array of players in this one region, all constructing particular narratives about the mountain for a variety of ends. While they share certain common goals, each has its own turf to defend, and each has it own economic and political stakes in the processes.

Protest at the Margins

It's good to see each and every one of you here on the land. We the people today are really concerned, otherwise you wouldn't be setting here if you weren't concerned. You are concerned people just like we are. The Shoshone people of this land, we began to get concern from the nuclear testing on the land—killing life and all the living things. We know it's dangerous. We know how it's going to work if we don't unite ourself together as one people. We are one. Remember. We all drinking the same water 'round the globe. It's not a different water on the other side—above us, below us, whatever. It's one water we all survive on.
—CORBIN HARNEY, spiritual leader of the Western Shoshone, addressing antinuclear protesters and supporters of Western Shoshone land rights, 15 April 1995, Cactus Springs, Nevada

Boundaries, borders, and zones apply not only to institutions and land but also to people, and people inhabit society's margins intentionally (if only for brief periods) to express opposition. They, too, offer a perspective on the dominant powers of the region and on Yucca Mountain. Such marginal zones of opposition also serve as fragile meeting grounds for multicultural and multiracial alliances. The Nevada Test Site, in particular, acts as a magnet drawing people together from widely different backgrounds, both cultural and political.

Religious groups—Franciscans, Quakers, Catholics, and others—have held vigils outside the gates of the Nevada Test Site since the late 1970s to protest war and nuclear weapons. Antinuclear activists—first, members of the national nuclear freeze movement, later, American Peace Test, and others—in conjunction with Western Shoshone Indians have held nonviolent direct action protests there since 1985.[23] In 1992 (the beginning of the international nuclear weapons testing moratorium) the Western Shoshone invited concerned people from around the world to a ten-day gathering called "Healing Global Wounds," which was organized by Global Anti-Nuclear Alliance. To date, the Healing Global Wounds gatherings continue to be held in the area at least twice a year, in the spring and fall. They are sponsored by a diverse array of groups, including Citizen Alert of Nevada, Citizen Alert Native American Project, the Western Shoshone National Council, the Alliance of Atomic Veterans, High County Citizen's Alliance, the Nevada Desert Experience, Nuremberg Actions, Seeds of Peace, the Shundahai Network, the Western Shoshone Defense Project, and others. Since 1987 more than 10,000 people have been arrested crossing the cattle guard at the gates of Mercury, the entrance to NTS. Such protest gatherings and actions signify the larger dimension of nuclear politics in the region, a dimension whose scope makes these gatherings part of the cultural politics of the twentieth century.

Indian people of the Yucca Mountain region do not assume a unified position regarding opposition to nuclear activity on their traditional homelands. Their views range from no-compromise opposition to reluctant cooperation with the Department of Energy, as will become especially clear in the following chapter, which examines the cultural resource studies conducted at Yucca Mountain. This section, however, identifies Indian groups and other groups engaged in direct opposition against high-level nuclear waste at Yucca Mountain, since—although on the margins—they form one of the most visible aspects of cultural politics within the nuclear landscape.

Cultural politics at Yucca Mountain takes different forms. It takes place representationally in the construction of legal documents such as the cultural resource studies, in persistent attempts by Indian tribes to work within "the system" in the pursuit of land claims (as the Timbisha Shoshone have attempted to do at Death Valley), and also in nonviolent direct protest that combines Indian land rights with antinuclear activism. To date, in the Indian community, direct protest has largely rested with the Western Shoshone, aided by the crucial (if complicated) support of many different grass-roots groups, both Indian and non-Indian. Here, nuclear politics expands into cultural politics when positions against nuclearism in the region are woven into Indian land rights, which are, themselves, inextricably part of Indian cultural identity and survival.

Western Shoshone Land Rights

In addition to the Indian groups mentioned earlier as opposing nuclear activities in the region—the (mostly Western Shoshone) Citizen Alert Native American Project (in alliance with Nevada's Citizen Alert organization), the Western Shoshone National Council, and the Western Shoshone National Defense Project—are a number of other active Native antinuclear groups. The Nevada Indian Environmental Coalition opposes the Yucca Mountain Project and seeks reparations for Indian tribes under the Nuclear Waste Policy Act's "affected tribe status" clause.[24] Outside of Nevada, but also attempting to pressure the DOE on nuclear-and toxic waste issues, is the National Congress of American Indians.

Though the Western Shoshone as a nation stand at the forefront of active protest, not all Western Shoshone are interested in nuclear politics; many are busy with other sovereignty struggles and land rights. Some couldn't care less, and many balk at making any kind of political alliances with white people, even those supporting them.

Although Western Shoshone are not present in great numbers at protest gatherings such as "Healing Global Wounds," the Western Shoshone National Council has consistently taken a public antinuclear stand for many years, a stand that they recognize allies them with white activists.

Existing already on the social margins, some Western Shoshone maintain serious doubts about forming alliances with those who have voluntarily placed themselves on the political margins, as have many white antinuclear protesters. Such alliances can be difficult. By allying themselves with other marginal groups, Western Shoshone run the risk of being ridiculed (and dismissed) by those with power. More important, issues of sovereignty tend to get overlooked in the dramatic confrontation over nuclear testing. Combining forces, however, results in larger numbers at demonstrations and thus greater visibility. (And besides, antinuclearism *is* part of their Indian ecological position.) For the foreseeable future, however, alliances between Indians of this region and antinuclear protesters promise to continue, with Yucca Mountain itself becoming the next target of protest. In the past, public protest has occurred outside the gates of Mercury (entryway to the Nevada Test Site). If Yucca Mountain becomes the site for the country's high-level nuclear waste, protests will most likely shift to the entryway to Yucca Mountain. In March of 1997, 80 indigenous people from across the Great Basin gathered at the base of Yucca Mountain to discuss the nuclear threat to Indian communities. Shoshone leaders have called on activists to block shipments of nuclear waste-bearing canisters. As in the nonviolent direct action of the '70s, '80s, and '90s, protesters will once again be arrested in the ritualized act of civil disobedience.[25]

The Western Shoshone land base includes the Nevada Test Site, Yucca Mountain, and beyond (actually, 24 million acres). The "legal" claim to the Nevada Test Site area stems from the 1863 Treaty of Ruby Valley, which is a peace and friendship treaty allowing settlers to travel through Shoshone territory, not to withdraw it from Indian use.[26] The treaty identifies the territory but does not cede the territory to any U.S. political entity. In the 1970s the U.S. government initially offered to the Western Shoshone a sum of $26,145,189 to buy the land, but the money still sits in the bank. The Shoshone refuse to accept money for something they refuse to sell. Not taking "no" for an answer, the U.S. government, under the auspices of the Indian Claims Commission, proceeded to accept the money on behalf of the Western Shoshone so that it (the U.S. government) could proceed with establishing title to the land. The Western Shoshone see this ruse as U.S. usurpation of their land, an infringement on their sovereignty that threatens a fragile cultural identity and survival. As noted by anthropologist Catherine Fowler, who has written about the Shoshone case:

> In 1985, because of the steadfast refusal of the Western Shoshone to accept the ICC payment, the Supreme Court took up the very narrow questions to "whether the appropriation of funds into a Treasury account . . . constitutes 'payment' under Section 22(a) of the Indian Claims Commission Act . . .", deciding in the affirmative (United States-v-Dann, 470 U.S. 39, 40–41, 44 [1985]). However the court did not go beyond this to decide the legal effect of this action on Western Shoshone land title. In fact, the next year, the District Court ruled that "[t]he government has admitted that the 1863 Treaty of Ruby Valley is in full force and effect." . . .
>
> Thus from various legal perspectives it is not at all clear that the DOE or federal government in general has the right to proceed with the Yucca Mountain project without first clearing the title to land or otherwise negotiating with the Western Shoshones.[27]

To reestablish presence on and claim to the land, the Western Shoshone proceed with actions that underscore their sovereignty on the land. When protesters cross the border into the Nevada Test Site, they flash their Western Shoshone visas, which the Western Shoshone National Council have printed out for this purpose, to the military guards. In addition, the Western Shoshone "police" their own lands with appointed Indian "marshals," and they print their own international passports, although they must leave the continent via Canada because the passports aren't recognized by the United States. Western Shoshone representatives have traveled abroad extensively in their quest for international recognition and have, indeed, been recognized by many countries outside the United States. The Yucca Mountain Project, however, expressly denies Western Shoshone land rights based on the Treaty of Ruby Valley. When questioned about the legal basis for this denial, project representatives offer only a blanket rejection of the Treaty of Ruby Valley.[28] Rejection here is no surprise. As noted by Mander, "From the late eighteenth to the late nineteenth centuries, the United States made 370 formal treaties with Indian nations."[29] As with the Treaty of Ruby Valley, the United States has violated virtually all of them.

Although not universally recognized, Western Shoshone land rights enjoy broad support. However, because of the publicity surrounding these claims, some Southern Paiute neighbors have been offended by the Western Shoshone's claims to the land. Although they accepted payment by the Indian Claims Commission in 1965, the Southern Paiute tribes—appealing to traditional rights—feel that some of the land belongs as much to them as to the Western Shoshone. One protest I witnessed at NTS that was broadcast by a Las Vegas TV station was seen by elders at the Moapa Paiute tribe on the other side (the eastern side) of the Nevada Test Site. When I interviewed Moapa Paiute elders at their reservation a few days later, they complained of the Western Shoshone having publicly claimed the Nevada Test Site. To the Moapa Paiute, the Nevada Test Site is part of their ancestral homeland, which has always been seen as their "backyard," something the Western Shoshone do not deny. As one Western Shoshone man said: "Relations [between the Shoshone and Paiute] were pretty consistent. People would go and use an area [of the Nevada Test Site/Yucca Mountain region] and avoid another tribe. The Department of Energy has created a conflict . . . where there are now lines in the ground, and they're trying to define who owns what."

It is unfortunate that a shared area, such as the Nevada Test Site/Yucca Mountain area, should become a wedge between ethnic groups who, if left to their own ends (and as they did historically), would willingly share it with one another. As described by anthropologist Richard Stoffle:

> The Ogwe'pi people, who had their primary residences in Oasis Valley [where there were many springs], were the principal users of the harvesting territories and the camps on Yucca Mountain, though visitors from neighboring districts were able to arrange to use the area on the basis of kinship ties and/or long-term ties of exchange. These reciprocal agreements to share harvesting areas with neighboring groups made it possible to compensate for unpredictable year-to-year variations in the yield of important species.[30]

However, today, resisting the U.S. government requires strong language supported by legal documents. The Western Shoshone feel compelled to appeal to the Ruby Valley Treaty even when it silences and, ironically, makes invisible their longtime coinhabitants of the region, the Southern

Paiute. The tensions between the two Indian groups brought about by this issue gets played out in the cultural politics of the Yucca Mountain Project as well. When the Yucca Mountain Project expressly denies the Western Shoshone's claims, it allies itself more closely with Southern Paiutes. Groups that might otherwise be allies end up in opposition to one another—at least in this one instance—while groups that might be adversaries form temporary alliances of convenience.

This is not to say that Southern Paiutes are happy with, or complacent concerning, the activities of the DOE on their traditional homelands. They are not. Tensions between the two Indian groups are simply exacerbated by the DOE's presence here, as well as by the history of Euroamerican land appropriations in this region. Unfortunately, because the Western Shoshone feel they must press their claim to the land at the expense of the Southern Paiute, they end up more estranged than ever in the DOE-controlled Yucca Mountain Studies, as will be evident in the next chapter. In the end, the DOE benefits from this weakening of intertribal alliances that might—in another configuration—have been a more potent political and cultural force of resistance. At other times, however, the two Indian nations cooperate, for instance, in attempts to develop an Indian epidemiological study of the effects of nuclear testing on Indian tribes of the surrounding area. Similarly, in May 1990, "two Southern Paiutes, including the Chair of the Paiute Tribe of Utah, [a]ttended with three Western Shoshones, international meetings in Moscow, in the Soviet Union, seeking to stop nuclear proliferation,"[31] demonstrating a shared concern over nuclear issues.

En Route to the Protest

Modern-day travelers going from California to Nevada via the north end of Death Valley have to cross the Funeral Mountains to get to the Nevada border that brings them into the mining towns of Rhyolite and Beatty. Behind the wild burrows off to the right of the highway and beneath the bright blue sky streaked by contrails from military jets appears a giant pyramid of a mountain with long horizontal steps cut across it—unmistakable signs of a mining operation. A nearby building features an Olympian-sized prospector holding the world in his hands as minerals— gold and silver—flow out into a receptacle with the mining company's initials writ large upon it. Welcome to Nevada. Before reaching the tiny gambling town of Beatty, the traveler passes cowboys, motorcycle gangs, a couple of casinos, and a smattering of downtrodden mobile homes. Heading south down U.S. 95, the traveler passes U.S. Ecology's (formerly Nuclear Engineering) recently closed low-level nuclear-waste dump, and the back entrance to Yucca Mountain. Another twenty-five miles brings her to the protest gathering at Cactus Springs. Just before the entryway to the Nevada Test Site, a postmodern description of Nevada in the form of a road sign pointing to the town of Pahrump reads: "the heart of the new old west." On the other side of the road the graffiti on the railing next to the fence enclosing the Nevada Test Site reads: "No More Nukes!" And the highway marker that was "Veteran's Memorial Highway" is changed to "*Atomic* Veteran's Memorial Highway." Near the graffiti rests a government plaque offering the "official" history of the Test Site. It reads:

THE NEVADA TEST SITE

Testing of devices for defense and for peaceful uses of nuclear explosives is conducted here. The nation's principal nuclear explosives testing laboratory is located within this 1,350 square mile, geographically complex, area in the isolated valleys of Jackass, Yucca, and Frenchman Flats. Selected as on-continent test site in 1950, the first test took place in 1951.

Archaeological studies of the NTS area have revealed continuous occupation by prehistoric man from about 9,500 years ago. Several prehistoric cultures are represented. The last aboriginal group to occupy the site was the Southern Paiute who foraged plant foods in season and occupied the area until the coming of the Pioneers.

Reading this sign one would think Indians had been extinct since the nineteenth century. The sign is misleading, which only those on their way to an antinuclear/indigenous rights gathering officiated by a Western Shoshone spiritual leader might notice. The Western Shoshone are not mentioned on the plaque. At one protest gathering, Western Shoshone Council member Bill Rosse Sr. refutes the history on this plaque when he says:

Our Mother Earth is all of ours, not just part of it . . . and a big part of it [NTS] we never have been able to use anymore since the '40s. Our people was moved off of it, and that was it!

The "Healing Global Wounds" Gatherings

The current Healing Global Wounds Gatherings are smaller than the anti-nuclear protests at the Nevada Test Site of the late 1980s and early 1990s that were held during the latest period of active nuclear testing. Since the moratorium on nuclear testing these protests have begun to focus more on local land rights and nuclearism—identifying intersecting issues of land, indigenous rights, environmental degradation, and the recent phenomenon of "subcritical" nuclear tests which, the DOE claims, are designed not to produce a self-sustaining nuclear reaction.

The gatherings last anywhere from three to four or five days, each day offering meetings on civil disobedience, strategy building for future events, and even consciousness-raising seminars on multicultural and interracial communication and alliance building. But mostly the daily meetings feature panels meant to teach the participants about nuclear issues, particularly those that are facing indigenous nations. Unlike many indigenous environmental gatherings that bring together mostly Indian participants, these gatherings are predominantly Euroamerican with Indian people in the role of teachers and leaders—an inversion of the usual positions, where whites are often in the role of the expert, for example in the Yucca Mountain Project's cultural resource studies. Virginia Sanchez, a Western Shoshone activist and organizer of a panel featuring indigenous speakers, was once asked why more Western Shoshone didn't attend the gatherings. She said:

> [T]he reason is that this portion of Native people working to regain or rebuild the environmental quality is only one facet of a very complex effort for us to reestablish or maintain our work and jurisdictions over our lives and our land. So I thought, "Well at least if I can get that message across, that might help," so that you can understand that there's so much more going on in our lives at home in our communities than just nuclear waste. And the best way to explain that is in understanding that we don't derive our rights as a nation, as a people, from the United States Constitution, or from any of the treaties that we signed with the United States. That these rights were derived as an inherent right, as people that lived in this land for thousands and thousands of years. So, but nuclear waste is a very very difficult problem that all of us are dealing with, and so I thought,

Figure 5.6 Multicultural demonstrations at the Nevada Test Site
Protesters, Indians, and Japanese survivors of atomic blasts march to the gates of
Mercury, Nevada, at the Nevada Test Site. October 1994.

Photo by Richard Rawles

> "Well my portion can at least be to put together a nuclear-waste day and bring in indigenous people to speak.[32]

Although Euroamericans are in the majority, these gatherings are also visited by members of different Indian tribes from around the Southwest and farther afield. In 1995, one gathering pulled together Indian individuals from the Gabrielino tribe (Southern California Channel Island area), Navajo, Lakota, Western Shoshone, Southern Paiute, Hopi, Mescalero Apache, and others.[33] White people are represented by young "hippie" types, older antinuclear activists, Jesuit brothers and priests trained in civil disobedience, religious groups from Quakers to Buddhists to Catholics, feminists, some academics interested in environmental justice issues, and often the deeply marginalized, those who are homeless, or nearly so, nomadic, and whose behavior might be classified "borderline" in another setting—all who, for a variety of reasons, identify with this particular form

Figure 5.7 Multicultural demonstrations at the Nevada Test Site
Western Shoshone Spiritual Leader Corbin Harney exchanging expressions of
peace and friendship with Japanese survivors of atomic blasts (known as
Hibakusha) and U.S. Atomic Vets (soldiers who had been placed in the vicinity of
atomic blasts on the Nevada Test Site during atmospheric explosions) outside the
Nevada Test Site. October 1994.

Photo by Richard Rawles

of injustice, or who just want to be near those who care about such things.
Also present are activists from Germany, Sweden, England, Southeast Asia,
the Philippines, and elsewhere. And then there are the Atomic Veterans
who witnessed the first nuclear bombs on the Nevada Test Site and who
have since collectively bought land adjacent to the Test Site to serve as a
kind of living memorial to the victims, foreign and domestic, of atomic
warfare and testing.

In October 1994, two busloads of Japanese atomic bomb survivors
(known as Hibakusha) from Hiroshima and Nagasaki visited a Healing
Global Wounds gathering. They marched in protest down to the gates of
Mercury at the border of the Nevada Test Site with Atomic Vets,
Shoshone Indians, and the rest of us. This accompanying entourage

included middle-age and older, well-dressed Japanese carrying banners that had been signed by hundreds of people in support of their tour "to stop all nuclear activity." Dispossessed Indians, veterans of war, veterans of atomic testing, survivors of nuclear bombings—all held hands in a huge circle in front of the cattle guard as fatigue-clad Army men, Wackenhuts (security personnel), and Nye County sheriff's deputies looked on at this remarkable confluence of people praying for peace in the desert. Japanese stepped forward to bear witness—some telling us about the glass shards still lodged within body and face from the Hiroshima blast fifty years previous. Indians stepped forward to tell their story. Translators were present to ease communication between cultures as key representatives from the different groups came forward to embrace inside the circle in a formal demonstration of peace. No television cameras were there. No radio station covered it. This remarkable event did not get relayed through the real-time channels of postmodern information-age communications vectors. Nobody saw it but us.

Networks on the Margins

The gatherings also offer different Indian activists a chance to make contact with one another. In comparison to the all-Indian gatherings—such as the annual American Indians Environmental Conference—the amount of networking between Indian activists here is small, but important nonetheless. For example, early one morning in 1994, as I stood next to Corbin Harney (Western Shoshone spiritual leader and key director of the gatherings), a Dineh woman came up to him to say good-bye. Their interchange was indicative of other networking at the margins of the gathering. The two whispered to one another, not speaking publicly. Corbin leaned over to the woman and told her that "his people were praying for hers." (The Dineh are engaged in serious confrontations with the Bureau of Land Management at Big Mountain over land-use issues, as well as ongoing struggles against the Peabody Coal mining company.) He said that the indigenous peoples were clearly being threatened with extinction, now more than ever before, in many overt and insidious ways, and that they would, together, need to fight it as best they could or else this would be the end of them. In a whispered interchange at dawn in the Nevada desert, the two sent messages of solidarity to their respective tribes and supported one another in the serious business of cultural survival.

The gatherings also allow white activists to meet with Indian activists, as well as with one another. Indeed, the gatherings are among the few places white and Indian activists get together, and one of the few places white people can learn about nuclearism on Native lands, as well as about other Indian land-rights struggles. Panel topics range from local to international issues, from environmental colonialism and environmental racism to more specific issues, such as the current environmental impact assessment on the Nevada Test Site, or legislation concerning high-level nuclear waste currently pending in Congress. Western Shoshone Chief Raymond Yowell talks about "exposing the nuclear industry for what it is"; Dineh Indians talk about confrontations with the Bureau of Land Management over land-use rights; Rufina Laws, of the Mescalero Apache Tribe, describes her efforts to oppose an MRS on her tribal lands; Indians from the Gabrielino tribe in the Los Angeles area inform the crowd about their sovereignty and land-claim struggles (over the sacred site Puvugna in Los Angeles); indigenous Alaskans tell of a history of nuclear activity that has affected their tribal nations, as do the Hopi and others.

The central organizer of the gatherings, longtime activist Jennifer Viereck, has, over the years, worked with members of the Western Shoshone National Council to bring together people from different cultures and different Indian tribes. These are not ideal demonstrations of multicultural alliance, but somehow, despite complex racial tensions barely beneath the surface of these events, the gatherings have managed to continue. The tensions here are not just about race but also about primary objectives. Though many Indians are concerned about environmental issues and feel that the destruction of land and its resources often means destruction of their culture, tensions exist between environmentalists and Indians concerning land uses such as cattle ranching. In this part of the country (Nevada and eastern California) Indians have assimilated into the cattle ranching business—a phenomenon that is itself the result of particular historical colonialist forces: U.S. governmental influence, the destruction of pinyon forests to make way for cattle ranching (decimating preexisting food sources), and last-ditch attempts at survival in a white man's world.[34]

Despite tensions, marginal spaces at the boundaries of powerful institutions can be places of freedom—if only for brief periods of time. This is one place where alternative narratives about this region get articulated and disseminated. What gets discussed in this odd setting includes anything from nuclear colonialism to Indian spiritual sites in the Los Angeles basin. What the networking reveals is not a completely coherent story, but many intersecting struggles. What the participants obtain—if they can put up with the bad food, the motley crowd, the heat, and the cold—is a sense of power and renewed energy to press their agendas.

The presence of the Western Shoshone at these protests has the effect of inserting into the debate over nuclearism a recognition of indigenous rights and another way of seeing the Nevada landscape. After all, the flag erected in the middle of the camp says "Support Shoshone Land Rights." Central to the argument the Shoshone make against any use of nuclear technology, including that used on their homelands, is that it violates "natural law."[35] Natural law and variations on the theme of natural law were called forth by many of the Indians I interviewed. It is an organizing principle for traditional Indian culture (and the Indian relationship between the human and the nonhuman world). Western Shoshone, Southern Paiute, and Owens Valley Paiute all appealed to this concept in our discussions about the environment and its relegation to a nuclear sacrifice zone.

Such protests demonstrate a clear line of resistance to both the DOE's plans for Yucca Mountain and the continued militarization of the Western Shoshone and Southern Paiute traditional lands. Such opposition is not readily evident in the official cultural resource documents on which I focus in the following chapter. Perhaps representation of this opposition was not seen as part of the mission of those who conducted the cultural resource studies. This book, however, finds it essential to a full understanding of cultural politics and presence in this part of the nuclear landscape. Direct opposition is part of the view from Yucca Mountain.

· 6 ·

Cultural Politics

Indian Perspectives on Yucca Mountain Cultural Resource Studies

> You know, the first thing we told them—"we" meaning the Indian represen-
> tatives of the 16 tribes that claim a cultural link to that land—the first thing
> we told them was that we were not supporting them, we did not condone
> what they use the land for, for the bombing and the use of nuclear weapons,
> and nuclear waste![1]

Indian opposition to nuclear waste at Yucca Mountain takes different
forms, not all of them reflected in official representations of the area. The
cultural narrative maps, also known as cultural resource studies, that represent the official record of the project (concerning Indian issues) tend to
leave out people whose perspectives may not support the assumptions of
those conducting the studies or those funding the studies. Indian
responses to textual accounts of themselves, their ancestors, and their culture in the Yucca Mountain region reveal the uses and abuses to which
cultural studies designed to preserve Indian heritage are subject.

Textual accounts of Indian life and history in the region discursively map a silenced people. Such representations cannot help but be influenced by the politically charged atmosphere around Yucca Mountain, by what the sponsors of such studies choose to emphasize or mute. Indian people of the region view such texts (and the way they are generated) with mixed feelings, and sometimes with outright rejection. In the view of many Native people, cultural resource studies not only account for lost histories but also illuminate underlying political tensions between Native people and the Department of Energy. Such tensions reveal the subtle mechanisms of exclusion built into the studies themselves. Paradoxically, such studies can exclude Indian voices while simultaneously including Indian concerns and legitimating Indian presence in the Yucca Mountain region. They suppress opposition even as they help promote some Indian interests. The net result, however, is that official documents on which decisions about the future of the region are based cover up Indian opposition to storing nuclear waste at Yucca Mountain.

By law, the Department of Energy must provide local communities with information about the Yucca Mountain Project. To do this, the DOE typically sets up shop in a small satellite office, usually in a strip mall next to the local hair salon, gambling casino, or furniture store. In this way, the long arm of the state (the nonlocal Department of Energy) reaches into the local (or "affected") community, in efforts to both inform the local population about the nuclear-waste project and convince locals of the mountain's safety and importance. Such offices can be found in Beatty (near Oasis Valley), Pahrump (near Ash Meadows), Las Vegas, Big Pine, and other places in the greater Yucca Mountain area. It was in the Beatty office—as I was on my way to a Western Shoshone-sponsored antinuclear protest gathering—that I first discovered the "official" cultural resource studies for Yucca Mountain.

The cultural resource studies I found comprised two very large spiral-bound documents, supplemented by a smaller book on the relationship between Native Americans and the Yucca Mountain region. These documents proved invaluable in writing this book, providing a travel guide through the "Land of Lost Borders."[2] Along with a similar set of studies commissioned by the state of Nevada, these texts are the kind of materials to which scholars turn for in-depth information about the relationship between Yucca Mountain and the Western Shoshone, the Southern Paiute, and the Owens Valley Paiute. Stuffing the DOE-commissioned documents into my backpack I continued down the highway to join the protesters at Cactus Springs. My interviews with Western Shoshone at the gathering threw into question many of the findings from these "reputable" documents, revealing a different story and, not surprisingly, a high-stakes political one at that.

If such a study were meant to document Indian cultural presence in the region—to substantiate it for the purpose of mitigating impact—then why was it condemned by many of those who stood to benefit from such documentation? What happened in the documentation process to compel one Moapa Paiute who participated in the cultural resource studies to say:

> They [the studies] are not saying how we really feel. . . . The government will say they're proposing this or that, but they're still going to go ahead and do it [build a repository at Yucca Mountain]! I mean, you know, even if there is opposition, they're still gonna go ahead. And here's the Moapa trying to oppose them, but they're still going to do it![3]

How could a document meant to give voice to Indian concerns stand accused of silencing them? And how did it come to be regarded as a form of cultural "blackmail?" As one Western Shoshone man noted:

> It's a difficult situation. You know, I used to go out with a lot of these groups [the Yucca Mountain Project Indian Program and the cultural resources activity] and I felt that to some degree they [the Indians] are being blackmailed or coerced.[4]

Cultural Narratives as Legal Documents
By law, the Department of Energy must conduct cultural resource studies to comply with the National Environmental Policy Act of 1969 (NEPA), which is meant to ensure satisfactory health, safety, and environmental quality, including cultural preservation, on federal lands for all United States citizens. Other laws that attempt to address cultural protection include the National Historic Preservation Act, the American Indian

Religious Freedom Act of 1979, and the Archaeological Resources Protection Act of 1978. Also important are the Native American Graves Protection and Repatriation Act of 1990 and the Advisory Council on Historic Preservation of 1985.

According to these laws, Indian cultural resources, including sacred sites, if found, cannot be destroyed without considering the alternatives. For instance, before the Department of Energy begins construction of a new road on or near Yucca Mountain, it must assess whether the project will harm the land, surrounding community, existing animal species, and so forth. If cultural resources are found—Indian artifacts, human remains, or evidence of religious practice—project personnel are required to consult with Indian representatives on how best to mitigate impact on affected resources. The DOE is not compelled, however, to cease operations. If no suitable alternative can be found (for instance, rerouting the road), then other measures, such as removing the resources, become options. In some cases, the DOE has repositioned roads at the Yucca Mountain Project for the protection of cultural artifacts. However, in the final analysis, concerning the Yucca Mountain Project and the eventual siting of a deep-geologic repository in this region, the Department of Energy is not bound by the cultural preservation and religious freedom laws noted above. The DOE decides whether implementation supersedes Native American interests. If Yucca Mountain is otherwise deemed "safe" for high-level nuclear waste, the existence of Native American cultural resources or sacred sites will not significantly alter construction plans for the repository.

Ironically, because the area has been closed off from public access by weapons testing (thereby preventing the usual plundering by both "legitimate" [that is, in Western scientific terms, not Indian] archaeological and nonlegitimate parties), Yucca Mountain's cultural resources are unusually well-preserved. However, land withdrawal doesn't always signify cultural resource preservation. For instance, no detailed record exists of how many sites of cultural significance have been destroyed on the Nevada Test Site during the nuclear-testing period. As noted by one Paiute woman: "In the '50s, they totally destroyed the cultural resources, and then they had the A-bomb there. . . . well, you can imagine."[5] Another example is found in Stoffle's comments on the impact that nuclear testing had on one specific site in the 1960s: "Unfortunately, testing of nuclear devices has disrupted and left an overburden of up to 50 feet over the McKinnis [archaeological] site. Worman [the archaeologist studying the site] was only able to carry out limited test excavations before the site was obliterated."[6] Indeed, whatever Indian presence was in evidence at the various ground zeros has been eradicated forever.

The Studies

The Literature Review and Ethnohistory of Native American Occupancy and Use of the Yucca Mountain Area, 1990, and its related ethnobotanical report *Native American Plant Resources in the Yucca Mountain Area, 1989,* identify the Native American ethnic groups that have traditional and historical ties to the site. The study, a chronological account of Native activities in the region during the late nineteenth and twentieth century, also helps identify the location of sacred, burial, and other archaeological sites in the area. Working closely with archaeological contractors and enlisting, in their own words, "active participation from representatives of each of the 16 identified tribes,"[7] the authors of the study reviewed and compiled a broad range of existing literatures on the area. The ethnobotanical study documents the botanical resources of the area, including the religious and medicinal uses of plants. Both of these reports make an effort to provide what they call the Indian "holistic" view of the landscape and plant life. However, they note important differences between the "rules of evidence" for social scientists and Indian people in interpreting the meaning of cultural resources and plants. As one archaeologist studying the mountain told me: "Science is one thing, religion another."

As I made contact with individuals of Indian tribes in the region, with the Department of Energy and its contractors and the state of Nevada Nuclear Waste Office—all the central players in this arena—I discovered two different sets of cultural/socioeconomic studies commissioned by opposing parties: the one given to me in Beatty, commissioned by the Department of Energy under the immediate direction of private contractor Desert Research Institute (subcontracted to anthropologists, led by Richard Stoffle, at the Institute for Social Research at the University of Michigan),[8] and a second one commissioned by the state of Nevada's Agency for Nuclear Projects/Nuclear Waste Project Office (using a team of anthropologists, led by Catherine Fowler, from the University of Nevada, Reno). The Department of Energy and the state of Nevada constitute opposing political entities in the Yucca Mountain political arena. The DOE report constitutes the official "cultural resource study," while the dissenting state of Nevada report seeks to document "Native American concerns" relating to the siting of a high-level nuclear waste repository at Yucca Mountain. Although more socioeconomic in nature, the state of Nevada report covers many of the same issues as the DOE report.

Because the DOE has more money and more distribution capacity, the Stoffle study is larger, more in-depth, and enjoys wider dissemination. Because of this greater level of funding, and because it is the document that satisfies National Environmental Protection Act requirements, it stands as the "official" representation of Indian culture at Yucca Mountain—the document of record. The Fowler study, on the other hand, lies somewhat hidden in the recesses of Nevada's Nuclear Waste Project office.

What distinguishes one set of cultural studies from another is not so much the details of the accounts as what gets left out. For instance, the Fowler report identifies the importance of the Treaty of Ruby Valley as the legal basis for Western Shoshone claims of sovereignty over Yucca Mountain. Fowler cites specific court rulings to substantiate the claim, while Stoffle ignores this contention, which is central to the Western Shoshone. In addition, Stoffle's study does not indicate that the Western Shoshone boycotted the studies. Thus, differences between the two cultural resource studies reflect opposition between the two commissioned parties.[9] By muting Western Shoshone opposition, the DOE reports imply cooperation between Indian tribes and the DOE, whereas the state of Nevada reports imply contestation at every turn. Similar differences between the two anthropological teams also emerged in the cultural resource studies for the Nevada Test Site. In that case, Fowler and her team "bowed out" for "ethical" reasons, leaving Stoffle and his team in charge. The leading anthropologist of each team (Richard Stoffle for the DOE and Catherine Fowler for the state of Nevada) also seem to reflect the political orientation of the tribes they have concentrated their studies on in the past (Western Shoshone for Fowler, and Southern Paiute for Stoffle).

While the Fowler text is an important source, a source I draw on extensively in Chapter 7 and 8, it does not have the same legal purchase as the DOE-commissioned studies. Indian representatives from the surrounding tribes took part in both studies but especially in the better-funded DOE studies, which have long-ranging and far-reaching impacts on perceptions of the region. Thus, Indian responses in my account focus on the DOE-commissioned official cultural resource studies conducted by the Stoffle team.

The Players

Rather than analyze the studies themselves, I have chosen to focus on the Indian responses to the DOE studies. Such responses bring into focus limitations of the studies and the processes by which the studies are conducted. The reader should bear in mind, however, that this account itself constitutes a discursive intervention in the region. Whereas the DOE-commissioned studies provide a cultural map of this region, my account—reflecting off of the DOE account—emphasizes statements of people who are not usually heard, as opposed to those who are.

However, my work is also partially constructed of—and indebted to—the very documents it investigates and sometimes criticizes, so that the textual field becomes complex. The fact that Indian people contest the methods of the DOE in constructing the documents does not mean the DOE studies are devoid of valuable and useful information.

Everyone—federal and state governmental institutions, ethnic groups, research groups, and individuals—all have something at stake in these documents. The Department of Energy has invested heavily in the Yucca Mountain Project and does not want to see its efforts go to naught. The researchers who contract with the Department of Energy are well aware of the limitations built into the parameters of their studies, but they are ultimately paid by the Department of Energy (through its contractors). On the other hand, these same researchers also have strong allegiances to the Indian communities with whom they have spent many years. The state of Nevada opposes nuclear waste in its borders and chooses researchers who protect its interests. The Indian people (most prominently the Western Shoshone) of the area have high stakes in protecting their traditional lands in hopes that one day they might reclaim them. Finally, growing up in a research community that used these desert lands as bombing fields has influenced my own interest in exposing such practices and their impact on marginalized peoples.

Though there are a variety of perspectives, the playing field for representation is not level. Studies described herein are not endowed equally. The conditions of production of these various representations also matter. Those studies conducted by whole teams of researchers have at their disposal greater resources than others. For instance, the Department of Energy has more resources than the state of Nevada, which has far more resources than I have as an independent researcher strategically wending my way through the backroads of the region. The Department of Energy studies are displayed in local information centers in the surrounding communities, but the state of Nevada studies are not, and so forth.

In the beginning, I chose a number of my informants from a list of people who had been Indian representatives for the Yucca Mountain cultural resource studies. The list was given to me (on a visit to the Yucca Mountain Project's offices) by a senior environmental manager with the Yucca Mountain Project in charge of the cultural resource studies and the related Native American Program.[10]

Many of the Indian cultural resource representatives I spoke with had also worked in this capacity with the cultural resource studies of the Nevada Test Site and, more recently, at Nellis Air Force Range, so they were quite well-versed in the process, knew the pitfalls, had lots to say, and tended to accept, or accommodate, at least some compromise with the institutional powers in the region.[11] This was particularly true for those I spoke with from Owens Valley and the Moapa Reservation. This was not the case with the Western Shoshone, who are adamantly opposed to the DOE and anyone contracting with the DOE. The statements from Ian Zabarte, the Western Shoshone Council's contact for high-level nuclear waste issues, is a case in point. As spokesperson for the Western Shoshone on issues concerning Yucca Mountain, Zabarte speaks in a way that demonstrates the oppositional nature of the official Western Shoshone position.

My contacts included the Owens Valley Paiutes in California, the Moapa Southern Paiutes in Nevada, and the Timbisha Shoshone in Death Valley, California. I also spoke with representatives from the Western Shoshone National Council. There are, of course, many more tribes involved in the cultural resource studies. Any documents that develop out of projects as massive as the Yucca Mountain Project are partial and depend on available resources. The following analysis attempts to fill in some of the gaps in the official record that even such a well-endowed agency as the Department of Energy, with a political bias in favor of the status quo, cannot or will not address.

Tribal Representation in Cultural Studies

Who is chosen to represent tribal knowledge of the environment, and how much do political forces influence this selection? The official cultural resource studies administered by Richard Stoffle included consultation with representatives of the 19 different tribes who were seen to have traditional cultural links to the area.[12] Even though the tribes choose their own representatives, individuals who most ardently criticize the DOE's activities and who oppose cooperation usually don't become representatives. The Yucca Mountain Project people I spoke with also identified favorites they considered to be "their Indians" (a term used by DOE contractors managing the studies). Thus, the DOE-sponsored studies tend to highlight cooperation as opposed to contestation. Those with the most contentious positions in respect to the repository are not represented. The DOE public relations materials reflect and exaggerate this tendency as in, for instance, the flier titled "Preservation Through Cooperation."[13] Such materials also demonstrate the very limited scope of the studies—emphasizing cultural preservation, not opposition to construction.

Indian representation in these "official" studies suffered a severe blow when the Western Shoshone National Council (the contemporary political body for most of the Western Shoshone tribes, in particular, the Duckwater Shoshone tribe) removed themselves from the study to protest federal authority and to assert their sovereignty over the affected region. One Western Shoshone elder explained the apparent lack of Western Shoshone representation:

> After they made their statements to Stoffle, the Western Shoshone National Council were invited to join the formal Yucca Mountain Native American Project, organized by the DOE, but no one showed up. Raymond Yowell [tribal chairman] didn't show up, and he was told to come. . . .

Yowell's statement about the project was that all the Shoshone should not even enter the DOE's project because all we were doing was rubber-stamping, so the project could be "in compliance." And it is true. Everyone has to be in compliance, you know, but they [the DOE] don't recognize any compliance with the Western Shoshone's Natural Law. It's like that recognition law I was talking about. We must be recognized under that [Euroamerican] system, but not under our system.[14]

As noted, Stoffle's study does not acknowledge the resistance and lack of representation on the part of the Western Shoshone.[15] Since the Western Shoshone are one of the three main ethnic groups involved, and one of the two ethnic groups in the immediate vicinity of Yucca Mountain and the project, such an omission would seem to seriously compromise the integrity of the study. In fact, in his book on Native American cultural resources at Yucca Mountain Stoffle states: "[T]here is no evidence that the cultural concerns of any ethnic or political groups is under-represented by the study."[16] Such a statement is skillfully crafted to substitute representation of people with "cultural concerns."

By not highlighting this important act of withdrawal, the cultural resource study effectively disallows opposition. Several Western Shoshone people expressed anger concerning this lack of representation in the cultural resource studies, including the fact that the whole process is orchestrated by white experts, and orchestrated in ways that allow some Indian representation but no real decision making. As one Western Shoshone man noted:

Because if you [Indian people] don't do anything, the researchers are unethical and immoral, as far as I'm concerned. They would come and tell a group of people [Indians] that the Department of Energy is going to come and do whatever they want anyway. And the sites are going to be destroyed if you don't participate in this program. At that time, [we would ask] "What sites?" [They would say,] "Oh, nothing specific, but we just know there are sites there." So these people [Indians] participate in the program. Now I got to the point in this program where I felt that we were doing more harm to ourselves than good, because it is not for one or two people to make a decision of such importance to the Shoshone people as a whole. [For instance,]

"What do we do with a burial site?" Well, traditionally, we're not supposed to bother them at all! But the Department of Energy, however, needs to do something, feels that it must do something. And [so] the researchers put into the minds of these people [the Indian representatives in the YMP], "Well, we can either lay cement over it, or move it, or not move it, or do something to try to protect it, and we need you to put a number next to these options in the order of greatest importance." So our people think, well, of course, we don't want it disturbed, which is the first option. But *they* [the researchers] put the ideas into their heads, put the process in front of them, and then [the researchers and the YMP people] are claiming, *or state,* through their multimillion dollar study, that *we* gave this input, that *we* made this decision! And, of course, at the bottom of all of this is the fact that it wasn't discussed on a tribal or a national level. And these people at the Department of Energy are going to use this type of information to state that this is how Indian remains are dealt with when you're dealing with Shoshone remains. And the gold mines will pick it up, and everyone else wants to pick up this same research and say, "Hey, this is an acceptable way to deal with Shoshone Indian remains." Because two or three Shoshone Indians said this is the way to do it—when they felt they had to do some-thing because the threat of imminent destruction was there anyway.[17]

In addition to revealing serious problems in tribal representation in the studies, Zabarte's statement identifies key mechanisms of exclusion built into the cultural resource studies themselves. Indian people aren't really given an opportunity to direct appropriate action; rather they are given a list of options from which to choose. None of these options is satisfactory. Thus, many feel they are not included in the studies at all, just used to rub-ber-stamp the DOE's activities. The presentation of options here is repre-sentative of "public participation" orchestrated by the DOE in other settings. Public hearings held to give local communities a chance to voice their concerns on whether to build a nuclear testing facility, for instance, are a public relations ruse. The DOE's discussion parameters never include the "option" of not building the facility. In the case of nuclear-waste dumps, the option of stopping the waste stream by stopping nuclear power production does not exist. Nor is the DOE bound by law to implement any suggestions made by the public.

Concerning the limitations of Indian participation in the studies, Stoffle, the principal anthropologist of the studies, notes:

> Although Indian people tend to resent proposed projects that from their perspective inappropriately use traditional lands, they tend to be realistic about the extent of their power to affect the process and the results of the projects. When provided with an opportunity to have input in the process Indian people have demonstrated a willingness to try to protect some cultural resources potentially affected by an unwanted project. This process has been termed "cultural triage" which is defined as a forced choice situation in which an ethnic group is faced with the decision to rank in importance equally valued cultural resources that could be affected by a proposed development project (Stoffle and Evans 1990). Cultural Triage can be both emotionally taxing for the Indian person and dangerous for the cultural resource.[18]

What Stoffle describes as "cultural triage," Western Shoshone National Council representative Ian Zabarte terms "ethnocide." Once again, serious opposition is muted while cooperation is highlighted. Stoffle's comment that Indian people "tend to be realistic about the extent of their power" also masks the frustration felt by almost all of the Indian people with whom I spoke, including Southern Paiutes and Owens Valley Paiutes. Clearly, Stoffle is conflicted; on the one hand he notes that Indian people are "realistic," while, on the other hand, the whole enterprise is "emotionally taxing" and culturally "dangerous." As the Western Shoshone spokesperson for high-level nuclear waste issues, Zabarte represents the official view of his people, many of whom have also used the term "ethnocide." Zabarte counters Stoffle's notion of "cultural triage" with an analogy describing the Western Shoshone holistic view:

> Well, all land is sacred, and you need to understand this in a much broader sense. That when you're taking away this mountain, or piece of this mountain—access to this mountain—you're diminishing the holistic value. . . . I mean it's like saying "Oh well, you can live without this arm." But that arm is who you are! That's the finger that your ring was on, or whatever it is, you know. That's the hand that you played baseball with or caught things with

or drank with, you know, whatever it is. "Oh well, you can live without your legs!" But those are the legs I walked on. . . . You've got to respect life. You've got to respect other people's ways. And you know if you take enough of it away there won't be enough cover for the little cottontails that are around here, and there won't be enough for the Shoshone people to continue being Shoshone.[19]

Zabarte, many Western Shoshone, and Southern Paiutes thus do not automatically welcome these studies as indicators of a new power and presence for Indian people in this region. Rather, they suggest that such studies *legitimate* the erasure of Indian presence on the land, relegating it to a mere ethnographic record or museum item. Zabarte said he was "pushed out" of the cultural resource studies by Richard Stoffle because he wouldn't cooperate, because he made too much trouble. Indeed, Zabarte is a "troublemaker" in the eyes of the Department of Energy; he's an activist unwilling to compromise. But this is how he put it:

He [Stoffle] tried to push me out of those. . . . You know I didn't want to have anything to do with him, but he did push me out of those activities because I was telling the people what was happening and what should be done. I would tell them, I said, "Hey we need to discuss this with all the people." The National Council needs to discuss this. We need the involvement and [need to have] a conference with just our own people. Where're we going to get the money to bring spiritual leaders—elders—here and try to discuss this thing? No, but *they* can bring one person—two people from Death Valley—a couple of Paiutes down the road here, as many as *they* can afford within their contract, whether it be Shoshone or Paiutes or whoever! There's different people and they all agree amongst themselves? [It's] different ethnic groups and backgrounds. . . . Well, yeah, [they say] "We'll agree with what Stoffle's proposing—it's okay."

It is not something that emanates from the mind of the Shoshone people! It is not! These places should be left alone! Period![20]

Pauline Esteves, a Timbisha Shoshone from Death Valley, was a reluctant participant in the Yucca Mountain resource studies, but only because as she put it: "If I don't do it, there won't be *any* Western Shoshone representation!" She knew, however, that her statements of opposition would show up only as a small paragraph in a very large document. And this made her bitter. Despite taking part in the studies, Esteves agreed with Zabarte's assessment of the cultural resource study process.

The Department of Energy's selection of a single Indian man (a Southern Paiute) as the DOE's only liaison between themselves and the Indian community provides another example of the department's selectivity in matters concerning Indian participation in cultural resource studies. Given that some tensions exist between the two main ethnic groups—the Western Shoshone and Southern Paiute—and that most of the Western Shoshone bowed out of the cultural resource study for political and ethical reasons—the DOE's decision to appoint only one liaison appears politically motivated. Although some Western Shoshone individuals cooperated with the DOE, the DOE regards the Western Shoshone as a whole to be uncooperative and consequently, consciously or not, excluded them from a process that the Western Shoshone viewed as unfair to begin with. Western Shoshone opposition was not even adequately noted in the document of record. In the end, appointing *only* a Southern Paiute man (regardless of the fact that he was also elected by Indian cultural resource representatives) has made it more difficult for the more contentious Western Shoshone voices to be heard. In addition, the DOE's Indian liaison maintained a very close and friendly relationship with his employer, the Department of Energy, further alienating many Western Shoshone who view the DOE with thinly disguised contempt. This tense political situation could have been partly remedied by appointing a second liaison of Western Shoshone descent (although it is quite possible that no Western Shoshone of sufficient standing would have agreed to such a position).

Manipulating cooperation through tribal representation—fostering communications with certain "good" Indian representatives at the expense of uncooperative "bad" Indians—is reminiscent of tactics used by past U.S. government agencies in negotiating with only those Indian "representatives" willing to compromise rather than those expressing politically uncomfortable demands. Similarly, refusing to adequately acknowledge Indian opposition (demonstrated by Indians' refusing to meet with government representatives) is another way of silencing that opposition. The Treaty of Ruby Valley itself demonstrates that tribal representation has always been a problem. As noted by Western Shoshone historian Steven Crumb, "Only one fourth of the Basin Shoshone population was involved in the treaty process [with the United States Government in 1863]." The U.S. treaty negotiators promised to meet with the remaining three-fourths of the Shoshone but never actually did.[21]

The Western Shoshone also felt discontent concerning whom the Department of Energy allows to speak for the Indians of the Yucca Mountain region. For example, although the Las Vegas Indian Center is treated as one of the twenty "tribes," it is not a tribe at all, but a conglomeration of different urban Indians. Its director, however, happens to be the DOE-Indian liaison, a paid consultant for the Department of Energy. Similarly, the Owens Valley Paiute have a good deal less connection to the immediate Yucca Mountain area than the Western Shoshone and the Southern Paiute but are nonetheless very active in the cultural resource studies. Interestingly, the cultural resource Indian representative from this more removed area of the Owens Valley made it a point to tell me that she didn't care about the politics of the nuclear activity at Yucca Mountain, only its cultural resources. Thus, it should come as no surprise to students of Indian history that the DOE fosters relations with less-political Indians, even when such Indians do not have as immediate an interest in the mountain as others geographically closer to it. Negotiations (and treaties) are first made with those Indians willing to cooperate. Increasing isolation eventually forces those remaining into submission.

Removal of Artifacts, Removal of Presence

Because they offer some of the few conduits for Indians to voice their concerns, cultural resource studies, including the designation or recognition of religious sites, are important practices—even when the laws that require them fall far short of their promise. The documents they create lend credence and legitimacy to claims of long-term Indian presence on the land, a presence too often eclipsed in the appropriation of their lands by Euroamericans. The existence of resources on the proposed site also provides Indians of the region some leverage (however small) with which to oppose activities at Yucca Mountain. The reemergence of Indian peoples in recent years has certainly been aided by these cultural resource studies and documents.[22] Even when nothing substantive actually results from the studies, they demonstrate that Indian claims to a much larger land base than that "given" to them under the reservation system have a legitimate historical foundation.

By acknowledging the presence of an "other" people, the United States, in turn, tacitly acknowledges an "other" landscape with boundaries different from those derived from the national security and energy demands of a "superpower." Such studies reveal an aboriginal geography beneath the sacrificial militarized geography of the interdesert region. At the very least, these studies force powerful political entities like the Department of Energy and the Department of Defense to recognize and interact with Indian people. Such recognition, in and of itself, stands as something of a major achievement when contrasted with past practices. From the perspective of many government agencies, it is still much more expedient to view Indians as a thing of the past (that is, as extinct) or as thoroughly assimilated.[23] Instead, artifacts must now be returned, and human bones, kept in dusty boxes crammed into storerooms, must be given back to the tribes; sacred and ceremonial sites must now be opened up to at least occasional visits by Indian groups. The Native American Graves Protection and Repatriation Act and the other cultural resource laws have stirred up the dust in this desert terrain where, as one Shoshone woman jokingly put it, "Indians are coming out from behind the bush."

The role of cultural resource studies in Native American political struggles is complex. On the one hand they help legitimate the preservation of Indian culture and history. But they can also be used politically to silence certain Indian concerns. They can give the appearance of responsible action when none is occurring. They can even legitimate the destruction of cultural presence by formalizing removal of artifacts.[24] Unfortunately, most studies are undertaken only when an area has been designated for development, and by then it is probably too late to stop "progress." In addition, though cultural resource laws act as a kind of power wedge into the smooth functioning of the state apparatus, they can simultaneously solidify the perception of Indian culture as an artifact of the past only. Indian people may gain new respectability based on archaeological discoveries of their ancestral culture, but this recognition does not translate into contemporary power.

The responses of Native people to the Yucca Mountain cultural resource studies reveal a great deal of frustration mixed with pride on the part of the Western Shoshone, Southern Paiute, and Owens Valley Paiute. Many view these studies more favorably than the all-too-familiar ethnographic studies of Indian people in this region. Unlike ethnographies, cultural resource studies are *legal* documents; they are mandated by the National Environmental Policy Act and by other laws regarding historic preservation. As official documents, they influence what gets preserved in its original place in the landscape and what is removed. Nevertheless, when cultural objects and human burial remains are removed, Indian people feel that the material link between the land and the presence of Indians on the land is severed, effectively erasing the history of Indian presence on the land. As one Indian said,

> At least we can say we tried our very best to say, "Leave this site alone!" The DOE says "We'll remove the baskets and store them away in some other places." We say, "No! Leave them right in there."[25]

Thus, removing artifacts or burial remains can hardly be considered an option at all. Material objects are traditionally left alone for use by ancestors and spirits who may need them. As Stoffle notes, this response by Indian people to cultural protection alternatives is "based on the belief that all plants, animals, and even physical elements have a consciousness, power, and purpose" and are thus best left undisturbed.

The whole process serves to remind Indians familiar with previous land appropriations of the bombing of undisclosed artifacts and burial grounds and of the presence of the federal government in the form of the military, the Bureau of Land Management, and the National Park Service. Though the government implies that Indians should be thankful for such costly, detailed studies, Indian people remain bitter. Such condescension on the part of the government compels those who were not already political activists to become more politicized. Three years after I met her, one elder Paiute woman who assured me at the beginning of our contact that she only cared about the "cultural part" began to talk politically about the need to stop government interference in her tribe's affairs.

The withdrawal of lands around Yucca Mountain, the Nellis Range, and the Nevada Test Site from Indian use since the 1940s makes it virtually impossible for Indians to possess contemporary knowledge of the area. As much as any single destructive act, this fencing off of the commons broke the continuity in knowledge about the landscape. Though Indians themselves were kept from this region, many archaeological studies were (and continue to be) conducted, as is demonstrated by the archaeological work done on the Nevada Test Site in the 1960s by Frederick Worman and others.[26]

The fact that the withdrawn area of Yucca Mountain, NTS, and the Nellis Range can be accessed by archaeologists but not its indigenous people heightens the tensions that already exist between Indians and archaeologists. Indian people are made to feel culturally legitimate only as objects of study. A Moapa Paiute woman who worked as a monitor of more recent archaeological digs[27] highlighted the sensitive nature of archaeological oversight:

> I've worked the test site as a monitor, and I've worked the Yucca Mountain as a monitor and the evidence is there. The pottery. On the test site I know there are some homes, lean-tos and whatnot. You can see it in the rock rings. [evidence of ancient encampment areas] It's there. There is evidence that our people were there. *But I mean that's just to pacify the tribes by having the monitors go out and work.*[28]

Similarly, others felt there was a discrepancy between what the DOE said were its policies about Indian monitoring and involvement and what actually took place. They felt there had been a breach of trust on the part of the DOE on more than one occasion.[29] Further, some Indian cultural resource representatives felt that the laws, while mandating studies, did not provide enough money for the preservation of artifacts. For instance, according to one Owens Valley Paiute woman, some artifacts weren't returned because the Indian communities didn't have the money to build adequate museums:

> Supposedly a lot of our things are supposed to have been returned. You know, and now they say, "We can't return it because you don't have a museum, it's not up to standard, you don't have a curator!" I mean even bones! Even a skull! You know, we'd like to bury them.

We don't have any money. We don't hardly have any land! So where are we going to put this supposedly big museum and get a curator and have it done like with [controlled] temperatures and the whole bit?

If they give this law to us, then they should give us the money to fulfill what we want. You know they make these laws, and then they block it all right there. Where we going to get all this money? We don't have any means. We have to get out and work just like everybody else.

And what bothers me is our youth. Our whole history as a people. If it's not with the tribe, it should be! Gosh, you know, you can go to the forest service, and they've got hundreds of bones![30]

Ultimately, if deemed "safe" by scientists, Yucca Mountain will be used for the purpose of entombing high-level nuclear waste, regardless of Indian opinions on the issue. The removal of artifacts or documentation of historical use by Indians are not enough to prevent cultural erasure. Yucca Mountain simply follows the pattern of land withdrawal already established, only now legalizing it with elaborate documents. The designation of a nuclear sacrifice zone—one that eradicates Indian presence— suggests that Zabarte's claim of ethnocide is closer to the mark than it might seem at first.

Different Ways of Knowing

Documents describing the scientific studies done at Yucca Mountain reveal a definite hierarchy of values assigned to the different components of those studies. The "environmental studies" associated with the environmental impact assessment and regulations appear at the bottom of the great chain of scientific being that exists at the Yucca Mountain Project. Far more prestigious are disciplines such as geology, hydrology, and volcanology, developed in the exploratory studies aspect of the project. The environmental studies part of the project is referred to disparagingly by some Yucca Mountain employees as the "bugs and bunnies" program. Within the environmental studies realm, cultural resource studies (mostly anthropology and archaeology) stand close to the bottom. At the very bottom of "scientific" analysis, of course, is the Native American Program, that aspect of the study that focuses on contemporary Native peoples in the area. Clearly, Indian people who are alive today—seen not just as inheritors of archaeological materials that inform us about human evolution—are of the least interest. Even some of the archaeologists I spoke with seemed to feel that working with contemporary Indian people is something of an imposition. Not only do cultural resource studies fare poorly in the hierarchy of scientific values, but their small domain is rife with tensions as well, particularly between Indians and archaeologists.

From beginning to end, Euroamerican anthropologists, archaeologists, ethnobotanists, ethnohistorians, and environmental science project managers orchestrate the whole process by which Indian presence is "historicized," only to be, in many cases, eradicated. All information gets organized and translated through white experts. Anthropologists and archaeologists often designate cultural resource sites on and around Yucca Mountain *prior* to communication with Indians. Indian representatives are simply brought in to validate the findings and interpret their relative significance. Some Indians are offended by this process. Recalling the time an archaeologist told two Indian cultural resource representatives to look at a "power rock," Owens Valley Paiute elders said:

> *They* tell us it's a power rock! The archaeologists tell *us*. But there's different people have different feelings about things. . . .
>
> How do the archaeologists know? They can't know the way we can. They say, oh yeah, this is so and so. How can they know? They're not Indians! We're Indians; we know.[31]

The ways in which Indians and social scientists understand the significance of particular cultural resource sites further contributes to tensions between the two groups. Designations of relative significance are attached to legal requirements such as those in the National Historic Preservation Act. As Fowler notes:

> Assessments of the archaeological properties on Yucca Mountain and decisions as to whether they are "significant" to preserve or mitigate will be made according to criteria set forth in regulations and policies that flow from NHPA (the National Historic Preservation Act). These regulations give primacy to the "scientific" significance of sites, something assessed

based on *the importance of any or all of them to answering research questions set forth in various plans for explaining prehistory and history.*[32] [My italics.]

Sites of mythological, spiritual, or healing significance (if considered at all) thus play a secondary role to research interests, and contribute to difficulties in communications between Indian representatives and Euroamerican scientists. Describing problems she has encountered working with archaeologists, Pauline Esteves notes:

> Well the archaeologists and anthropologists have to follow their system. And in order to do their work they fall under that. . . . Some things could be said so simply, but no, they have to come out with all these long-sounding terms. . . . There's that system they have to work with so they can be according to the law. And they're bound to that.

That "system" is understood as a very different one from the Native American system of belief. According to Esteves:

> We have clashed, he [Stoffle] and I. But I feel very alone when I do that because the others just tend to just go along. Sometimes I wonder, who are these people [meaning the other Indians involved in the Yucca Mountain Project cultural resources studies]? They are supposed to be people who are knowledgeable about the environment—the *whole* environment, as a whole. And they're not saying anything. All they were telling me after Richard [Stoffle] and I would clash, is "You sure told him off, Pauline." I says, told him off? I says I don't understand what you're saying! They don't talk my language, in other words. "Told him off"! I wasn't telling him off. I says, *look, I'm here to educate these people* [the anthropologists]. *I don't know what you people call it, I says, to me these people, they're coming from another world. Another educational system. And I'm trying to educate him about our way.*

The law works to reinscribe scientific narratives of human and cultural evolution in the region, not Indian culture or religion. It becomes a mechanism of exclusion built into the cultural resource studies themselves.

What it excludes is the other "system" to which Esteves alludes—a knowledge base that I will discuss more thoroughly in Chapter 8.

Richard Stoffle, director of the Yucca Mountain cultural resource studies, acknowledges the tension between the Indian and Euroamerican epistemological viewpoint when he writes:

> Archaeologists sometimes do not accept the interpretation and mitigation recommendations of American Indian people with whom they are working to assess cultural resources. These differences have become so common and so important to both Indian people and professional archaeologists that special conferences have been organized to help articulate the points of disagreement and to seek resolution.[33]

In the end, however, Stoffle feels differences can be bridged by the "common goals" of saving cultural artifacts from destruction. Some Western Shoshone charge, however, that Indians who participate in such efforts are simply rubber-stamping the assessments of archaeologists to the exclusion of other issues of cultural significance, including land rights.

The fact that Indian people in this region live in a border zone with powerful Euroamerican scientific cultures and defense institutions contributes to both intercultural and intertribal tensions. Indians in the region are partially assimilated, but not entirely; some are more so than others. Many are situated on the border between different ideological systems, and responses to cultural resource studies reveal tensions in this highly charged and fractured landscape. Interactions with social scientists to establish presence in the nuclear landscape inevitably alter and develop Indian identity in new ways, just as Indian people continue to press their views within a system that resists them. And both cultures change accordingly, although not at all proportionately.

Collaborations

Both of the cultural resource studies done at Yucca Mountain can be seen as complex ongoing postcolonial documents—only this time they are the co-(re)creation of a repressed culture by both the repressor and the repressed. A critical examination of the process allows us to see how culture actually changes and develops in the real world. Cultural identity is not a static, self-contained organic entity, but rather results from struggles within power relations, from alliances between unexpected agents from opposing ideological encampments, from a politics of care and compassion on both sides by those who attempt communication with the other—even when bound within agonistic constraints (as are the cultural resource anthropologists and Indian overseers). While such a positive spin may be difficult for many to accept because such studies seem like one more nail in the cultural coffin of Indian peoples, these documents (in some cases, at least) serve to help define Indian identity in the nuclear landscape and reestablish a historical presence that had been all but eradicated. For instance, Paiute women from the Owens Valley told me how compiling the ethnobotanical information into one volume (the DOE-funded report titled *Native American Plant Resources in the Yucca Mountain Area*[34]) helped them to learn about the flora of their own traditional area and how their ancestors used it for food, building materials, and medical purposes. Thus, white social science helps to both preserve and reconstruct a culture that white society itself has been, until very recently, and to some extent still is, hell-bent on destroying.

Without denying the problems inherent in one culture's narrating another when the other is colonized as severely as are American Indians, it is important to note that some Indian people view positively the disciplines of archaeology, anthropology, and ethnography that have charted these colonized cultural domains. Some felt that they learned a great deal from white experts and consequently praised their work. Unlike Western Shoshone, Owens Valley Paiute Indians expressed respect for Richard Stoffle and his work, citing his efforts to represent the Indian world view. Similarly, one woman told me how she had read all of Julian Steward's anthropological books on the Great Basin Indian cultures to learn about her tribe's past. Another felt that ethnographers actually saved a lot of Indian knowledge that would have otherwise been lost in the severity of forced assimilation:

> We didn't have a written language. I mean we didn't have any writing at all, so much of it [cultural knowledge] got lost. I figure that the people that came a long time ago and talked with the Indians that were around then, well, communication was nil at best. Because the Indians couldn't speak

English, and those white people couldn't speak Indian. So the early anthropologists did the best they could but the Indians told them then what they were doing way back. That's more than what we know. But that was a long time ago. That's why I feel sometimes a lot of that stuff some anthropologists got wrong in some places, they had it mixed up. But still those early ethnographers were closer to it than some of us [now] can say. They [the Indians of the past] were a spiritual culture telling at the time.[35]

This statement demonstrates the complex role the anthropologist has played as documenter of cultural knowledge while remaining inextricably bound to the colonizing culture. It also shows the inadequacy and frustration that many Indian people feel as representatives of a "different" culture, a different system of thought that even they have difficulty remembering.

Timbisha Shoshone elder Pauline Esteves spoke positively of how an experienced anthropologist can solicit forgotten memories, stories, and histories: "I remember certain things, but not all. I've forgotten. But an expert person can bring that out, I found that out!"[36]

However, at the same time, Esteves expressed anger and exasperation at how anthropological accounts of Indian people get published but often don't benefit contemporary Indian people in their struggles for sovereignty and recognition.[37] This distrust was palpable in my early discussions with Esteves.[38] She made very clear that she was utterly tired of being the subject of white people's books, mine included. She didn't want to exist just to keep all us "social scientists" employed:

And so I believe that anything that makes jobs, they're going to keep. So they [social scientists] are going to always keep us down on that level, so they can always use us. When are they going to stop studying us? They [the anthropologists] ask the same old questions over and over again. When are they going to stop? When am I going to stop answering the same old questions that I have answered throughout the many years, and it's still going on.[39]

In contrast, the Department of Energy representatives I interviewed preferred to highlight, propagandistically, the fact that they had created documents that were tools for Indians to use in exploring their own cultural history and knowledge. In the end, however, the Indian world view and way of knowing do not easily fit into the confines of social science language. There remains a gulf between Western scientific knowledge systems, epistemologies, and expression and Indian (Western Shoshone, Owens Valley, and Southern Paiute) ways of knowing and forms of expression. This difference deepens the social and political power inequities felt by Indian people because it constructs a knowledge hierarchy in which Indian knowledge ranks below that of Western science.

The many problems of the cultural resource studies examined in this chapter—those of hierarchy, of tribal representation, of the dominance of Euroamerican knowledge systems, and the way in which the DOE uses these studies to misrepresent the level of cooperation it enjoys with the surrounding Indian communities—contribute to the perception that the Yucca Mountain Project perpetuates politics as usual through the continuation of dominating practices.

Conclusion

Contrary to the DOE-produced image of cooperation, Indian accounts of the cultural resource studies depict a region rife with cultural and political divisions, not all of them obvious to the casual observer—whatever his or her political persuasion—who simply wants to put nuclear waste out of sight, out of mind. The power differential between players such as the Timbisha Shoshone and the United States Navy or the Moapa Paiute and the Department of Energy is immense. The average Western Shoshone family income is approximately $3,000 per year. Neither their numbers nor, with a few exceptions, their largely subsistence economies gives them any leverage to press forward with their agendas. Except for the archaeological evidence, or the fact that some are poorly kept wards of the state, they might as well not exist for the U.S. government.

Despite their weaknesses, cultural resource and religious freedom laws have opened a Pandora's box for the dominant institutional powers in the region. Indians' presence in the area—after years of forced assimilation and waves of colonization (including forced removal from Native lands)—must now be acknowledged by powerful institutions like the Department of Defense, the Department of Energy, and other agencies of the federal government. The greater irony is that U.S. law requires Indian people to prove their occupation of the land. That Indians must prove to their conquerors that they have occupied the land for millennia prior to the white man's arrival must seem to be the ultimate indignity in the history of repression of Indian cultural identity. That the proof should have to be made on Euroamerican scientific terms only aggravates that indignation.

The following statement should be understood within this context of internal colonialism, which, for some Indians of the area, goes to the root of all other issues, including nuclear colonialism:

> We still have a lot of work to do with a lot of groups. It's hard even for some of these groups . . . how do we demonstrate to them that we're Shoshone? We would like to be Shoshone. We want to be Shoshone. And that our ability in those things which make us Shoshone—being able to go on to the land, being able to go to our springs, our birth sites, our burial sites, our sacred sites, go hunting our animals—the things that make us who we are—gathering our berries, you know, praying, knowing how to pray, being able to build fires in Death Valley without the Park Service harassing people. These things are important. They make us who we are, and we have to do them. But it's hard to demonstrate to people that we have no way to defend such a simple way of life. Everything else is encroaching upon our rights, violating our rights, destroying our ability to be who we are. And it seems that the burden is put on us against all odds! *Prove it,* they say![40]

· 7 ·

The Country of Lost Borders

An Historical Sketch
The road to Yucca Mountain from the west moves around the China Lake Naval Weapons Center (which closes off the Coso and Argus mountain ranges), over the Panamints and down into Death Valley before forking. The northerly approach crosses over the Amargosa Range before turning south at the town of Beatty. Just past Beatty and U.S. Ecology's abandoned nuclear waste dump, everything on the east side of U.S. 95—more than 3 million acres—is strictly off-limits. It belongs to the Air Force and the Department of Energy.

In 1903 Mary Austin named this desert region "the Country of Lost Borders," but this is hardly the case now. Today, borders are everywhere. Except for Death Valley, this is now the land of geographic ellipses: inaccessible militarized dark zones—a place of intersecting and sometimes armed borders, behind which the memory of the land fades into silence. It wasn't always so. As Mary Austin's poetic evocation of the landscape suggests, what borders existed prior to the land's militarization were permeable and fluid, not fixed.

If, in the myopia of the present, the history of Indian people on this land is ignored, then Euroamericans unwittingly subscribe to the standard wasteland narrative so commonly invoked to justify the (mostly) military land withdrawals. This wasteland history is exemplified in the following passage—a 1963 publication commemorating the twentieth anniversary of the China Lake Naval Weapons Center:

> To those who first squinted their eyes at the *vast nothingness* which prevailed in 1943, it must have seemed an impossible task. But a world-wide war was on, and the order was: "We need it—build it." And the wind in the sagebrush seemed to snicker.

The above publication also uses subheads such as "OUT OF NOTHING-NESS . . . INTO HISTORY" and "Where sagebrush once grew now grow sages of science."[1]

In fact, it was not out of nothingness that China Lake, Nellis Air Force Base, the Nevada Test Site, and other military reservations in this region were created. By not taking into account the history of Indian occupation of this land—an alternative history of millennia-long human occupation—Euroamericans become accomplices in postcolonialist practices that have always erased presence. In this case the presence is that of the Western Shoshone, the Southern Paiute, and, farther afield, the Owens Valley Paiute tribes. As one Owens Valley Paiute elder told me:

> You know the Indians are nonpeople. When white people write anything—even people we went to school with and who lived with us in Big Pine—if they write something they usually write the Indians out of the picture. I think it's just that they didn't understand us. And they didn't really want to tangle with what they didn't understand.[2]

Different historical narratives illuminate different landscapes, as well as different ecological perspectives between Euroamericans and Indians of the Great Basin and Mojave deserts. This land, "good for nothing but bombing practices," has been a field of social and economic struggle between Indian people and Euroamericans, between land as a commodity for private and government enterprise and land as homeland, source of sustenance, and "holy land." Once the region is populated in our own minds, different patterns of land use can be compared with different cultural narratives that legitimate specific uses and, ultimately, different knowledge systems. For example, close examination of the capitalist ideology beneath the Euroamerican wasteland narrative reveals an ecological ethos used to support land appropriation. Today, that "wasteland" has been transformed into a much-valued commodity for the burial of high-level nuclear waste. Yet this region offers an alternative story, as exemplified in the Western Shoshone statement:

> Newe Segobia, the name given by the Western Shoshone people to the land they have lived upon, roughly translates as "the people's earth mother." . . . Non-natives have often regarded this subtle, beautiful landscape as barren, worthless, or empty, and Federal policy from the beginning through the present day reflects this hostile misunderstanding of the Great Basin and its Native people.[3]

Not all Euroamericans think, or thought, of this land as a wasteland. Certainly different people within various ethnic groups have seen the same land through different lenses. However, the wasteland narrative, the narrative that describes this land as alien to human life, was and is too powerful to ignore. It has played too great a role in the depiction of this landscape as one fit only for bombs and waste.

Ancient History

Archaeologists and anthropologists trace Western Shoshone and Southern Paiute occupation of the Yucca Mountain region back more than 10,000 years. As opposed to white occupation of the region, which began in earnest only after the 1848 Gold Rush, indigenous habitation and associated knowledge and experience of this landscape has far greater historical depth— indeed, is of another order altogether. This difference must be taken into account when assessing competing knowledge claims about the land.

Archaeological data indicate indigenous occupation of the Yucca Mountain region as far back as 12,000 years ago.[4] In her summary report on the Yucca Mountain region, Catherine Fowler provides the archaeological benchmarks of 12,000, 6,000, and 2,000 years prior to the present to identify changes in the character of indigenous occupation.[5] She notes that within a span of 10,000 years—from 12,000 to 2,000 years ago—Indian use of the mountain appears to have progressed upward from its base to its ridge. For instance, archaeologists have found 12,000-year-old evidence of human occupation such as projectiles, tools, and other implements around the base of the mountain near "ephemeral washes" such as Fortymile Wash. Six-thousand-year-old evidence of temporary camping sites and hunting activities (in addition to evidence of occupation around the mountain's base) has been found on the "saddles and low passes [of] the mountain itself." Here, too, archaeologists note the presence of tinajas or potholes—natural rock formations used as water tanks—dating as far back as 6,000 years.

Around 2,000 years ago "the Indian settlement pattern appears to shift again toward occupation of small rock shelters at the top of steep slopes on Yucca Mountain and outlying ridges." Intermountain brownware, a Western Shoshone and Southern Paiute pottery, was also found from this period; and at this time, too, Indian activities seemed to be oriented more toward seed gathering than hunting.

As indicated in the cultural resource studies described in Chapter 6 (and the archaeological maps in Chapter 5), there is ample archaeological evidence of Indian occupation of the Yucca Mountain region and throughout the Nevada Test Site. Burial sites have been found at Paiute Mesa and Cane Springs; ceremonial rock circles have been found in Fortymile Canyon, along with rock shelters, petroglyphs, glass beads, baskets, other kinds of woven articles, and much more. All of this evidence links the Western Shoshone, Southern Paiute, and Owens Valley Paiute to this region. This 10,000-year-old heritage of sustained occupation influences many contemporary Indian people's ecological frame of reference. Though they may not always know how to interpret petroglyphs or other signs from the past, many Indians of the region speak from a sense of their people having been in one place from time immemorial. In contrast, the Euroamerican historical experience of this land is a mere 150 years—a relatively recent encounter with a foreign and alien landscape that was never perceived as a land of sustenance. The difference between these two historical frameworks greatly affects each culture's ecological perceptions.

> I remember every morning before she'd wash her face, my mother would get up and just right before the sun comes up she's out there praying, you know. Feeding, feeding the Spirit, you know.[6]

Recognition of this deep historical context is important if we are to understand at least part of why Indian people of this region describe the land as sacred, or why the Western Shoshone and Southern Paiute remain steadfastly bound to this particular geographic domain, even after multiple efforts to relocate them and after years of bombing by nuclear and conventional weapons. When Timbisha Shoshone elder Pauline Esteves tells the story about her mother using the nearby Coso Hot Springs as a place of healing, she is, in part, calling forth this memory of place, this historical occupation—even when she, herself, has never been to the hot springs:

> My mother said when she was a young girl in Darwin [the town near Coso], they would go up there [Coso]. And I says, "What did you do?" She says, "The old people out there were talking and everything, and we young girls were told to get down into the mud and be cured and get purified and it's good for us and we won't have no bad dreams and we will be better people," and all this kind of stuff. She said they stayed out there for two or three days. They didn't have to gather wood or anything because they cooked right over the boiling mud in their pots. And they even drank some of the water, but very little of it, she said, and then they would come on home. They did a lot of rabbit hunting there also and gathering of some seeds. And then they would come on home.[7]

Her mother's use and perception of the hot springs as both a spiritual healing ground as well as a site to gather plant seeds and to hunt rabbits show the intricate weave of subsistence and spirituality that characterizes traditional Western Shoshone and Southern Paiute statements about the land. The Coso Hot Springs have also been used by other Indian tribes with links to Yucca Mountain, and they, too, describe it as being "many hundreds of years old," and as an important place of healing:

The religious spirit power is there . . . put by Mother Earth to provide for the Indians . . . to remove sickness. We have to make a special prayer, by taking ten flint . . . each one for prayer . . . talk to the water . . . sometimes the water waves pray to the world. The Earth will keep moving. . . . Indians have to pray to the water to keep the earth together. Indians have to talk to the Spirit Power . . . when you pray at Coso with the flints, it is to thank the Spirits and the Springs for the benefits given for the broken health . . . Mother Earth put these places all over the country . . . but Coso is a main one . . . has lots of power. It is many hundreds of years old. That water is life. Indians used other hot springs, Long Valley, Mono Valley, Keough . . . but they are not Coso.[8]

Rather than romanticize Indian earth-centered spirituality, implying that Indians of the region are *naturally* more spiritual than Euroamericans, I suggest that what accounts for such perceptions comes, in part, from an exceptionally long-term habitation and commitment to place. In the next chapter, I will also suggest that reliance on oral traditions plays a role in the development of a socioecological perspective among Indian people in this domain. I do not presume to explain Indian spirituality in material terms alone, but I suggest that such factors (long-term habitation and consequent commitment to place) influence religious perceptions of the land (which, in turn, influence ecological perceptions) and may account for the wide differences between Indian people and Euroamerican narratives about the region.

Use of such terms as "Mother Earth," "sacred land," "traditionalist," "power (Puha)," and "Indian ecological ethos" are viewed with skepticism by many Western scholars. Such terms have been abused and can potentially dehumanize their subjects. They cannot, however, be discarded— first, because Indian people themselves use them, and second, because, when used in the proper context, they help to describe at least some aspects of the relationship many Indian people of this region have with the non-human world in general, and with specific sites in the landscape in particular. Indian spirituality is not the only reason for keeping nuclear waste out of Yucca Mountain, but it is one aspect of a complex set of differences between two groups of players in this contested terrain. Articulating its presence helps non-Indian people comprehend the Indian landscape.[9]

Proactive Environmental Practices

Anthropological and ethnohistorical scholars of this region (including Native American scholars)[10] draw upon a variety of archaeological studies, historical accounts, observations, and documents combined with ethnographic reports to construct their narratives about precontact times in this region. Historical sources include early traveler reports such as diaries and records from those who traveled through the Nevada Test Site area and Fortymile Canyon, government documents, early government reports of reconnaissance expeditions, local newspaper accounts, and other archival materials.[11] Early ethnographic accounts of Western Shoshone and Southern Paiutes—by John Wesley Powell and G. W. Ingalls in 1869, and by I. T. Kelly and Julian Steward in the 1930s—are also major sources of information.[12] The ethnographic accounts, of course, are based on (and indebted to) the testimony of Indian elders who have preserved knowledge of Indian history within their oral traditions.

In general, accounts of life among these Indian groups before contact with Euroamericans indicate a socially peaceful, and what we might now call an environmentally sustainable, existence. Because of the demanding environmental conditions of this desert region, life was not easy; but its inhabitants managed to survive and even—as many Shoshone and Paiute songs suggest—to flourish and develop a deep attachment to the land that maintained life.[13] Indeed, because finding sustenance was difficult, maintaining life required a great deal of knowledge about the land's resources and the best ways to ensure continuation of those resources. Often this meant a seminomadic existence that conserved the resources of a particular area while people searched for food elsewhere. Indians learned not to exhaust the resources of an area. Their patterns of seasonal migrations and annual returns suggest that survival was intimately bound up with knowledge of the availability of game and plants throughout the yearly cycle.[14] Like many other indigenous people, knowledge of the land and its resources was necessarily woven into the daily lives of precontact Indians. This intimate relationship between Indians and their environment was carried over, through daily practices and oral tradition, into postcontact life—even to the twentieth century.

Indian people in this region before and after contact with Euroamericans should not be viewed romantically as existing within an Edenic symbiosis with nature—as somehow synonymous with nature, making no distinction between themselves and their environment. *That* story is a Euroamerican construction of "primitive" peoples. Rather, recent investigations into Indian ecological practices show evidence of a high degree of environmental management predating any Euroamerican influence.[15] Long before contact with white people, Owens Valley Paiutes irrigated fields, and Shoshone and Southern Paiutes sowed wild seed in areas to which they returned seasonally to harvest. For example, the following 1859 report demonstrates the astonishment of some white people as they first encountered the Owens Valley Paiutes:

> Large tracts of land are here irrigated by the natives to secure the growth of the grass seeds and grass nuts—a small tuberous root of fine taste and nutritious qualities, which grows here in abundance. Their ditches for irrigation are in some cases carried for miles, displaying as much accuracy and judgment as if laid out by an engineer, and distributing the water with great regularity over their grounds.[16]

Clearly, Indian ecological practice has never meant the absence of human activity and development. Indian "ecology," at least in part, comes from an intimate interaction with a local land base and the continuity of that relationship through time. Longtime habitation of an environment inevitably requires sustainable practices, even for seminomadic peoples. For instance, harvesting of wild plant life did not mean complete harvesting but leaving enough plant life for regeneration.[17] Pruning of trees and the use of fire for clearing were used judiciously and expertly. Water sources were recognized as a resource for wild animals, not just humans, and so were maintained by Indian people for these purposes, a practice that continues in some places today.[18] Elder Indian consultants for the Yucca Mountain cultural resource studies expressed concern that because the creation of the Nevada Test Site made the area inaccessible to them, they had not been able to fulfill their "responsibility" to the wildlife of the area (by keeping the natural water tanks clean). These kinds of practices—that is, active Indian development and maintenance of the land—have to be recognized before one can understand the impact that Euroamerican land appropriations and ownership practices have had on Indian people. Proactive environmental practices by Indian people also help us to better understand the perceived relationship between nature and culture concerning the Western Shoshone, Southern Paiute, and Owens Valley Paiute in this region. The Euroamerican myth that Indian people of the region could not cultivate land and were thus little better than "wild animals" historically legitimized appropriation of Indian land.[19] Representing Indians as "primitive" or "wild" creatures effectively depopulated the land, opening it up to the "civilizing" presence of Euroamerican settlers. Given the history of colonization and the colonial representation of Indian peoples, it is important to stress the proactive character of Indian interactions with the environment. As will be shown in the next chapter, Indian people clearly see themselves nondualistically as both part of and distinct from the natural environment. This perception is, of course, very different from the problematic representation of "nature" and "culture" in at least some of the more predominant strains of thought within the Euroamerican tradition, where the two realms are largely conceived of as separate antagonistic entities. This dualism manifests in the Euroamerican "fear" of falling back into a state of primitivism, barbarism, wildness (the way Euroamericans have often historically represented Indian people). Oddly, this is also the source of Euroamerican Edenic dreams of a return to an original pure state of nature, a more wholesome, untainted existence closer to God (the way many Euroamericans often represent Indian people today). Nostalgia for the past and demonization of the other find representation in people of many races and ethnicities, not just Euroamericans. What is important here is the deployment of such representations within the colonialist context.[20]

Contact with Euroamericans

Long before any Euroamericans traveled across the Western Shoshone and Southern Paiute domain, the land had been appropriated by non-Indians—on paper, at least—and passed from one imperialist player to the next, effectively pulling the region into the world imperialist system. In 1492 the Western Shoshone and Southern Paiute aboriginal homelands became—by "right of discovery"—the property of Spain. In 1821 Mexico claimed them until the 1848 gold rush when Mexico ceded the land to the

United States in accordance with the Treaty of Hidalgo.[21] When "the white man" finally appeared in this Western region, social, cultural, and environmental disasters followed in his wake: from the trappers to the pioneers, from the Mormon settlers to the U.S. Cavalry and the Gold Rush miners. Colonization of the West continued into the twentieth century with the advent of Sunbelt-bound urban refugees, massive military war-game theaters, and scientists testing nuclear bombs in the desert.

Indians in this region have been subject to forced relocation and assimilation and have been cut off from the means of sustaining a livelihood based on the subsistence techniques honed through the centuries by their ancestors. Through privatization and government redistribution of their remaining land holdings, they have been driven into tiny "colonies." Finally, through the military land withdrawals, Indians of the region were denied an adequate land base from which to practice an environmentally sustainable economy. Add to this the deliberate destruction of pinyon forests to make way for cattle grazing and the radiation poisoning of vast tracts of foraging areas, and an environmental disaster of epic proportions emerges when viewed from its effects on the original inhabitants of the land. This environmental transformation, with its attendant social dislocation, is not often recognized as such because it has taken place over time— 150 years. The pattern only promises to continue into the twenty-first century with the importation of high-level nuclear waste at Yucca Mountain and low-level waste at Ward Valley.

The history of contact for both the Shoshone and Paiute people was, like most other Indian contacts with Euroamericans, disastrous. As Western Shoshone historian Steven Crum has noted, Shoshone contact with Euroamericans began in 1827 and 1828 with Jedediah Smith and Peter Skene Ogden, trappers who characterized the indigenous people they encountered as something less than human. In the words of Smith, they were "the most miserable of the human race having nothing to subsist on (nor any clothing) except grass seeds, grasshoppers, etc."[22] It is noteworthy that both men came to the region on behalf of their employers, the Rocky Mountain Fur Company and the British-owned Hudson's Bay Company, respectively, thereby inserting into the region capitalist practices that had not existed before.[23] The Indian space organized according to a subsistence economy (where some form of sustainable practice was necessary to ensure continuation of food sources) was thus reorganized according to not only a national, but (even at that time) an international economy of capitalism, where the profit motive supplanted maintenance of resources as the central objective. The trapper companies' relationship to the land based on capital accumulation and an orientation toward natural resources as "exchange value" came into conflict with an Indian relationship based on a subsistence economy and an orientation toward natural resources as "use value."

From this time forward, the capitalist economy of exchange value and the Euroamerican ethic of private ownership (or in its current form in Nevada, "private" government ownership) intruded upon, dominated, and all but destroyed the Indian organization of land according to commons regions and usufruct rights. Euroamericans in this region bent the land and its elements to their will, with large-scale mining operations, monumental alterations of waterways, the sucking dry of underground water tables, and the uprooting of pinyon forests to make way for cattle-grazing land. In contrast, Indians adopted what Stoffle calls a "transhumant *adaptive* strategy," one that accords with the seasons, the life cycles of the flora, and migratory patterns of the fauna. Indigenous people, forced to assimilate to survive, learned by necessity the so-called law of supply and demand, the profit motive, cattle ranching, casino entrepeneurship, and the fine points of hosting a nuclear-waste facility.

As in many other regions in the Americas, the alien diseases that white people brought decimated Shoshone and Paiute populations (in the midnineteenth century) especially in the permanent spring districts where such "water sources often served as the loci for the communication of disease."[24] Oasis Valley, Ash Meadows, and Pahrump (areas noted in Chapter 5) were all affected. The brutal killing of Native Americans by Euroamericans in the region also reduced their population. Life-sustaining flora and fauna were severely depleted so that in addition to epidemics, the Indians suffered from starvation or near-starvation at various times in the latter half of the nineteenth century; and waterways were polluted by the introduction of stock animals, as successive waves of Euroamericans moved across their land en route to the West Coast. What little arable land could be found in the region around Yucca Mountain was quickly appropriated. The Indian population was "proletarianized" into labor camps at the outskirts of newly laid Euroamerican townships. (That is, Euroamerican townships were *overlaid* onto preexisting Indian villages.)

Indians were also forcibly rounded up and relocated to distant areas. Many, however, found ways to hide or return home secretly. Many of the Indian people I interviewed told stories that had been passed down to them by grandparents about the forced removal of ancestors. According to one group of Owens Valley Paiutes:

> Back then they called the Indians squatters. In 1870 or thereabouts the military came in at Fort Independence and they did take the Indians and had them march out of this valley. They literally herded them like cattle. And they went to take them to another reservation that was called Fort Tejon. And they wanted the Indians to live there. The white people did not want the Indians in this valley. Because they wanted this valley. So they literally took the Indians, together, and pushed them out. And they killed a lot of Indians and a lot of children and women.
>
> I also got this from the records of the military themselves, so you know we're not just saying it. It did happen. Close to a thousand Indians! And a lot died. Hundreds of them died.[25]

This story of forced relocation was also relayed to me by another elder Paiute woman:

> My great-grandmother, you know, she and her family was in that march, that trip out. But her father told her and her mother to hide out and then travel only at night and come back and he would meet them here [at Big Pine], and he would go on with them [on the march] a little bit further. And at one point they [the Army] told the women and the children to separate from the men, because they were going to slaughter the men. But there was some one [of the Indians] who understood English a little bit, so he told the Indians, and he probably sensed it too, and he told them that they—the women—shouldn't separate from the men at all. So they just all stayed together, saying, "If you're going to kill them, you can kill us." So they stayed together. And a lot of people came back. They sneaked back at night. My

great-grandmother did, and they were really tough, anyway, you had to be tough! And they came back.[26]

Referring to practices of forced assimilation in the 1930s, Timbisha Shoshone elder Pauline Esteves told similar stories about her parent's generation "hiding" from Euroamerican government agents:

My grandfather made it a point that his children weren't going to be placed into those institutions. He hid them out, so my aunts and my mother weren't oriented into that other life [Euroamerican]. They just gradually got into it as they got older. But their knowledge was directly from their next generation back.[27]

Esteves emphasized that her mother and aunt resisted the white man's education in order to preserve a knowledge base that was distinctively Indian and that included a view of the landscape unlike anything a Euroamerican might have access to, or even imagine. Anthropologists studying the region also note that although Indian people of the area adopted many aspects of Euroamerican culture, they retained many traditional hunting, gathering, and ceremonial practices; by no means could one assert unequivocally that the Indians of the area had fully assimilated into the settler lifestyle and world view. As Stoffle notes, "Native American people achieved a new synthesis of traditional Native American culture and Euroamerican culture, functioning in two overlapping cultural worlds."[28] This "overlapping" is also evident in contemporary Indian statements about Yucca Mountain, which often combine mythopoetic knowledge with scientific knowledge.

Appropriation of the Springs

As described in previous chapters, the desert areas of the Great Basin/Mojave region, including the Nevada Test Site and Yucca Mountain areas, hold important oases around springs and waterways where Indian people maintained permanent and temporary homes. In the immediate Yucca Mountain region these core oases consist of the three spring districts of Ash Meadows, Oasis Valley, and the Eso District. From these centers

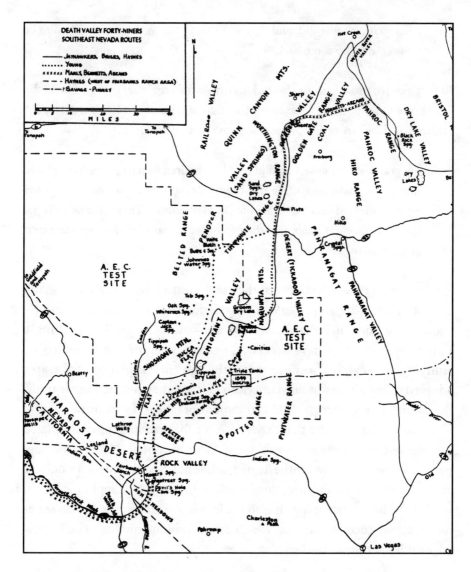

Figure 7.1 Springs in the Fortymile Canyon and Ash Meadows districts
The Forty-Niners' travel routes illustrate the numerous springs clustered through-out the Yucca Mountain and Nevada Test Site region, as well as springs in outlying areas such as Ash Meadows

From: Stoffle et al., *Native American Resource Studies at Yucca Mountain, Nevada* (Koenig, 1984)

Indians traveled to outlying areas to hunt and forage, returning periodically to these permanent camps. (See Fig. 5.2 for a map of the districts.)

Because of Euroamerican encroachment and an explosion in Euroamerican population, by the turn of the twentieth century, Native Americans in the Yucca Mountain region had become a minority in the core oasis areas (except in the Eso District, which was too dry and remote for Euroamerican tastes). Indians lost control over most of the springs and, thus, their base of subsistence, and were forced to live at these same oasis areas in labor camps. To survive, many Indians supplemented their low wages by gathering resources in "refuge regions" on what is now the Nevada Test Site. Corroborating what many Indian people told me, Stoffle (himself referring to the work of Julian Steward) notes that, at the turn of the century and later, Indians made full use of this "wasteland" region:

> Native American families from the Oasis Valley area had harvested Salvia on Bare Mountain and Yucca Mountain. In July, families from the Belted Range harvested hu:gwhi, a large grass seed resembling wheat. Later the families harvested rye grass seeds in the area around the Ammonia Tanks. In September, Oasis Valley people went to the Belted Range to harvest piñon nuts. Fall rabbit drives were held on the flats south of Whiterock Spring, "under the direction of Wangagwana, the local chief." Rabbit drives lasted about a month and often included participants from Ash Meadows, Death Valley, Lida, and the Kawich Mountains.[29]

All of the areas mentioned—the Belted Range, the Ammonia Tanks, Whiterock spring, and so on—are now inaccessible regions on or around Yucca Mountain.

Clearly, these activities demonstrate the importance of this now inaccessible environment to its Indian inhabitants—inhabitants whose ecological practices were characterized by Stoffle's "transhumant adaptive strategy" even while they worked as part-time wage laborers for Euroamericans.

Because springs were smaller and fewer in the area of the Nevada Test Site, Euroamericans were not usually enticed to farm and ranch there. But even this refuge was eventually taken from the Indians:

Some Native American people continued to live within the area of the Nevada Test Site, and many continued to harvest wild resources there, up until the area was withdrawn from public use in the 1940s.

Beginning in the 1940s, the area of the Nevada Test Site began to be withdrawn from public use, with the creation of the Tonopah Bombing and Gunnery Range, the Nellis Air Force Range, and the Nevada Test Site. The withdrawals of land decisively reduced Native American access to wild plant and animal resources *and contributed to a diaspora of Indian people from the region of the Nevada Test Site* that had already begun with the establishment of reservations—all of which were at considerable distances from the later Nevada Test Site.[30] [My italics.]

Thus, the area we now call the Nevada Test Site and Yucca Mountain served as a region of wild resource harvesting for Indians well into the twentieth century. For the Western Shoshone, it served as a permanent habitation area in the Eso District of the Belted Range, right up to the time the land was withdrawn by the military and Department of Energy. As one Western Shoshone elder put it:

> We used to live out in that area [the Nevada Test Site] in the '40s. But then we had to be moved out of it. See, when they made this test range and such, that's when we had to move off the land. The land's ours yet.[31]

Such appropriation occurred in places farther afield as well. In the early part of the twentieth century in the Owens Valley, water resources were siphoned off by Los Angeles, profoundly altering the lives of the Owens Valley Indian population. The story of the decimation of Owens Lake is well documented, but not usually from the perspective of the Indians of the area. In the words of Bertha Moose, an elder interviewed at Big Pine in the Owens Valley:

> When LA bought out the land, they took everything. They took the water, and then we didn't have the seeds like we used to do. We used to eat the seeds and use the willows for making the baskets, and then things were all drying up. So now we only have some pine nut trees.[32]

Coso Hot Springs was fenced off at roughly the same time as the Yucca Mountain region. Like the shared areas of Yucca Mountain, the Coso Hot Springs were used as a resource and spiritual commons by different Indian tribes for a variety of purposes and, most importantly, for healing. But like many commons throughout the world, they were withdrawn for use by those who appropriated the land and fenced them out—in this case, by the China Lake Naval Weapons Center. As Esteves remembers:

> The Navy wanted to get the Indian people off of their land, not to be hunting out there anymore, not to be taking their horses out there, and were telling them to move their horses and they [Indians] weren't going to do that, of course, and that's when they clashed with the Navy and has been clashing with the Navy for a long time. And it's still ongoing, not in the same way, not really clashing [now] but talking with the Navy.
>
> But in those days they had big problems with the Navy because what the Navy were doing was building fences and, of course, when you build fences, you can't use the land. And from this side, of course, that was the entrance into Coso. And so that's what happened. First they was telling them that they could no longer use their lands because it was all Navy, and then they expanded into Coso and we were told not to be going in there, that it was all Navy, and then finally—a few years ago—they started to do the geothermal operations there, and when they started to do that there was various meetings among the Indian people protesting it.[33]

Keep in mind that this "closing of the commons" occurred relatively recently—only forty to fifty years ago.

Today, when Indian tribes want to hold ceremonial gatherings at Coso Hot Springs, they must undergo an elaborate process of government supervision and clearance. The rules and regulations attached to their visitation rights (granted by the nearby Naval Weapons Center) make them furious, but not as much as the devastation of the Hot Springs by the Navy's geothermal operations there. According to Gaylene Moose:

> Then you've got to have permission. You've got to have permission from the Department of Energy, or the military, and then you have to have your

Social Security number, your name, your license number, everything just to go in there and use the spiritual grounds that was there for the Indian people.

Now it's destroyed! Them putting those geothermal energy things up. You can't even get into the ponds and soak anymore like you used to. Or heal. Because it's so hot that the buildup is just making those ponds bubble up! I was there last month. It's even scary to walk on the ground anymore. The holes are drying up, the clay's getting so hard that it's like boom! like a bomb going off. The ground is shaking, the ground's got burned crust where you're scared to walk, and now it's just really scary. I think it's just from the buildup from them taking the energy up higher. But the lower ponds are just exploding because of the air. One of the holes sounds like a big jet. It's the air, the hot air, and now it sounds like a big jet.

We stayed the night, and the ground that we slept on was hot, warm. In our tents it was warm, the ground was warm. So you can see what they've done to it. The only way some of the elders soaked was to allow the water to bubble out and cool, and then that's how they got to it. They made little ponds for themselves. But it's just, it's not like it used to be.[34]

Esteves described the visitation procedures this way:

Then before we know it, we hear that an agreement was made, that we were only supposed to be escorted in [to Coso], and we kind of thought that rather funny. We were to be escorted in like little children so we could be watched over and all that.[35]

Treating the Indians like "little children," of course, recalls a familiar paternalistic pattern of colonialist practices throughout the world where identification of the native population as children calls for oversight by the paternalistic colonialist power, legitimating appropriation of land and resources.

In nearby Death Valley, during this same period (the '30s and '40s), more water places were taken, this time by the National Park Service. However, rather than being fenced out, the indigenous Timbisha Shoshone were fenced in. They were corralled into what the National Park Service calls a "squatter village" outside of Furnace Creek. This process of colonization continues to the present. I spoke with Pauline Esteves at the

Timbisha Tribe's "squatter" community in Death Valley for hours in her mobile home—coffee boiling on the stove, prayer hoop in the kitchen window. She told me how the Timbisha were considered squatters:

> I don't know if you know or not, but we are federally recognized like I said, but we don't have a land base. We're known as "squatters" here.
>
> We've been squatting for, oh ever since we've been here. They've attempted to move us, but we've told them if they don't like us, they can move on. We were here before them. Thousands of years. There are [archaeologists] saying they've got us marked down in four different periods of time. We're finally in the Shoshonean period. [Lots of laughter.] I can't believe how they do this!

Esteves went on to tell how the Timbisha tribe recently alarmed even environmentalists by requesting to be included in the Desert Protection Act of 1994.

> At first [U.S. Senator] Feinstein and some of the people balked, especially the Department of the Interior. They were shocked when we said we wanted a land base within a national park and on its exterior boundaries which we also recognize as our original homelands. We recognize it *all* as our original homelands. They said "Those people must be crazy!" Within the National Park, you know! [Lots of laughter] So it's crazy.[36]

The Coso Hot Springs, Death Valley, and the greater Yucca Mountain region are sites of a larger set of land-based cultural struggles that concern this portion of the militarized and nuclear landscape. In fact there is a whole web of springs with traditional importance to the Indian peoples of this arid land that together form an Indian landscape beneath the militarized zone. This network of springs will become more visible when we look directly at Indian representations of the landscape in following chapters.

The pattern of land appropriations in this region begins to take shape and provide historical coordinates from which to chart Indian occupation and history in the now forbidden zones. Los Angeles takes the Owens Valley from the Owens Valley tribes and the other occupants of the valley; China Lake Naval Weapons Center takes Coso Hot Springs, the Coso

Range, and much more from the Owens Valley tribes, the Timbisha Shoshone, and other surrounding tribes; the U.S. Air Force and the Atomic Energy Commission take the Nevada backcountry from the Western Shoshone and the Southern Paiute; and the National Park Service takes Death Valley from the Timbisha Shoshone, making them squatters on their own homeland. All of this happened in the first half of the twentieth century, and represents only the middle section of Zone Two of the nuclear wasteland.

This brief sketch of Indian occupation in the greater Yucca Mountain region takes us into the middle of the twentieth century, when the land was appropriated for use as a nuclear-testing arena, a weapons-testing arena, and a national park, a time not in the far distant past, knowable only by interpretation of Indian artifacts, but a recent history whose threads of imperialism extend back into the nineteenth century.

Though tragic, this history is not only one of victims and conquerors. As Western Shoshone historian Steven Crum has pointed out, Indian people in this large area should not be seen only as passive agents. When they were encroached upon, they resisted; and when they were forced to assimilate, they modified their own assimilation in a variety of ways. Although the social and environmental impact on Indian people in Zone Two of the nuclear landscape—a region including the Nevada Test Site, Nellis Air Force Range, Yucca Mountain, China Lake Naval Weapons Center, Ward Valley low-level nuclear-waste dump and other imposing institutions—is severe and the military and government agencies in this region are immensely powerful, many Indian people have actively resisted them, and continue to do so today, even while being pushed to the margins of their boundaries.

·8·

Aboriginal Homeland

How beautiful is our land
how beautiful is our land,
forever, beside the water, the water,
how beautiful is our land.

How beautiful is our land,
how beautiful is our land,
Earth, with flowers on it, next to the water,
how beautiful is our land.
—IMAA HUPIA (The Early Morning Song)
  Western Shoshone song[1]

Barren, remote and of limited intellectual appeal, Yucca
Mountain in far southern Nevada is fast becoming the
world's most intensely studied piece of real estate.
—SCIENCE[2]

The Cultural Politics of Difference

The above evocations of desert lands starkly illustrate the disparity
between different cultures' views of the same region. Juxtaposition of
Western scientific and Indian perspectives of Yucca Mountain and of the
desert in which it resides bring into sharp contrast different narratives
concerning what constitutes not only historical truth but natural fact in
the nuclear landscape. Highlighting this contrast allows westerners to see
an alternative landscape, to reconsider the legitimacy of each way of representing the natural world. That this region might appear as something
other than barren, empty, and remote lets Euroamericans see how they
might approach it as something other than land fit only for disposal of
nuclear waste. Although worlds apart, the two perspectives with which
this book is concerned—Shoshone and Paiute and, for lack of a better

term, Western scientific—have each created a set of understandings, an ecology, that defines its own relationship to the natural world. They are both constructed out of social (including political) contexts. This chapter, in conjunction with the next one, highlights some of the differences between the belief systems and knowledge practices that inform each ecological perspective.

As a methodological strategy, a comparative cultural analysis of different ecological knowledges disrupts dominant discourses on nature. Though environmental science remains a powerful and useful narrative, it is subject to cultural and political influences beyond scientific inquiry itself. At the same time, the environmental sciences hold virtually absolute power of representation in this particular terrain. To whatever extent scientific accounts may be legitimate in their own right, they are—like Indian accounts—not without cultural biases and cultural foundations. When Euroamerican scientific representations are not automatically aligned with fact and Native American representations with "fiction" or myth (seen as false knowledge), a very different view of the contested landscape emerges, and Indian constructions of nature become equally legitimate narratives. Like scientific narratives, Indian narratives are practices for shaping partial and consequential knowledge.

Differences

Of the many differences between the two cultural perspectives one of the most fundamental is that which exists between a primarily oral-based culture and a text-based culture. Orality, like literacy, is a mode of communication about the world that has unique characteristics. Unlike textuality, it requires embodied transmission of knowledge through speech. For the Western Shoshone and Southern Paiute, knowledge about the environment was conveyed orally for thousands of years before the relatively recent introduction of printed texts into their cultures. Prior to contact with Euroamericans (and even long afterward), the central form of transmitting knowledge about the natural world came from elders who claimed direct communication with that world. Thus, for the purposes of understanding the traditional Western Shoshone and Southern Paiute relationship with the environment, it is useful briefly to examine some oral-based stories, tales, and songs. These provide (among other things) a "mytho-graphic" map of the landscape. Here, Indian place-names and traditional activities associated with particular places depict an alternative landscape. Such stories describe movement through the landscape and how the land-scape was created. They portray a geography different from that which is articulated through Euroamerican texts and electronic representations, through grid-based maps, computerized models, infrared photographic images, and earth sciences such as geology or hydrology.

A related and equally significant difference between the two cultures concerns the concept of the self and its relationship with the nonhuman world. For traditional Western Shoshone and Southern Paiute people of this region, this relationship is characterized by what Western philoso-phers term *intersubjectivity*. The natural world is perceived as possessing a level of subjectivity that Euroamericans usually grant only to other humans. Elements in the natural world are thus traditionally accorded respect and consideration as autonomous entities, endowed with "voices" that particularly gifted individuals can hear. This intersubjective relation-ship manifests in ritual and religious practices. It also manifests materially in traditional stewardship practices. Ethnoecologists have shown how "indigenous" plant species have been able to survive to the present day only because of interventions by indigenous people of this region. In other words, both human and nonhuman communities have sometimes evolved *together* for mutual survival over a 10,000-year history.[3] As noted in the preceding chapter, this exceptionally long land tenure has also had a pro-found impact on Western Shoshone and Southern Paiute ecological per-spectives and environmental practices.

Often relying on memories of their grandparents' stories, the voices of Indian elders in this chapter reflect the fragility of their perspective. Obvi-ously, colonization has taken its toll. Nevertheless, a distinctive Western Shoshone and Southern Paiute ecological ethos continues to exist today. For many Indians, this ethos isn't exactly the same as that of their elders or the elders of two generations ago, but neither is it altogether different. In some cases it has become part of their highly synthetic world view—which fuels their activism for land rights and makes use of Western modes of communication, such as faxes, computers, and the English language, to communicate that world view.

Isolating Traditional Indian Perspectives

Out of necessity, the Western Shoshone, Southern Paiute, and Owens Valley Paiute have adjusted to many Euroamerican traditions, economic orientations, values, customs, and habits. To suggest that there is an Indian socioecology, or an Indian ecological ethos, outside of the reality of this culturally synthetic world is both accurate and misleading. And, of course, like all cultures, the Indian world is made up of differently situated people (and groups of people) with different historical experiences, so that—even if it could be isolated from Euroamerican influences—a single monolithic "Indian" conception of nature would not exist. While Indian tribes in the Yucca Mountain region have adopted many Euroamerican ways, they have also altered their own assimilation to form a synthesis of the two cultures. But this cultural synthesis is not a seamless weave. It does not necessarily produce a coherent alternative the way the colors blue and red, for example, produce violet. It's more messy, patchy, and stitched together—as when Paiute elders break into their native tongue in the middle of an English sentence during an interview. While some Indian people speed along the information highway, others may work in silver mines during the week and lead sweat lodges at weekend ceremonial gatherings. In either case, traditional forms of knowledge and daily practices often persist intact in recognizable forms.[4] Traditional practices and beliefs—that is, those handed down from precontact times—can be as much a part of contemporary Indian people as are assimilated customs and beliefs. For instance, from listening to elders talk I came to see that many of them (while they have assimilated in numerous respects) continue to inhabit a world animated by *Puha*, perceived as "sacred," informed by visions and dreams, ordered by Indian ceremony and ritual, and governed by what some Indians call "natural law." While this distinctively different perception of the environment often accompanies a patchy knowledge about "ecosystems" and the "science" of natural resource management, it also remains identifiably unique—so that one can begin to articulate an "Indian ecology" distinct from Western scientific ecosystems ecology.

The following accounts emphasize what Indian people themselves call the "traditional" perspective. Once this is established we will see how it combines with other—Euroamerican—representations of nature to form a rich and versatile (and successfully assembled) ecological knowledge.

Indian Geography and Mythopoetic Knowledge

> Our history is not what has been written in books. Our history is in the Creator's belongings: the rocks and the mountains, the springs and in all living things.[5]

In the previous chapter I argued that a unique ecological perspective exists among the Indian inhabitants of the Yucca Mountain region and that this perspective grew out of a long land tenure. In thus historicizing Indian ecology, I linked what I term an ecological ethos to the material conditions of survival. Similarly, by emphasizing the oral quality of Indian discourses on the environment, I hope to avoid naturalizing the Indian ecological perspective. As a cultural, not a natural, phenomenon, the Indian ecological ethos sheds some of its romantic trappings, but not its difference. The oral quality of Indian ecological communication as reflected in stories, songs, and tales demonstrates that the way Indians view the landscape is mediated by their cultural heritage, not that their culture is informed by an Edenic, prelapsarian proximity to the natural world, as our Judeo-Christian heritage might have it.[6]

As narrative techniques the story and the song reveal crucial elements in the transmission of knowledge about the environment and the place of humans within the environment. Such communications are not quaint, entertaining "fairy tales" or myths only; they also serve as pedagogical tools for the transmission of ecological and social precepts and moral action—"right living." Though often highly entertaining and amusing, Shoshone stories, not unlike German fairy tales, serve often as cautionary narratives. Unlike their German counterpart, however, Indian tales are not so much about what dangers lurk within the natural world but instead what comes from transgressing what some Indians call "natural law"—a concept I will explain more fully later in this chapter.

Stories that require oral techniques for the retention of knowledge often appear to Western literate minds as the stuff of tall tales, verse, music—anything but serious knowledge. In fact such techniques are essential for the retention of knowledge and information in oral cultures. Rhythm, patterns, repetition, alliterations, formulary expressions in standard thematic settings, such as the Coyote and Wolf tales and the like, act as "memory systems" intertwined with serious thought and at times valuable ecological insights.[7] The combination of knowledge (such as seasonal environmental change, the medicinal properties of plants, and so on) with moral instruction also differentiates traditional Western Shoshone and Southern Paiute perspectives on the environment from Euroamerican science. Jean-François Lyotard sees this combination of "factual" knowledge and moral instruction as characteristic of oral-based forms of knowledge and identifies it as "narrative knowledge." Contrasting it with scientific knowledge, Lyotard sees narrative knowledge as "a question of competence that goes beyond the simple determination and application of the criterion of truth."[8]

Different perceptions influence the creation of different landscapes.[9] Where the print-mediated world view of Western desert travelers (and of Western science) often produces a discourse on barren wasteland, the oral narratives of indigenous inhabitants often depict the land's life-sustaining and healing properties. Frederick Turner, in *Beyond Geography*, describes the way in which the Judeo-Christian emphasis on the book and recorded history reinforces the separation from nature and inscribes the struggle against nature in the pioneer mentality that saw in the West an empty "terra incognita"—a wilderness to be conquered, settled, and civilized.[10] In sharp contrast, orally transmitted stories by descendants of the original inhabitants of that "wilderness" reveal a landscape teeming with springs, food sources, and medicines; a land alive with animal life, spirits, and power. In short, recorded history literally inscribes itself on our perceptions of the land.

The Storied Land

In contrast to the historicized landscape of settler discourse, the Southern Paiute refer to the extended region around Yucca Mountain as "The Storied Land" or *Tuwiiny aruvipu*. It is the home of mythic entities like Wolf and Coyote, whose primary place of habitation is the sacred Spring Mountains where Charleston Peak—called *Nuvagantu*—is said to be the Southern Paiute's place of origin, only twenty-five miles from Yucca Mountain.[11] Along with the Southern Paiute, the Western Shoshone, including the Timbisha Shoshone in Death Valley, and the Owen's Valley Paiute are also the people of Wolf and Coyote—people of the "Trickster Tales."[12] Like the sacred site of *Nuvagantu*, the Timbisha's homeland is very near Yucca Mountain, only 30 miles away. In fact the Timbisha are the closest tribe to the Yucca Mountain Project installation. The Timbisha's (or Tumpisattsi's) descriptions of their homeland—only recently recorded by the tribe itself—offer non-Indians a way to begin to understand this region from the perspective of the "Storied Land."

> The *Tumpisattsi* live in their valley where their ancestors have lived since the time of Creation. Some archaeologists have written that our ancestors came here less than one thousand years ago from the Great Basin, but we learned differently. It was told by the old ones that Coyote brought the people to this place in his basket. When he fell asleep, the people crawled out of the basket and went away in all four directions. This happened at *Wosa* (Coyote's "burden basket"), now called Ubehebe Crater on the maps of the [Death Valley] Monument.
>
> Our history is not what has been written in books. Our history is in the Creator's belongings: the rocks and the mountains, the springs and in all living things. The old ones taught us that Coyote did not leave the people until he finished his job and traveled through *Tupippuh Nummu* ("our homeland"), naming all the places for the people to use for places to stay and to obtain all they needed.
>
> At the places that Coyote named for them, the *Nummu* found a good living in their homeland.
>
> —*The Timbisha Shoshone Tribe and Their Living Valley*[13]

Although this record is obviously a text, its source is a tale "told by the old ones," and meant only to be spoken. It mythologizes a prominent feature of the landscape as the place of origin, but it also marks out the Timbisha's homeland as that which sustains life and provides the material conditions for their continued existence. And because it addresses and "corrects" the written archaeological record of the tribe's origins, this story stands as a defiant statement directed to not only the Department of the Interior (via the National Park Service) who corralled the tribe into a forty-acre plot, but to the scientific community as well.

Until 1933, when the Interior Department took possession of Death Valley, the Timbisha Shoshone enjoyed an expansive movement across the desert terrain and into the adjoining mountains. As evident in the quotation above, this terrain is often expressed in animistic and mythopoetic language, as well as in terms of use value. In this way, cultural origins and the history of Indian occupation and use are mapped geographically through oral recitation. (The Timbisha's recently written account is largely in response to unrelenting suppression of their presence by the National Park Service.) Using traditional stories, the Timbisha's strategy here has been to remap, and thus "reclaim," land that Euroamericans have appropriated with pioneer names and narratives as well as "scientific" archaeological interpretations of cultural artifacts. In those instances where Euroamericans have retained Indian words as place names, their original meanings are usually lost. For instance, most people aren't aware that the place name "Inyo" (the county in which Death Valley resides) is a Paiute word meaning "Dwelling place of the Great Spirit"—indicating a sacred geography beneath the pioneer legacy of death and the struggle against nature that Western histories commemorate. In contrast to pioneer narratives, Indian movement through the landscape as depicted in tales and orally transmitted stories reveals a mythical-spiritual dimension to the ethos of sustainability discussed in the previous chapter. Timbisha accounts, stories, and songs describe pathways that lead to good camping sites where berries, seeds, rabbits, bighorn sheep, prickly pears, "honey-sweet" mesquite beans, and fresh water can be found. Not coincidentally, many of these are also sites of spiritual significance imbued with *Puha* (power). For instance, *Tumpitina*, now called Nevares Spring, was a place of healing and dance, as well as a place to hunt bighorn sheep.

Although Euroamerican histories depict a pioneer environment of hellish character, the pamphlet titled "The Timbisha Shoshone Tribe and Their Living Valley" provides an alternative narrative map (enhanced with photographs). Directed toward tourists visiting the valley, this pamphlet uses Indian place names to describe Indian uses of the landscape. The very same land that appears to non-Indians as a *terra incognita* and as hostile wilderness suddenly assumes a life of its own with inhabitants of long standing. Veils of meaning made heavy with Euroamerican cultural signs of death (Death Valley, Funeral Mountains, Devil's Golf Course, Hell's Hole, Coffin Canyon, Dante's Inferno) fall away to reveal a "Living Valley" of fresh water springs, abundant fauna, and edible flora. Other place names are stripped away as well. Wildrose campground and spring becomes *Suunapatun* ("Where the willows are growing"); Ubehebe Crater becomes *Wosa*, Coyote's "burden basket," the Timbisha origin site; Travertine Spring becomes *Potoin* or *Poto'inna*; Emigrant Spring becomes *Papikku*; and so on. Making a dry land life-sustaining, springs are everywhere present. As the Timbisha note:

> Before outsiders changed our valley, it was described in the names of the places that were important for our survival here. Many are the names of springs. If the Manly Party, who traveled across our valley in 1849, had known our stories and trails, they would have found water, and *Tumpisa* ("red rock") might not be known as a Valley of Death.
>
> The water from *Potion* or *Poto'inna* (shown on the Monument maps as Travertine Spring) used to flow down what is now called Furnace Creek Wash into the mesquite groves just to the south. There were also smaller channels. There was enough water for many animals and migrating birds.
>
> *Suunapatun* ("where willows are growing"), is now the location of the Wildrose campground and spring. It was an important place to go in the summer for food. People could get rabbits there, as well as gather berries and seeds. The canyon goes from the spring up into our good pine nut gathering place.[14]

Significantly, this pamphlet is not available at the national park's Visitor's Center bookstore, although plenty of books on pioneer life are available. Since the Timbisha don't have the money for more printings, the pamphlet—the only "voice" of the contemporary Indians native to the valley—has been discontinued. Locked into land-use struggles with the Timbisha, the Death Valley Park Service is apparently uninterested in promoting recognition of its only native tribe. Indeed, the National Park Service prefers a version of history that usually erases the tribe from current occupancy.

Ethnoecologists have commented on the mythopoetic character of place names and how they reflect "conspicuous environmental conditioning."[15] As noted by anthropologist Catherine Fowler, whose work was informed by Indian consultants at Yucca Mountain between 1986 and 1988:

> Animal progenitors. . .[w]ere considered to be "bosses," "owners," "masters," "beautiful progenitors" of present-day species. Each set the course for its

species, and at the same time set human customs through a series of adventures and misadventures. Particularly active in this period were Coyote and Wolf, often portrayed as dueling brothers, but also Mountain Lion, Badger, water beings such as Frog, raptorial birds, and a host of others. Their activities, myth-specific, were mapped onto the landscape in a myriad of place-names, often associated with individual features of the geography such as rock formations, specific caves or springs, petroglyph and pictograph panels, trails, washes or arroyos, and much more. People [Indians], even today if they have been properly instructed, cannot move about the landscape without thinking of and feeling these links to the past. They also feel the power emanating from these specific features as well as more generally.[16]

In addition to specific use-value-oriented mythographic mapping found in place names (exemplified by the Timbisha's use of place names), Shoshone and Paiute tales offer interpreters another narrative thread to follow—one that supports the claim that Indian people's experience of the Great Basin and Mojave Desert region is marked by cooperation with the environment and not a pioneering mythical struggle against nature. While Timbisha Shoshone mapping relates place names to specific activities and tends to localize environmental characteristics, Shoshone and Paiute mythological tales tend to be more general in nature, effectively resisting the urge to "possess" the landscape by incessant naming of places and things. These tales focus more on moral instruction—what constitutes socially correct behavior *vis-à-vis* the natural world.

The tale "Coyote Learns to Fly" provides a good, if complex, example of moral instruction related to the environment.[17] In this tale, the nasty "Sky Boys" wantonly kill Coyote's nephew, Mountain Sheep Boy, without needing to eat him. Even worse, they leave the carcass to rot despite Mountain Sheep Boy's dying wish that they "use him." Coyote plots revenge, and his brother, Wolf, helps by giving him some sinew. Coyote gives the sinew to Spider, who uses it to spin a web over the "skyhole" that then entraps the Sky Boys when they come down to earth for water, allowing Coyote to exact revenge by killing them. One "moral" suggested by the tale (there are many) would seem to be to warn young hunters that they should kill only to obtain food, and not merely for the thrill of the hunt. In so doing, they should make use of every part of the animal, including the offal (the sinew).[18] This phantasmagorical tale, with its many events and levels of meaning, arises out of the problematic that humans face in killing animals with whom (in the Indian view) they are related.[19] Another tale, called "Eagle Hunting," offers perhaps a simpler example of a "ecological" moral: A man falls to death as he attempts to obtain eagle feathers from a nest. Clearly this suggests that disturbing eagles in their nest is not the proper way to obtain feathers.

Traditionally told by "old men" in the wintertime, the tales persist to this day and are told by men and women of various ages.[20] As noted by Catherine Fowler, although there are few Western Shoshone living today "who can tell the tales in their native language . . . some younger people are helping to perpetuate the traditions by telling the stories in English. They, too, add considerable style, humor, and grace to their presentations."[21]

Together, narrative place name maps of the local landscape (such as those used by the Timbisha to inform the traveler of food and water sources) and the Trickster Tales (featuring a host of animal characters, but especially Coyote and Wolf) help in forming a picture of the region's native socioecological ethos. They provide "proper instruction in human behavior and interrelationships" (Fowler, 1990), including the relations between humans and nonhumans, as well as geographic information for long-term survival.

It should be noted that the Trickster Tales and other stories are not reducible to environmental "realities" or determined by environmental conditions. Such deterministic approaches are too limited in scope and have been rightfully criticized. Neither should the tales and other ceremonial practices be viewed functionally only—as that which "stabilizes peoples' relationships with their ecosystems" so that culture itself becomes a self-regulating system reflecting that of the natural ecosystem around it.[22] Recognizing the problems of such functionalist anthropologies, one must still acknowledge the importance of the tales in transmitting knowledge about the environment. They have functioned in this manner, although not only in this manner.

By approaching these myths and stories as sources of knowledge about the land, non-Native people can begin to appreciate a different lived environment than the *terra incognita* of the pioneer histories or the wastelands of scientific discourse, where this desert region stands at the bottom of a hierarchically organized and economistic productivity register. Knowledge of this other landscape has been preserved through a specifically oral tradition. If the oral transmission of knowledge—the oral mode of communication—is lost, as it threatens to become, we risk losing a unique cultural perception of this landscape. In this region, a geography of sacrifice includes sacrifice of oral-based forms of perception and knowledge, further contributing to our understanding of "nuclear colonialism."

Intersubjectivity and Ecological Ethos

Long used by the Western Shoshone as a "sacred place" for ceremony, song, visions, and healing, Rock Creek (*Bah-tza-gohm-bah* or "otter water") in Northern Nevada is a clear, clean watercourse flowing through an ancient canyon. It is fed by natural springs in the middle of an otherwise arid Great Basin desert.[23] During a visit there in the spring of 1994, I witnessed Western Shoshone ranging from preteens to elders in their late nineties participating in sweat lodges, healings, song, and dance. Unlike the antinuclear protests at the Nevada Test Site, the Rock Creek gatherings are attended mostly by Indian people, not whites.

As in the Yucca Mountain region, the water itself serves as the focus of cultural and spiritual activity at Rock Creek. People entered the creek for healing purposes as a kind of baptism after ceremonial sweats, which were conducted at least twice daily, in the morning and late afternoon. Full of chanting in the Shoshone language, these cathartic ceremonies echoed with prayers directed toward both the human and nonhuman worlds. Elders too frail to endure the sweat itself participated by strategically stationing themselves outside the sweat lodge at the four directions.

In addition, sunrise circle dances formed part of the ceremonial activities. These dances, which are simple but require coordination and cooperation with one's neighbors, began before dawn and lasted until the sun came over the canyon walls, accompanied by the drumming and chanting of Shoshone Spiritual Leader Corbin Harney. For the benefit of the uninitiated Harney described how the syncopated stomping of the dancers, traditionally performed by Indian ancestors in the late winter, served to gently shake the earth awake, beginning the regenerative processes of Spring. Describing these rituals and practices, he was later quoted as saying:

Wherever you go, in places like these, there are spirits out there trying to hold themselves together. We are the ones with the voices, and we have to talk to those spirits, and so that's what we're doing by having our spiritual gatherings. When we get together and pray and talk to the spirits of everything that's out here for a few days, then the spirit is happy. The water is happy. The air is happy, and so on. This practice is very important to the people. [We have to] keep this spirit alive here, so it will have a voice and keep talking to us and helping us. That part is very important to us all. . . .

People were brought here because this is medicine water. It's a medicine canyon, a medicine rock, and medicine water.[24]

For Corbin Harney, the natural environment is, as his words suggest, his "medicine." Reciprocally, it is the voices of the people—in prayer—that enable the nonhuman environment (also understood as "the spirits") to "hold themselves together"—that is, to maintain health. In his role as the Western Shoshone Spiritual Leader Harney serves as a link—an intermediary—between the nonhuman world (nature) and the human community. As David Abrams has pointed out, this role is articulated in the shaman's special ability to communicate not with the "supernatural" (as Euroamericans so commonly misunderstand it) but with the fully "natural:"

The traditional or tribal shaman, I came to discern, acts as an intermediary between the human community and the larger ecological field, ensuring that there is an appropriate flow of nourishment, not just from the landscape to the human inhabitants, but from the human community back to the local earth. By his constant rituals, trances, ecstasies, and "journeys," he ensures that the relations between human society and the larger society of beings is balanced and reciprocal.[25]

For the Western Shoshone people, Harney does, in fact, act as just such an "intermediary." He speaks of his communications with rocks, water, ashes, insects, birds, and plant life, relaying messages from these animals and elements (and from the spirits within them) back to his tribe. Significantly, Corbin Harney did not learn to speak English until he was in his late thirties. Because he "ran away" from the "cruel" Euroamerican boarding schools of his youth, which tried to imprint "book learning" on him, he remaines uneducated in the Euroamerican tradition, and he describes himself as mostly illiterate.[26] In these ways he is closer to the oral culture of his Shoshone ancestors than many contemporary Western Shoshone. That Harney perceives himself to be (and is perceived by others to be) an intermediary between the natural and human worlds in part explains why he became an antinuclear activist and has led demonstrations against nuclear activities at the Nevada Test Site for more than a decade.[27]

If one "medicine" stands out in the natural world, for Harney, it is water. The metaphor of water as medicine runs throughout his speeches. It is an idea white people seem most easily to grasp. It is not exotic—it is ubiquitous, and crucial to survival.

In his crusade against nuclear activity in the Yucca Mountain/Nevada Test Site region, Harney has for years warned against the dangers of polluting the water:

> I never have spoken out until lately here, the Spirit coming to me and telling me, "Well, you are going to have to give us a hand here." It was in a vision, Water said to me, "I'm going to look like water, but pretty soon nobody's going to use me."

Harney's conversation with the water further demonstrates the intersubjective nature of the relationship he has with the natural elements. That the basis of that relationship is a kind of spoken dialogue or exchange reinforces the concept that it is the speaking subject that constitutes at least one side of the intersubjective experience of the natural world. It is not that oral cultures are by nature closer to nature (nonhuman nature) but that the mode of communication lends itself to an intersubjective relationship with what we in the West call "nature" (as other).

Not only their spiritual leader but many traditional Indian elders (and those of younger generations who follow "traditional" customs) perceive water in this landscape as a sacred cleansing and healing resource, as is beautifully expressed in the Indian elder's comment: "*Sometimes the water waves pray to the world.*" Whether water is perceived as a spiritual or a utilitarian element, even nonnatives recognize that water pollution is pollution of life. As Harney often says, water from plastic jugs bought at the grocery store isn't an adequate replacement, not for the body or the Spirit. Fear of water contamination is a recurring theme in Indian statements in cultural resource studies (Stoffle's and Fowler's) of Yucca Mountain. In Yucca Mountain environmental risk assessment questionnaires, Western Shoshone and Southern Paiutes expressed concern over how contaminated water would affect plants and animals as much as how it will affect humans, suggesting that a more reciprocal relationship exists between humans and nonhuman life than it does for many white people. Again, these concerns are articulated by Harney in prayers such as the following one, which he addresses to the water:

> Be pure and clean, so that when we use you, you keep us healthy, and so you can continue to be clean for us and all the living things.
>
> Make sure that when you come from within the earth, make sure you're clean. When we use you, when we drink you, make sure you give us strength and energy, and when we take a bath with you, I'm asking you, Water, to continue to give us a good feeling, with whatever we do with you, in whatever way we use you, so that all the living things, all the plant life, everything that uses you in any way, that everything can be clean.

The desire expressed in this prayer is not that of some mystical yearning for transcendence but a commonsense ecological ethos that even a hydrologist working at Yucca Mountain would find hard to fault.

Any consideration of Shoshone and Paiute ecological ethos, or environmental knowledge at Yucca Mountain, therefore, necessitates a consideration of water. In the Yucca Mountain area, as at Rock Creek, water (in all its geographic configurations) forms the basis upon which many cultural geographic maps are built. It is even deeply intertwined with subjective identity, as noted in the following passage:

> Not surprisingly, to desert people, water is exceedingly important. The morpheme *paa* (*pa-*, "water") is one of the most common in both the Western Shoshone and Southern Paiute language. It is found in countless place names (springs, areas with/without water, lakes, seeps, etc.); it also occurs in the related term for human and animal blood (SP: *pai*(<-)*pi*; WS: *paopi*).[28]

The importance of the springs and all water sources in the Yucca Mountain region ("found in countless [Indian] place names") cannot be overemphasized. Even though such watery oases are not readily seen by the casual traveler, their mere existence effectively argues against the wasteland discourse. In addition to Yucca Mountain's proximity to numerous springs clustered on all sides in the surrounding area, the mountain is located near the Amargosa River, an important "ephemeral" subterranean river running through the Amargosa Valley. In fact, Yucca Mountain rests upon the third largest aquifer in the United States (a deep regional aquifer extending from Utah down into Death Valley, California, and southern Nevada), as well as on top of a series of more shallow volcanic aquifers.[29] This is ecological knowledge that the Department of Energy downplays, but is, nevertheless, ubiquitous in Indian statements about the area.[30]

Obviously, the Yucca Mountain region is not wetlands, but neither is it devoid of water or water movement. In a practical sense, the existence of water in this desert environment is local knowledge. Of course, the Department of Energy knows about it, and the Yucca Mountain Project has teams of people studying it, but the general public outside the Amargosa Valley sees only the driest of landscapes. Discounting the presence of water in the region forms the underpinnings of the wasteland discourse. Knowledge based on intersubjective relationship tends to be local, although not all local knowledge comes from intersubjective experiences such as Corbin Harney's.

Listening to Indian descriptions of this region ultimately leads us to water. As the Timbisha say: "Many are the names of springs." Just as a dry desert wash leads to a canyon spring, Indian geography helps us to perceive a living environment. Water and its integrity surfaces time and again as the chief concern regarding nuclear practices in the desert, whether those practices include testing or waste burial. As one Indian consultant for the state of Nevada put it:

> The water worries me. There's an underground ocean under the Test Site, like the Amargosa River at Beatty, and there are artesian wells at Kimball and Springdale (in Oasis Valley). All of them had Indian names. None of that water is pumped. It just comes out of the ground. If they keep messing around in there, they'll murder the land they're living on by ruining the

water. Water is life. When they ruin that, they might as well just drain the juice out of their own system.[31]

Although it may seem ironic that in a desert environment water appears everywhere in the Indian perception of place, it also makes sense that water should be highly regarded because of its very scarcity. As noted earlier, what Stoffle calls the "core" areas of Indian habitation around Yucca Mountain (the Belted Range, Oasis Valley, and Ash Meadows) offered enough water to support numerous Indian villages. However, there are also springs that are less concentrated, dispersed to the east and north of Yucca Mountain, that were used seasonally by Indians when they had access to this region. As Stoffle notes:

> To the east and north of Yucca Mountain are several springs that were used by Native American people from pre-contact times to the 1950s. Some of these springs were occupied year-round, others seasonally, and still others on a regular but intermittent basis. These springs include *Tippipah Spring* and *Toboban Spring* on the slopes of Shoshone Mountain; *Cane Spring* on the slope of Skull Mountain; the *Ammonia Tanks, Captain Jack Spring, Whiterock Spring,* and *Oak Spring* around the southern end of the Belted Range; and numerous other smaller springs and water catchments.
>
> Some families apparently made their primary residence at one of these springs. Other families apparently resided at one of these springs only during the winter season. Still other families came to the area and used the springs only during the fall season to conduct rabbit drives on the flats, harvest piñon nuts in the mountains, and harvest wild grains at a variety of locations. A fall festival held in the Ammonia Tanks area in some years drew people to the area from Oasis Valley and elsewhere.[32]

(See Fig. 7.1 for the location of the arc of springs described here.)

Given the scarcity of water and its centrality for life in the region, a cultural map emerges that suggests a "sacred" geography—one defined and articulated by water sources. Water is present in tinajas (natural rock water containers), called *po?o* in Western Shoshone and *pikapo* in Southern Paiute (there are at least nineteen of these on Yucca Mountain alone);[33] it is present in fresh water springs, and in hot springs; and it is present invisibly (though suggestively) in dry washes or underground rivers, as well as in such ephemeral and elusive sources as creeks and seeps. Subterranean movement of water in this land can be perceived as linking all places to one another. Medicine people are said to travel from one spring to another via underground waterways, although such journeys require special powers and are considered dangerous.[34] "Water babies" are said to live in springs, so one must take care not to offend them or they may cause harm.[35] Most significantly, water is perceived as a major source of healing, as that which cleanses the body of impurities and renews life. In whatever form, in the desert, water *is* life. For the desert's indigenous inhabitants the tragic irony is that, if contaminated with radionuclides, water also becomes the vector of illness and death as it carries transuranic toxins to all parts of the landscape.

Indian descriptions of the healing properties of water are important in understanding the loss felt by Indian people over inaccessible or destroyed sources of water. As one Paiute elder comments on Coso Hot Springs: "Our grandparents used it as a bathing area and blessing. It's a very sacred place for our tribes. We've had it as a healing place. They believed it was a healing spirit that stayed at Coso."[36] And, as noted earlier by Pauline Esteves (quoting her mother's words): "We were told to get down into the mud and be cured and get purified and it's good for us and we won't have no bad dreams and we will be better people." One Paiute couple said simply: "Coso was a place to pray and be healed."[37] But as the Paiute man, Dewey Charlie, notes: "Coso is losing power because it is not free. It should be left alone for the Indians."[38] Recently, when the Navy allowed Indians of the area to visit the springs (for a day), the Indian pilgrims, as noted by one participant, "stopped first at a sacred hill, at Devil's Kitchen, which overlooked Coso Hot Springs. A spiritual man and four helpers climbed to the top of the hill to offer their prayers to the spirits. The elders in the group climbed the hill as far as they could manage, with the rest of the group remaining at the base of the hill to offer their prayers." Although mostly closed off from the Indian people who "feed the springs" by offering prayers and religious tokens, the springs continue—even today under military occupation—to elicit a sense of spirituality and obligation. Such water sources are marked by an intersubjective relationship with the land, a sense of reciprocity.

Like Coso Hot Springs and Rock Creek, the springs at Ash Meadows near Pahrump, Nevada, are regarded as "spiritual" places, healing places. "I remember when my dad took me over there to show me the hot springs when I had got sick for a whole week," said one Moapa Paiute elder. "I had to go in there and talk [with the springs] so I could get well. That's where he took me, so I could get well. . . . But like I say, they've taken them all away."[39]

One of the three important spring districts traditionally occupied by Indian people before Euroamerican appropriation (and shared, to some extent, after contact), Ash Meadows, today a National Wildlife Refuge in the southern end of the Amargosa Valley, stands as a testament to the beauty of these watered districts—oases that have become increasingly uncommon in the southwestern United States.

Like Rock Creek, the crystalline aqua-blue springs clustered at different points in Ash Meadows connote anything but wasteland. The springs are surrounded by lush green reeds rustling in the breeze, wildflowers with bees, watery grottoes, and bird life. Amid the deep desert silence, one hears the sound of water bubbling up out of the earth, gliding down hills in thin watery sheets, or coursing through the valley in creeks. The valley is alive with frogs, pupfish, lizards, coyotes, rabbits, and other creatures. According to an information sheet at the refuge, the valley "provides habitat for at least 24 plants and animals found nowhere else in the world. Four fishes and one plant are currently listed as endangered."[40] Ash meadows has a "greater concentration of endemic species than any other local area in the United States, and the second greatest in all of North America."[41] Each spring is an oasis in the desert and, with Mt. Charleston presiding, even the casual visitor can imagine its importance as a place of both sustenance and spirituality for the Indians of the past. It remains significant to the Indians of the present as well, although it is not accessible except within National Wildlife Refuge regulations, which bar camping or water use. Recently bought by the Nature Conservancy, Ash Meadows is in the process of being restored to its "natural" state, which, of course, does not include Indian people. Official natural histories of the area do not mention the area's significance as a site of *cultural* history, and recent history at that. Once again, Indian presence is eclipsed—this time by environmentalists, who, in writing "natural" histories, unwittingly contribute to the erasure of an oral-based culture.

It is no accident that Ash Meadows makes us conscious of the presence of water in the Amargosa Desert where Yucca Mountain resides. As the National Wildlife Refuge literature notes:

> The refuge is a major discharge point for a vast underground water system stretching 100 miles to the northeast [the direction of Yucca Mountain which is less than 20 miles away]. . . . Water bearing strata comes to the surface in more than 30 seeps and springs, providing a rich and complex variety of habitats. . . . Many stream channels and wetlands are scattered throughout the area. Mesquite and ash tree groves flourish near the wetlands, and saltbrush and creosote shrubs grow in the drier upland soils.

Together with Indian discourses of water babies and shamanic journeys through underground waterways, a picture emerges of a landscape not of isolated water sources but one connected *by* water—an integrated, if often invisible, nexus that permeates the land like capillaries (to use an organic metaphor). This network of moving water obstructs scientific validation of Yucca Mountain as safe for storage of high-level nuclear waste. Though this region is one of the driest in the country, it is still a place where water can move through fissures and faults deep within the earth.

Indian historical use and understanding of Yucca Mountain and its immediate region give rise to an alternative geography whose disparate spaces are woven into a single weave by a delicate network of watercourses and water places. From the core water districts (from Pahrump, Indian Springs, Oasis Valley, and Ash Meadows) extend trails and pathways that wind around, over, and through Yucca Mountain. Fortymile Wash forms a major access trail to the backcountry; other trails transect numerous washes and canyons in the area. For the Western Shoshone and Southern Paiute, this landscape is not, as the writer of *Science* magazine claimed, of "limited intellectual appeal." Nor is it "barren." It is an aboriginal homeland, a storied land, not a nuclear sacrifice zone—although it may be all three, simultaneously, in the near future. As the Timbisha say: "If the [Euroamericans who crossed the desert in the nineteenth century] had known of our stories and trails, they would have found water." Since they never bothered to ask, they found death.

Figure 8.1 Spring at Ash Meadows
At places like Ash Meadows, water "erupts" as springs in numerous places, revealing the vast underground water source in the region
Photo by Valerie Kuletz

Intersubjectivity

Intersubjective, direct communication with the nonhuman world—exemplified by Corbin Harney not only praying to but *talking with* the water (implying that the water experiences him as much as he experiences it)—should be understood as part of a parallel system of understanding the natural world that is not necessarily inferior to a Euroamerican science that objectifies the natural environment. Originating from a very different mode of communication for obtaining and transmitting knowledge—from a base of orality as opposed to literacy—it is different, not just less developed, than text-based knowledge systems.

Asserted by Claude Lévi-Strauss over thirty years ago, in his book ironically titled *The Savage Mind*, the perception of indigenous epistemologies as parallel forms of knowledge (as opposed to immature forms of knowledge) is not new. As Lévi-Strauss notes:

> [T]here are two distinct modes of scientific thought. These are certainly not
> a function of different stages of development of the human mind but rather
> at two strategic levels at which nature is accessible to scientific inquiry: one
> roughly adapted to that of perception and the imagination; the other at a

remove from it. It is as if the necessary connections which are the object of all science, Neolithic or modern, could be arrived at by two different routes, one very close to, and the other very remote from sensible intuition.

Myths and rites are far from being, as has often been held, the product of man's "myth-making faculty," turning its back on reality. Their principle value is indeed to preserve until the present time the remains of methods of observation and reflection which were (and no doubt still are) precisely adapted to discoveries of a certain type: those which nature authorized from the starting point of speculative organization and exploitation of the sensible world in sensible terms. This science of the concrete was necessarily restricted by its essence to results other than those destined to be achieved by the exact natural sciences but it was no less scientific and its results no less genuine. They were secured ten thousand years earlier and still remain at the basis of our own civilization.[42]

While I do not wish to infer (as does Lévi-Strauss) that Indian traditional knowledge is "science"—as though science is the field of truth upon which all epistemological practices must eventually come to rest if they are to be legitimate—Levi-Strauss's disruption of hierarchy and the common belief that modern science is part of a linear progression toward perfect knowledge marks a turning point in Western conceptions of indigenous cultures.

My use of the term intersubjectivity should not be equated with the various ways this term has been used in the branch of western philosophy known as phenomenology, particularly in the work of Husserl and Merleau-Ponty. However, there have recently been interpretations of Merleau-Ponty's work, particularly his later (unfinished) work, that show how Merleau-Ponty's direction in phenomenology resonate with what I have described as an indigenous ecological perspective. David Abrams's reading and reworking of Merleau-Ponty's writings is particularly promising in this regard. Abrams's work demonstrates that there do exist in western thought and terms the seeds of an understanding of the relationship with the nonhuman world similar to that of Native peoples. This may be one way non-Natives might begin to articulate a philosophy of sustainability.[43]

Western philosophy aside, the Native intersubjective relationship is characterized by a perception of the world as animate, a nonhuman world that is engaged in an active relationship with the perceiver of that world.

The human being is not separate from that world but both separate and part of it at one and the same time. The world takes part in the embodied, sensual perceiver and the perceiver in the existence of the world. That is, they are interconstitutive, they make each other. In this dynamic relationship both entities are continually in process, responding to one another; they are not static, unchanging, and dualistically separated from one another. My use of the term intersubjectivity here helps to describe the socioecological ethos found historically among many Western Shoshone and Southern Paiutes, and currently among the elders of the Yucca Mountain region.

Rather than romanticize Indian people as essentially closer to nature, I would suggest that their concern for, and feelings of responsibility to, the earth and its well-being is a byproduct of the traditional Indian recognition of humans as engaged in an intersubjective relationship with the nonhuman world. When Indian consultants in the Yucca Mountain cultural resource studies give offerings and prayers to specific sites (plants, rocks, or springs, for example) to which they have been taken for identification and interpretation purposes, they engage in a ritualized act of *reciprocity* with the natural world, an act reflecting a world view that sees the relationship between humans and nature as intersubjective. Similarly, when Indian people insist that they must actively care for a particular water source for it to continue to exist (in a healthy state), and, reciprocally, when they say that that water source must take care of them so that they can continue to live, their words bespeak an intersubjective relationship with the nonhuman world on the level of daily practice. Orality helps maintain this practice by facilitating communication between the human and nonhuman. When Indian people talk to and pray with nonhuman entities, and when they claim to listen and then hear what the "spirit" has to say in return, they recognize the self as interdependent with and inter-constitutive of the world outside the self. For example, Corbin Harney says: "I talk to rocks in my prayers. I ask the rocks, *Make sure that you are in such a way that we hear from you. Make your voices heard; make sure that I hear what you're saying.*"

Because orality tends to foster greater direct communication (and reciprocity, ritualized or not) between humans and nonhuman nature on a daily lived basis, it is not implausible to suggest that it may be orality that makes the intersubjective world view more accessible, or at least easier to achieve. Although language still mediates perception, and culture (through technologies developed to sustain survival) still shapes interaction with the environment, the lack of heavily codified binary systems of thought that are the hallmark of literate and especially print cultures makes possible a more unified, "holistic" world view animated by *Puha* or "spirit."[44] The natural world in oral cultures is perceived more directly by being in it; perception occurs by hands-on experience as opposed to the mediation of textual accounts, which presumes a distance between sender and receiver. For the Indian, the rock becomes more than an instance of a type—such as granite or feldspar—it becomes not only porous or smooth, but warm or cold, an entity in relationship to other phenomena—a snake's nest perhaps, or a lush outcrop of medicinal herbs—near and around it, or the whole intersubjective matrix of the perceiver herself who touches it, smells it, sees it, indeed, adds to it in myriad ways. It can—in this world—become a "power rock," as the Paiute elders suggested. In this world, the power rock is always given an offering, or the hot springs are always offered "ten flint" so that, in return, "the water waves pray to the world."

As environmental risk-perception studies of the Yucca Mountain Project underscore, Indians of the region view a "proper relationship" with the natural world as one not hierarchically organized in relation to the human being.[45] The animals, plants, rocks, and insects are perceived as being as important as human beings because they are interrelated within a matrix of mutually reinforced perceptions. Clearly, this is not a world view that produces a Great Chain of Being with humans near the top and all others below.

The intersubjective world view that appears to characterize certain Indian perceptions of the Yucca Mountain region does not radically separate the natural world from human existence (that is, it does not totally objectify it). Neither does it bespeak a perception of human existence as one that is completely absorbed into "nature" (without any consciousness of individuality).[46] Rather, it is a world view exemplified by interrelationship. Elements of the natural world are referred to as relations: "We have been born and raised here, the Mountains, and Valleys, with their Springs and Creeks, are our Fathers and Brothers."[47] Or, as a Shoshone song expresses it: "Song Woman/ Sits beating the rhythm of her song/ There in a distant place/ Next to her cousin, the water (Hupia waimpentsi/Hupia wentsetuih hainna/ Pennan napaatuintsi/ Okwaitemmayenten. . .).["]48

For Indian people of this region, a tradition of recognition of intersubjective relations with the earth symbolically constructs the earth as part of the cultural body (as noted in the examples above). The concept of "Mother Earth," while not unknown in Western cultures, is much more prevalent in contemporary Indian religious expressions. It can be viewed as a unitary metaphor that ties all relations within both the human and nonhuman worlds together in a truly "worldwide web."[49] Emphasis on relations between the people and the land helps explain why the loss of aboriginal homeland is perceived as the loss of Indian culture. Indeed, when their homelands are appropriated today the Western Shoshone don't just describe it as a "loss" but as "ethnic cleansing." The body politic, the cultural body, is the land itself.

"Natural Law," Puha, and Contracts with Nature

A number of metaphors used by Shoshone and Paiute elders in this region speak to a kind of ecological ethos that derives from intersubjectivity and the persistence of orality as a predominant mode of communication. These are the concepts of "natural law," and the practice of what one Paiute elder called "making contracts with nature." Both illuminate the reciprocity between the self and the natural (and often the spiritual) world. As one Paiute elder says:

> And the Indian people were doing spiritual things. They were *making a contract with mother nature* when they went out to get pine nuts! They say, "We're going to do this if you do this for us," you know, they were making all these little contracts. And the white people would just go in there and back their trucks into the trees and knock everything down [laughs], and do anything to it! And the Indians didn't do that. And that was the difference between the two races and that's why it was so hard! We still haven't gotten to a handshake, I don't think.[50]

To make a "contract with nature" implies an understanding of the self as capable of communication with nature, a nature that has a similar subjectivity, so that one can "communicate" with that nature. This composition of self and nature as intersubjective requires of the individual a set of responsibilities the likes of which Euroamericans usually understand as necessary only for "social" relations, and which are formalized as written documents. The Indian contract with nature, on the other hand, extends these responsibilities to the natural environment. In one interview with women from the Owens Valley Big Pine tribe, Bertha Moose recalled how her mother went out every morning at sunrise to "feed the Spirit." Responding to this, another Paiute elder said:

> Like I say, we were out making contracts, you know.
>
> The Indian ancestors weren't really saying: "Help me, help me, help me," and that was all. They were saying, "I'm going to do this if you [the spirit] do this." You know, and making contracts. And things like "I've been bad, and I want you to cleanse me from that bad, and I will do such and such . . ." But then we [the younger generation] didn't carry through with it. But they would say it every morning as the sun was coming up . . . And you know that kind of a spiritual thing, it's ingrained into even our children. They want to be sophisticated and be with the "now" generation, but still they come back, and they want to know who they are.[51]

To make a contract with nature, of course, is a metaphor, one that borrows from another culture the idea of a written contract to convey a sense of a binding agreement, one that abides. The tension between what we understand by the terms "nature" and "contract" allows a new meaning to emerge—one that is foreign to Western conceptions of having to dominate and subdue nature through conquest (in the pioneer sense), or control nature through science (in the Baconian sense).

The related concept of *natural law* also speaks to an ecological ethos. Not to be confused with natural law as law that has been naturalized by Western legal scholars, the Indian conception of natural law is a set of commitments that refers to a code of ethics for how human and nonhumans should conduct relations.

Characterized as "spiritual," the concept of natural law is founded upon a perception of the earth as animated by *Puha*, by spirit-power. This being the case, the earth cannot be owned by any individual. Though primary land use rights can be established, they differ from claims of private property. *Newe Segobia*, as the Shoshone say, is not for sale, because it cannot be owned. Obviously, many Indians and tribes now possess title to land and take part in the buying and selling of land. Indian tribes have historically occupied territories and have engaged in skirmishes over land access. Such land politics have occurred for various reasons and are different for various Indian communities. However, for the Indians of the Yucca Mountain region, while not without territorial boundaries, land use has traditionally been flexible, sometimes communal, and informed by a philosophy of inalienability, as explained in the following statement:

> And another thing about the land is that we consider it everybody's, you know. We don't say, "Well oh you got that place so you can take it as yours." We still don't have that mentality. We feel that it belongs to everybody. And I think maybe sometimes we should grab what we can and have something, but we don't. Like with the town of Big Pine. We have to work together to keep the town of Big Pine going and work with the white people! We have to work together because Big Pine doesn't have that much to draw people in. But we still have that little veil in there that separates the Indians and the white people.[52]

The Indian concept of "natural law" marks a fundamental difference with Euroamericans, who are seen to constantly transgress it. Natural law is the opposite of Western progress and materiality; the opposite of private property, of nature as resource only, and of incessant experimentation. As one Paiute elder notes:

> The white people have one set of values, and the Indians have another set of responsibilities to their own people. And the white people feel that you have to progress constantly. Whatever you find, you've got to improve it. No matter what it is, you either have to add to it or improve it or whatever. It doesn't matter if it's spiritual. They don't, I hate to say this, but White people are not very spiritual. They have looked all over the world for their religions, so they really don't have that thing about them. So what they're doing is doing material things and carnal things.[53]

Similarly, a Western Shoshone man comments on natural law as that which forbids certain kinds of experimentation on nature:

> You know, you don't tamper with making tomatoes bigger and brighter and redder and lasting longer. You don't try and make a pig-cow. You don't tamper with genetics. You don't do those insane things over there at the Nevada Test Site. You don't try to figure out how fast you can make a nuclear bomb explode, whether it's one ten thousands of a second faster, or two ten thousands of a second. Those things all violate natural law.[54]

In the outdoor laboratories of the Nevada Test Site and the Naval Weapons Center at China Lake, violations of natural law occur daily. The experiment that is the Yucca Mountain Project violates the Indian concept of natural law.

Another, somewhat different, description by a Western Shoshone man (and reiterated by other Western Shoshone I interviewed) identifies the concept of natural law more directly in contestation with Euroamerican "common law":

> Well, we have our way of looking at things, which is based on natural law. However, the Western world pretty much runs on a common law which came out of Europe and headed this way. It deals with commerce and a lot of other types of things. Our natural law, of course, is based on nature. And the threat to the law which the West uses (and the rest of the world, as a matter of fact) is that if they follow natural law then they have to recognize that indigenous peoples' beliefs and values and the laws by which they run their lives are the laws they must follow. And these are all the laws they [the white people] have been breaking for at least the last 500 years and probably the last 10,000 years. So natural law is really a threat to those people . . .[55]

Indeed, that Shoshone natural law can be transgressed so easily is, in part, because it is not codified, not written. It serves as a metaphor in the same way as contracts with nature, signifying not only a binding relationship but also a profoundly ethical one—one founded on respect for the integrity of the natural world.[56]

For the Western Shoshone in particular, the focus on natural law (explicitly codifying the concept) may well be a response to ongoing confrontation with a Euroamerican legal system that has been used to validate and legitimate land appropriation and outright theft, as exemplified by the recent "payment" by the United States for *Newe Segobia*.[57] To combat the powerful Euroamerican legal apparatus, Western Shoshone have rearticulated the unspoken, uncodified, background knowledge of the earth as sacred and inalienable (and, in this region, as Shoshone homeland and territory) into "natural law," Indian law. This move illuminates two things. First, it shows the flexibility and malleability of "culture"—that culture is not static but always changing in response to mutually transforming interrelationships with others. Second, the attempt to transform background commonsense knowledge into "law" is a move toward power, a move toward what Bourdieu calls "symbolic power."

Pierre Bourdieu identifies the differences between doxa (commonsense knowledge) and orthodoxy (codified knowledge) when examining the power of law in society.[58] In contradistinction to doxa, orthodoxy is the codification of doxa; it is background (usually unspoken) knowledge made explicit. Orthodoxy gives *authority* to commonsense knowledge. This move toward juridical language and power by the Western Shoshone is an attempt to play the game of law, an attempt to produce a legal codified structure necessary in their bid to combat the U.S. government's encroachments into their lands, perhaps exemplified most by their appeals to the 1863 Treaty of Ruby Valley. However, this move toward orthodoxy is problematic because it propels the Shoshone out of the world of orality and the authority of immediate presence, and into the world of literate significations open to different and unceasing interpretations of "natural law."

The problem, or contradiction, for the Western Shoshone is this: If the "sacred" quality of "natural law" is the result of powerful orally transmitted doxa and related action, then the Western Shoshone appropriation of Euroamerican conceptions of law as a strategy (making the sacred a written codified "law") may provide a tool to counter American legal claims, but it undercuts the spiritual authority of the orally transmitted background knowledge (what Derrida would call the metaphysics of presence).

It is unclear in this scenario what kind of compromise might be possible—that is, whether Indian people in this region, particularly the Western Shoshone, can maintain the knowledge and perception of certain aspects of traditional culture passed down as doxa, while simultaneously appropriating authority-granting structures such as legal orthodoxy in their struggle for existence as a culture. In this case, traditional doxa (the Indian subject as positioned within a "spiritual" earth) and contemporary orthodoxy (the Indian as subject to the authority of a law of the earth, or "natural law") each imply a different theory of the subject, which is inextricably tied to specific philosophies of justice. This move toward a kind of legitimacy, power, and authority vested in the written word may have a detrimental impact on traditional Indian subjectivity, which, I have argued, provides a unique model of intersubjective ecological ethos.

Aside from the complications in certain articulations of natural law, such terms and practices (making contracts with nature, reciprocity, the practice of actively communicating with the nonhuman) have their basis in an intersubjective perspective, which itself forms the foundation of what we can begin to see as a socioecological ethos characteristic of traditional Indian culture—particularly that of the elders—in this region. Intersubjectivity need not necessarily look like the traditional Indian rituals at Rock Creek in order to exist. Ecological ethos, based on intersubjective consciousness, is bound to take on a different character and appearance among different cultures. Thus, although Euroamericans can learn from traditional Indian people, imitation of traditional Indian ways won't necessarily give them the same experiential results.

Type, Trope, and Topos

Because most Euroamericans are situated primarily within a textual and literate world, how are we to understand Corbin Harney's talking with the rocks, or the statement "the water waves pray to the world," or even "making contracts with nature," without falling back on our cultural bias, which perceives such statements as "merely" fiction, poetic fancy, or just plain crazy—certainly not as legitimate articulations of nature and our relationship to it? Being so far removed from any oral traditions of our own, how can we grant legitimacy to the oral-based knowledge of the Indian elders of this region with their particular form of ecological ethos and intersubjective practice? Does an oral-based culture produce a more ethical, ecologically healthy perspective than a hypertextual one?

The relationship between orality and literacy, and between intersubjectivity and radical objectivity opens up possibilities for answers to these questions. While a number of critics have discounted the Indian ecological ethos as mere posturing, it should be evident from the discussion thus far that the role of metaphor in the organization of knowledge is central to any discussion of how the different epistemological worlds of orality and literacy convey and in some sense determine the socioecological ethos of a culture.

In this chapter, I have described the Indian ecological ethos as one that comes out of an intersubjective perspective. In turn, I have suggested that an intersubjective perspective may be easier to achieve within an oral-based culture. The connection between intersubjectivity and an alternative ecological ethos is clear: Not privileging the separation between subject and object disallows extreme objectification of nature. But what is the connection between orality and intersubjectivity? Why do people in oral cultures appear more easily to view the world from an intersubjective perspective? Perhaps it has to do with the fact that oral knowledge—that is, knowledge produced out of an oral culture—or what has been called "narrative knowledge" (Lyotard)—*embraces* metaphor when producing knowledge about the world. This approach can be distinguished from scientific knowledge, which, while also employing metaphor, does not embrace it, but rather uses it only because it must, to explain the unknown in terms of the known, and indeed tries to *constrain* it.[59]

Why is embracing metaphor as a central technique for describing the world important in the production of an intersubjective perspective? Metaphor, as many theorists have pointed out (particularly Ricoeur), conflates categories. Metaphor blurs boundaries. Its use fosters intersubjective perception because intersubjectivity requires the blurring of boundaries between subject and object. Concerning the intersubjective nature of ecological ethos: If we do not radically separate ourselves from the world (for instance, creating "nature" as objectified Other) we enter a realm of blurred boundaries—a poetical, metaphorical world.

Metaphor is central to the kind of mythological language that is found in oral cultures such as the Western Shoshone and Southern Paiute. We can see the conflation of categories most clearly in the case of the Shoshone and Paiute Trickster Tales. Coyote is both man and animal, and perhaps god, from a time when "men were animals." Certainly this appreciation of metaphor gives new meaning to the storied land as the land of lost borders. In the Trickster Tales the *play* of metaphor can be seen in its illegitimate couplings (Coyote as man and beast, Coyote consorting with his relatives). These couplings constitute not only the linguistic blurring of boundaries characteristic of descriptions of intersubjectivity but also the creative and playful articulations of the world that tend to expand in meaning (the entity is no longer just Coyote but also a human). The oral delivery of the tale also allows expansion; each telling is slightly different, with the teller often adding on to or altering the original tale to suit the occasion. The tales constitute a poetic knowledge as opposed to scientific knowledge.

Mythological knowledge, as used by the Southern Paiute and Western Shoshone, is not the only type of communication to employ metaphor. All communications about the world employ metaphor. Metaphor is essential to language, including what we call scientific language. However, metaphorical language is subject to different processes within different systems of constructing knowledge and to different modes of communication. Scientific discourse, residing in a textual world, must proceed rigorously in defining its metaphors to accomplish accurate representation, or at least communication of its meaning. The metaphors of scientific discourse, as opposed to mythological discourse, must be argued and continually redefined within the context of a particular discipline, which is layered, as it were, with numerous textual assertions until the metaphor (for instance, the scientific use of the metaphorical term "field") assumes a precise, or at least stable, meaning.[60] Interestingly, from this perspective we see that the Indian field of knowledge (while not voluminous compared to science) is structured to expand in meanings, while the scientific (voluminous compared to Indian tales) is structured to narrow meaning. Scientific meaning-making comes from ever-contracting written definitions symbolized in the typologizing of the object: Granite is a *type* of igneous rock.

The capacity for expansion, implied by metaphor, is often perceived as threatening to Euroamerican conceptions of rationality. Similarly, Indian communication with nonhuman objects opens up the possibility of multiple interpretations of what constitutes a significant site in the landscape, or historical fact. Such multiplicity clearly presented a problem for the archaeologists working on cultural resource studies at Yucca Mountain.

The question of irrational knowledge, and especially the fear of expanding meanings, including the polysemy of words, has been of interest to various Western philosophers, including certain strands of feminist philosophy (Irigary, Kristeva). The "slippage of the signifier" may be particularly vexing to textual cultures because of the absence of the speaking subject to explain, reinterpret, clarify—which is what the teller of the tale is capable of doing in an oral culture, that is, responding to the listener.

Merleau-Ponty perceives of the world of language—both oral and textual—as being founded upon a network of unspoken and unwritten commonsense knowledge that "precedes perception." Making meaning of this world, he posits, has proceeded along at least two paths: the path that constructs "geometrical space" and the path that constructs "mythical space," also called anthropological space. Anthropological space is characterized by a shrinkage in the space directly experienced, "a rooting of things in our body," a conflation of the subject with the object.[61] This is what I interpret as intersubjective space that blurs boundaries, and is thus best articulated by metaphor. It is in this world that one dreams, has visions, communicates with nonhuman nature, makes contracts with nature.

It is in this world—the world of mythological or anthropological space—that the Indian phrase "all my relations" can logically include nonhuman entities. This is the space, the landscape, wherein reciprocity is practiced with nonhuman entities; the space from which an ecological ethos might emerge based on mutual respect between the human and the nonhuman. Clearly, this world is threatening to Western sensibilities. The classic definition of schizophrenia is a world of totally blurred boundaries where outside objects are perceived as extensions of the body, where dementia can overcome even commonsense capacities to maintain one's own life, one's own survival. As Merleau-Ponty notes:

> What brings about both hallucinations and myths is a shrinkage in the space directly experienced, a rooting of things in our body, the overwhelming proximity of the object, the oneness of man and the world.[62]

This phantasmagorical, hallucinatory space of mythological perception coexists with, in fact is actually repressed by, what Merleau-Ponty calls "everyday perception," also known as "objective thought." The two "paths" (one might say, poetic and scientific) are thus seen to inhabit what he calls the same "natural space," contributing to the multidimensionality of lived experience. As Merleau-Ponty suggests, mythological consciousness "opens onto a horizon of possible objectifications." Myths occur against a background of activities rooted in the lived environment, where survival depends on knowledge of where water is in the desert, for instance, on how to find medicinal herbs to heal the sick, on how and when to harvest pinyon nuts to stave off starvation, and on how to prune the trees to ensure future harvests. When the Indian elders read signs in the environment— by reading meaning in the presence of a bird passing overhead, or in the absence of certain plants, or in the peculiar formation of a particular out- cropping of rocks—they do so against a background of environmental knowledge and interaction spanning thousands of years. This tacit back- ground knowledge is not unlike that represented in myth. The metaphori- cal, mythological blurring of boundaries does not constitute what for Westerners would seem insanity, or the "supernatural," because it is almost always grounded in practical knowledge, whether it be ecological or ethical in nature—in other words, in the practice of living and survival (not only in the past but in the present, as well). Thus, Indian elders quoted herein do not live in some irrational, purely "fictive" world—in what Carl Sagan pejoratively calls the "demon-haunted world" (the world he fears we will all fall back into if we give credence to any world view outside of the scien- tific rationalistic one). Rather, they inhabit a geography of multiple dimensions, both objective and mythological.

The fact that Indian people accept Euroamerican knowledge today and even incorporate it into their own representations of the world is not just the result of total assimilation, but a continuation of a centuries-long practice of adapting to a world they did not create and which now includes automobiles and various forms of electronic communications. Many Indian people live in both worlds (that of objective thought and poetic thought) without feeling that one invalidates the other. Indeed, they know on the level of everyday practice that metaphorical, mythological, and poetic thought can open a space for producing knowledge about the world that embraces nondualistic, nonhierarchical ethical values.

(Re)Assembling Knowledge

Isolating traditional geographic perspectives—ones that may have originated before contact with Euroamericans but have certainly been influenced by conquest—has been a purposeful strategy enabling us to see the unique cultural geography of Yucca Mountain. But such a strategy is fraught with conceptual and representational traps, especially those found in the rhetoric of lost origins in which traditional practices, knowledge, and customs become idealized cultural models marked by stability, grace, nobility, and purity. These attributes are seen to preexist the fall into modernity, with its constant change, rupture, dislocation, and fragmentation. This dualistic rhetoric opposes the cultural stasis of the native to the dynamism of the invader, as though each culture's (perceived) distinguishing characteristics were mutually exclusive. Attempting to establish an Indian ecological perspective is meant only to make an alternative geography visible, not to idealize indigenous peoples. Indeed, I have argued that such a perspective may result, at least in part, from a particular cultural mode of communication, as well as long-term historical occupation.

In truth, cultures and landscapes are always dynamic (and intersubjective). But this does not mean that certain ways of seeing the world and being in the world do not endure through time, because they do—both changing and staying the same with each passing generation. The unique ecological-cultural perspectives described in this chapter continue to exert an influence on Indian people today, influencing everything from Indian civil disobedience to environmental-impact reports and the adoption of sustainable development practices. Indian people in this region are also using traditional concepts (commonsense environmental knowledge, "natural law," the practice of "making contracts with nature," as well as an intersubjective consciousness of human and nonhuman relations) to reconstruct and reassert their own identity in opposition to Euroamerican presence and occupation. As we have seen, this identity is intertwined with the immediate local landscape. As such, it becomes a strategic countermeasure to the deterritorialized space represented by the nuclear-waste repository.

Whether they are oppositional or compatible with Euroamerican views, these local Indian ecological perspectives now form part of a field of articulations about this landscape that is global in scale. While the Yucca Mountain region is a local area, it is also always expanding outward to include the world capitalist (or advanced industrialist) system. For Indian people in this region, life after 1840 can never be fully explained on the local level without reference to the global. Trappers, miners, settlers, and missionaries widened the field of encounter in the nineteenth century; high-tech military operators, nuclear scientists, urban developers, and tourists blew it apart in the twentieth. Indeed, a nuclear-waste repository is nothing if not a geographic space where the expansionist requirements of capitalism are revealed as self-destructing—subsuming everything in its path, including the desert's indigenous inhabitants.

In the midst of such territorial transformation, durable, traditionalist mythopoetic narratives proceed forward as they are woven by Indian people into new, sometimes even parascientific descriptions of the nuclear landscape at Yucca Mountain, as is evident in the following Western Shoshone statement, which combines giant mythological snakes with geological fault lines:

> They're determined to put it [nuclear waste] there. It's not a safe place or anything. And to Native Americans, Shoshone people, it's sacred. We believe that Yucca Mountain has a snake under there, asleep, and that the serpent will wake up. . . . I believe if that there serpent is disturbed that they're going to have all kinds of stuff there. I believe that. Because see this is all earthquake faults along here. We've got about thirty-five or forty different faults in this area. It's not good.
> —WILLIAM ROSSE SR., Western Shoshone spokesperson[63]

Like a bird's nest constructed out of scraps and bits of trash—synthetic materials produced in the human environment, twigs, mud, and other materials from the nonhuman environment, and the feathery detritus of the bird's own body—perceptions and representations of Yucca Mountain and its surrounding region have been assembled over time and reinforced with the mud of cultural repetition. Each culture (Indian and Euroamerican) projects the image of its nest back to itself through representations—stories, reports, investigations, myths, models, petroglyphs, diagrams, paintings, flow charts, maps, songs, aerial infrared photographs, and circle dances at sunrise. The nest is constantly in need of repair, sometimes nearly destroyed, and often so close to other nests that its walls and edges merge in asymmetrical communion with the nests of alien birds.

As exemplified in Mr. Rosse's comment, Native American statements about high-level nuclear waste at Yucca Mountain demonstrate how Indian mythopoetic knowledge is often interwoven with the nest of an alien bird—that is, with Western scientific knowledge. Here, giant mythological snakes merge with earthquake fault lines. Such statements are emblematic of the way knowledge about the world is patched together, or assembled, out of seemingly incompatible narratives. In this case, the result makes sense but is not seamless. Lévi-Strauss called this way of assembling knowledge "bricolage"—referring particularly to the knowledge constructions of "primitive" (nonindustrialized) peoples. The same tendency is evident here in statements from so-called "modernized" Indians. Nor are such expressions all that different from what contemporary sociologists of science (such as Latour, 1987) term "assembling," "layering," and "collage" to describe the fabrication of scientific facts and technical artifacts used in the *process* of producing modern scientific knowledge about the world.

While sociological observations of scientific process focus on particular practices within particular scientific disciplines, assemblages can also be observed at the intercultural level. Statements like Mr. Rosse's demonstrate how knowledge is culled from different cultures (different metaphorical "nests") and combined to describe the natural world. Such terms and phrases as "biodiversity," "sustainable land restoration practices," "environmental management," and "ecosystems" become interwoven with traditionalist discourses.[64] In the Western Shoshone National Defense Project's land and restoration efforts, a core group of Indian traditionalist/environmentalists build gabions (check dams to "heal" gullies) to protect hot springs and other riparian environments. They establish sustainable livestock management practices to, as they put it, "promote ecological health of the land [thereby] maintaining its natural biodiversity." They are "engaged in the preservation of Rock Creek," "battle against irresponsible mineral development," protect "riparian zones," and work toward the "prevention of a nuclear waste dump at Yucca Mountain."

All these practices are, in part, based on contemporary environmental science. However, they are also based on what the Western Shoshone Defense Project themselves call their 10,000 year history of habitation in one place—the place they know as their homeland, *Newe Segobia*, over which they insist they maintain sovereignty:

> We will continue to work to protect the riparian zones surrounding springs and creeks, incredibly important areas biologically. . . . *Ecological health cannot be assessed until the intricacies of the relationships between all the parts of an ecosystem are learned by years and generations of living on the land.* It is for this reason that we feel it is imperative that Western Shoshone sovereignty be recognized because they possess the experience and the long term commitment to protect this place called Newe Segobia. *The healing of the land and of the people cannot begin while transnational corporations and the U.S. Government refuses to acknowledge the rights and responsibilities of the Western Shoshone Nation.*[65] [My italics.]

This statement demonstrates another way narrative knowledge is assembled with contemporary environmental discourse. Environmental discourse and practice is used not only to augment but also to reinterpret an older environmental practice and knowledge (in effect, redescribing reality). Springs and waterways are both "important areas biologically" *and* places in need of healing. The intersubjectivity of human and nonhuman is reflected in the phrase "the healing of the land *and* the people."

Using a comparative and critical approach to the "ecology" of the region shows that it is a product of cultural and historical forces behind the "assemblages" of knowledge constructions that produce Yucca Mountain as, on the one hand, an Indian (sometimes referred to as a "sacred") landscape, and, on the other hand, as a "sacrificial" landscape. "Knowledge" should be understood as specifically *not* constituted by a single, coherent narrative (or theoretical field) about, in this case, the natural environment. Rather, it should be understood as a collage of practices that evolve over time. Recognizing the assembled collage-like character of all statements about the natural world—whether they be Indian or (as will be shown in the next chapter) Western scientific—makes it easier to see how our gerrymandered narrative creations about nature and ourselves are informed by cultural influences.[66]

"Ecology" for both cultures constitutes a language for understanding "nature," as well as a set of spatial practices for constructing landscapes. Even when Indian ecological perspectives are mixed together (assembled) with Euroamerican scientific perspectives, behind each articulation of the natural world (and our relationship to it) lie different ideologies concerning property, and human and nonhuman relations as well as other political, cultural, and social influences that help to construct the material world in different ways.

Although Indian people in this area have been forced—often brutally—to assimilate, their long history in the region shows that recent assimilation rests on top of a tradition of comparatively mountainous proportions. This is not to deny the imposing power of colonialism on indigenous peoples and traditional practices. Many Indians, through forced and sometimes voluntary assimilation, became cattle ranchers and have earned their livelihood in that way for generations; others worked (and still work) in the mines of Nevada. One Southern Paiute tribe has attempted to build a golf course in the desert to accompany a new luxury resort on the outskirts of Las Vegas; and Colorado Indian tribes are building casinos for the booming gambling tourist trade along the banks of the Colorado River. Such practices often place the Indians in opposition to environmentalists, and sometimes even to their own tribal traditionalists. However, such practices do not erase a 10,000 year history. They exist because Indians now exist within, and at the edges of, Euroamerican society. As noted, culture—always already filled with contradictions—is altered and changed by intermingling with other cultures. Even so, focusing only on contemporary assimilation tendencies (most popular in today's academic world) cannot eclipse a sustained cultural history. Deep traditions persist; they are the ground upon which contemporary influences take root. The power of this traditional field has to be recognized if we are to fully understand both this region and its occupants. Trivializing such a tradition by calling it ingenuous "New Age" spiritualism has too often become an excuse to deny it legitimacy. For instance, the Western Shoshone claim that Lander

County uses just such an argument to push the county's development agenda for the Rock Creek site.[67]

By recognizing the links between orality and certain aspects of environmental ethos, it is possible to move beyond seeing Indian people as "by nature" more ecological than non-Indians. Instead, it becomes possible to consider the Indian mode of communication (in theory available to anyone, although not in the same manner) as the special circumstance that allows a particular ecological ethos to flourish. In this way Native environmentalism would not be naturalized but grounded in practice.

The move from orality to literacy to electronic information systems need not destroy previous knowledge with each succeeding phase. Today, some Indian people in the Yucca Mountain region are standing (albeit uncomfortably) in all three worlds. They attend sunrise dances, teach their language and stories by oral transmission, record their history in English as well as in the native language, help "write" environmental-impact statements (inserting into the Euroamerican documents traditional Indian interpretations of the land), attend ceremonial sweats, make pilgrimages to sacred springs, use faxes, computers, and computerized mapping programs. Some work to maintain all these forms of communication simultaneously. And this is where intercultural *assemblage* of knowledge production is most interesting, because it is here that oral-based knowledge is interwoven with literate-based knowledge. For instance, when the Western Shoshone Defense Project talks about "protecting Mother Earth" by "restoring riparian habitats," it is engaged in a rhetorical strategy closely akin to the semantic clash of ideas found in metaphor. This practice is not one of empty rhetoric, however, but a practice that allows new meanings and new spaces for meaning to emerge. These new vistas opened up can harbor meanings for a "Western" culture that has run out of new frontiers to overrun and that has turned back upon itself with such lethal consequences. Nonetheless, this may be the last generation to see if such an explicitly multilayered practice can actually survive and thrive and, perhaps, serve as a model for a world that offers equal legitimacy to different forms of communication and knowledge production.

· 9 ·

The Experimental Landscape

On October 3, 1995, the U.S. government offered an official public apology to victims of radiation experiments conducted between 1944 and 1974, an extraordinary event that was overshadowed by the announcement of a verdict in the O.J. Simpson trial. During that public apology, then Secretary of Energy Hazel O'Leary (using a mythological metaphor) stood before an image of a Janus-like face representing nuclear energy—one side happy and smiling, the other side monstrous, mean, and frowning. As the camera zoomed in on the Janus face, O'Leary gestured with her long pointer stick toward the happy side and said nuclear energy could be "good," but, pointing to the monster side, it could also be "bad." Its use in medicine was "good," for instance, but the deliberate injection of radioactive isotopes into unwitting human subjects was "bad."

Although lost in the fray over the Simpson trial, this public apology provided a glimpse into some of the more troubling aspects of nuclear scientific research and the pursuit of knowledge at all costs. It also shed light on a period in the history of U.S. military and scientific research when science could proceed with little, if any, critical oversight from agents outside its hallowed domain. But contradictions and omissions abound in O'Leary's apology. Radiation has caused some of the harm that the medical community tries to remedy using radiation. O'Leary also chose to ignore the fact that the "bad" side of the Janus face represents far more than human experimentation. The specter of nuclear war and the reality of thousands of tons of lethal, enduring waste account for nothing in O'Leary's sanitized version of the nuclear complex. The good side of the Janus face (medical uses of nuclear technologies) produces only 1 percent of the nuclear-waste stream, and the downwind victims of over 100 above-ground on-continent atomic tests received short shrift in her watered-down version of events.

The full report presents a more comprehensive picture. In addition to seeking an investigation of human radiation experiments, President Clinton in 1995 asked that "intentional environmental releases of radiation" also be investigated. Intentional environmental releases of radiation resulted from both atmospheric testing and underground testing of nuclear bombs, including many previously undisclosed tests across the country. The investigaton also brought to light other intentional (and often secret) controlled releases of radioactive materials—such as radiation warfare field experiments (Oak Ridge, Tennessee), diffusion of radioactive gases for "detectability" tests (Hanford, Washington), radiation-tracking tests (Los Alamos, New Mexico), and tests of radiation warfare ballistic dispersal devices (Dugway, Utah).[1] Radiation was released into the environment for various purposes, including to study the effects of nuclear accidents that the government feared might occur at the nuclear weapons facilities, and the possible effects of radiation caused by the meltdown of a nuclear reactor. Largely neglected (although noted) by the President's Advisory Committee's investigation, however, were the intentional releases that were conducted by environmental scientists studying ecological energy flows.

During much of the Cold War period, irradiated human subjects and irradiated landscapes (as large as Frenchman Flats at NTS, or as small as the deliberately contaminated alfalfa field at the University of Rochester in New York[2]) were often hidden within the secret and expanding domain of government-sponsored science. These experiments in radiation ecology are linked historically, sociologically, and scientifically to nuclear weapons testing and the nuclear complex. They provide a window into the scientific culture that produces large-scale environmental experiments such as those at Yucca Mountain. Radioecology, as it is also known, influenced Euroamerican studies and representations of nature in the postwar era. These representations have come to dominate the field of ecology (and other fields in the earth sciences) and belie the American fascination with energy, power, and control.

Indeed, Indians, with their concept of *Puha*, aren't the only ones in this region for whom energy and power are of significance. With the advent of the Atomic Age—after the Second World War—the words *energy* and *power* became deeply inscribed with an enhanced metaphorical potency in the culture of Euroamericans. The atomic blasts on the "proving grounds" of White Sands, New Mexico, and the Nevada Test Site released profoundly destructive energy that was "harnessed" to create nuclear power—the bad side and the good side of O'Leary's Janus face, respectively. At the same time, and in some cases slightly earlier, different intellectual fields started interpreting a variety of life processes (natural and social) using a language of energy flows and cycles.[3] Within the discipline of ecology—the branch of biology that deals with living organisms and their environment—the cybernetic concept of the "ecosystem" exercises an ever-widening influence on certain scientific constructions of nature—at least until the 1980s. Nature is viewed as a complex system (or systems) of circular feedback loops and cybernetic energy flows. Keeping the metaphorical density of such terms as energy and power in mind—and the correspondence between the two cultures (Indian and Western scientific) in conceiving of different kinds of energy as the basis of all life—this chapter briefly explores the links between the experimental ethos of nuclear science, nuclear politics, and the post-WWII environmental discourse on nature, specifically the discourse that represents nature as a system, an ecosystem—a construction for nature that (although no longer dominant in ecological theory[4]) remains prevalent in the wider Euroamerican culture of today.[5]

Isolating and magnifying the link between ecosystems ecology and experimental studies in nuclear science helps to illuminate the cultural context of scientific representations of nature in general and the Yucca Mountain region in particular. The way the natural environment at Yucca

Mountain is represented and the kind of human (scientific) interventions prevalent in that region reveal a cultural and scientific history that is very different from the Indian one of the previous two chapters. Instead of homeland, Yucca Mountain is perceived and represented as a system that can be monitored and controlled, a site of experimentation—an outside laboratory of monumental proportions.

Nuclear materials are not new to the Yucca Mountain area. Their presence has always been linked to the scientific community—including those, for instance ecosystems radioecologists, who have wielded great influence over the way Euroamericans perceive the natural world. How Euroamerican scientists think about the natural environment, the "ecosystem," and our relationship to it was linked to nuclearism long before we needed to find a place for nuclear waste.

Intellectual Precursors to the Experiment at Yucca Mountain: Ecology, Energy, and Radiation

The ecosystem concept is today most often associated with the work of brother ecologists Eugene and Howard Odum and with a period lasting approximately thirty years, from the 1940s to the '60s, when it dominated ecological theory. Although it governed the ecological scene in the United States during this time, the Odums's functionalist ecosystems articulations were never free from critical scrutiny, nor were the Odums the first to represent nature as an ecological *system*. Indeed, the field of ecology and the notion of an ecosystem (a term dating only to the 1930s) has always been fraught with seriously divisive debates internal to the discipline, and has changed over time.[6]

The concept of an ecological community was introduced by Frederick Clements in the first half of the twentieth century. Clements argued, holistically, that different groups of species come together to inhabit an environment in an interdependent, organized, and integrated way, forming what he called *communities*. The emphasis on communities as the unit of analysis, as opposed to individual organisms, offered a holistic approach because it asserted that the integrated whole, the community, is more than the sum of its parts. Indeed, Clements compared the community to a single organism, thus producing an organic functionalist interpretation of nature. The Clementian perspective posits that ecological communities—in addition to being ordered and balanced entities—are also dynamic. If disturbed, and then left alone, they will eventually return to a balanced state through a process called "succession." If left undisturbed the "community" achieves a mature, stable "climax state." Clements's articulation of an integrated environmental community through which materials move (analogous to the metabolism of an organism), as well as his concept of the biome, proved to be powerfully suggestive to many ecologists of his time and later. Ecologists such as Tansley (who actually coined the term "ecosystem"), Elton, Lindeman, Hutchinson, and others, however, rejected Clements's organismal analogy, progression of the community toward a stable climax state, even the notion of the community itself, as well as other aspects of his work. Nevertheless, these ecologists also developed their theories based on Clements's work, particularly on the concept of environmental metabolic-like energy flows. For instance, Hutchinson and others adapted V. I. Vernadsky's work with biogeochemical cycles to the ecosystems model, thereby widening the concept of the community to include abiotic entities (nonliving components of the ecosystem).

Although ecosystems ecology was strengthened by numerous practitioners, it wasn't until Eugene and Howard Odum began to demonstrate the "productivity" and "trophic efficiency" of ecological communities that the functioning of an ecosystem could be adequately described and, more importantly, measured, and thereby gain dominance in the field.[7] Significantly, it was the atmospheric nuclear testing in the Marshall Islands, at Eniwetok Atoll, that provided the Odums with, in their own words, the opportunity "for critical assays of the effects of radiations due to fission products *on whole populations and entire ecological systems in the field*."[8] By tracing the movement of radionuclides they were able to see and begin to measure the movement of energy through an entire ecosystem.

Knowledge Assemblages, Redux

Radiation ecology and ecosystems ecology form aspects of a historically situated and very heterogeneous group of articulations about the natural world that fall under the somewhat vague umbrella of environmental science. As noted in one prominent textbook: Environmental science envisions itself a "holistic" science as it "requires knowledge of many scientific fields . . . offer[ing] an integrated view of the world and our part in it."[9]

In reality, the field is not as integrated as this textbook writer would like. As noted in the previous chapter, in a discussion of Indian knowledge assemblages, knowledge about the "natural environment" whether Indian or Euroamerican is rarely (or only within narrow disciplinary boundaries) constituted by a single coherent narrative, theoretical field, or set of practices.[10] Many nonscientists expect science to present uncontested truths and consistent historical narratives. Instead, while some forms of continuity do exist, scientific disciplines are also often characterized by tangential theoretical movements, divergent and competing conceptual paths, and what Kuhn called "paradigm shifts."[11] And, as in any knowledge system, science is also subject to "outside" influences, including cultural trends and political agendas, as the Atomic Energy Commission's funding of radiation ecology exemplifies, in which the politically expedient need to find "peaceful" uses of nuclear energy propels research into the nuclear arena.

Almost by definition, environmental science is an assemblage, a heterogeneous collage of concepts and practices gleaned from its constitutive disciplines. Environmental science's foundational field—ecology—exemplifies how scientific narratives and practices change over time and are beset by internal debates about truth claims. Ecosystems have moved historically from being perceived as superorganisms (Clements) to self-regulating cybernetic systems (E. P. and H. T. Odum) to—in the jargon of chaos theorists—complex adaptive systems (Santa Fe Institute theorists); many theoretical ecologists do not currently believe in ecosystems at all. Ecosystems have been represented as progressing in an orderly fashion toward balanced equilibrium or, conversely, as chaotic systems prone to acute disturbances, far from equilibrium. Similarly, debates within the field of ecology range from approaches considered "holistic" to those considered "individualistic." Nature has been metaphorically represented as cooperative and as competitive, as ordered and as chaotic, as systemic and as individualistic. Indeed, debates as to whether an ecological community actually exists in nature or is simply a human construct imposed on nature continue to this day.

The point here is not to show that biology and ecology are lesser sciences than, for instance, physics or chemistry, but that scientific knowledge itself moves, changes (sometimes gradually, sometimes abruptly), and is influenced by cultural factors. For example, one of the central criticisms of

Clements's work (and, later, of the Odums's work) was that he imposed a functionalist order onto the natural world—an order perceived (from some perspectives) as desirable for the social world. Such transferences, of course, carry serious political implications if we consider power relations and the normalization (naturalization) of submissive roles within socially ordered hierarchies of power. Along with the influences of granting agencies, the importance of metaphors (organismic, social, or mechanistic) in the articulation of nature in the field of ecology and at Yucca Mountain cannot be overlooked. For now, it is enough to note that the collage-like character of the discipline itself, its history of contested truths, and multiple views of nature reflect a field in flux.

By the 1960s the ecosystems concept, as represented by the Odums, had come under attack by population biologists and evolutionary ecologists. Even so, ecosystems science survives as an important conceptual and practical organizing principle in many articulations of applied ecological study, including those at Yucca Mountain. The biogeochemical cycle, the emphasis on energy pathways, and the use of computer simulations for predicting complex interchanges among biotic and abiotic systems and for quantifying field observations are all basic tools derived from the ecosystems tool kit.

So infused with the language of ecosystems ecology has U.S. culture become, irrespective of the status of ecosystems concepts among theoretical ecologists, that politicians and other nonscientists routinely speak of ecosystems when discussing the natural environment. The word *ecosystem* itself has been thoroughly naturalized and accepted within the culture at large, coloring people's understanding and knowledge of the natural world. Ecosystems ecology's development from a specific set of experiments initiated in military operations research and weapons development at the start of WWII, and its link to military-inspired and funded cybernetics and information theoretic researches is, today, completely obscured.[12] Its associated terminology—power, energy, productivity, efficiency, and work—have likewise been naturalized within an ecological context, making possible the discourse on ecological economics and a managerial ethos in which control of these factors becomes the primary mission of environmental managers in late industrialist capitalist society.[13] Indeed, use of these economic terms within the discourse on ecology helps bring the whole of the natural world within the capitalist "system" of production, in which waste, however lethal, can be seen as a "natural" byproduct of our energy consumption. On a more theoretical level, in Baudrillard's *For a Critique of the Political Economy of the Sign* capital construes nature as a "productive force to be mastered" by designating the environment through such economistic signs. Mastering the signs (through calculation) translates to mastery of the environment.[14]

Systems Ecology and Economistic Metaphors

Although originally marshaled in the cause of antiaircraft targeting and developed into logistics for WWII troop mobilization (operations research), after the war, in the 1950s cybernetic systems theory took other disciplines by storm, including that of ecology (and its subfield, radioecology).[15] As applied to natural environments, systems theory articulates nature as an electrical feedback system. Nature can thus be analyzed by a systems ecologist much the same way an engineer might analyze the workings of an electromechanical system.[16] Kitching said that systems ecology can be defined as "the approach to the study of the ecology of organisms using the techniques and philosophy of systems analysis: that is, the methods and tools developed largely in engineering."[17] Haraway, Taylor, Mitman, and others have demonstrated how, during this period (1930s to the 1950s and beyond), "nature" was transformed from a community of organisms to a system of cybernetic/information feedback loops—a transformation that demonstrates the impact of social and political influences on the reconstruction of scientific representations.[18] (Not coincidentally, cybernetics contributed to the development of the computer, which of course was in part driven by the need to model the physics of nuclear reactions in weapons development.)

In the work of systems analysts such as Eugene and H. T. Odum, both living and nonliving entities (biotic and abiotic) compose nature within a self-regulating, complex system characterized by (usually) numerous feedback loops that encompass biological, geological, and chemical materials and elements (hence the term "biogeochemical"). Even today, in many textbooks, the biosphere is compared to a giant, complex, but ultimately closed system. The system is composed of "flows of energy." Energy is defined as the capacity to do work. As noted by H. T. Odum: "Energy is the

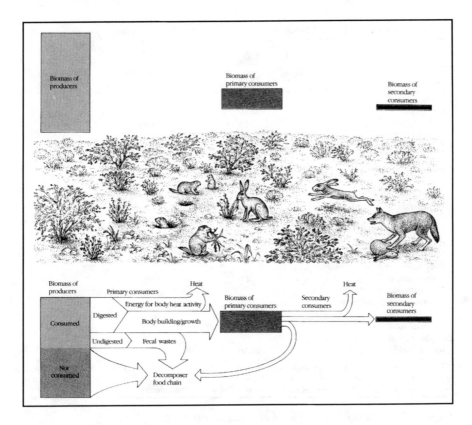

Figure 9.1 Textbook example of energy and nutrient flow through an ecosystem

From: Chiras, *Environmental Science*, 3rd ed. (adapted from Nebel)

primary, most universal measure of all kinds of work by human beings and nature."[19] Biomass (the organic matter produced by living things measured as dry weight, and a form of potential energy) flows through a food chain in an ecosystem. It decreases as it flows from one "trophic level" (the feeding level an organism occupies in a food chain) to the next—according to the laws of thermodynamics.

Some systems are seen to be more *productive* than others, and some more *efficient* than others. Productivity is the measure of biomass, most commonly measured in kilocalories.[20] An ecosystems approach will represent all of this with flow diagrams (essentially energy circuit diagrams) that include purely physical processes, such as soil degradation. As noted by Taylor: "The flow diagrams, when transformed into computer models,

Estimated Annual Gross Primary Productivity of the Biosphere and Major Ecosystems

Ecosystem	Area (10^6km²)	Gross Primary Productivity (kcal/m²/year)	Worldwide Annual Gross Primary Production (10^{16}kcal)*
Marine			
Open ocean	326.0	1,000	32.6
Coastal zones	34.0	2,000	6.8
Upwelling zones	0.4	6,000	0.2
Estuaries and reefs	2.0	20,000	4.0
Marine total	362.4		43.6
Terrestrial			
Deserts and tundras	40.0	200	0.8
Grasslands and pastures	42.0	2,500	10.5
Dry forests	9.4	2,500	2.4
Boreal coniferous forests	10.0	3,000	3.0
Cultivated lands with little or no energy subsidy	10.0	3,000	3.0
Moist temperate forests	4.9	8,000	3.9
Fuel-subsidized (mechanized) agriculture	4.0	12,000	4.8
Wet tropical and subtropical (broadleaved evergreen) forests	14.7	20,000	29.0
Terrestrial total	135.0		57.4
Biosphere total (round figures, not including ice caps)	500.0	2,000	100.0

*This column is calculated by multiplying the area by the productivity of each region. It tells the relative importance of each zone to total biospheric productivity.
Source: Odum, E. (1971). *Fundamentals of Ecology* (3rd ed.). Philadelphia: Saunders

Figure 9.2 Textbook example of ecosystems productivity hierarchy
In this scheme deserts and tundra are at the bottom of the productivity scale producing only ø.8 percent of "worldwide annual gross primary production."

From: Chiras, *Environmental Science*, 3rd ed. (Adapted from *Fundamentals of Ecology*, Second Edition by Eugene P. Odum and Howard T. Odum, 1959 by Saunders College Publishing and renewed 1987 by Eugene P. Odum and Howard T. Odum. Reproduced by permission of the publisher.)

could be used by systems ecologists to generate predictions about the future or about responses to perturbations [in the environment]."[21] Perturbations can be anything from drought to the intrusion of a roaming predator to a nuclear bomb.

How nature is represented gets transformed in this shift from organismic to cybernetic analogies, which is coupled with a move toward more economistic analogies and metaphors, as demonstrated in the following textbook ecosystem description:

In an ecosystem, then, *productivity* is the rate at which sunlight energy is converted into the potential energy of biomass. The overall rate of biomass production is called the gross primary productivity (GPP). Like a worker's gross pay, the GPP is subject to some deductions. . . . Much like your net pay, the Net Primary Productivity is what's left over after deductions.[22]

The bioeconomic ecological model forms a particularly disturbing trajectory through the latter half of the twentieth century. As noted by Donald Worster, bioeconomic ecology regards all creatures on the earth as "related to one another essentially as producers and consumers; interdependence in such a world must mean sharing a common energy income. . . . man [sic] must be considered primarily as an economic animal—he is one with all life in a push for greater productivity."[23]

This language for describing ecosystems clearly derives from market economics, and recalls criticism leveled at so-called "native" and Third World peoples, who, in market terms, are perceived as low producers. Indeed, this particular kind of discourse undermines the integrity of a place such as Yucca Mountain, which registers low on the hierarchy of productivity and biomass. Deserts in general, of course, don't receive high marks in this scheme, as the phrase "deserts as dumps" implies.

As the systems management model suggests, the bioeconomic world order pushes not only for greater productivity but also for greater control. It is an integrated circuit, a system of energy transfers, a self-regulating system with efficiency as its highest goal. In this way, Western culture can be seen to naturalize such economic concepts as competition and self-interest, turning our economic system into our ecology. A society with a different ecology (for instance, the Western Shoshone and Southern Paiute) maintains a different economy and different subjectivity (sense of self).

Following trends to extrapolate cybernetics into different areas of human concern,[24] both Howard and Eugene Odum extended their textual models and systems diagrams of natural ecosystems to represent other social and cultural systems with obvious bias about how the world might best be ordered and managed. H. T. Odum's *Environment, Power, and Society*, while considered somewhat marginal in the scientific community precisely because of its extension from the "natural world" to the social world, nevertheless demonstrates the cultural kernel (only magnified) at the center of ecosystems analysis. Lest we think only Indians concern themselves with the connections between spirituality and nature, we need only consider Odum's ecosystems world view applied to religion. Odum's ecosystems vision is a universal vision, a prophetic vision that encompasses all of life. As he states:

> The key program of a surviving pattern of nature and man is a subsystem of religious teaching which follows the laws of the energy ethics. Whereas the earlier tenets of religions were based on the simple energy realms of their time, the new sources and large magnitudes of power require revisions of some of the mores and the personifications used in teaching them. *We can teach the energy truths through general science in the schools and teach love of system and its requirements of us in the changing churches.* System survival makes right and the energy commandments guide the system to survival. The classical struggle between order and disorder, between angels and devils is still with us.[25] [My italics.]

The diagram on the following page, provides a cybernetic systems flowchart for the realm of angelic work leading to heaven, and the realm of disordering hell's fire. [See figure 9.3]

Radioecology: Tracing the Atom through the Landscape

Although radioactive isotopes were used to study ecosystems before the Odums employed the technique, Eugene and Howard Odum were central to the advancement of radiation ecology. After the Western Shoshone and Southern Paiute were removed from the Nevada Test Site and the Yucca Mountain region in the 1940s, and after a decade of atmospheric testing, environmental ecosystems scientists, most prominently the Odums, began to study the Nevada Test Site along with other zones of nuclear contamination.

The meteoric rise of ecosystems analysis owes its momentum to the U.S. post-WWII nuclear weapons complex and the Atoms for Peace program, along with funding from the National Science Foundation and the Atomic Energy Commission, which made many ecosystems studies possible. The field of radiation ecology—the quantitative basis of postwar ecosystems ecology—owed its existence in great measure to the Nevada Test Site Proving Grounds, the Hanford Plutonium Complex, the nuclear tests at Eniwetok Atoll, and the nuclear weapons laboratories at Oak Ridge, Tennessee,

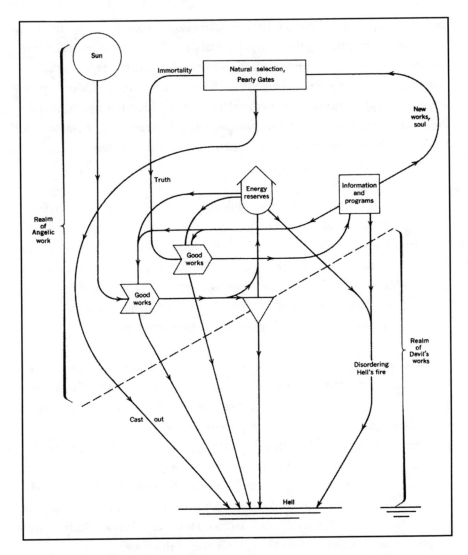

Figure 9.3 Howard Odum's use of energetics to depict cultural beliefs
[From the original] "Common abstractions of energetics and religious teachings
showing angelic operations of order, evolution, and selection of information
above and the evil processes of disorder, dissipation, and heat death below."

From: Howard T. Odum, *Environment, Power, and Society* (Wiley-Interscience, 1991). Reprinted by permission of
John Wiley and Sons, Inc.

and Savannah River, Georgia. Because radiation ecology plays such a pivotal role in formulating the energetic basis for the ecosystems argument, the second edition of Eugene Odum's immensely influential textbook *Fundamentals of Ecology* devoted an entire chapter to it.[26] Eugene Odum's preface to the 1959 edition of the textbook specifically identifies the Atoms for Peace program, and the vital importance of using radioactive isotopes as tracers in the environment for advancing scientific knowledge of ecosystems. As he notes in the preface:

> Fortunately, biologists and the public alike are beginning to realize that ecological research of the most basic nature is vital to the solution of mankind's environmental problems. Some of the things which we fear most in the future, radioactivity, for example, if intelligently studied, help solve the very problems they create. Thus, isotopes used as tracers in the environment elucidate turnover processes which we must understand before radioactive waste materials can be safely released into the environment.[27]

Although Odum warns against the hazards of radioactivity and is concerned about a future reliance on nuclear energy, he is simultaneously bound within a systems discourse that naturalizes the nuclear fuel cycle with his suggestion that "radioactive waste materials can be safely released into the environment." This in effect naturalizes the nuclear fuel cycle into a biogeochemical cycle within the environment—one that includes not only humans but their energy needs for production and consumption. His brother was instrumental in developing the sections on energy flows in biogeochemical cycles using radioactive isotopes. Howard Odum was employed by the Puerto Rico Nuclear Center at the time.

In the aftermath of the Second World War, when science in the United States had metamorphosed into the "big science" network of government-funded projects, national laboratories, and even secret science cities devoted to defense-oriented agendas,[28] the Odums received funding from the national defense and nuclear research program through departments like the Office of Naval Research, but most especially through the Atomic Energy Commission (AEC). As the Final Report on human radiation experiments notes: "[R]adioecology [b]egan during the Manhattan Project with research on the radiosensitivity of aquatic life around the

Hanford Reservation and extended to research on flora and fauna in and around other AEC sites."[29]

Almost immediately after the bomb was dropped on Hiroshima in 1945, the U.S. government began the process of establishing a nonmilitary domestic agency—the AEC—under which nuclear energy could be controlled. But the links between the military (and its interests) and the Atomic Energy Commission (precursor to the Department of Energy) have always been especially strong. The Atoms for Peace program was started in 1953 (under the Eisenhower Administration) to explore the potential for industrial uses of nuclear power. In part, this was meant to assuage public uneasiness with military control of atomic energy, along with fears of its destructive and contaminating aspects.

Through this program the Odums (and others) found an adequate supply of radioactive isotopes with which to experiment—something not possible before the wide-scale establishment of military and commercial-oriented nuclear science.[30] After 1948, until the mid-1960s, research programs in ecology were established at Oak Ridge National Laboratory, Savannah River National Laboratory, and Hanford—all nuclear complexes. Indeed, the "new tool" for many ecologists at the advent of the Atomic Age was none other than radiation itself. As noted in the final report of the *Advisory Committee on Human Radiation Experiments*:

> After the war's end, the network of radiation researchers, government and military officials, and physicians mobilized for the Manhattan Project did not disband. Rather, they began working on government programs to promote both peaceful uses of atomic energy and nuclear weapons development.
>
> Having harnessed the atom in secret for war, the federal government turned enthusiastically to providing government and nongovernmental researchers, corporations, and farmers with new tools for peace—radioisotopes—mass-produced with the same machinery that produced essential materials for the nation's nuclear weapons. Radioisotopes, the newly established Atomic Energy Commission (AEC) promised, would create new businesses, improve agricultural production, and through "human uses" in medical research, save lives.[31]

Cybernetic models of ecosystems were created from data derived from radioecological studies conducted at places such as Eniwetok Atoll and the Nevada Test Site, where radionuclides leached into the environment. Others were derived from data gathered after deliberate injections into the environment. Regardless of the means, the importance of radiation ecology for determining energy flow within a given system was revolutionary for the discipline of ecology because it allowed the modeling and quantification of dynamic systems.[32]

Radioactive "tags" were used to track the movements of animals and for estimating population densities. After WWII, radioactive isotopes were also used to trace "metabolic" pathways within an ecosystem, much the same way they were used, before and after the war, to study the metabolism of plants and animals (including human beings such as retarded children, Army personnel, prisoners, and other people considered marginal and expendable). As described by Hagen:

> While [radioactive] tracers could be used to measure directly the movement of materials through the ecosystem, they could also be used to measure indirectly the flow of energy. Plants, the producers in the ecosystem, were labeled with a radioactive isotope. At subsequent time intervals the various consumers in the community were then sampled for radiation. This type of study yielded two important types of information about the internal workings of the ecosystem. First it could be used to isolate individual food chains. If a particular species of plant was labeled, then only herbivores feeding on the plant and the carnivores feeding upon those herbivores would later become radioactive. Second, tracer studies could be used to answer the question: How long does it take for energy to move through the ecosystem? By continuously monitoring the various animal populations for radiation, one could estimate the time required for elements originally in the plants to reach the end of the food chain . . . [B]y following the movement of tracer elements, the ecologist could accurately determine the actual pathways of energy flow, the rates at which the energy flowed, the amount of time that various elements remained within particular compartments of the ecosystem (residence time), and rates at which these elements moved from one compartment to another (turnover rate).[33]

As noted by Hagen, Taylor, and others, the "Age of Ecology" and the "Atomic Age" coincide.[34] Radioecology can be mapped onto the land by identifying the irradiated landscapes used for its experiments. The Eniwetok Atoll in the Marshall Islands and the Alaska tundra on the North Slope provided the Odums and others with ecosystems (outdoor) laboratories, as did the "buffer zones" around the nuclear weapons laboratories in the United States.[35] Such buffer zones—forests, rivers, deserts—were subjected to radioactive isotopes, which acted as tracers, allowing scientists to measure and identify the "dynamics" of the ecosystem. Sometimes these experimental landscapes were subjected to a steady emission of low-level radiation into the air (El Verde Forest, Puerto Rico), sometimes to large amounts of heated water from nuclear reactors (Savannah River, Georgia). Sometimes isotopes were introduced into the soil, sometimes into the waterways. Radioisotopes were pumped into farmland, grassland, ponds, tropical coral reefs, forests, island environments, and desert and Arctic regions. From the 1940s to the 1970s there appeared to be no end to what experiments one could perform. Experimental landscapes can be found in Nevada, Washington, Tennessee, Georgia, South Carolina, New York, Alaska, New Mexico, Idaho, Utah, and elsewhere in the United States.

Overseas, in addition to the South Pacific and Japan (where the effects of the Hiroshima and Nagasaki blasts were studied), the El Verde forest in Puerto Rico became the site of a premier radioisotope study. This study (conducted between 1963–67) featured continuous irradiation of a section of the forest for the duration of three months. The study employed more than 100 scientists, was directed by Howard T. Odum, and was funded by the Atomic Energy Commission. Ecology had become "Big Science."[36]

The Odums and others maintained that radioecological experimentation used insignificant amounts of radioactive elements, so insignificant that they were incapable of causing harm to the experimental environment. But some of these studies were done to observe the *stress* of radioactive fallout on the environment—on animals and plant life. Clearly there is a circular quality to atomic research and use—the need to control the atom justifies its continued use.

While scientists such as the Odums promoted the use of radiation for experimental purposes, they were also some of the first to sound the alarm of the dangers of continued production of nuclear power and testing of nuclear weapons. The energy flow diagrams produced by way of observing radioisotope movement began to show that radionuclides from fallout, waste, and pollution could not easily be diffused safely within the system, posing no threat to organic life forms. Instead, they could become concentrated, magnified, and very dangerous.[37]

The Nuclear Fuel Cycle and Systems Ideology

Inevitably the risks associated with experimentation are subsumed under a higher purpose—be it national security, economic competitiveness, the need to understand the effects of radiation in case of attack, or, in our case, solving the nuclear-waste crisis. Even in the 1950s the promise of a cheap, abundant, and virtually limitless supply of energy to fuel the engines of capital was a "higher purpose" far too seductive for government and business to pass up. As Joseph Camilleri notes in *The State and Nuclear Power*:

> The prodigious sums of public money, the enormous scientific, technical, and industrial resources, and the broad powers invested in the Atomic Energy Commission reflected the conviction that the energy of the atom represented an overriding national interest deserving special status and the highest policy priority.[38]

With the Navy leading the way in reactor technology, questions centered on obtaining and ensuring a sufficient supply of nuclear fuel, particularly for military purposes. Plutonium (converted into fissionable materials) is needed to build nuclear bombs, and it is a byproduct of the fission process used in reactors (commercial and military). Since it was costly for the military to develop its own reactors to produce plutonium for weapons, at the very beginning of the Atomic Age there were economic incentives to develop commercial reactors, thereby creating a steady supply of cheap weapons-grade plutonium—at least that was the idea behind the nuclear fuel cycle in the early days.[39] The United States (via the AEC) very early on engaged the services of corporations such as General Electric (Hanford contractor), Union Carbide, and DuPont in the production of fissionable materials, setting the stage for the development of commercial reactors.

According to Allen, in 1948, General Electric's general research facilities at Schenectady, New York, was "often cited by AEC chiefs as evidence that their munitions enterprise was also interested in the constructive use of atomic energy."[40]

Before plutonium waste can be recycled into fuel for either energy production or weapons, it must be reprocessed. As Camilleri explains:

> Until the mid-1970s, the major nuclear states had operated on the assumption that commercial reprocessing, or more specifically the extraction of uranium and plutonium from irradiated fuel and the recycling of these materials for use in thermal or breeder reactors, would enhance the economic competitiveness of nuclear power. Reprocessing was also viewed as part of a comprehensive waste management strategy.[41]

The idea that waste could be efficiently managed through reprocessing (the "back end" of the nuclear cycle) testifies to a technological over-optimism fueled by the systems paradigm—the belief that atomic energy, like other forms of energy, was part of or could be made part of a "natural" cycle that included economic consumption and production. While this notion may seem farfetched today, Odum's diagram of the "energy basis for the system of humanity and nature of the United States of America" [See figure 9.4] shows just how prevalent such ideas were.[42] Uranium, derived from "Land, Mountains" is shown entering a fuel process that branches off into electric power, waste processes, and mineral processes. The fuel process converts to electric power for use by the military and other sectors. Significantly, however, the waste finds its way back into natural weather and water systems. Nothing is wasted in this attempt to bring nature and culture into the capitalist system. Odum's diagram suggests that it all starts with the sun and ends with that most important of capitalist processes: "exports."

As has been shown, this cybernetic systems "ideology" pervaded scientific culture well before it was popularized as "ecology" for the masses. It was directly influenced by nuclear experimentation and in fact represents an ethos that can be summed up in the statement: "Nothing exists outside the system." If nothing exists outside the system, there can be no waste; everything, theoretically, finds some use value.

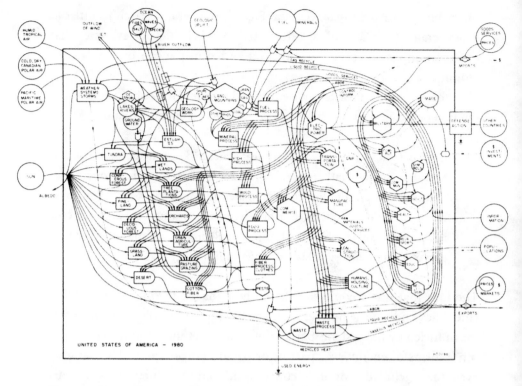

Figure 9.4 H.T. Odum's "energy basis for the system of humanity and nature of the United States of America"

From: H.T. Odum and E.C. Odum, *Energy Basis for Man and Nature*, 2nd ed., 1981 (originally 1976). Reproduced with permission of The McGraw-Hill Companies.

Scientists would never claim that all nuclear waste could be recycled, but the belief that it could be managed efficiently helped build a case for commercialization of nuclear energy, which ensured a ready supply of potential fuel for nuclear weapons. Of course, reprocessing turned out to be economically inefficient; it was cheaper in the long run to rely on uranium reserves. More importantly, reprocessing is politically dangerous—it discharges too much weapons-grade plutonium into a politically unstable world. In the end, the *system* (including its cultural and political spheres) didn't behave as predicted. We live with the consequences of that miscalculation today—70,000 tons of high-level radioactive waste, and counting.

This brief history of the precursors to the experiment at Yucca Mountain shows three things: (1) it shows the link between the Atomic Age and the scientific field of ecology, (2) it demonstrates some of the political pressures (in the form of financial and institutional support) exerted upon ecosystems scientists in the postwar era—influence that eventually shapes our representations of nature by directing research toward nuclear issues and the use of nuclear materials, and (3) it demonstrates the transformation of the discipline from one socially influenced metaphor (from organic functionalism) toward a different socially influenced metaphor based on cybernetic systems and economistic processes. Aside from the multiple ironies implied by a mechanistic model of an organic model used as a social model to model the natural world, this last transformation underlies the technocratic ethos of experimentation. In a sense, all of "nature" becomes a cybernetic feedback system, one that, theoretically, can be fine-tuned and controlled—if we can come to chart all of its functions by means of experimentation. As the metaphors imply, and as Baudrillard has argued, the environment becomes a system of signs to be manipulated. Knowledge of the system is knowledge of power and energy, which are terms used in modeling both nature and the economy. The postwar discourse on nature is essentially the reduction of nature to power, energy, and information. Control and power are at the center of the contradiction that is the Yucca Mountain experiment. That we cannot control this waste, this "spent" fuel—which is not spent at all since it's highly radioactive—reveals the contradiction deep within the rhetoric of control used by the nuclear industry.

Managing the System:
The Yucca Mountain Project and the Technology of Knowing

The Yucca Mountain site has been the object of study for sixteen years; by 1995 the cost of feasibility studies totaled $1.7 billion; the cost per day of feasibility studies in 1995 came to $1.46 million; no other sites are being studied for possible waste containment.[43] In 1994 twenty states filed suit to force the federal government to open a repository by 1998. Waste containers and cooling ponds for high-level radioactive fuel rods are leaking at existing power plants. Because power plants continue on line and thus produce high-level radioactive waste, utility companies are running out of room in which to store it. Developing countries are shipping their weapons-grade plutonium (from U.S.-sponsored nuclear power plants) back to the United States as promised in accordance with U.S. nonproliferation policy; and nuclear warheads are being decommissioned, leaving a substantial amount of plutonium and other waste to contend with. *This* is the background against which scientific studies are conducted at Yucca Mountain. Together, these factors make finding a solution to the nuclear-waste crisis urgent and of the highest national priority, whatever the scientific merits of the proposed solution. To pretend that scientists and government decision makers can remain objective in such an environment simply compounds any errors discovered in the process by adding a larger layer of self-delusion.

In addition to existing within this highly charged political environment (this looming crisis), science at Yucca Mountain is also conducted within a cultural ethos of experimentation that has in the past justified exposing humans to high levels of radiation. Whether these past transgressions were undertaken in pursuit of knowledge or in the name of national security, entombing nuclear waste at Yucca Mountain represents as much of an experiment as medical experiments performed on unsuspecting humans, or those carried out with intentional releases of radioactive gases on downwind populations, or those conducted in above-ground tests in front of troops. While the rationale may have changed to suit the times, the fact that we do not know, indeed cannot know, in what state radioactive materials will survive entombed inside Yucca Mountain beyond a few hundred years (if that) constitutes an experiment of immense scope. And what we do know from past experiments with radioactive materials is not reassuring. Radiation is the gift that keeps on giving. Burying radioactive materials in Yucca Mountain constitutes an injection—on a grand scale—of radioisotopes into an experimental ecosystem.

The challenge now appears to be how humans can best manage this land of "low productivity" so that it will be suitable for radioactive waste. This requires yet more experimentation to make accurate predictions. Management is the fine art of control based on prediction. As the Yucca Mountain promotional material says:

> What is challenging about this project is using different fields of science to predict complex environmental interactions for thousands of years. Specialists in different fields of science must understand how their findings interact, then make their predictions based on those interactions.

I would offer this piece of advice, and that is be skeptical of what you hear from the [Yucca Mountain] project people when you go on the site. They always put on the best, most optimistic face about the site. They only talk about the good aspects of the site, and they only talk about the wonderful things they're going to do in the future and the wonderful data they're going to collect. But there's not a whole lot about the problems, the issues, the great uncertainties in the data and even the techniques being used.

—KARL JOHNSON, Technical Director,
Nevada's Nuclear Waste Project Office[44]

Just as the politics of nuclear culture influence science, science tries to influence cultural perceptions of itself and the objects of its studies. As a serious display of big-science assemblage, the Yucca Mountain Project is touted by the Department of Energy as an historically unprecedented science project. And it is impressive. Partly because this rather small mountain has undergone intense scientific scrutiny for more than ten years, public relations materials rightfully claim it as "one of the most intensive scientific investigations ever conducted!"[45] Unfortunately, the intensity of the public relations campaign often seems to rival that of the scientific studies of the mountain. Unlike previous scientific investigations of nuclear elements, for instance the Manhattan Project, this project is highly publicized. In some ways its public relations campaign can be compared to media coverage of the Gulf War. People were treated to a lot of technical expertise as they watched televised bombings of targets from the nose of a "smart" bomb, but the coverage was intensely controlled and manipulated by the U.S. government. Similarly, science at Yucca Mountain is publicized and promoted everywhere with ample technical explanations and demonstrations, but it is orchestrated like a propaganda campaign. The DOE promotes the site as a repository while simultaneously claiming to be engaged in objective study. The conflicting agenda is rather transparent.

The publicity may be deployed in part to justify the high cost of the study; and at $1.46 million a day,[46] justifications are necessary. Similarly, the "spin-off" knowledge from these studies alone (like that from basic weapons research) is used to justify some of the high costs of the project.

In effect, it becomes more than just a nuclear-waste project; it becomes, in the jargon of the DOE's public relations, that which expands the frontiers of science itself. By making the mountain a center of advanced earth science and ecological research, the DOE softens the edge of its unpopular and difficult mandate to find a safe haven for high-level nuclear waste.

Public outreach information offices, scattered throughout Nevada and other states, are constructed as "science centers," with models, charts, videos, computer simulations, and educational materials. Ostensibly, these centers exist to answer all questions, clear up any confusions, and dispel any fears about what is going on at Yucca Mountain, so that the average citizen can come to her own conclusions. The information office purports to function as an information center, a museum, and a public relations satellite office all in one—a microworld of rational inquiry and explanation, a symbol of cool detached science in the hot desert sun. All aspects of the Yucca Mountain Project are illuminated with texts, pictures, videos, diagrams of the nuclear-fuel cycle, and models of all kinds. Models are especially big. The information centers feature models of the inside of nuclear power plants, models of uranium pellet-filled tubes bundled together to form a nuclear fuel assembly, models of the mountain itself with its network of storage tunnels exposed to show how the waste will be positioned inside the mountain. Videos show how the great tunnel-boring machine eats through the mountain. There are interactive display exhibits, glass box-encased displays of stuffed animals indigenous to the desert region, antique tools and implements from the days of the pioneers, as well as displays of arrowheads and Shoshonean basketry. Explaining everything from molecular physics to local Native American community organizations, the information office is there to inform *and* persuade. The Yucca Mountain Project also directs numerous educational outreach programs to public schools in Nevada and sponsors special open-house days, designed as family entertainment, such as "Discovery Day, a day of hands-on fun for the whole family," where "scientists [are] on hand to help you delve even further into some of this land's most wondrous features." [See figure 9.5]

The Yucca Mountain Project public relations people use a variety of methods to try to dispel dis-ease and resistance over the issue of nuclear waste at Yucca Mountain. They make the project seem an educational science project and a high-level basic science research project. They attempt

Figure 9.5 Example of Yucca Mountain Project public relations effort

Department of Energy/Yucca Mountain Project

to naturalize nuclear reactors and deep-geologic containment of nuclear waste. For instance, one public information flier features a story of how, in Gabon, Africa, site of Oklo, there exists a "natural nuclear reactor." In this, "nature" has "beaten humans to the punch by creating the world's first nuclear reactor":

> Two billion years ago, nature not only appears to have created her first nuclear reactor, she also found a way to successfully isolate the waste produced deep underground.

Some scientists have suggested that 1.7 billion years ago at the Gabon site natural conditions prompted an underground nuclear reaction. In the words of the DOE flyer:

> Once the natural reactors burned themselves out by consuming needed amounts of the U-235 [a uranium isotope needed in sufficient amounts to permit fission, if other conditions are right], the highly radioactive wastes they generated stayed in place. Confined by the granite, sandstone, and clays surrounding the reactor areas, plutonium and other long-lived radioactive elements created during fission remained in place deep under Oklo.

The DOE contends that this provides a "model" for deep-geologic containment for high-level radioactive wastes such as at Yucca Mountain. The obvious problem is that it's not a comparable situation at all. The rock types at the Gabon site are different from Yucca Mountain, and we now have far more radioactive isotopes (produced from continuous production) than those produced from the small number of nuclear reactions thought to have occurred at the Gabon site. Besides, just because something has occurred in nature doesn't make it safe for human replication. Naturalizing nuclear processes in this way is a common DOE strategy to assuage public concerns, as, for instance, when the DOE talks about the existence of "natural" background radiation in discussions with concerned citizens over nuclear fallout or radioactive pollution near the weapons labs. This kind of public relations effort has a frantic quality about it as it spins itself tighter and tighter to make the visitor believe in the credibility of the DOE's endeavor. It is a frenzied assurance.

Scientists: Public and Private

On one visit to the Hydrologic Research Facility I asked scientists from the U.S. Geologic Survey if they felt the pressures of the nuclear-waste crisis as they studied the mountain. Did the political pressure to find a suitable site for nuclear-waste influence their work? Responses were characterized by defensiveness and epitomized by one meteorologist, who said: "Most scientists are deeply ethical people." This type of statement, meant to reassure the public of the quality of science at the Yucca Mountain site, is ubiquitous and has the effect of precluding further discussion. How political influence affects scientific work at a place like Yucca Mountain is an obvious and understandable question, but some scientists take it as a personal affront, an attack on their integrity. A geologist for the USGS who mapped faults within 100 kilometers of the test site told me that in the early stages of the project, before the state of Nevada was allowed to station its own scientists in the field to ensure quality, DOE-contracted geologists tended to see themselves as beyond any criticism and brooked no questions from outside parties. Their attitude, he said, was: "How dare they interfere with us because we are pure [doing pure science]." Such statements as "We're not in the business of showing the site as safe if it's not" appear in all of the DOE publications, in outreach information, and in individual statements by some scientists in public settings. (Public tours of the project include opportunities to talk with the scientists.) Meanwhile, Congress keeps pushing for a repository, and bills keep accumulating.

Objectivity in the face of outside pressures is clearly a point of contention because it is always being questioned. As one scientist (who shall remain anonymous) said to me:

> You know, we scientists on this project certainly say that the job we're doing is good honest science. If I find a disqualifying factor associated with the site, whether my salary is paid by this project or not, I have to get up and say "This site is not going to be safe if we build it here." Okay?

After about an hour of discussion, however, the scientist who made this statement revealed concerns about issues that he clearly felt compromised objectivity, such as the fact that no other sites are being investigated. "DOE has all its eggs in one basket, and that basket is Yucca Mountain," he said. "And they did that for almost purely economical reasons."

Serious questions about the kind of science being conducted at Yucca Mountain lie just underneath the project's public relations façade. Interviews with scientists who have worked on various aspects of the project revealed more concern than the DOE's public face shows about issues that cannot be explained away—questions about earthquake activity, future mineral exploration, and especially about gaseous releases of radioactive materials and underground water movement at the mountain. Privately, some scientists (both "inside" employees and outside contractors) acknowledged the political pressure under which studies are conducted. Time and money present incontestable pressures.[47] Some scientists complained that important studies are not conducted because of these pressures.[48] One senior environmental scientist in a management position told me that it simply wasn't economically feasible to perform site characterization studies on more than one site in the nation. Thus, in 1987, the 1982 Nuclear Waste Policy Act was amended to consider and study only Yucca Mountain.[49] Scientists working under this policy understood well the implications of this limited research scenario. As one scientist told me:

> The idea was if Yucca Mountain didn't pass the test [of safety], then we had to go back to Congress, and they would tell us what to do. But that's scary, because if you have to start over you've got another three decades [of studies]. All the while this spent fuel is just piling up.

Such fears that Yucca Mountain might not pass the test were once again forcing Congress (in 1996) to amend the Nuclear Waste Policy Act:

> Well, frankly, there is a movement in the federal government right now to look at amending the Nuclear Waste Policy Act to make it, I shouldn't say easier, but to make it, ah, to make some contingencies if the site doesn't pass the test, but also to make it a little more realistic.

Making it "a little more realistic" for this scientist meant lowering the radiation standards to accommodate Congress's need to stamp Yucca Mountain safe for waste.[50]

Contestations over scientific data and findings at Yucca Mountain have emerged from time to time. In the late 1980s project geologist Jerry S. Szymanski suggested that water upsurges in the mountain brought on by earthquakes could conceivably flood the repository chambers.[51] In the early 1990s the *New York Times* science section reported that Los Alamos scientists suggested that the close proximity of casks could result in "criticality" and set off a nuclear explosion. But such criticisms—and almost all others—are consistently refuted by panels of experts (such as the National Research Council), allowing business to proceed as usual. (Szymanski, disagreeing with the panel, resigned from the project.)

Scientists who oppose siting the repository at Yucca Mountain have argued that ample evidence has existed for some time to disqualify the site as a repository.[52] Karl Johnson, technical director for the Nevada Nuclear Waste Project Office, himself a geologist and hydrologist, claims that scientists who disagree with the DOE management schedule and who want to conduct further studies that might slow down the DOE's schedule to site a repository are routinely ignored:

> I wouldn't go so far as to say they're being kept quiet. I think that's not appropriate. But I think while their views are listened to, that the DOE and especially the engineering side feels that there is this higher priority and this outweighs the need to collect the scientific data.[53]

Thus, in addition to the overriding concern of the national interest to find a permanent solution to the waste crisis, concern for achieving more limited goals (such as tunnel construction) overrides the need for more information. This pattern of hierarchizing goals ripples throughout a project subsumed by the national interest.

Johnson also accused the DOE of hiring "consultant hired guns"—that is, "consultants who will express the point of view of the client." He felt strongly that the 25-foot-diameter tunnel under construction at Yucca Mountain for the exploratory studies facility will compromise important scientific studies. The EIS chambers are to consist of 14 miles of tunnels, part of an eventual 1,400-acre mine under the mountain. Starting construction of the tunnels before "designation" of the site is, according to Johnson, the clearest indicator yet that the project will go ahead regardless of scientific "findings." Yucca Mountain Project literature (Winter 1996) claims that tunnel excavations "will provide valuable data" about, among other things, "how rock and systems for moving waste into a repository will perform over time."

Two years after this particular discussion with Johnson, and after funding for Yucca Mountain had been severely cut by Congress to demonstrate its dissatisfaction with the duration and cost of the project, I visited a Yucca Mountain information office. The office sported a big map of the repository showing how fast tunnel construction was proceeding. There was no doubt that the repository was being built, even though it still hadn't been deemed "safe." As another scientist—one who opposes Johnson's position—admitted in 1994:

> As soon as we go underground we spend billions of dollars, and so you're going to make the site pass the test. Because you're going to be under there, and you're already making those tunnels big enough for a repository . . . And we're doing that for cost sake, because if the site is suitable, why should we redrill things, you know? And so the state of Nevada wants us to stay on the surface doing only surface drilling, if that even. But it's a real concern—the NRC [Nuclear Regulatory Commission] is concerned about it too—we can potentially mess up the result, the test that we need to do.

Where the Ghost Dance Fault Meets the Repository Horizon: Water at Yucca Mountain

The Yucca Mountain Project produces a quarterly report, or newsletter, titled *Of Mountains & Science*, meant to give interested parties (specifically the nonscientific public) updates on the ongoing studies and issues of concern. Scientists are portrayed as reporting facts, but any perusal of the newsletter shows consistent effort (by the scientists themselves) to explain away any and all problems that emerge in studies of the mountain. Public acknowledgment of "problems" by the DOE is handled so carefully that they are allowed to be revealed only after they can be adequately contained or explained. For instance, in October 1994, as I toured the mountain with a senior environmental scientist, I learned that scientists had recently found tritium in the water table at Yucca Mountain (discovered in a borehole drilled near the Ghost Dance Fault on the southeast side of the mountain), and that such a discovery was capable of, in his words, "shutting the whole operation down." It wasn't until the winter of 1996 that the tritium problem appeared in *Of Mountains & Science*. Finding high amounts of tritium in the water meant that the water source was hydrologically "young" (less than forty years old; that is, young enough to have been polluted by tritium due to radiation testing in the latter half of the twentieth century). The unsettling implications of tritium in the groundwater were quickly explained away: Tritium-contaminated water was found in only one borehole (so far), so it wasn't yet perceived as a threat. Further, any water that might move into the repository, potentially corroding the waste canisters, and moving out into the environment (polluting it) could be dealt with by redirecting the tunnels away from the water path or sites of accumulation. As the acting chief of the Geological Survey blithely commented, "It is not a difficult situation at all—yet." Still, it "remains a concern" for him, since, he notes, "We're not in the business of trying to show the site is suitable if it's not." Like Odum's studies with radioisotopes, it is the "trace" of radioactivity within the system that reveals how dangerous radioactivity is to the environment.

The deep-geologic "natural" solution to the waste crisis necessitates human mediation to shore up the system (mediation such as reinforcing rock, venting systems for gases, or redirecting tunnels away from water sources). If "human mediation" is used repeatedly, it weakens the argument that a 10,000 year (more accurately a 250,000-year) stable "natural barrier" can be found to contain the waste. And since human mediation is relatively short-lived, its increase at the Yucca Mountain site is problematic. As one scientist at the project told me: "Humans can only take credit for a safe engineered barrier for 300 years. After that time, you have to assume radioactive material will bust out." The impermanence of any human-made container illustrates why a natural barrier is the barrier of choice. However, the dynamic nature of the "system," to use an ecological term, argues against containment. Earthquakes (the shifting of fault lines) create new fissures in the rock, and water travels through the mountain via fissures. If water enters the repository at some time in the future (because of new fractures caused by earthquakes), then arguments for natural barrier containment become moot. If water can move into the repository then it can also move out of it—taking radioactive elements with it.

In addition to showing that Yucca Mountain may not be impermeable, the discovery of tritium in the groundwater at Yucca Mountain reveals that so much tritium was released in thermonuclear tests worldwide since the 1960s that hydrologists can date water accordingly: thus, "A pocket of water containing substantial amounts of tritium can be characterized as less than forty years old. This is because water isolated before the 1960s would contain significantly less tritium than water isolated afterwards."[54] The same article also tells us that, today, "significant portions of existing tritium are produced in the nuclear reactors." The tritium is absorbed in coolant water, which evaporates and returns to the Earth in the form of rain and sinks into the ground into the aquifers that sustain us all. As the newsletter notes: "Tritium makes its way through air, water, food, and into virtually all living things."[55]

Tritium in the water at Yucca Mountain reveals more about the movement of water than the danger from the polluting radioisotope itself. Just as radioisotopes were purposefully used to chart ecosystems' pathways and "metabolism" in the Cold War years, another radioisotope (tritium) once again helps scientists to see the internal workings of the Earth's "system": water movement through *nearly* impenetrable rock at Yucca Mountain. Dating of the water is important. Forty-year-old water shows that it hasn't taken very long for water to move from the surface of the mountain into the so-called "unsaturated zone."

Although a dry region, Yucca Mountain is not without water, as the hydrologic studies show (and as we know from Indian narrations of the region).[56] Before the tritium discovery, hydrologists had studied the occurrence of "perched" water pockets or "zones" situated beneath the proposed repository (the unsaturated zone) but above the water table (the saturated zone). Concern over perched water focuses on the rate at which the water is moving, whether it is interconnected with other water sources, or whether it could potentially move through the repository site and beyond. To determine the movement of water into these zones, scientists pump it out of existing pockets of water and wait a period of time before remeasuring water levels, which allows them to determine whether or not these same pockets of water have filled back up, indicating water movement. According to the literature, tests are done using time periods measured in hours and weeks. From such tests, scientists predict water movement over thousands of years. Scientists rely greatly on computer models here. In tests conducted in 1995, some water did return to partially fill up the pockets, but not in "vast quantities." Scientists are quoted as saying that water "is probably moving, but is it moving fast enough over the next several thousand years for us to be concerned about?"[57]

The water pathways of concern, with their high concentrations of tritium, form a strange kind of geologic poetry. The Ghost Dance—after which the Ghost Dance Fault is named—was a powerful North American Indian millenarian movement. In 1870, a Paiute holy man, Wovoka, saw in a vision a "peace and prosperity" ritual. He prophesied the end of the world, return of the dead, and the destruction of white people. In the throes of enormous cultural upheaval, large numbers of Native peoples gathered at ritual centers to dance the Ghost Dance. It was a lament as well as a last effort to resuscitate indigenous cultures. Perhaps one can see poetic justice in the tritium-laced water traveling through the Ghost Dance Fault line at Yucca Mountain—Indian power come back to wreak havoc on the colonizer. The name of the fault also recalls the Indians who, in this context, continue to be concerned about the water and who assert that water connects all things deep beneath the Earth. It is the water, after all, that the Western Shoshone and the Southern Paiute fear will become contaminated and spread the contamination to "all the living things."

The Experimental Ethos and the Logic of Control

> The 10,000-year test: federal scientists focus their scrutiny and more than $1 billion on Nevada's Yucca Mountain, the probable site of the nation's first high-level radioactive waste dump.
> —RICHARD MONASTERSKY, *Science News*[58]

The problem of water flow into the repository site—as suggested by the borehole studies at the Ghost Dance Fault area and in the Calico Hills area—is potentially serious enough to disqualify Yucca Mountain as a repository site. Models of water moving through fissures and along pathways are crucial in predicting future scenarios. Simulation of future scenarios is a powerful tool, but simulations are not "reality"; they are stories. Models show us one of the ways scientists tell stories about the mountain, and about nature. Their computed predictions may even be highly probable, but they remain educated guesses based on incomplete information. The use of models to predict future scenarios shows that placing a repository at Yucca Mountain is essentially an experiment. As one senior scientist at the project told me:

> Some say it's impossible. Some say if you really want to build a repository, forget about the guidelines and just build the thing. It's just such a monumental project. . . . I mean, we have a better understanding of how this table [pointing to his office desk] is going to react sitting out there in the open, than we do about a natural system. I mean, there's just too many variables, but we're being asked to do that.

Scientists don't really know how the water will move through this environment thousands of years from now, how gases will move through it along pneumatic pathways, or how stable the earth itself is. These are model-produced stories with very high stakes.

The importance of water and predicting what water will do in the future has been of interest to indigenous people of this region since they can remember. It is central to their life and their culture, and it is deeply embedded into the structure of their linguistic system. The hydrologic studies of water at Yucca Mountain show that it is important to scientists, too. But their relationship with it is quite different. The scientific interest in water focuses on controlling the system. Control is necessary, but it is especially necessary because of our previous "experiments" with nuclear power. This experiment with nuclear materials is ongoing, forcing us to predict events into a future longer than previous recorded history and for as long as humans have lived in the region. The Yucca Mountain Project is radioecology on a grand scale.

Like the models used to determine water pathways at Yucca Mountain today, the models used by the Odums and others in ecosystems ecology promised control. The managerial ethos conceptually transforms nature into an integrated circuit, hardwired for work and productivity, a cybernetic system—a predictable, self-regulating system. Yucca Mountain, for its scientific practitioners, is every bit as much a cybernetic system as the nearby Nevada Proving Grounds were for Eugene Odum. The experimentation at Yucca Mountain is necessary to provide "feedback" that can be recycled into the system to make future predictions that will determine what actions to take. In this way the experimental ethos is connected to the manipulation of the system.[59] It is an ethos of control. But once the repository is sealed (after only 50 years), humans relinquish all control, and "nature" takes over. The concept of a closed system, suggesting containment, and the idea of feedback loops suggesting mediation and control are in this case mutually exclusive. A system of feedback loops remains a concept useful for today's technocrats who want to convey the illusion that they can safely contain the uncontainable transuranic elements. It is only from this skewed perspective, however, that Yucca Mountain can be regarded as a "system" with completely observable and predictable functions. Like the idea of a nuclear fuel "cycle" whose legacy is 70,000 tons of waste, the Yucca Mountain Project is a product of the "cybernetic technological functionalism" that began with the explosion of systems theory around the middle of the twentieth century.[60]

The model and the simple or complex *system* the model represents should be understood as text. Unlike the traditional Indian discourse on nature concerning this region, the scientific perspective here is textual-laden. As noted earlier, textuality and orality are cultural matrices through which one begins to know the nonhuman world. Neither contemporary Euroamericans or Western Shoshone exist exclusively in one mode of communication. However, social groups will rely on one mode more than the other, and some are more extreme in their concentration of a single mode. For instance, Western scientific nature at Yucca Mountain is represented and known almost exclusively through computational scripts, written reports and documents, computer models, and laboratory experiments that produce "data." Data are text. Textual mediation can have the effect of separating the distance between the perceiver and the perceived, between subject and object. The separation between subject and object is an inevitable separation within a literate society. The mountain and its environs are constantly mediated by computerized models, textual accounts, ultrasound waves, geologic boring drills taking core samples from layered rock, and tunnel-boring machines—an impressive variety of technologies employed to simulate, dissect, diagram, chart, and interpret the mountain's complex organization as a biogeochemical system prone to disturbances such as earthquakes and volcanoes. These technologies of knowledge metaphorically fragment the landscape, taking it apart in order to reassemble it into a simulated landscape. And they also separate the environment from the human within it. Mapping the landscape in this way also produces knowledge committed to containment, as opposed to that of expansion and movement characteristic of Indian narrative maps. However, in a complex way, both are committed to survival.

My interest in Indian claims about and representations of nature in the preceding chapter was meant not to determine their absolute truth value but rather to understand how they work and have worked historically in the lives of Indian people of the area—that is, how they work as practical, legitimate, culturally embedded representations of, and relations with, nature. Since Euroamericans usually perceive Indian knowledge as culturally determined, stressing the cultural embeddedness of Indian knowledge productions will not be perceived as problematic to the majority of the reading public. But this is not the case when it comes to Euroamerican truth claims and scientific knowledge assertions. Here, one finds powerful resistance to perceiving knowledge production as culturally embedded. Nevertheless, scientific work at Yucca Mountain is a cultural and political practice.

The "deserts as dumps" doctrine serves, as so many times before, as a backdrop to the Yucca Mountain Project. Compatible with the wasteland narrative, scientists promoting nuclear waste in the world's deserts rely on the economistic metaphors of productivity and efficiency to identify and represent the Yucca Mountain environment. Low productivity creates marginality in late industrial, hypercapitalist society. According to some environmental scientists today, a desert environment such as Yucca Mountain is worth sacrificing to the national interest because it is perceived as an unproductive ecosystem, and therefore expendable. While the scientists who wrote *Deserts as Dumps?* do not simplify the issue, in the end, they answer the question in the affirmative. For them, deserts, in general, are the best *ecosystems* for toxic-waste disposal. Though they admit that "it is inappropriate to think of these arid ecosystems as waste lands of no value, or to interpret their apparent barrenness as a lack of complexity," they go on to assert because of human mismanagement there has been a "loss of productivity of these *already marginally productive lands*."[61] (My italics.)

Thus, the preceding review of this experimental landscape does not ask whether, for instance, models of geochemical or hydrological processes are in and of themselves valid representations but, rather, how is the culture built into the model? How is it reflected in the *system*? And, in what way do political and cultural perspectives limit the field investigated by scientists? Validity of science is not the point here; the limitations of the scientific view and its malleability in the face of political power and technocratic ideologies are.

Conclusion

There is one special "model" that must be seen as never having worked, and that is epitomized in the Yucca Mountain experiment itself. At the beginning of the Nuclear Age, the public was told a story—a graphic model—about something called the "nuclear fuel cycle." This story promised us that we could recycle nuclear waste back into the system. The story was used to justify the obviously dangerous use of nuclear weapons and of nuclear power. And the story of the nuclear fuel cycle epitomized the myth of control of atomic energy. This myth guided policy decisions, the consequences of which we live with today.

Whatever model simulation we devise, it remains a text that we can tinker with and revise, but the outcome will elude us much as it did for those who devised and over the years revised the nuclear fuel cycle. It ceased being a cycle virtually from its inception. It became a spiral—spiraling out of control, because the "cycle" existed only in the minds of its creators, who demanded that reality conform to their ideal of a safe, clean, efficient, and replenishable source of energy to fuel what they believed to be a natural economy of production and consumption, supply and demand. By attempting to naturalize technology and the economy, humans (Euroamericans) only demonstrate that they cannot control nature. The power of the atom—the force within nature itself—unleashed cannot be put back in the ground as though it had never been called forth to do our bidding.

"Closing the circle of the atom" (a phrase recently used by the DOE to describe its "cleanup" strategies of the nuclear weapons complex) is not yet possible. As Odum's systems eventually demonstrated, and as tritium in the moving and "perched" waters at Yucca Mountain also shows, we have not been able to close the loop. The outdoor laboratories of the Department of Energy and the Department of Defense, laced with tritium, plutonium, and other radioactive elements, are living proof of this. Complete control, once again, evades us—but the ethos, or the fantasy, remains.

· 10 ·

Conclusion

In the 1959 textbook *Fundamentals of Ecology* Eugene Odum described ecosystems contamination resulting from nuclear testing fallout. One of the areas he studied was the Nevada Test Site. In the chapter "Radiation Ecology," Odum described the kind of lifestyle and place of habitation that would produce the highest risk of radiation contamination. His description matched, almost exactly, the contamination scenario experienced by Native Americans in that area. The irony of this is that Odum offered his description as a *hypothetical* scenario, because Native Americans were, for him, invisible. He wrote:

> [T]he peak level of radioiodine in the thyroids of humans during the 1955 test series was about 0.005 millimicrocuries per gram wet tissue . . . the maximum permissible level in man for continuous exposure is now listed as 15 millimicrocuries per gram. Note . . . that jack rabbits living at the 60 miles point along the fallout path had about 20 millimicrocuries per gram; kangaroo rats were found to have as much as 200 in the same study. *Therefore, we see that if man were forced to obtain all his food from a restricted contaminated*

area, he might easily be obtaining at least temporary levels which he would not want to risk. . . . Thus, we see that while there seems to be little to worry about radiation in average worldwide levels, local situations could change the picture drastically. Young children under four years of age accumulate Sr^{90} more rapidly than adults and are presumably more radiosensitive.[1]

The Moapa Paiute Reservation, along with other Indian tribes, constituted just such a "local situation." As the Moapa elder women said at the beginning of this book, "All of our activities were outside during those times." The Moapa Paiutes ate rabbit and deer and other animals from this region, and their drinking water was local. "Our water ran down along in front of our homes in ditches, so that was our water." All of the people—adults and children—lived outside in the summertime. They slept outside. Their lives are not hypothetical; nor are the deaths of those lost to cancer.

Just as radioactive isotopes were used in the 1960s to isolate food chains in radioecology (with herbivores feeding on plants and carnivores feeding on herbivores), recent locally initiated epidemiological studies on Indian cancer groups rely on radioactive isotopes in their studies. But in their case irradiation is not initiated by the researchers; rather it results from past government testing of nuclear bombs. We must ask: Where does the experimental field begin, and where does it end?

However unwitting, many scientists, including some of those studying nuclear fallout, are at least as complicit in making Indians invisible as the rest of us. Even today there are scientists working on the Yucca Mountain Project (in that same experimental landscape) who are unaware of contemporary Indian claims on that mountain, unaware of the close proximity of Indian communities to it.

Euroamericans expect science to predict the future and to protect us from harm, but clearly science does not possess such omnipotence. By separating science from the world around it—the cultural and political world—we have misjudged and misrepresented the role of science and its capabilities. Indeed, science has proved too often the handmaid of governmental, military, and corporate expansionist interests. Science has been deployed repeatedly in the national interest, but who and what determines the national interest, and who and what gets sacrificed to it? Many of the Indians interviewed for this book feel that their families and their lands have been sacrificed. In this sense, science contributes to the political and economic oppression of Indian people that began in the eighteenth century with the so-called Enlightenment and Manifest Destiny.

The complicity of science and the military for political and economic ends in the postwar era should be evident by now. We have seen, for example, how Indian issues and concerns about the region around Yucca Mountain have been ignored or discounted through various mechanisms of exclusion, including DOE-sponsored reports that are meant to include their perspectives on certain limited issues such as historical occupation.

We have seen how comparing two sets of perceptions about the environment and their intellectual lineages—the traditional Indian (specifically, the Western Shoshone, Southern Paiute, and Owens Valley Paiute) and the Western scientific—illuminates the limitations of each perspective, while simultaneously placing the two discourses on equal epistemological footing in such a way that one does not dominate the other due to its greater political power, or, as Bourdieu would say, "cultural capital."[2] In some respects, this balancing act is an artificial one since Euroamerican scientific representations of the region enjoy far more legitimacy and political prestige than those of the region's indigenous populations. Nevertheless, moving from one view to the other assists us in opening intellectual horizons onto the diversity of knowledge about place and nature that exist in this desert region. Comparing the two knowledge systems shows how environmental science, as a discipline and as practiced at Yucca Mountain, exists within a specific cultural and political context (and is a product of a specific cultural tradition), in the same way that Indian traditional knowledge about this environment exists within a cultural context. However, because environmental science is the dominant narrative, its truth claims are "naturalized," that is, taken out of their cultural context and perceived as self-evident, so much so that the narratives that science constructs about the natural world become resistant to critical scrutiny, especially from those outside the discipline itself.[3] The brief history of ecology, and ecosystems ecology in particular, in Chapter 9 illuminates some of the cultural and political factors that influence the Euroamerican perception of nature and that inform the Yucca Mountain Project—factors that exclude alternative perspectives that might jeopardize the project's implied political objective. By examining these factors in the larger context, we begin to see the powerful role of metaphors in scientific knowledge productions. They reveal the unstated assumptions from which we grasp the natural world and interpret it.

When we describe the extended Yucca Mountain region as an "outdoor laboratory," the experimental landscape becomes a metaphorical landscape as much as a material reality. Metaphoricity and materiality are not, for human beings, separate entities. In using language science situates itself within culture and manifests a cultural production. Cybernetic terminology imposes human mechanistic, electrochemical conceptualizations onto nature; to a large extent people comprehend nature through their cultural productions—texts and machines. In this respect nature is what we make it. The ecosystem perspective identifies nature with energy conceptualized as work, with productivity conceptualized as the capacity to produce consumable materials, and with efficiency—all words that help to build an industrial, cybernetic-oriented, and economistic society. As the metaphors used to describe natural processes change through time from Clements's organism to Odum's electro-chemical circuit machine, it becomes impossible not to see our current late industrial, technocratic society reflected in our science. Today, the environmental economic discourse on productivity, with its organization of ecosystems according to capacities of "worldwide annual gross primary production"[4] (see Figure 9.5) places Yucca Mountain as exceedingly low in the hierarchy of productivity, and thus deems it appropriate for nuclear waste disposal. But whose "productivity" are we talking about? Certainly not that of the Western Shoshone or Southern Paiute who have subsisted on the mountain's plants, animals, and water and who value the land in quite a different way.

Science relies heavily on metaphors when representing nature.[5] Ecology and, more specifically, the concept of the ecosystem are no exceptions. Here, economic and social metaphors proliferate to describe and explain nature. Many of these linguistic terms are politically motivated and are assertions of the status quo (stability, functionalist order, capitalist economics). Ironically, today, Indian pronouncements about nature are often dismissed as politically motivated. Why isn't such a phrase as "productive hierarchy" not seen as politically and culturally motivated, crafted to organize nature according to consumer interests? Indians claim that the land is sacred or holy homeland and thus should be under the care of the Native peoples. Capitalist Euroamericans say the land is resource rich and highly productive or unproductive and therefore should be used in various ways: for human consumption or for waste dumps. Which group—Native Americans or Euroameircans— is the more politically motivated?

Our representations of the world wield great power. By identifying Yucca Mountain as a wasteland we legitimate actions that turn it into a wasteland. When we fill it with high-level nuclear waste, our actions suggest a belief that the earth is inert (because we need it to be) despite our knowledge of its dynamism. We downplay or ignore knowledge of a huge regional aquifer, numerous shallow volcanic aquifers, earthquake activity, and potential volcanic activity. Even in this dry, quiet landscape with its dense enduring rock, water moves—in its various forms. And the materials we fill the rock with also move, change with time. Heat and gases are emitted from decaying radioisotopes, moisture accumulates, and canisters corrode.

The systems ecologists were right about one thing: Nature is dynamic, and high-level radioactive waste won't disappear. Eventually, it will be recycled back into the "system." It will accumulate in animals and humans down the food chain. If industry and the military continue to produce radioactive elements such as plutonium, they will become lively agents in a new kind of system that includes the transuranic elements, if not those who unleashed them. What the systems theorists mistook was the extent to which humans could control the system. Control in the cybernetic sense is different from "working with." It is analogous to the human control of other humans as governors of slaves. Eventually, the slaves revolt, become free radicals.

If we can learn anything from the Indian perspective in this region it is that we need to afford all things some degree of subjectivity. Even when today's scientists well understand the limits of "objectivity," Euroamerican culture—including scientists—continue to proceed as though humans live outside the world they attempt to manipulate and control. Control is not all bad. But the belief in the right to control an objectified Other is dangerously illusory. The experiment at Yucca Mountain, and the history of that region show the illusion (indeed, the fantasy) of control for what it is. Much like the "Sorcerer's Apprentice" of the Disney cartoon, the product of our meddling with forces we don't entirely understand escapes our control—multiplying and taking on a life of its own.

Nuclear Waste: So What Do We Do with It Now That We Have It?

A solution to the crisis of nuclear waste must be found. This is not a point of contention. What is contentious is how we go about solving this intractable problem. Pretending that burying 70,000 tons of high-level radioactive waste in a desert mountain will take care of our problem reveals the same kind of intellectual hubris that created the problem. We know radionuclides will eventually escape any type of containment, yet we continue to produce this waste and will need to find more and more places to put it. Sealing off the waste and hoping "nature" will contain it is the equivalent of sweeping the dirt under the rug. The dirt remains, and it is only a matter of time before it gets out from under. So what do we do?

People who oppose continued production of nuclear power and nuclear weapons do not ignore the fact that we have this waste on our hands and must do something with it. What they suggest we do is stop production and keep the waste where it is until suitable storage can be found, monitoring it carefully, and adjusting storage procedures as we learn more about possible solutions.[6] We need to be sure nongovernmental oversight is included in the decision-making process. And, I would add, some of that oversight should be conducted by nonscientists. The problem of nuclear waste has wide-ranging ethical, social, and cultural dimensions; it is a mistake to assume that storage and disposal are merely technical problems, just as it is a mistake to assume that science can contend with all the social ramifications of the problems. Finally, we need to recognize the pattern of environmental racism that has emerged in the desert regions currently targeted for containment of nuclear waste and make decisions commensurate with social equity and justice. These "experimental landscapes" are becoming sacrificial landscapes as are—once again—the people for whom the land is traditional homeland.

The Semiotics of Fear

Yucca Mountain in Nevada and the Waste Isolation Pilot Project (WIPP) in New Mexico—the two central nodes in the two zones of concentration in the nuclear landscape—must be seen as this country's unacknowledged monuments to the Cold War, to "progress," and to power as conceived in the Euroamerican tradition. Indeed, the cost of the Cold War requires a reckoning before "we" can be declared victors. These two sites call victory into question in a serious way.

In 1992, the Environmental Protection Agency assembled a "blue-ribbon panel" consisting of two anthropologists, an archaeologist, two astronomers, two materials scientists, a geologist, a linguist, an artist, and a cognitive psychologist to come up with a "permanent marker," a monumental and identifiable sign for future humans that would signal danger concerning the 240,000-year lethal waste stored at the WIPP facility (and at Yucca Mountain)—one that would serve as a sign for any future inhabitants when presumably any presently existing language would be extinct. The panel broke up into two teams to work on the mother of all DO NOT ENTER signs for the hottest of hot spots in the nuclear landscape. Among the various proposals were: *The Landscape of Thorns, The Spike Field, The Black Hole,* and last but not least, *The Menacing Earthworks.* These were described as follows:

> *The Landscape of Thorns:* One square mile of randomly spaced basalt spikes, 80 feet high, erupting from the ground at all angles.
>   Or, its cousin, *The Spike Field,* with thorns evenly spaced and erectile.
> *The Black Hole:* A boundless pad of black concrete that would absorb so much heat it would be impossible to even approach.
> *The Menacing Earthworks:* An expansive empty square, surrounded by 50-foot-high earthen berms jolting outward like jagged bolts of lightning. And at the center of the square, a 2,000-foot-long, walk-on, global map displaying all the world's nuclear dumps, including this one. Rudimentary message kiosks would dot the periphery. A sealed room just below ground would harbor the most intimate details of the repository's contents.[7]

Such is the human imagination for signifying the nuclear landscape. A walk-on global map displaying all the world's nuclear dumps stands as a heartbreaking vision of the future, and it demonstrates the international scope of this burgeoning problem. The territories that once were called the Soviet Union are dotted with nuclear dumps and contaminated zones—a nuclear landscape as great as that in the United States, if not greater. Many nations rely on nuclear power to a much greater extent than does the United States—France, for instance, which now must contend with thousands of tons of high-level nuclear waste. And in many cases—whether it be disposal of nuclear waste or testing of nuclear weapons (such as the recent tests by China and France)—indigenous populations, and the desert and oceanic regions of the Third World and Fourth World, will continue to bear the burden. Clearly, much more needs to be written and investigated about international geographies of sacrifice. Kazakhstan served as a nuclear testing ground for the former Soviet Union, the Pacific Islands served France and the United States, the Western Shoshone and Southern Paiute desert lands served the United States, and Tibet continues to serve China. Many of these same regions will be the dumping grounds for nuclear waste from the failed experiment in nuclear energy in the twenty-first century. In addition, Africa will provide dumps for the First World, and Orchid Island already provides an indigenous dump for Taiwan (with its U.S.-backed nuclear power companies). The list goes on. All these providers are indigenous peoples and indigenous lands. And at the rate nuclear fuel is processed throughout the world, nuclear colonialism will expand into and beyond the twenty-first century—unless production is stopped.

The pursuit of nuclear power in both its militaristic and economic forms has had and will continue to have tragic consequences for life in the American desert and beyond. A fundamental redefinition of our relationship between the human and nonhuman is needed to find solutions to the problems that the radical separation between them has helped create. Otherwise, in the American West, we will continue to project those tragic consequences into the future and lay waste a desert whose secret source of life—water—is our common bond and heritage.

Notes

Preface

1. The term *nuclearism* here refers to the entire complex of nuclear weapons testing, research and development, production, stockpiling, and waste disposal from nuclear weapons development and nuclear power plants.

2. Steve Boster, "CLPP Produced High Explosives for First A-Bombs: Manhattan Project Remembered as 50-Year Anniversary Approaches," *The Rocketeer*, 27 January 1995.

3. Criticizing one's home community is difficult. I have much respect and love for many who live here, and with whom I grew up. I recognize that some form of national defense is necessary; nevertheless, the enterprise of weapons creation and its impact on the region's land and people need to be illuminated. Ultimately, it must fall on those who come from within these communities to speak out, since they are the ones who have had access to such environments. My critique of the Naval Weapons Center at China Lake is not targeted at any individuals, living or deceased. It is simply meant to make visible the invisible powers that exist in these desert regions.

4. Although blindness to ethnic diversity still dominates cultural attitudes in the area, there have been recent signs of interest, recognition, and concern among some people in the China Lake community. And to my astonishment, there was actually a powwow in Ridgecrest, a town outside of China Lake, in the fall of 1995—the first ever since the Navy's occupation of the land—an indication of the reemergence of the Indian populations of the area. (A second powwow was held in the fall of 1996.)

Chapter 1

1. Evelyn Samalar, interview by author, tape recording, Moapa Paiute reservation, Nevada, 18 April 1995.

2. Lalovi Miller, interview by author, tape recording, Moapa Paiute reservation, Nevada, 18 April 1995.

3. A nongovernmental epidemiological study of the health problems of Indian communities surrounding the Nevada Test Site was recently initiated by the Citizen Alert Native American Project and the Childhood Cancer Research Institute. A related program, Nuclear Risk Management for Native Communities, is an ongoing Indian-initiated project responding to the health concerns of several native communities dealing with radiation contamination risks.

4. U. S. Department of Energy, *Environmental Management* 1995, February 1995, DOE/EM-0228.

5. Advisory Committee on Human Radiation Experiments, "Final Report, " October 1995 (Washington, D.C.: Government Printing Office, report no. 061-000-00-848-9).

6. The term "nuclear colonialism" links nuclearism to colonialist practices. The term began to be used in the early 1990s and appeared to emerge simultaneously among activists and Indians. I have encountered it in the writing of Ward Churchill, as well as in the work of Jennifer Viereck (an antinuclear and Indian land-rights activist and political writer), but others have used it also.

7. Ward Churchill, *Struggle for the Land: Indigenous Resistance to Genocide, Ecocide and Expropriation in Contemporary North America* (Monroe, Maine: Common Courage 1993), 23–26. Churchill uses the term "radioactive colonialism" in the same way that I use "nuclear colonialism." His analysis of radioactive colonialism is embedded within the framework of internal colonialism.

8. I purposefully use local and activist maps and perspectives to identify the nuclear landscape. This methodological strategy is meant to open a space for further investigation. Activist claims are not without bias; however, they are particularly important because they usually erupt out of dire, often life-threatening circumstances.

9. For example, on the international level, as Africanist scholar Paul Lubeck has suggested, much of Africa has become "deterritorialized," or made into an international sacrifice zone.

10. Because deserts are targeted for nuclear testing and waste disposal, my geographic focus is on the interdesert region, as opposed to the more commonly studied intermountain region.

11. Nuclear power plants and their cooling ponds (for the spent-fuel rods), as well as processing centers on the East Coast of the United States, constitute a nuclear landscape in their own right. However, this study is focused on the West and Southwest desert region.

12. Donna J. Haraway, *Modest_Witness@Second_Millennium.FemaleMan©_Meets_Onco-Mouse*™ (New York: Routledge, 1996).

13. Jerry Mander, *In the Absence of the Sacred: The Failure of Technology and the Survival of the Indian Nations* (San Francisco: Sierra Club Books, 1991), 6–7.

14. Of course, the U.S. nuclear landscape is not limited to the continental United States, but also exists in significant concentration in Hawaii, Alaska, and U.S. territories in the Pacific and elsewhere.

15. Samuel H. Day, ed., *Nuclear Heartland: A Guide to 1,000 Missile Silos of the United States* (Madison, Wis.: Nukewatch, 1988), 6.

16. "Because the federal government has never created a storage site for high-level radioactive waste, fuel pools in nuclear plants across the country have become de facto nuclear dumps—with many filled nearly to capacity. The pools weren't designed for this purpose, and risk is involved: the rods must be submerged at all times. A cooling system must dissipate the intense heat they give off. If the system failed, the pool could boil, turning the plant into a lethal sauna filled with clouds of radioactive steam. And if earthquake, human error or mechanical failure drained the pool, the result could be catastrophic: a meltdown of multiple cores taking place outside the reactor containment, releasing massive amounts of radiation and rendering hundreds of square miles uninhabitable." Eric Pooley, "Nuclear Warriors," *Time*, 4 March 1996.

17. An analysis of (and argument for) deserts as nuclear and toxic waste dumps in the United States, as well as in the world, can be found in Charles C. Reith and Bruce M. Thomson, eds., *Deserts as Dumps? The Disposal of Hazardous Materials in Arid Ecosystems* (Albuquerque: University of New Mexico Press, 1992).

18. On July 16, 1979, the United Nuclear Corporation's tailings dam failure at Church Rock, New Mexico, resulted in 100 million gallons of radioactive water spilling into the Rio Puerco.

19. The reprocessing of nuclear materials is perhaps the only stage not present here.

20. Specifically, WIPP is outside the towns of Carlsbad and Loving, New Mexico, approximately 85 miles from the Mescalero Apache reservation. The reservation is therefore between two important nuclear sites—WIPP and the Trinity Site on the White Sands Missile Range.

21. Bureau of the Census, Population Division, Racial Statistics Branch, *A Statistical Portrait of the American Indian Population* (Washington, D.C.: Government Printing Office, 1984); Department of Health and Human Services, *Chart Series Book* (Washington, D.C.: Public Health Service HE20.9409.988, 1988), cited in Churchill, *Struggle for the Land*, 262.

22. Department of Interior, *Indian Lands Map: Oil, Gas, and Minerals on Indian Reservations* (Washington, D.C.: Government Printing Office, 1978), cited in Churchill, *Struggle for the Land*, 261.

23. Churchill's account of "internal colonialism" also makes important connections between the way in which Indians are viewed as expendable labor for extractive industries and the way the U.S. government uses its "trust" authority over reservations to support outside corporate—not Indian—profitability. Churchill, *Struggle for the Land*, 262.

24. Of course, Indians aren't the only people in this area. Many Spanish-speaking Americans live here along with Euroamericans and others. I focus on the Indian population because they are rarely recognized, are concentrated in this area, are profoundly impoverished, and have far more compelling historical ties to this land than do other populations in the area.

25. Hal Rothman, *On Rims and Ridges: The Los Alamos Area Since 1880* (Lincoln: University of Nebraska Press, 1992), 208.

26. Although I refer to the energy companies as a "third player" here, they are, in fact, closely tied to and protected by the state in matters of "national security."

27. K. S. Shrader-Frechette, *Burying Uncertainty* (Berkeley: University of California Press, 1993), 15, citing: House Subcommittee on Energy and Power of the Committee on Energy and Commerce, *Safety of DOE Nuclear Facilities*, 101st Congress, 1st sess., 1989, serial no. 101-1 (Washington, D.C.: Government Printing Office, 1989); House Subcommittee on Energy and Environment of the Committee on Interior and Insular Affairs, *Nuclear Waste Policy Act*, 100th Congress, 1st sess., 1988 (Washington, D.C.: Government Printing Office, 1988), 3ff., 45ff., 46–47, 97, 211ff., 393; U.S. Congress, NWP, 31, 73, 41ff., 185.

28. Although consisting of separate "players," both military and commercial uses of nuclear power were weapons in the strategic aim to "roll back" the Soviet Empire.

29. Although plans for new domestic nuclear power plants have momentarily ceased, the United States government, along with the nuclear industry, is still actively promoting so-called "peaceful" nuclear energy in developing nations; most recently, in China.

30. Shrader-Frechette, *Burying Uncertainty*, 15, citing S. Novik, *The Electric War* (San Francisco: Sierra, 1976), 32–33.

31. Ibid.

32. Ibid. 15–16.

33. Ibid. 18–19, citing Henry Kendall, "Calling Nuclear Power to Account," *Calypso Log* 18, no. 5 (October 1991).

34. Shrader-Frechette, in *Burying Uncertainty*, estimates that this figure has already been reached. Projections vary widely in part because of the system used to classify waste levels. What is classified as "high-level" nuclear waste usually comes from electricity-generating nuclear power plants. Fuel for power plants consists of solid pellets of enriched uranium that have been sealed in tubes that are bundled together to form a nuclear fuel assembly. The fuel is "spent" in about one year, at which time it is removed from the reactor and replaced. The spent fuel rods are highly radioactive. (See also Chapter 4 on problems relating to the classification of radioactive waste.)

Chapter 2

1. Dorothy A. Purley, interview by author, tape recording, Paguate Village, Laguna Pueblo reservation, New Mexico, 16 September 1995.

2. Dorothy Purley's testimony should be read as a personal discussion with the author only, not as an official statement from the Laguna Pueblo. Dorothy's outspoken stand and her criticism of the uranium mines are not necessarily shared by all Pueblo or Navajo people.

3. Reith and Thomson, *Deserts as Dumps?*, 38–39.

4. Churchill, *Struggle for the Land*, 264. For an excellent account (with footnote resources) of the uranium industry in Indian country, see all of the chapter titled "Radioactive Colonization: Hidden Holocaust in Native North America." Other sources cited by Churchill to substantiate this claim are Richard Hoppe, "A Stretch of Desert along Route 66—the Grants Belt—Is Chief Locale for U.S. Uranium," *Engineering and Mining Journal* 79, no. 11 (1978), 79–93. Also see Winona LaDuke, "A History of Uranium Mining," *Black Hills/Paha Sapa Report*, vol. 1, no. 1 (1979).

5. [Hosteen Kinlichee], "An Overview of Uranium and Nuclear Development on Indian Lands in the Southwest," in *Southwest Indigenous Uranium Forum Newsletter* (Gallup, N.Mex.: September 1993), 5.

6. This was the famous Project Trinity. The Alamagordo Range site was, and of course still is, near the Mescalero Apache reservation in Southern New Mexico. Because of their proximity to the explosion site some Mescalero Apache claim to be among the first victims (along with the Atomic Veterans present at this site during the explosion) of atmospheric nuclear weapons testing because of downwind contamination.

7. [Kinlichee], "Overview of Uranium," 6.

8. Ibid.

9. Marjane Ambler, *Breaking the Iron Bonds* (Lawrence: University Press of Kansas, 1990), 152.

10. Department of the Interior, *Final Report* Environmental Impact Statement for the Jackpile-Paguate Uranium Mine Reclamation Project, vol. II (Albuquerque, N.Mex.: October 1986), A–35. Statement by Chester T. Fernando, governor of Pueblo Laguna.

11. Department of the Interior, *Final Report* Environmental Impact Statement for the Jackpile-Paguate Uranium Mine Reclamation Project, vol. II, A–36.

12. "Colorado and Utah led the country in uranium production in the 1950s and early 1960s, with New Mexico and Wyoming gaining first place in the 1970s." Arjun Makhijani, Howard Hu, and Katherine Yih, *Nuclear Wastelands* (Cambridge, Mass: MIT Press, 1995), 113.

13. Churchill, *Struggle for the Land*, 264.

14. Ibid., 262. Citing Joseph G. Jorgenson, "The Political Economy of the Native American Energy Business," in *Native Americans and Energy Development*, II, ed. Joseph G. Jorgenson (Boston: Anthropology Resource Center/Seventh Generation Fund, 1984), 9–20.

15. For more information on the health risks associated with uranium mining and milling, see Linda Taylor, "Uranium Legacy," *The Workbook*, vol. VIII, no. 6 (Albuquerque, N.Mex: Southwest Research and Information Center, Nov./Dec. 1983); Jonathan M. Samet et al., "Uranium Mining and Lung Cancer in Navajo Men," *The New England Journal of Medicine*, 310, no. 23 (7 June, 1984); Navajo Health Authority, "Neoplasms Among Navajo Children," grant proposal (Window Rock, Ariz.: 24 February, 1981); Paul Robinson, "Uranium Production and Its Effects on Navajo Communities Along the Rio Puerco in Western New Mexico," *The Proceedings of the Michigan Conference on Race and the Incidence of Environmental Hazards*, ed. Bunyan Bryant and Paul Nohai (Ann Arbor: University of Michigan School of Natural Resources, 1990). See also: Arjun Makhijani, Howard Hu, and Katherine Yih, *Nuclear Wastelands* (Cambridge, Mass: MIT Press, 1995), Chapter 5. Makhijani's *Nuclear Wastelands* identifies the major health studies conducted on uranium miners. It also documents the historical disregard of the studies' results (that certain aspects of uranium mining were dangerous to miners and should be altered) by the uranium companies and the Atomic Energy Commission.

16. *Radiological Quality of the Environment in the United States*, U.S. Environmental Protection Agency (Washington, D.C.: Government Printing Office, 1977), 62–66. (Cited in Churchill, 1993, p. 266.) See also L.M. Shields et. al., "Navajo Birth Outcomes in the Shiprock Uranium Mining Area," *Health Physics*, vol. 63, 542–551; and Donald Calloway, "Neoplasms Among Navajo Children," submitted to the Division of Health Improvement Services, Navajo Tribe (Fort Defiance, Arizona), February 1981.

17. Donald Calloway, "Neoplasms Among Navajo Children," submitted to the Division of Health Improvement Services, Navajo Tribe (Fort Defiance, Arizona), February 1981. Cited in *The Workbook*, Southwest Research and Information Center, vol. VIII, no. 6, November-December 1983.

18. *The Workbook*, Southwest Research and Information Center, Vol. VIII, No. 6, November-December 1983.

19. Marjane Ambler, *Breaking the Iron Bonds*, 174.

20. Rita Begay qouted in Melissa Schlanger, "'Right Off We Could Tell It Was Unusual,'" *Gallup (N.M.) Independent*, 18 July 1989.

21. Chris Shuey, "The Puerco River: Where Did the Water Go?" *The Workbook*, vol. XI, no. 1, (Albuquerque, N.Mex: Southwest Research and Information Center, January/March, 1986).

22. Arjun Makhijani, Howard Hu, and Katherine Yih, *Nuclear Wastelands*, 121.

23. Churchill, *Struggle for the Land*, 271, citing Environmental Protection Agency, *Potential Health and Environmental Hazards of Uranium Mine Wastes* (Washington, D.C.: Government Printing Office, 1983), 1–23.

24. D. R. Dreeson, "Uranium Mill Tailings: Environmental Implications," *Los Alamos Scientific Laboratory Mini-Report* (February 1978), 1–4. Cited in Churchill, *Struggle for the Land*, 275.

25. Churchill, *Struggle for the Land*, 275, citing Thadias Box et al., *Rehabilitation Potential for Western Coal Lands* (Cambridge, Mass: Ballinger, 1974).

26. L. M. Shields et al., "Navajo Birth Outcomes in the Shiprock Uranium Mining Area," *Health Physics* 63, no. 5 (1992).

27. Taylor, "Uranium Legacy," 199.

28. L. M. Shields et al., "Navajo Birth Outcomes," 550.

29. Department of the Interior, *Final Report* Environmental Impact Statement for the Jackpile-Paguate Uranium Mine Reclamation Project, A–10.

30. This kind of collaboration between scientists and private or government interests also occurred in lawsuits between the Department of Energy and downwind victims of nuclear testing at the Nevada Test Site area (described in Chapter 3).

31. Even though the final settlement with the Anaconda Company gave the Laguna Pueblo Indians enough money to unsatisfactorily reclaim the mine, they are still left working with uranium tailings as one of their primary means of making a living. Again, they appear to be at risk, excluded, and expendable.

32. Department of the Interior, *Final Report* Environmental Impact Statement for the Jackpile-Paguate Uranium Mine Reclamation Project, A–62 and 63. Statement by Mr. Herman Garcia of Paguate village.

33. *Final Report* Environmental Impact Statement for the Jackpile-Paguate Uranium Mine Reclamation Project, A–48. Statement by Mr. Harold Lockwood of the Laguna tribe.

34. Susan Pearce and Karen Navarro, "The Legacy of Uranium Mining for Nuclear Weapons," *Enchanted Times*, Summer 1993 (Albuquerque, N.Mex.).

35. And, of course, much traditional Indian land is now national park land and wildlife preserve, which doesn't make it exempt from contamination. For example near Moab, Utah, sits a site (owned by Denver Atlas Corp.) harboring 10 million tons of uranium mill waste, which are slowly leaking contaminants into the Colorado River. The radioactive dump (a 130-acre radioactive legacy of the Cold War) sits between Arches National Park and a wildlife preserve. Canyonlands national parks, the Grand Canyon National Park, Glen Canyon, and Lake Mead

national recreation area are all downstream from the tailings pile. The U.S. Nuclear Regulatory Commission has determined that moving the dump would be too expensive, and so it remains in this fragile landscape on a waterway that feeds millions of people.

36. Phone interview with Chris Shuey, 19 November 1996. Shuey is Community Water, Wastes and Toxics project director at the Southwest Research and Information Center, Albuquerque, New Mexico. See also Paul Robinson, "Review of Recent Uranium Production and Market Trends." This report was prepared on behalf of the Inter-Church Uranium Committee. It was presented at the Joint Federal Provincial Panel on Uranium Mining Development in Northern Saskatchewan, 13–14 June, 1996. Paul Robinson is research director for the Southwest Research and Information Center in Albuquerque, New Mexico.

37. Winona LaDuke, "Native Environmentalism," *Earth Island Journal* (Summer, 1993), 35.

38. Richard Nafziger, "Transnational Energy Corporations and American Indian Development," *American Indian Energy Resources and Development*, Development Series no. 2, ed. Ortiz (Albuquerque: Native American Studies Dept., University of New Mexico, 1980), 14.

39. Ibid., 14.

40. Paul Robinson, "Uranium Production and Its Effects on Navajo Communities Along the Rio Puerco in Western New Mexico," in *The Proceedings of the Michigan Conference on Race and the Incidence of Environmental Hazards*, ed. Bunyan Bryant and Paul Nohai (Ann Arbor: University of Michigan School of Natural Resources, 1990), 176.

Chapter 3

1. Michael Renner, "Tarnished Armories," *Environmental Action*, May/June 1991, cited in William Thomas, *Scorched Earth: The Military's Assault on the Environment* (Philadelphia, PA: New Society Publishers, 1995), 17–18. For a visual image of U.S. militarized airspace, see: Richard Bargen, *Airspace Blues* (privately printed, 1989) as shown in Richard Misrach, *Bravo 20: The Bombing of the American West* (Baltimore and London: Johns Hopkins University Press, 1990), 9.

2. Gerald D. Nash, *The American West Transformed: The Impact of the Second World War* , 157.

3. Ibid., 157.

4. Concerned Citizens for Nuclear Safety, *The Nuclear Reactor*, vol. 3, no. 2 (Santa Fe, N.Mex., May/June 1994).

5. Nash, *The American West Transformed*, 177. My inclusion of China Lake is added to Nash's description. China Lake is often omitted from these kinds of accounts, not because of its size and position (it was and is one of the largest centers of weapons development in the world) but because of its secrecy.

6. The Department of Energy has, over the past five years, spent $7.5 billion in attempts to clean up Hanford's radioactive contaminants. Still, very little has actually been cleaned up. For a brief overview of Hanford's legacy see Kenneth J. Garcia, "The Cold War Colonies: America's Nuclear Legacy" and "Hanford's Poisoned Landscape," *San Francisco Chronicle*, 2 April 1995. For a more in-depth overview see Michele Stenehjem Gerber, *On the Home Front: The Cold War Legacy of the Hanford Nuclear Site* (Lincoln: University of Nebraska Press, 1992). See also Michael D'Antonio, *Atomic Harvest: Hanford and the Lethal Toll of America's Nuclear Arsenal* (New York: Crown, 1993).

7. "Valley of the Rockets: The Jewel In the Navy's Crown," from "China Lake Commemorates 50 Years" in *The Ridgecrest* (Calif.) *News Review*, November, 1993.

8. R. E. Kistler and R. M. Glen, *Notable Achievements of the Naval Weapons Center*, NWC TP 7088 (China Lake, Calif.: Naval Weapons Center, August 1990), 16.

9. Rothman, *On Rims and Ridges*, 225.

10. The government has acknowledged these tests in a stunning investigation of radiation experimentation culminating in a final report published in 1995. Most references to intentional

radiation releases in this chapter are documented in this report, including previously secret and undisclosed releases at Los Alamos, the AEC's Oak Ridge facilities in Tennessee, the Dugway Proving Grounds in Utah, the Hanford facility, and in Alaska. See Advisory Committee on Human Radiation Experiments "Final Report," Washington, D.C.: Government Printing Office, October, 1995. Report no. 061-000-00-848-9.

11. Advisory Committee on Human Radiation Experiments "Final Report," Washington, D.C.: Government Printing Office, October, 1995. Report no. 061-000-00-848-9, 255–531. These tests are also noted in: John Fleck, "Lab Sent N-Clouds Adrift Over New Mexico," *Albuquerque Journal*, 16 December, 1993, cited in Tad Ensign and Glenn Alcalay, "Duck and Cover(up): U.S. Radiation Testing on Humans," *Covert Action Quarterly*, no. 49 (Summer 1994).

12. Though reports of government abuse do sometimes reach fantastic proportions, my experience has been that most accounts that emerge from "concerned citizens" usually can be substantiated, making "anecdotal evidence" an important thread to pull on when attempting to unravel the cloak of darkness surrounding the nuclear weapons complex.

13. Tyler Mercer, Advisory Committee on Human Radiation Experiments, transcript of proceedings of 30 January 1995, Santa Fe, New Mexico, 35.

14. Advisory Committee on Human Radiation Experiments, 529–530.

15. Ensign and Alcalay, "Duck and Cover(up)," citing R. Jeffrey Smith, "U.S. Discloses 204 Secret Nuclear Tests," *Washington Post*, 8 December, 1993; General Accounting Office, "Nuclear Health and Safety: Examples of Post World War II Radiation Releases at U.S. Nuclear Sites," November 1993, RCED 94-51FS.

16. Garcia, "The Cold War Colonies," citing 1986 Department of Energy documents that revealed the Green Run experiment and other releases.

17. Advisory Committee on Human Radiation Experiments, 514–518.

18. This expansion is, in part, ironically the result of the end of the Cold War and the dismantling of the armed forces' presence abroad. See Michael DiGregorio and Jim Rosenthal, "The Final Frontier: The Cold War's Over, but the Armed Forces Continue Their Expansion at Home," *Mother Jones*, October 1996.

19. The term "squatter community" has been used by the National Park Service in Death Valley to refer to the Timbisha Shoshone band of the Western Shoshone Indians, which preexists the Park Service in the area.

20. The Spanish name "Pajarito" is derived from the Tewa Indian "Tsirege" of AD 1300. Tsirege means "little bird" and was translated from the Tewa language into the Spanish "Pajarito" by the archaeologist Edgar L. Hewett.

21. Los Alamos is also near traditional Spanish-speaking communities such as Espanola and others. These are identified in Rothman, *On Rims and Ridges*. The pueblo communities closest to the labs are the San Ildefonso and Santa Clara pueblos. Other pueblos in the surrounding area are also affected by the labs' activities, especially those downstream in the Rio Grande Valley.

22. Suzanne Ruta, "Fear and Silence in Los Alamos," *The Nation*, 4-11 January 1993. For a brief overview of environmental management programs currently planned for the Nuclear Complex, including Los Alamos, see U.S. Department of Energy, Office of Environmental Management, February 1995. DOE/EM-0228.

23. Suzanne Ruta, "Fear and Silence in Los Alamos," *The Nation*, 4-11 January 1993.

24. Concerned Citizens for Nuclear Safety, *The Nuclear Reactor* (Fall 1996).

25. Jay Coghlin, phone conversation with author, 9 December 1996. Jay Coghlin is Concerned Citizens for Nuclear Safety's LANL program director.

26. Los Alamos Study Group, All People's Coalition, *Enchanted Times*, Fall/Winter 1993 (Albuquerque, N.Mex.), p. 6.

27. Concerned Citizens for Nuclear Safety, *The Nuclear Reactor*, vol. 3, no. 3 (September/October 1994) and vol. 4, no. 1 (Spring 1995).310

28. Concerned Citizens for Nuclear Safety, "LANL Deliberately, Secretly Released Radiation on at Least Three Separate Occasions in 1950," *The Nuclear Reactor*, vol. 3, no. 1 (February/March 1994).

29. Mary Riseley, "LANL Gropes to Find a New Way," *Enchanted Times*, Fall/Winter 1993 (Albuquerque, N.Mex.: All People's Coalition, Los Alamos Study Group), 6.

30. The expansion of Area G has also been momentarily abated because LANL scientists have decided to practice waste compaction, reducing the volume of waste so that it requires less room for burial. Though this practice may delay the expansion, it is not a long-term solution to waste reduction.

31. Riseley, "LANL Gropes to Find a New Way," 7.

32. Louis Freedberg, "Livermore: Panel Recommends Ending Nuclear Arms Work," *San Francisco Chronicle*, 2 February 1995. Despite the recommendation of the commission, neither facility will lose its command post as a premiere weapons laboratory. The Stockpile Stewardship PEIS report designates new subcritical nuclear testing facilities to be built at Livermore, Los Alamos, and other sites in the West. (See: United States Department of Energy, *Final Programmatic Environmental Impact Statement for Stockpile Stewardship and Management*, September 1996. DOE/EIS-0236.)

33. Ruta, "Fear and Silence in Los Alamos."

34. Ruta, "Fear and Silence in Los Alamos."

35. United States Department of Energy, *Final Programmatic Environmental Impact Statement for Stockpile Stewardship and Management*, September 1996, vol. I, 4–407, DOE/EIS-0236.

36. Debra Rosenthal, *At the Heart of the Bomb: The Dangerous Allure of Weapons Work* (Menlo Park, Calif: Addison-Wesley, 1990), 10.

37. Rosenthal, *At the Heart of the Bomb*, 9. For a good introduction to Sandia Labs and Manzano Mountain, see Chapter 2, "Sandia Bomb & Novelty," which is the nickname given Sandia Labs by its own engineers.

38. *Albuquerque Journal*, 24 April 1992 and *Albuquerque Tribune*, 13 April 1993, cited in All People's Coalition, "Communities Concerned about Potential Radioactive Dumping in Albuquerque Sewers," *Enchanted Times*, Summer 1993.

39. All People's Coalition, "People's Emergency Response Committee," *Enchanted Times*, Summer 1993 (Albuquerque, N.Mex.)

40. That it takes the presence of white, middle-class activists to make such issues visible is unfortunate and reveals the racism of U.S. society. However, evidence exists that coalitions composed exclusively of communities of color are gaining ground in influencing environmental policy. Such coalitions in the United States may face powerful obstacles in the near future, however, because of the current ultraconservative composition of Congress.

41. Tad Bartimus and Scott McCartney, *Trinity's Children: Living Along America's Nuclear Highway* (New York: Harcourt Brace Jovanovich, 1991), 32.

42. "Missile Range Serves as Model for T&E," *Aviation Week & Space Technology*, 140/24, 13 June, 1994, 49.

43. Tad Bartimus and Scott McCartney, *Trinity's Children: Living Along America's Nuclear Highway*, 40.

44. Joseph Masco's work on nuclearism and militarism in "Indian Country" in New Mexico illustrates the scope and impact of current practice battlefields, especially the Army's Theater Missile Defense Extended Test Range Proposal on the Navajo community. Masco has written of the Army's campaign to "elicit support for a program to test a new generation of PATRIOT missile interceptors" over the entire northwestern half of New Mexico. From paper submitted to the 1996 American Anthropological Association; panel titled: "The Space of History and Identity in Native American Futures."

45. This was especially true in the early years (late 1940s to 1960s). However, many of the scientists—living in these regions for decades—have also made these lands their home, and so have

come to regard the desert with a mixture of appreciation and utilitarianism. Weapons work is filled with such contradictory feelings.

46. "Naval Weapons Center Silver Anniversary," Technical Information Department Publishing Division, China Lake Naval Weapons Center, October 1968.

47. David Loomis, *Combat Zoning: Military Land-Use Planning in Nevada* (Reno/Las Vegas: University of Nevada Press, 1994), 70.

48. For more on the rock art in the Coso area see David S. Whitley and Ronald I. Dorn, "Rock Art Chronology in Easter California," *World Archaeology*, 16 (2) 1987; David S. Whitley et al., "The Late Prehistoric Period in the Coso Range and Environs, *Pacific Coast Archaeological Society Quarterly*, 24 (1), January 1988; Ronald I. Dorn and David S. Whitley, "Chronometric and Relative Age Determination of Petroglyphs in the Western United States," *Annals of the Association of American Geographers*, 74 (2) 1984.

49. "Valley of the Rockets: The Jewel In the Navy's Crown," *The Ridgecrest* (Calif.) *News Review.*

50. Gaylene Moose, interview by author, tape recording, Bishop Paiute Tribe of the Owens Valley, Big Pine, California, 20 November 1994.

51. R. E. Kistler and R. M. Glen., *Notable Achievements of the Naval Weapons Center*, NWC TP 7088 (China Lake, Calif: Naval Weapons Center, August 1990), 17.

52. William Thomas, *Scorched Earth: The Military's Assault on the Environment* (Philadelphia: New Society Publishers, 1995), 17, citing Kristen Ostling and Joanna Miller, "Taking Stock: The Impact of Militarism on the Environment," *Science for Peace*, February 1992.

53. Richard W. Stoffle et al., *Native American Cultural Resource Studies at Yucca Mountain, Nevada* (Ann Arbor: Institute for Social Research, University of Michigan, 1990).

54. Loomis, *Combat Zoning*, 9–10.

55. Michael Skinner, *Red Flag* (Novato, Calif: Presidio, 1984), 52, cited in Loomis, *Combat Zoning*, 10.

56. Steven J. Crum, *The Road on Which We Came: A History of the Western Shoshone* (Salt Lake City: University of Utah Press, 1994), 1.

57. For an explanation of the Western Shoshone sisters Mary and Carrie Dann and of how their legal battles over land use represent Western Shoshone sovereignty in Nevada, see Jerry Mander, *In the Absence of the Sacred*, 311–312.

58. Julian H. Steward, *Basin-Plateau Aboriginal Sociopolitical Groups*, Bureau of American Ethnology, Bulletin 120. Washington, D.C.: Smithsonian Institution, 1938; Warren L. D'Azevedo et al., ed, "Tribal Distribution and Boundaries in the Great Basin," *The Current Status of Anthropological Research in the Great Basin 1964*, Desert Research Institute Technical Report Series S-H. Social Sciences and Humanities Publications No. 1 (Reno, Nev.: Desert Research Institute, 1966), 167–239; Stoffle et al., *Native American Cultural Resource Studies at Yucca Mountain, Nevada.*

59. Loomis, *Combat Zoning*, viii.

60. A statement made by congressional investigators, under the Carter administration, of the Atomic Energy Commission's operational records, 1978. Keith Schneider, foreword to Carole Gallagher, *America Ground Zero: The Secret Nuclear War* (New York: Random House, 1993).

61. Citizen Alert, "Human and Environmental Effects of Nuclear Testing," January 1991, activist handout citing Dr. Joseph Lyons, "Childhood Leukemia Rates," 1979, for childhood leukemias and EPA Off-site Monitoring Report, 1990, for Wildlife contamination.

62. Loomis, *Combat Zoning*, 31.

63. United States Department of Energy, *Final Programmatic Environmental Impact Statement for Stockpile Stewardship and Management*, September 1996, vol. I, 4–454, DOE/EIS-0236.

64. As the most invisible of the downwind residents, Native Americans near NTS who suffered greatly under the testing regime were not included fully in the few epidemiological studies done (cultural living conditions were not adjusted for higher rates of exposure), nor were they included in the law suit brought against the government by Utah's downwinders.

65. Howard Ball, *Justice Downwind: America's Atomic Testing Program in the 1950s* (New York/Oxford: Oxford University Press, 1986), 85.

66. Valerie Taliman, "Nuclear Guinea Pigs: Native People Were on Front Lines of Exploitation," *Native American Smoke Signals*, January 1994.

67. Richard W. Stoffle et al., *Native American Cultural Resource Studies at Yucca Mountain, Nevada* , 29–31.

68. Schneider, "Foreword," *America Ground Zero*, xviii.

69. James W. Hulse, *Forty Years in the Wilderness* (Reno: University of Nevada Press, 1986), 61.

70. Pauline Esteves, interview by author, tape recording, Timbisha Shoshone tribe, Death Valley, California, 22 November 1994.

71. For more on the epidemiological studies that were done see Makhijani et al., *Nuclear Wasteland*, 280–281.

72. Information about native culture and problems with Euroamerican epidemiological studies of the Nevada Test Site area was first conveyed to me in a phone interview on 29 April 1994 with Heidi Blackeye, staff person for the Citizen's Alert Native American Project. Today, Southern Pauites and Western Shoshone have organized the "Nuclear Risk Management for Native Communities Project" with Virginia Sanchez as program director.

73. "Report: Feds Snub Tribe's Radiation Exposure," *Reno Gazette-Journal*, 7 June 1994.

74. "Executive Summary, National Cancer Institute Study Estimating Thyroid Doses of I–131 Received by "Americans From Nevada Atmospheric Nuclear Bomb Tests," National Cancer Institute, Washington D.C, July 1997.

75. *Milwaukee Journal*, 11 October 1993.

76. David Hulen, "After the Bombs: Questions Linger about Amchitka Nuclear Tests," *Anchorage Daily News*, 7 February 1994.

77. Dan O'Neill, *The Firecracker Boys* (New York: St. Martin's Press, 1994).

78. Tim Beardsley, "Science and the Citizen," *Scientific American*, April 1994, 14.

79. From 1993 to 1995 I attended DOE "scoping sessions" for this reconfiguration in Las Vegas, Nevada; Los Alamos and Albuquerque, New Mexico; and Livermore, California. Where the center of the new and improved "nuclear weapons complex for the twenty-first century" will be placed is (at the time of this writing) not completely clear.

80. *Report on the Roles, Missions, and the Armed Forces of the United States*, Chairman of The Joint Chiefs of Staff, February 1993.

81. There are grass-roots groups monitoring this militarization, for instance the Rural Alliance for Military Accountability (RAMA) based in Reno, Nevada. I was informed of current military expansion plans by Grace Bukowski of RAMA. Other grass-roots groups include Citizen Alert (NV) and Progressive Alliance for Community Empowerment (NM).

Chapter 4

1. Joanna Rogers Macy, *Despair and Personal Power in the Nuclear Age* (Baltimore: New Society, 1983).

2. P. Grossman and E. Cassedy, "Cost Benefit Analysis of Nuclear Waste Disposal," *Science, Technology, and Human Values* 10, no. 4 (Fall 1985): 48, cited in Shrader-Frechette, *Burying Uncertainty*, 17.

3. William J. Broad, "Plutonium Predicament," *San Jose Mercury News*, 2 May 1995, reprinted from *New York Times*. Statement by Arjun Makhijani, nuclear physicist and president of the Institute for Energy and Environmental Research.

4. For an assessment of some of the health risks for those living near nuclear reactors, for instance, see Jay M. Gould, *The Enemy Within: The High Cost of Living Near Nuclear Reactors* (New York/London: Four Walls Eight Windows, 1996).

5. Charles Pope, "Nuclear Arms Cleanup Bill: A Tidy $230 Billion," *San Jose Mercury News*, 4 April 1995. The $230 billion estimate is for the kind of cleanup that still would not allow any of

the sites to be accessible to the public (meaning that the sites would remain dangerous to human health and safety). Returning all of the sites to their prior condition has been estimated by the Department of Energy to run approximately $500 billion. In other words, these, too, will form a dispersed web of national sacrifice areas across the U.S. landscape.

6. For more information on the environmental legacy of the Cold War, see Department of Energy, "Executive Summary," *Estimating the Cold War Mortgage: The 1995 Baseline Environmental Management Report*, March 1995, DOE/EM–0232; Department of Energy, *Closing the Circle of the Splitting of the Atom: The Environmental Legacy of Nuclear Weapons Production in the United States and What the Department of Energy is Doing About It*, January 1995; and Department of Energy/Office of Environmental Management, *Environmental Management 1995*, February 1995, DOE/EM-0228.

7. The Groundwork Collective, "The Illusion of Cleanup: A Case Study at Hanford," *Groundwork*, 4 (San Francisco, the Groundwork Collective, March 1994), 14. See also Gerber and D'Antonio.

8. Michel Foucault, "Nietzsche, Genealogy, History," trans. Donald F. Bouchard and Sherry Simon, in *The Foucault Reader*, ed. Paul Rabinow (New York: Pantheon, 1994), 96.

9. Lewis Mumford, "The Morals of Extermination," *Atlantic Monthly*, October 1959.

10. Shrader-Frechette, *Burying Uncertainty*, 14. For a comprehensive technical review of health hazards related to radiation and to weapons production in general, see Makhijani et al., *Nuclear Wasteland*, Chapter 4, "Health Hazards of Nuclear Weapons Production," 65–104.

11. David L. Chandler, "Frightening Chernobyl Findings," *San Francisco Examiner*, 30 January 1994 (reprinted from the *Boston Globe*). For more on Chernobyl, see Alla Yaroshinskaya, *Chernobyl: The Forbidden Truth*, trans. Michele Kahn and Julia Sallabank (Lincoln: University of Nebraska Press, 1995).

12. Carol J. Williams, "9 Years Later, Chernobyl Toll Goes On," *San Jose Mercury News*, 27 April 1995 (reprinted from the *Los Angeles Times*).

13. Bartimus and McCartney, *Trinity's Children*, 190–191.

14. Ibid.

15. Ibid., 194.

16. For a list of some specific studies, see Gould, 7; see also Makhijani et al.

17. Statistics from The National Breast Cancer Coalition, 1995. In *The Enemy Within*, Gould also documents and studies the link between radiation exposure and breast cancer.

18. An article by Jeff Wheelwright, "For Our Nuclear Waste, There's Gridlock on the Road to the Dump," *Smithsonian*, May 1995, demonstrates the way in which science (and its promoters, science writers) collaborate with the industry that supports it (and them). The article could have been written by a DOE public relations firm. Wheelwright is a former science editor for *Life* magazine.

19. For an excellent, in-depth review of the Nuclear Waste Policy Act and its failure to extricate nuclear waste regulation from control of the nuclear industry, see Jacob, *Site Unseen*, in particular, Chapter 5, "The Failure of the 1982 Nuclear Waste Policy Act," 95–121.

20. Good sources for information on the nuclear power industry, including some sources on the waste issue, are: Shrader-Frechette, *Burying Uncertainty*; Jacob, *Site Unseen* ; J. Samuel Walker, *Containing the Atom* (Berkeley: University of California Press, 1992); Gene I. Rochlin, *Plutonium, Power, and Politics* (Berkeley: University of California Press, 1979). See also the work of Arjun Makhijani and the Institute for Energy and Environmental Research.

21. This waste classification information was taken directly (modified slightly) from Concerned Citizens for Nuclear Safety, *The Nuclear Reactor*, early Spring, 1995, 5.

22. Arjun Makhijani and Scott Saleska, *High-Level Dollars, Low-Level Sense: A Critique of Present Policy for the Management of Long-Lived Radioactive Wastes and Discussion of an Alternative Approach* (Takoma Park, Md.: Institute for Energy and Environmental Research, 1992), 8–9.

23. Arjun Makhijani and Scott Saleska, *High-Level Dollars, Low-Level Sense*, 8–9.

24. Jacob, *Site Unseen*, 95–120.

25. Ibid., 100.

26. The slippery language found in the NWPA is dissected at length in Jacob's *Site Unseen*. I was made aware of these examples in his critical assessment of the NWPA.

27. Department of Energy/Office of Civilian Radioactive Waste Management, "Overview—Nuclear Waste Policy Act," DOE/RW-0104.

28. "Nuke Deadline Looms," *Las Vegas Sun*, 21 June 1994.

29. House Committee on Appropriations, *Energy and Water Development Appropriations for 1995*, 103rd Cong., 2nd sess., 1995, 1790.

30. Ibid., 1794. Statement by Rep. Douglas "Pete" Peterson.

31. Shrader-Frechette, *Burying Uncertainty*.

32. Reith and Thomson, *Deserts as Dumps?*

33. Grace Thorpe, "Radioactive Racism? Native Americans and the Nuclear Waste Legacy," *The Circle*, 16, no. 4 (April 1995).

34. Winona LaDuke, "Native Environmentalism," *Earth Island Journal*, Summer 1993, 34–35.

35. Reese Erlich, "Native Americans and the Nuclear Waste Battle," *Horizons*, National Public Radio, 1993.

36. Thorpe, "Radioactive Racism?"

37. Although the Department of Energy expects WIPP to open in 1998, the DOE must cross many hurdles for this to be the case.

38. Concerned Citizens for Nuclear Safety, "What is WIPP?" *The Radioactive Rag*, IV, no. 1, (Santa Fe, N.Mex., Winter-Spring, 1992).

39. There have been various congressional maneuvers to rush WIPP into opening such as the Bingaman/Domenici WIPP amendment passed in the Senate on June 20, 1996. Significantly, the amendment was passed with no public hearings.

40. New Mexico is "saturated" because it contains the radioactive research materials and waste of Los Alamos National Labs, Sandia National Labs, and the radioactive legacy of the uranium industry discussed in earlier chapters.

41. National Academy of Science, *The Disposal of Radioactive Waste on Land*, Report of the Committee on Waste Disposal of the Division of Earth Science, NAS-NRC pub. 519, Washington, D.C., 1957.

42. See Rosenthal, *At the Heart of the Bomb*, 198, n. 8: "The water at WIPP became a political issue when the Scientists' Review Panel on WIPP issued its *Evaluation of the Waste Isolation Pilot Plant (WIPP) as a Water-Saturated Nuclear Waste Repository* (Albuquerque, N.Mex., January 1988)."

43. John Cushman Jr., "U.S. Drops Test Plan at Bomb Waste Site," *New York Times*, 22 October 1993. Scientific source appears in: Scientists' Review Panel on WIPP, *Evaluation of the Waste Isolation Pilot Plant (WIPP) as a Water-Saturated Nuclear Waste Repository* (Albuquerque, N.Mex., January 1988).

44. Reith and Thomson, *Deserts as Dumps?* 314.

45. Rosenthal, *At the Heart of the Bomb*, 195.

46. Susan Hirschberg, phone interview by author, 30 March 1995. Hirschberg, at the time of this interview, was waste and contamination director for Concerned Citizens for Nuclear Safety, Santa Fe, New Mexico.

47. Don Hancock, phone interview by author, 17 June 1997. Hancock is with the Southwest Research and Information Center, Albuquerque, New Mexico.

48. In 1997 it appears that the Mescalero are no longer considering harboring temporary above-ground high-level nuclear waste on their reservation. However, because they came very close to doing so it is important to consider why and how this happened (as will be detailed in the following section of this book).

49. Winifred E. Frick, "Native Americans Approve Nuclear Waste Dump on Tribal Lands," (University of California, Santa Cruz) *City on a Hill Press*, 16 March 1995.

50. Jacob, *Site Unseen*, 138.

51. House Committee on *Appropriations, Energy and Water Development Appropriations for 1995*, 103rd Cong., 2nd sess., 1995.

52. William J. Broad, *New York Times*, 18 November 1990.

53. "Scientists Fear Atomic Explosion of Buried Waste," *New York Times*, 5 March 1995. (Although this scenario was suggested by numerous scientists, it has been discounted as unlikely, allowing business as usual to continue at the Yucca Mountain Project.)

54. Not accepting its designation as a nuclear waste dump is almost universal among Indian groups in the area. All social impact and cultural resource studies corroborate this finding.

55. Broad, "A Mountain of Trouble."

56. In addition to tritium, in September of 1997 scientists reported finding plutonium in a water well on the Nevada Test Site. This finding has sparked new debates among scientists as to the feasability and danger of storing waste at Yucca Mountain.

57. My projection for the outcome of the Nuclear Waste Policy Act is substantiated by one of my contacts, a senior scientist/environmental study manager for the Yucca Mountain Project. He has told me repeatedly that this is the only way they will be able to proceed with the project.

58. One might argue that such a practice does not alter the fact of the amount of radioactivity measured in curies or roentgens but nonetheless alters public perception of the significance of such "facts," which has the same effect where public health is concerned.

59. Monitored Retrievable Storage Review Commission, "Nuclear Waste: Is There a Need for Federal Interim Storage?" *Report of the Monitored Retrievable Storage Review Commission* (Washington, D.C.: Government Printing Office, 1989), no. 022-003-01164-1.

60. One exception was Lincoln County, Nevada, which in 1995 attempted to lobby for an MRS. Even in this case, however, the state of Nevada was able to override the county's plans.

61. Valerie Taliman, "Nine Tribes Look at Storage: Signs Point to Nuclear Dump on Native Land," *Smoke Signals: Voice of The Nations*, vol. 1, no. 5 (August 1993), 17.

62. Ibid., 17.

63. Randel D. Hanson, "The Mescalero Apache: Nuclear Waste and the Privatization of Genocide," *The Circle*, vol. 15, no. 8 (August 1994), 6–7.

64. Karl Johnson, phone interview by author, October 1994. Johnson is technical director for Nevada's Nuclear Waste Project Office.

65. Matthew L. Wald, "Nuclear Storage Divides Apaches and Neighbors," *The New York Times*.

66. Joseph Geronimo, great-grandson of the famous nineteenth-century Apache warrior, spoke compellingly about the poverty on the reservation in Erlich, "Native Americans and the Nuclear Waste Battle."

67. This reservation member was quoted in Winifred F. Frick, "Native Americans Approve Nuclear Waste Dump on Tribal Lands."

68. Beth Enson, "The Nuclear Waste Struggle Continues on the Mescalero Apache Reservation," *The Workbook*, vol. 20, no. 1, Southwest Research and Information Center (Albuquerque, N.Mex., Spring 1995).

69. Joseph Masco, "Nuclear Reservations: Plutonium and 'National Security' in Post-Cold War New Mexico," presented at the American Anthropology Association Annual Meeting, Washington, D.C., November 15–19, 1995.

70. This surprising statement (surprising because of its source) was made to me by a high-level contractor for the Department of Energy who requested anonymity.

71. Randel D. Hanson, "Nuclear Agreement Continues U.S. Policy of Dumping on Goshutes," *The Circle*, vol. 16, no. 1 (January 1995), 8. See also Randel D. Hanson, "Gathering Focuses on Environmental Racism," *The Circle*, vol. 16, no. 10 (October 1995), 10–11.

72. Recently, members of the Skull Valley Band of Goshute—a group called "Ohngo Gaudadeh Devia"—have come together to oppose their tribal council's plan to accept an MRS. As with the Mescalero Apache the debate over hosting an MRS is creating serious friction among tribal members.

73. For readings on the environmental justice movement and environmental racism, see Andrew Szasz, *Ecopopulism: Toxic Waste and the Movement for Environmental Justice* (Minneapolis: University of Minnesota Press, 1994); Robert D. Bullard, ed., *Confronting Environmental Racism: Voices from the Grassroots* (Boston: South End, 1993). In addition see Lois Gibbs and the Citizens Clearinghouse for Hazardous Waste, *Dying from Dioxin: A Citizen's Guide to Reclaiming Our Health and Rebuilding Community* (Boston: South End, 1995), as well as others.

74. Reith and Thomson, *Deserts as Dumps?*, p. 106.

75. Richard W. Stoffle et al., *Native American Cultural Resource Studies at Yucca Mountain, Nevada* , 85.

76. Philip M. Klasky, "The Eagle's View of Ward Valley: Environmentalists and Native American Tribes Fight Proposed Nuclear Dump in the Mojave Desert," *Wild Earth*, Spring 1994.

77. Ibid.

78. Statement made by Llewellyn Barrackman of the Fort Mojave Indian Tribe. The statement appeared in Robert Stebbins, "The Desert Tortoise," *Terrain* (Summer 1995).

79. For more information on transportation of nuclear waste, see: Department of Energy, *OCRWM Transportation Report*, June 1995, DOE/RW-0473.

80. More information about the complex relationship between U.S. commercial policies regarding nuclear technology and power and U.S. nonproliferation policy can be obtained from the Western States Legal Foundation in Oakland, California.

Chapter 5

1. This alternative, historical, narrative map of the region (based on Indian occupation) was taken from Catherine S. Fowler, *Native Americans and Yucca Mountain: A Summary Report* (State of Nevada, Nevada Nuclear Waste Project Office, September 1990), NWPO-SE-026-90.

2. Fowler, *Native Americans and Yucca Mountain*, 45.

3. For more on attempts to place the MX missile on Western Shoshone land, see Rebecca Solnit, *Savage Dreams* (San Francisco: Sierra Club Books, 1994), and Mander, *In the Absence of the Sacred*.

4. Jay Miller, "Basin Religion and Theology: A Comparative Study of Power (Puha)," *Journal of California and Great Basin Anthropology* 5(1, 2): 66–86, and Jay Miller, "Numic Religion: An Overview of Power in the Great Basin of Native North America," *Anthropos* 78: 337–354, cited in Fowler, *Native Americans and Yucca Mountain*, 14–15.

5. Arnold is executive director of the Las Vegas Indian Center and liaison between the DOE and the surrounding Indian community for the Yucca Mountain Project. Our meeting took place on Yucca Mountain in October 1994.

6. Fowler, *Native Americans and Yucca Mountain*, 17.

7. Stoffle et al., *Yucca Mountain Project: Literature Review and Ethnohistory of Native American Occupancy and Use of the Yucca Mountain Region*, interim report (Department of Energy), 17, available from OTIS, DOE/NV-10576-21.

8. Stoffle et al., *Yucca Mountain Project*, 17.

9. Fowler, *Native Americans and Yucca Mountain*, 76.

10. Stoffle et al., *Yucca Mountain Project*, 17.

11. Ian Zabarte, interview by author, tape recording, 24 October, 1994, Cactus Springs, Nevada. Zabarte is the high-level nuclear waste contact for the Western Shoshone National Council.

12. For theoretical articulations of the social construction of space see Henri Lefebvre, *The Production of Space*, trans. Donald Nicholson-Smith (Oxford, UK: Basil Blackwell, 1991); Edward W. Soja, *Postmodern Geographies: The Reassertion of Space in Critical Social Theory* (London: Verso, 1980); Kathleen M. Kirby, *Indifferent Boundaries: Spatial Concepts and Human Subjectivity* (New York/London: Guilford, 1996); Patricia Yaeger, ed., *The Geography of Identity* (Ann Arbor: University of Michigan Press, 1996); Alexander Wilson, *The Culture of Nature* (Cambridge, Mass.: Blackwell, 1992).

13. Although I have used the unifying term "Euroamerican" here, these different land uses are the product of different agencies with different objectives. While all are "Euroamerican" some have opposing interests and concerns, illuminating the diversity of Euroamerican attitudes toward the environment.

14. Solnit, *Savage Dreams*, 57.

15. Wilderness as a concept and its relation to American ideology have been explored by many scholars, for instance Roderick Nash, *Wilderness and the American Mind* (New Haven, Conn.: Yale University Press, 1967); Carolyn Merchant, *Ecological Revolutions* (Chapel Hill: University of North Carolina Press, 1989); Frederick Turner, *Beyond Geography: The Western Spirit Against the Wilderness* (New York: The Viking Press, 1980); William Cronon, *Changes in the Land: Indians, Colonists, and the Ecology of New England* (New York: Hill and Wang, 1983); Patricia Nelson Limerick, *Desert Passages* (Albuquerque: University of New Mexico Press, 1985); R. White and P. L. Limerick, *The Frontier in American Culture* (Berkeley: University of California Press, 1994); C. Vecesey and R. W. Venables, eds., *American Indian Environments* (Syracuse, N.Y.: Syracuse University Press, 1980).

16. David Abram, *The Spell of the Sensuous* (New York: Pantheon, 1996).

17. As with the term "social system," I understand the term "world view" as being composed of a variety of signifying systems that can be examined independently. That which is similar between the different systems is understood as a world view, although it, too, is commonly contested. (See Raymond Williams, "Culture as Signifying System," in his *The Sociology of Culture* [New York: Schocken, 1981], 207–214.)

18. Most ethnographic work on the Western Shoshone and Southern Paiute was conducted after 1930—rather late by most standards. Early accounts of Native life in the Great Basin can be found in the work of Julian H. Steward and I. T. Kelley. There is a great store of subsequent work as well.

19. Pauline Esteves, interview by author, tape recording, at the Timbisha Shoshone village, Death Valley, California, 22 November 1994. Esteves is the Timbisha's acting tribal chairperson.

20. For an historical example of the impact of different economic regimes on Indian cultures see Cronon, *Changes in the Land*, and Merchant, *Ecological Revolutions*.

21. Department of Energy, *Environmental Impact Statement for a Proposed Repository at Yucca Mountain, Nevada*, July 1995, RW-0364P.

22. Gregory A. Fasano, interview by author, tape recording, 17 October 1994, Las Vegas, Nevada. Fasano is a senior environmental scientist with SAIC working on the Yucca Mountain Project and, until recently, coordinator of the Yucca Mountain Indian Project.

23. Solnit, *Savage Dreams*. See also Mike Davis, "Dead West: Ecocide in Marlboro Country," *New Left Review*, no. 200 (July/August 1993).

24. Department of Energy, *Nuclear Waste Policy Act, as Amended*, February 1995, DOE/RW-0438 Rev. 1, sec. 117 and sec. 219.

25. For a history of nonviolent direct action in the 1970s and 1980s, see Barbara Epstein, *Political Protest and Cultural Revolution: Nonviolent Direct Action in the 1970s and 1980s* (Berkeley: University of California Press, 1991).

26. For more on the Treaty of Ruby Valley and how the U.S. government bypassed it by "buying" Newe Segobia from the Western Shoshone, see Fowler, *Native Americans and Yucca Mountain*, 37–45, and "The Theft of Nevada: the Case of the Western Shoshone" in Mander, *In the Absence of the Sacred*.

27. Fowler, *Native Americans and Yucca Mountain*, 42.

28. Fasano, interview by author, 17 October 1994.

29. Mander, *In the Absence of the Sacred*, 199.

30. Stoffle et al., *Native American Cultural Resource Studies at Yucca Mountain*, 96.

31. Fowler, *Native Americans and Yucca Mountain*, 48.

32. Virginia Sanchez, addressing Healing Global Wounds gathering, 15 April 1995, Mercury, Nevada.

33. Except for the Western Shoshone, these Indian speakers are usually not tribal council representatives, but individual activists. Direct action politics is itself a marginalizing activity that many tribes prefer not to be involved in.

34. Although a phenomenon resulting from assimilation, cattle ranching has become intertwined with Western Shoshone sovereignty rights, as exemplified by the Dann case. See "The Dann Sisters Case" in Mander, *In the Absence of the Sacred*.

35. "Natural law" is a term that will be explained (and problematized) in more detail in Chapter 8, "Aboriginal Homeland." It should not be confused with Euroamerican legal or scientific uses of the term.

Chapter 6

1. Marion Zucco, interview by author, tape recording, Big Pine Paiute Tribe of the Owen's Valley, Big Pine, California, 20 November 1994.

2. Mary Austin used this term in 1903 to describe the Indian land of the Mojave Desert (in *The Land of Little Rain*). The term applies to much of the Nevada Test Site region as well.

3. Lalovi Miller, Moapa Paiute elder, interview by author, tape recording, Moapa Paiute reservation, Nevada, 18 April 1995.

4. Ian Zabarte, interview by author, tape recording, Indian Springs, Nevada, 10 October 1994.

5. Marion Zucco, interview by author, 20 November 1994.

6. Stoffle et al., *Literature Review and Ethnohistory of Native American Occupancy and Use of the Yucca Mountain Area*, 49.

7. "Identified tribes" of the area had by 1996 been increased to nineteen (twenty if the Las Vegas Indian Center is included).

8. The hierarchy of contracts demonstrates some of the complexity of these studies. The DOE contracts with SAIC to conduct cultural resource studies, and that company contracts with the Institute for Social Research at the University of Michigan, Ann Arbor. Anthropologists Richard W. Stoffle, John E. Olmstead, and Michael Evans produced the final report mentioned here.

9. The state of Nevada and the Western Shoshone both oppose storing nuclear waste at Yucca Mountain, although for partly different reasons. The state of Nevada does not support the Western Shoshone land claim (although some anthropologists who contract with the state do).

10. At the time of my visit, I was taken on a private tour of Yucca Mountain in which we visited a number of cultural resource sites in the region. I was accompanied by a senior environmental scientist, the DOE-Indian liaison for the studies, and two senior archaeologists (one of whom flew in from Reno especially for the visit). The men on this tour were all accommodating, polite, and a bit defensive as I asked questions about the DOE's relationship to the Indian people in the region. It was clear to me that for both the DOE contractors and the Indian people with ties to the mountain, the cultural resource studies (along with Western Shoshone protest gatherings) were an important place to start my investigation.

11. The DOE pays the cultural resource representatives for their services.

12. For a list of tribes associated with this study, see the map of ethnic territories and corresponding tribes, Fig. 5.5.

13. This flier is distributed by the DOE in an information packet on the Yucca Mountain Project titled "Why Are Scientists Studying Yucca Mountain?", Department of Energy/Office of Civilian Radioactive Waste Management, DOE/RW-0340P, April 1993.

14. Pauline Esteves, interview by author, tape recording, Timbisha village, Death Valley, California, 22 November 1994. Esteves is acting chairperson of the Timbisha Shoshone tribe.

15. Catherine Fowler (an anthropologist working with the Western Shoshone) confirmed that the Western Shoshone did feel they were inadequately represented.

16. Stoffle et al., *Native American Cultural Resource Studies at Yucca Mountain*, 9.

17. Ian Zabarte, interview by author, 10 October 1994.

18. Stoffle et al., *Native American Cultural Resource Studies at Yucca Mountain*, 168.

19. Zabarte, interview by author, 10 October 1994.

20. Ibid.

21. Crum, *The Road on Which We Came*, 26.

22. There are many reasons for the vigorous rise of American Indian ethnic identity since the 1960s, such as changes in federal Indian policy, American ethnic politics, and American Indian activism (encouraged by the civil rights movement). For more on this issue, see Joan Nagel, "American Indian Ethnic Renewal: Politics and the Resurgence of Identity," *American Sociological Review* 60 (December), 947–965.

23. A case in point is the Timbisha, who, while living in Death Valley, are not acknowledged by the Park Service, which (at the Visitor's Information Center) usually refers to Indians of the region as having existed only in the past.

24. The feeling that compliance with cultural resource laws was more harmful than helpful was expressed by Indian people who appeared on panels with archaeologists at the Eleventh Annual California Indian Conference held at the University of California, Los Angeles, 6–7 October, 1995. Numerous Indian people claimed they were used to merely oversee and legitimate the elimination of their material and historical presence on the land. Tensions between Indians and archaeologists were especially high at some sessions of this conference.

25. Pauline Esteves, interview by author, 22 November 1994.

26. Frederick C. Worman, *Archaeological Investigations at the U.S. Atomic Energy Commission's Nevada Test Site and Nuclear Rocket Development Station.* (Los Alamos, N.Mex.: Los Alamos National Laboratory, 1969).

27. In accordance with the cultural resource laws mentioned earlier, Indian monitors are supposed to be hired prior to significant project construction that might threaten artifacts. These Indian monitors are supposed to accompany the archaeologists in their initial study of the proposed construction site. The Yucca Mountain site characterization project is a huge project and has numerous ongoing construction projects associated with it.

28. Lalovi Miller, interview by author, 18 April 1995.

29. Big Pine Paiute tribal elders, interview by author, tape recording, Big Pine, California, 20 November 1994; Moapa Paiute elders, interview by author, tape recording, Moapa Paiute reservation, Nevada, 18 April 1995.

30. Marion Zucco, interview by author, 20 November 1994.

31. Bertha and Gaylene Moose, interview by author, tape recording, Big Pine, California, 20 November 1994.

32. Fowler, *Native Americans and Yucca Mountain*, 30.

33. Stoffle et al., *Native American Cultural Resource Studies at Yucca Mountain*, 20. For more on the conference proceedings regarding these disagreements, see: Polly Quick, ed., *Proceedings: Conference On Reburial Issues* (Society for American Archaeology and Society for Professional Archaeologists, Chicago: Newberry Library, 1985).

34. Stoffle et al.; Wesley E. Niles and Joan T. O'Farrell, *Yucca Mountain Project Native American Plant Resources in the Yucca Mountain Area, Nevada*, Department of Energy interim report, November 1989, DOE/NV-10576-19.

35. Clara Rambeau, Big Pine Paiute tribal elder, interview by author, Big Pine, Calif., 20 November 1994.

36. Pauline Esteves, interview by author, 22 November 1994. Esteves is here referring to the Timbisha's anthropologist, Catherine S. Fowler.

37. It should be noted that Pauline Esteves's comment was not directed at Catherine Fowler, who has helped the Timbisha Shoshone in extensive efforts to claim a land base in Death Valley. Indeed, Fowler's work exemplifies how anthropology can be deployed for social justice purposes.

38. Although she can be quite blunt and critical, in the end, Esteves was unfailingly generous, capable of passionately discussing these issues for hours.

39. Esteves, interview by author, 22 November 1994.

40. Ian Zabarte, interview by author, 10 October 1994.

Chapter 7

1. Naval Ordnance Test Station, "NOTS 20 Years," *China Lake* (Calif.) *Rocketeer*, 8 November 1963. (Prior to being called the Naval Weapons Center, China Lake was referred to as Naval Ordnance Test Station, or NOTS.)

2. Clara Rambeau, Owens Valley Paiute elder, interview by author, 20 November 1994.

3. Western Shoshone National Defense Project, *Newe Seogobia Is Not For Sale!* (Crescent Valley, Nevada).

4. Fowler, *Native Americans and Yucca Mountain,* citing Lonnie C. Pippin, ed., *Limited Test Excavations at Selected Archaeological Sites in the NNWSI Yucca Mountain Project Area, Southern Nye County, Nevada* (Reno: University of Nevada, Desert Research Institute, Social Sciences Center publication no. 40, 1984) and L. C. Pippin, R. L. Clerico, and R. L. Reno, *An Archaeological Reconnaissance of the NNWSI Yucca Mountain Project Area, Southern Nye County, Nevada* (Reno: University of Nevada, Desert Research Institute, Social Sciences Center publication no. 28, 1982).

5. For extensive bibliographies of archaeology, ethnohistory, and anthropology of the Yucca Mountain area, see Stoffle et al., *Native American Cultural Resource Studies at Yucca Mountain* and Fowler, *Native Americans and Yucca Mountain.*

6. Bertha Moose, Owens Valley Paiute elder, interview by author, 20 November 1994.

7. Pauline Esteves, interview by author, 22 November 1994.

8. Dewey Charlie (Inyo County elder Paiute resident), *Land Use History of Coso Hot Springs, Inyo County, California,* interview by Iroquois Research Institute, Public Works Department, Naval Weapons Center, January 1979, 92.

9. The problem of misrepresenting Indian spirituality associated with some aspects of the New Age movement and some environmentalists has been examined by a number of scholars. I found this issue covered in J. Peter Brosius, "Negotiating Citizenship in a Commodified Landscape: The Case of Penan Hunter-Gatherers in Sarawak, East Malaysia" (prepared for the Social Science Research Council conference "Cultural Citizenship in Southeast Asia," Honolulu, Hawaii, 2–4 May, 1993), 19–26; and Robert Henry (Hank) Stevens (Osage Nation), "Sacred Landscapes: Continuity and Change" (unpublished paper presented at the 11th Annual American Indian Conference, University of California, Los Angeles, 7 October, 1995).

10. Contemporary regional scholars whose work I have drawn on include Catherine S. Fowler, Richard Stoffle, and, for Western Shoshone history, Steven Crum.

11. For a description of sources see Stoffle, *Literature Review and Ethnohistory of Native American Occupancy and Use of the Yucca Mountain Area,* and Fowler, *Native Americans and Yucca Mountain.*

12. Fowler, *Native Americans and Yucca Mountain,* citing I. T. Kelly, "Southern Paiute Field Notes," 1932–33, in author's possession, Reno, Nevada, and J. H. Steward, *Basin-Plateau Aboriginal Sociopolitical Groups* (Washington D.C.: Bureau of American Ethnology Bulletin 120, 1938, 1941). See also Stoffle et al., *Literature Review and Ethnohistory of Native American Occupancy and Use of the Yucca Mountain Area.*

13. Although an account of Owens Valley Paiutes *after* contact with Euroamericans, the story "The Basket Maker" in Mary Austin's *Land of Little Rain* offers a compelling narrative depicting the hardships and pleasures of a local Paiute woman. This account gives a sense of what it may have been like to survive and thrive in such a harsh environment. See Mary Austin, *Land of Little Rain* (New York: Penguin, 1988; originally published by Houghton Mifflin, 1903).

14. See Stoffle et al., *Native American Cultural Resource Studies at Yucca Mountain,* and Fowler, *Native Americans and Yucca Mountain.*

15. Thomas C. Blackburn and Kat Anderson, eds., *Before the Wilderness: Environmental Management by Native Californians* (Menlo Park, Calif: Ballena, 1993).

16. Ibid., 354.

17. Catherine Fowler, unpublished ethnoecology of the Timbisha (presented in a meeting at the Timbisha Shoshone colony at Death Valley, Calif., May 1996). (Information also from personal conversations with Fowler.)

18. Indians I interviewed brought my attention to such practices. The cultural resource reports by the Stoffle team and the Fowler team also make note of this practice.

19. Crum, *The Road on Which We Came*.

20. See Nash, *Wilderness and the American Mind*; White and Limerick, *The Frontier in American Culture*; and Frederick Turner, *Beyond Geography*. Critical assessments of Euroamerican representations of Indians can also be found in the work of Gerald Visenor, *Manifest Manners: Postindian Warriors of Survivance* (Hanover, N.H.: University Press of New England, 1994) and Robert F. Berkhoter, Jr., *The White Man's Indian* (New York: Vintage Books, 1978).

21. This brief historical sketch was derived from the more detailed work of Crum, *The Road on Which We Came*.

22. Susan R. Sharrock, "A History of the Indians of Nevada from First White Contact to the Reservation Period: Extracted from Eye-Witness Accounts" (unpublished paper, June 1, 1967), 4, cited in Crum, *The Road on Which We Came*.

23. For more on this subject concerning other Indian peoples see Cronon, *Changes in the Land* and Merchant, *Ecological Revolutions*.

24. Stoffle et al., *Literature Review and Ethnohistory of Native American Occupancy and Use of the Yucca Mountain Area*.

25. Gaylene Moose, interview by author, 20 November 1994. For a local historical account, see W. A. Chalfant, *The Story of Inyo: Its Pioneering, Its Indians, Its Struggles Over Water* (Bishop, Calif: Chalfant, 1959).

26. Clara Rambeau, Big Pine Paiute Tribe of the Owens Valley, interview by author, 20 November 1994.

27. Pauline Esteves, interview by author, 22 November 1994.

28. Stoffle et al., *Literature Review and Ethnohistory of Native American Occupancy and Use of the Yucca Mountain Area*, 31.

29. More specific information on resource use in the region can be found in Stoffle et al., *Native American Cultural Resource Studies at Yucca Mountain*, Nevada, 1990, 29–35, citing Julian H. Steward, *Basin-Plateau Aboriginal Sociopolitical Groups* (Washington, D.C.: Smithsonian Institution, Bureau of American Ethnology Bulletin 120, 1938), 96–98.

30. Stoffle et al., *Native American Cultural Resource Studies at Yucca Mountain*, 38–39.

31. William Rosse Jr., interview by author, tape recording, 10 October 1994, Cactus Springs, Nevada.

32. Bertha Moose, interview by author, 20 November 1994.

33. Pauline Esteves, interview by author, 22 November 1994.

34. Gaylene Moose, interview by author, 20 November 1994.

35. Pauline Esteves, interview by author, 22 November 1994. Of course, the Navy's demands stem in part from the frequent test bombing missions practiced over the area.

36. Pauline Esteves, interview by author, 22 November 1994.

Chapter 8

1. Crum, *The Road on Which We Came*, 4–5, song trans. Beverly Crum.

2. "Another Panel Rejects Nevada Disaster Theory," *Science* 256, 24 April 1992.

3. Catherine Fowler, unpublished paper on Timbisha Shoshone ethnoecology (presented at a panel on Timbisha Land Restoration, Timbisha tribal village, Death Valley, Calif., 26 May 1996). For a description of her theory (using the Timbisha Shoshone example), refer to Chapter 7.

4. For example, in May 1996, before marching against the Park Service at Death Valley Monument in support of land rights, young adult members of the Timbisha Shoshone tribe

participated in a sunrise ceremony featuring traditional prayers and songs to "mother earth," to the rocks, sky, the plant life, and so forth. I received the day's itinerary via fax, including an invitation to the sunrise ceremony. The Timbisha Shoshone also use their computer Internet Web site to inform others of their land restoration activities and rights.

5. Historic Preservation Committee of the Timbisha Shoshone Tribe, *The Timbisha Shoshone Tribe and Their Living Valley* (Death Valley '49ers Inc., published as Keepsake No. 34 for the 45th Annual Death Valley '49ers Encampment, 9–13 November 1994, Death Valley, Calif.)

6. For examples of how early Euroamerican travelers encountered and recorded the desert of this region, see Limerick, *Desert Passages.*

7. These techniques, and others, that are used for sustained thought in oral cultures have been articulated by Walter J. Ong, *Orality and Literacy* (London and New York: Routledge, 1982), 34. Ong's discussion of such techniques is partially based on the work of Eric A. Havelock, *Preface to Plato* (Cambridge, Mass.: Belknap Press of Harvard University Press, 1963).

8. Jean-Francois Lyotard, *The Postmodern Condition: A Report on Knowledge,* trans. Geoff Bennington and Brian Massumi (Minneapolis: University of Minnesota Press, 1984), 18.

9. The very use of the word "landscapes" in this context connotes a frame of reference. As Ricoeur notes: "Because we have seen paintings we can now perceive the universe as landscape." Paul Ricoeur, "The Functions of Fiction in Shaping Reality," *A Ricoeur Reader: Reflection and Imagination,* ed. Mario J. Valdes (Toronto/Buffalo: University of Toronto Press, 1991).

10. Turner, *Beyond Geography,* 31–47.

11. Stoffle et al., *Literature Review and Ethnohistory of Native American Occupancy and Use of the Yucca Mountain Area,* 14.

12. There are many literary accounts of Indian narrative, geography, and sacred places. A few examples are Keith H. Basso, "Stalking with Stories: Names, Places, and Moral Narratives among the Western Apache," "Text, Play, and Story: The Construction and Reconstruction of Self and Society," ed. Stuart Plattner, *1983 Proceedings of the American Ethnological Society* (Washington D.C.: American Ethnological Society, 1984); Klara Bonsack Kelly and Harris Francis, *Navajo Sacred Places* (Bloomington and Indianapolis: Indiana University Press, 1994); Vecsey and Venables, *American Indian Environments;* D. Tedlock and B. Tedlock, eds., *Teachings from the American Earth: Indian Religion and Philosophy* (New York: Liveright, 1975).

13. Historic Preservation Committee of the Timbisha Shoshone Tribe, *The Timbisha Tribe and Their Living Valley.*

14. Ibid.

15. See Fowler, September 1990, *Native Americans and Yucca Mountain;* A. Hultkrantz, 1996, "An Ethnoecological Approach to Religion," *Ethnos* 31:131–40.

16. Fowler, *Native Americans and Yucca Mountain,* 15–16. Note: Because of this "environmental conditioning," it is no surprise that the subdiscipline of "ethnoecology"—an anthropological orientation especially focused on the intersection between culture and ecology—initially grew out of the work of those studying the Great Basin Native tribes, for instance Julian Steward.

17. Anne M. Smith, *Shoshone Tales* (Salt Lake City: University of Utah Press, 1993), 129.

18. This mythopoetic interpretation was suggested to me by Richard Rawles. Depending on the version, the tale also tells of the origin of the menstrual cycle, as well as rules for childbirth. No single interpretation exhausts its meanings.

19. Note: When Coyote accidentally dies (in the same tale) and comes back to life only to find a hole in his head from his fall, he scoops out pieces of his brain to eat (saying "That's pretty good gravy"), suggesting that to eat animals is akin to eating oneself (he promptly vomits).

20. According to Anna Premo (Western Shoshone) in Smith, *Shoshone Tales,* 79.

21. Catherine Fowler, Foreword to Smith, *Shoshone Tales,* xxxi.

22. Cronon, *Changes in the Land.*

23. Highly unusual natural phenomena, such as water in extremely arid regions or flowers in snow-covered alpine regions, have historically been perceived to mark places of power in many parts of the world. Birnbaum calls such occurrences "eruptions" of power. Raoul Birnbaum, "Signs of Power in the Natural World: Indicator Plants in the Wutai Mountains," ed. Françiscus Verellen, *Culte des sites, culte des saints* (Paris: Ecole Française d'Extreme-Orient, forthcoming).

24. Corbin Harney, *The Way It Is: One Water . . .One Air . . . One Mother Earth* (Nevada City, Calif.: Blue Dolphin, 1995).

25. Abrams, *The Spell of the Sensuous*, 7.

26. At the Rock Creek gathering that I attended, Harney took a group of us on a walk through the canyon, at which time he described his past and how he came to be concerned with—recognized in himself—the "gift" of healing. He told this story about his escape from boarding school and his own description of himself as "illiterate" at this time.

27. While Harney is a man of the spirit, he is also very practical. The small group of white people who were invited to the Rock Creek gatherings included those who had supported Western Shoshone land rights at earlier demonstrations. Harney's position is that there aren't enough Indian people alive to make the kinds of changes that will ensure survival. He therefore makes alliances with Euroamericans, as well as with other people in different parts of the world such as Khazahkstan, Puerto Rico, Japan, the South Pacific, and elsewhere (usually those who have been affected by nuclear colonialism). And though he invites some white people to participate in Indian ceremonial practices, he makes clear that white people aren't Indians. His interest is in, as he says, "educating the white man" about the "Indian spiritual relationship with nature." New Age appropriation of Indian ritual is not acceptable. Rather, Harney always asks white people to "pray in their own way, not in ours." Inviting white people to the Rock Creek ceremonies was never an attempt to accommodate Indian "wannabes." It began as a small-scale practice of inter-racial alliance building when the springs, creek, and canyon became threatened by Lander County's efforts to build a multiuse recreational reservoir/dam that would result in flooding the canyon, including Shoshone ancestral burial grounds. This project was dropped after officials found that the creek's gravel beds do not sufficiently hold water. Today, the creek and surrounding area continue to be threatened, this time by mining interests, which have become as destructive to Indian lands in recent years as nuclearism and militarism have been in the second half of this century.

28. Fowler, *Native Americans and Yucca Mountain*, 47.

29. Debbie Edwards (USGS hydrologist, USGS Headquarters, Las Vegas, Nevada) phone interview by author, August 1996. For more on water in the Yucca Mountain/Nevada Test Site region, see I. J. Winograd and W. Thordarson, "Hydrogeologic and Hydrochemical Framework, South-Central Great Basin, Nevada-California; with Special Reference to the Nevada Test Site," *Hydrology of Nuclear Test Sites*, Geologic Survey Professional Paper 712–C, prepared on behalf of the U.S. Atomic Energy Commission (Washington D.C.: Government Printing Office, 1975).

30. Since radiation readily moves through water, including ground water, the DOE "is banking on" what they describe as the "natural dryness of the Yucca Mountain area" as the "first layer of protection" against escaping radionuclides from the repository. They admit that human barriers will eventually break down. "Once that happens, natural barriers, including the mountain itself, will be counted on to stop or slow the movement of radioactive particles." See Department of Energy, "Could Radioactive Materials Get Out of a Repository?" *DOE's Yucca Mountain Studies* (Las Vegas, Nev.: Yucca Mountain Site Characterization Project).

31. Fowler, *Native Americans and Yucca Mountain*, 84.

32. Stoffle et al., *Literature Review and Ethnohistory of Native American Occupancy and Use of the Yucca Mountain Area*.

33. Fowler, *Native Americans and Yucca Mountain*, 26, citing Pippin, *Limited Test Excavations at Selected Archaeological Sites in the NNWSI Yucca Mountain Project Area*, 13.

34. This was described to me by Corbin Harney in a conversation that took place in Santa Cruz, Calif., in 1995.

35. Information about water babies can be found in statements by elders working with Catherine Fowler on cultural resource studies of Yucca Mountain. They also appear in Smith, *Shoshone Tales*, 78–79.

36. Owens Valley Paiute-Shoshone elders, interview by author, 20 November 1994.

37. Iroquois Research Institute, *A Land Use History of Coso Hot Springs* (Naval Weapons Center, China Lake, Calif.: administrative publication number 200, 1979), 98.

38. Ibid., 92.

39. Evelyn Samalar, Moapa Paiute elder, interview by author, 18 April 1995.

40. Ash Meadows National Wildlife Refuge information sheet, July 1995.

41. Ibid.

42. Claude Lévi-Strauss, *The Savage Mind* (Chicago: University of Chicago Press, 1962), 15–16.

43. See David Abrams, *The Spell of the Sensuous*; and "Merleau-Ponty and the Voice of the Earth," *Minding Nature: The Philosophers of Ecology*, ed. David Macauley (New York: Guilford, 1996).

44. This is not a nostalgic explanation of Indian culture and knowledge, but rather an attempt to speak about difference without resorting to romanticism. The current loss of such world views is indeed lamentable, not for nostalgic reasons, but because they contain important insights that are not readily available in the dominant culture.

Many scholars today are rightfully weary of nostalgia concerning Indian culture, but caution against this form of dehumanization has become so pronounced as to deny any authentic cultural difference. For instance, in *Environment and History* (Routledge, 1995) the environmental historians William Beinart and Peter Coates write: "The resurrection by the descendants of indigenous peoples of 'aboriginal' ideas about nature is a powerful ideological statement rather than good history. It has proved especially seductive for the disenchanted who seek inspiration in a precapitalist symbiosis of humankind and nature." First, such a statement delegitimizes the interventions of the "descendants of indigenous peoples"—essentially accusing all descendants of cultural posturing and "ideological statements" as opposed to making "good history"; second, it implies that anyone inspired by Native American cultures must be ignorant of the realities of their shortcomings. One need not be a romantic to respect or admire aspects of another culture's ways. It is clear what authors such as the above are warning against, but their zeal keeps them completely encased in their own cultural perspective, incapable of recognizing beauty where it does exist, or tragedy of loss when real loss occurs.

45. "When concerns are ranked by Indian people, environmental risks from the repository are placed *above* those involving personal health and economic aspects. When people discuss the topic outside the formal structure of a questionnaire, it is also the risks to the land, the water, plants, and animals that are raised first. These feelings are deep-seated and [g]o back to old cultural themes: proper relationships to the land and resources." Fowler, *Native Americans and Yucca Mountain*, 47.

46. The intersubjective ecological ethos disallows either side of the debate between ecocentrism and anthropocentrism. (Such a dichotomy positions, on the one hand, the *merger* of subject and object, as in the case of ecocentrism where the human is merged with nature, and, on the other hand, the radical *separation* of subject from object, as in the anthropocentric view where the human subject is separated from nature as object.)

47. Crum, *The Road on Which We Came*.

48. Ibid., 10–11. (Crum notes: "Sung by a Shoshone elder who wishes to remain anonymous.")

49. For a controversial but stimulating critical analysis of Indian use of the term "Mother Earth" (and its strategic use in Pan Indianism today) see Sam D. Gill, *Mother Earth: An American Story* (Chicago/London: University of Chicago Press, 1987).

50. Clara Rambeau (Owens Valley Paiute elder), interview by author, 20 November 1994.

51. Ibid.

52. Ibid.

53. Ibid.

54. Ian Zabarte, interview by author, 24 October 1994.

55. Ibid.

56. From my own observations in my work with Western Shoshone and Southern Paiute people, this respect and integrity is not absolutist; that is, it does not appear to deny the use of all technologies, just those that are clearly harmful to humans and nonhumans. Certainly, for Western scholars, this calls forth all sorts of philosophical questions about what constitutes integrity, harm, and even "nature."

57. The "sale" of Newe Segobia was described in Chapter 5, "The View from Yucca Mountain."

58. Pierre Bourdieu, *Outline of a Theory of Practice*, trans. Richard Nice (Cambridge, UK: Cambridge University Press, 1972).

59. Unlike the Indian people of this region, Euroamericans do not have a *primary* tradition of active communication with the nonhuman world. However, Euroamericans do have certain philosophical articulations that have attempted to reconstruct how we understand being in the world, as well as how we know the world (epistemology) that come close to the intersubjective consciousness of traditional Indian practices. This can be found in aspects of the phenomenologies of Husserl, Merleau-Ponty, Heidegger, and others. Similarly, ethicists, such as Hans Jonas and Karen Warren, among others, have attempted to articulate various aspects of intersubjectivity and its relation to sustainable ecological practices. In addition, feminist theorists examining the objectification of nature have posited an essentially intersubjective, alternative representation of epistemological practice. From within these discursive interventions an examination of the role of metaphor in language has emerged. Feminist epistemologists such as Haraway and Keller, in particular, have illuminated the metaphoricity of scientific discourse. Others have examined the role of metaphor in oral-based knowledge productions.

60. In posing the question of the function of metaphor, Ricoeur hypothesizes that "scientific language aims at univocity in argumentation by suppressing equivocity." (In "Word, Polysemy, Metaphor: Creativity in Language," *A Ricoeur Reader*, 83.)

61. Merleau-Ponty, *Phenomenology of Perception*, 291.

62. Ibid., 291.

63. William Rosse Jr. (Western Shoshone elder), interview by author, tape recording, 10 October 1994, at Cactus Springs, Nevada.

64. Western Shoshone Defense Project newsletter, vol. 4, no. 1 (Winter/Spring/Summer 1996), 22. (All quotes in this paragraph reference this citation.)

65. Ibid.

66. For more on the concept of "collage" see Helen Watson-Verran and David Turnbull, "Science and Other Indigenous Knowledge Systems," in *Handbook of Science and Technology Studies*, eds. S. Jasanoff, G. E. Markle, J. C. Petersen, and Trevor Pence (Thousand Oaks, Calif.: Sage, 1995), 115–139. Watson-Verran and Turnbull adopt Deleuze and Guattari's term "assemblage," "which in their usage is like an episteme with technologies added but that connotes the ad hoc contingency of a collage in its capacity to embrace a wide variety of incompatible components."

67. "Save Bah-tza-gohm-bah," *Citizen Alert Newsletter*, vol. 2, no. 1 (March 1996), 8.

Chapter 9

1. Advisory Committee on Human Radiation Experiments, *Final Report*, 506–562.

2. Ibid., 29.

3. The application of cybernetics to various life processes was explored by social, psychological, and biological theorists in the well-known Macy Foundation conferences held between 1946 and 1953. For an introduction and interpretation of these meetings, see: Donna Haraway, *Primate Visions* (New York: Routledge, 1989), 103–104; and Steve Heims, *The Cybernetics Group* (Cambridge, Mass.: MIT Press, 1991).

4. The cybernetic view of midcentury ecologists has since transmogrified into what some observers have called "second-order cybernetics"—or open systems that take into account concepts from evolutionary biology to suggest models that are "complex adaptive systems," for instance, or that see organisms as largely autopoetic (self-organizing) structures. For more on the so-called "sciences of complexity," see Heinz R. Pagels, *The Dreams of Reason: The Computer and the Rise of the Sciences of Complexity* (New York: Bantam, 1988); David Pines, ed., *Emerging Synthesis in Science*, proceedings of the founding workshops for the Santa Fe Institute, Santa Fe, New Mexico (Redwood City, Calif.: Addison-Wesley, 1988); Gregoire Nicolis and Ilya Prigogine, *Exploring Complexity: An Introduction* (New York: W. H. Freeman, 1989); and for a more critical analysis, Katherine N. Hayles, *Chaos Bound: Orderly Disorder in Contemporary Literature and Science* (Ithaca, N.Y.: Cornell University Press, 1990).

5. Hence, the popularity of the Gaia Hypothesis—the earth as a cybernetic self-organizing system, for instance. How the Gaia Hypothesis has been reinterpreted by many nonscientists is itself quite instructive. Although the Gaia Hypothesis is deeply rooted in cybernetic systems theory, it has in the minds of many of its adherents been transformed back into an organismic entity demonstrating a continued (if confused) resistance to the mechanistic world view. See J. E. Lovelock, *Gaia: A New Look At Life on Earth* (Oxford/New York: Oxford University Press, 1979).

6. For discussions of the debates in and the history of the ecological sciences, see Joel B. Hagen, *An Entangled Bank: The Origins of Ecosystem Ecology* (New Brunswick, N.J.: Rutgers University Press, 1992); Leslie A. Real and James H. Brown, eds., *Foundations of Ecology: Classic Papers with Commentaries* (Chicago/London: University of Chicago Press, 1991); Michael G. Barbour, "Ecological Fragmentation in the Fifties," in *Uncommon Ground*, ed. William Cronon (New York: W.W. Norton, 1995), 233–255; Carolyn Merchant, ed., "The Emergence of Ecology in the Twentieth Century," *Major Problems in American Environmental History* (Lexington, Mass.: D.C. Heath, 1993), 444–484; Gregg Mitman, "From the Population to Society: The Cooperative Metaphors of W. C. Allee and A.E. Emerson," *Journal of the History of Biology* 21, no. 2 (Summer 1988), 173–194; Anna Bramwell, *Ecology in the 20th Century: A History* (New Haven, Conn.: Yale University Press, 1989); Richard H. Grove, "Origins of Western Environmentalism," *Scientific American* 267, no. 1 (July 1992), 42–47; Frank Benjamin Golley, *A History of the Ecosystem Concept in Ecology* (New Haven, Conn.: Yale University Press, 1993).

7. As noted by Hagen, the measuring of productivity and trophic efficiency of an ecosystem was first proposed by Raymond Lindeman, but he was only able to develop rough estimates. See Hagen, *An Entangled Bank*, 101.

8. This quote is from Howard T. Odum and Eugene P. Odum, "Trophic Structure and Productivity of a Windward Coral Reef Community on Eniwetok Atoll," *Ecological Monographs* 25 (1955): 291–320, cited in Hagen, *An Entangled Bank*, 102. (Emphasis in original.) Hagen's book provides a good introduction to ecology in the Atomic Age.

9. Chiras, Daniel D., *Environmental Science*, 3rd ed. (Redwood City, Calif: Benjamin-Cummings, 1991), 4.

10. See Watson-Verran and Turnbull, "Science and Other Indigenous Knowledge Systems," 116–117.

11. Thomas S. Kuhn, *The Structure of Scientific Revolutions*, 2nd ed. (Chicago: University of Chicago Press, 1970).

12. See Robert Lilienfeld, *The Rise of Systems Theory: An Ideological Analysis* (New York: John Wiley & Sons, 1978), especially "Operations Research and Systems Analysis," 103–135.

13. It is through such an ecological ethos that it becomes possible for companies to trade pollution credits.

14. Jean Baudrillard, *For a Critique of the Political Economy of the Sign*, trans. Charles Levin (St. Louis, Mo.: Telos, 1981).

15. Although its mechanical metaphors abound, cybernetics owes some of its advances to warm-blooded animals who were "sacrificed" to its advancement. Cybernetics was originally derived, at least in part, from Norbert Wiener's often macabre studies of the behavior of the nervous systems of animals (studies performed in Mexico because they were illegal in the United States). Using a process of "decerberation" (the severing of the brain from the spinal cord) Wiener was able to measure what amounted to the death throes of cats, "in which the cat's leg jerks involuntarily in increasingly rapid spasms until ceasing altogether." In this way "he arrived at a formula of the reflex arc that described a phenomenon of feedback, called *hunting* in servomechanisms such as steerage systems—a crucial "advance" in the development of cybernetic control theory." Richard Rawles, "Cybernetics Killed The Cat," unpublished paper, 1993, citing Wiener, Norbert, *Cybernetics* (Cambridge, Mass.: MIT Press, 1948), 7 and 19–20.

16. The most cited example of a cybernetic system is a thermostat control—the temperature of a room triggers a heating or cooling unit that in turn raises or lowers the temperature of the room. Such a system regulates the amount of energy so as to achieve efficiency, neither overheating or overcooling the room.

17. R. L. Kitching, *Systems Ecology: An Introduction to Ecological Modeling* (New York and London: University of Queensland Press, 1983).

18. See Donna J. Haraway, "The High Cost of Information in Post-World War II Evolutionary Biology: Ergonomics, Semiotics, and the Sociobiology of Communications Systems," *The Philosophical Forum* XIII, nos. 2–3 (Winter-Spring 1981–82), 244–278; Peter J. Taylor, "Technocratic Optimism, H. T. Odum, and the Partial Transformation of Ecological Metaphor after World War II," *Journal of the History of Biology* 21, no. 1 (Spring 1988), 245–265; Mitman, "From the Population to Society."

19. Howard T. Odum and Elizabeth C. Odum, *Energy Basis for Man and Nature* (New York: McGraw-Hill, 1981).

20. Any college-level environmental science textbook will offer this basic ecosystems depiction. This particular skeletal description of ecosystems analysis was culled from Chiras, *Environmental Science*.

21. Taylor, "Technocratic Optimism."

22. Chiras, *Environmental Science*, 65.

23. Donald Worster, *Nature's Economy: A History of Ecological Ideas* (Cambridge, UK: Cambridge University Press, 1977), 314.

24. Cybernetic theory was extended to the social realm as general system theory by Ludwig von Bertalanffy and others. See Ludwig von Bertalanffy, *General System Theory: Foundations, Development, Applications* (New York: George Braziller, 1968). A good overview of various applications of cybernetics can be found in Heims, *The Cybernetics Group*.

25. Howard T. Odum, *Environment, Power, and Society* (New York: Wiley Interscience, 1971). The quote appears in Chapter 8, "Energetic Basis for Religion," 236–253. In this chapter Odum also provides "The Ten Commandments of the Energy Ethic for Survival of Man in Nature," the first of which is: "Thou shall not waste potential energy" (p. 244).

26. Eugene P. Odum, *Fundamentals of Ecology*, 2nd edition (Philadelphia: W. B. Saunders, 1959).

27. Ibid., v–vi.

28. See Chapter 3, "Science Cities in the Desert: Outdoor Laboratories and Theaters of War."

29. Advisory Committee on Human Radiation Experiments, "Final Report," 547, n. 3. See also J. Newell Stannard, "Survey of Radioecology: Environmental Studies Around Production Sites," *Radioactivity and Health: A History* (Springfield, Va.: Office of Science and Technical Information, 1988).

30. For example, Hagen identifies experiments that were cut short due to lack of available isotopes (Hagen, *An Entangled Bank*).

31. Advisory Committee on Human Radiation Experiments, "Final Report," 19.

32. For an overview of ecosystems ecology, with specific analyses of the work of Eugene and Howard Odum (and the role of radiation-related research to their work), see *An Entangled Bank*, specifically Chapter 6, "Ecology and the Atomic Age"; Taylor, "Technocratic Optimism"; and Haraway, "The High Cost of Information in Post-World War II Evolutionary Biology."

33. Hagen, *An Entangled Bank*; 114.

34. Hagen, *An Entangled Bank*; Mitman, "From the Population to Society"; and Taylor, "Technocratic Optimism."

35. Hagen, *An Entangled Bank*, 10; Advisory Committee on Human Radiation Experiments, "Final Report."

36. Howard T. Odum and Robert F. Pigeon, eds., *A Tropical Rain Forest: A Study of Irradiation and Ecology at El Verde, Puerto Rico* (Springfield, Va.: U.S. Atomic Energy Commission, 1970).

37. For instance, radionuclides can become magnified (concentrated) as they move through the food chain. Hagen offers the example of radioactive phosphorous found in the Columbia River near Hanford: "[T]he concentrations of radioactive phosphorous were often hundreds of times greater in vertebrates at the ends of aquatic food chains than in the cooling water leaving the nuclear reactors. . . . As Odum pointed out, 'we could give "nature" an apparently innocuous amount of radioactivity and have her give it back to us in a lethal package.'" (*An Entangled Bank*, 116.) Magnification of radionuclides is also covered in Odum, "Radiation Ecology," *Fundamentals of Ecology*, 452–486.

38. Joseph A. Camilleri, *The State and Nuclear Power: Conflict and Control in the Western World* (Seattle: University of Washington Press, 1984), 10.

39. For more on the nuclear-fuel cycle and its corresponding national and international policy implications, see Rochlin, *Plutonium, Power, and Politics*. See also Shrader-Frechette, *Burying Uncertainty*, 15–19.

40. James S. Allen, *Atomic Imperialism: The State, Monopoly, and the Bomb* (New York: International Press, 1952), 84–85.

41. Camilleri, *The State and Nuclear Power*, 202–3.

42. Today, in 1996, these notions of recycling military nuclear materials back into the commercial sector (using plutonium wastes from bomb dismantling for nuclear power plant fuel) are once again being pursued by the Department of Energy. Critics note the poor judgment of linking military nuclear production with commercial needs. The cycle justifies continued use of nuclear power, which still leaves us with massive amounts of high-level nuclear waste for which we have no solution.

43. House Committee on Appropriations, *Energy and Water Development Appropriations for 1995*, 1787.

44. As noted in pervious chapters, the Nevada Nuclear Waste Project Office is in direct opposition to the Yucca Mountain Project and the burial of radioactive waste in Nevada. Even though their opposition is openly stated, the Nevada agency's scientists must be considered in the scientific evaluation of the mountain. Their credentials are as sound as those working for the Yucca Mountain Project.

45. The Yucca Mountain project consists of two different "processes:" the site characterization and the environmental-impact statement. Site characterization is conducted to "determine the suitability of the site for a spent nuclear fuel and high-level radioactive waste repository." Scientists study the "structural, mechanical, chemical, and hydrological characteristics" of Yucca Mountain. The mountain is assessed on the surface, underground, in laboratories, and from computer models. Of interest to researchers are underground water movement, earthquakes, volcanoes, and climate changes. The other "process," the environmental-impact statement, is a legal process based on The National Environmental Policy Act. It seeks to determine environmental impacts that might occur if a repository were "constructed, operated, and eventually closed at Yucca Mountain." The EIS uses knowledge of the mountain gained from the site

characterization study in addition to its own studies. Both scientific processes are conducted by reputable, well-trained scientists.

46. The daily costs fluctuate over time. This is the cost per day for 1995.

47. Of course, the fact that the necessary technology does not yet exist for answers to questions about the mountain's capacity to store high-level nuclear waste presents another obstacle to scientists studying the mountain.

48. For instance one USGS scientist told me of her worries that the DOE was not conducting adequate hydrological studies of the large regional aquifer under the mountain. According to this source the main reasons for not doing the studies were time and, more especially, money. Severe congressional appropriations cutbacks in 1995–96 further reduced scientists' ability to conduct appropriate tests of the area. Complaints about the project by scientists working for or contracting with the Department of Energy are attributed to "anonymous" sources for obvious reasons.

49. For a good description of how Yucca Mountain became the only object of investigation, see Jacob, *Site Unseen.*

50. As noted earlier, on August 1, 1996, the Senate passed another bill (S. #1936) to amend the Nuclear Waste Policy Act yet again. The new bill allows nuclear power companies to ship their nuclear waste to an "interim" storage site on the Nevada Test Site next to Yucca Mountain. In September 1997, the House passed the bill. If President Clinton does not veto it, the waste will be prepared for deep-geologic containment right at the site itself. It should be noted that passage of this bill has preceded designation of the Yucca Mountain site as safe and suitable for nuclear waste. In the previous bill it was illegal to have an interim waste storage site in the same state that hosts a deep-geologic repository. Apparently, inequitable burden on a single state (Nevada) is no longer an issue.

51. "Another Panel Rejects Nevada Disaster Theory," *Science*, 24 April 1992.

52. Karl Johnson, phone interview by author, 14 October 1994. See also *Geotimes*, January 1989, and *Geotimes*, August 1991.

53. Karl Johnson, phone interview by author, 14 October 1994.

54. *Of Mountains and Science*, Winter 1996, 134.

55. The same is true for other radioisotopes. For instance, radioactive carbon (^{14}C) and chlorine (^{36}Cl) were also atmospherically dispersed in fallout from nuclear testing. See J. T. Fabryka-Martin et al., "Infiltration Processes at Yucca Mountain Inferred from Chloride and Chlorine-36 Distribution" (Los Alamos National Laboratory, N.Mex., December 21, 1994), LA-CST-TIP-94-019/Milestone Report 3417.

56. The winter of 1995 was the wettest for Yucca Mountain in 55 years. *The Site Characterization Progress Report* of April 1, 1996, reported that the tributaries of Fortymile Wash and the Amargosa River "flowed simultaneously throughout their entire Nevada reaches." *Site Characterization Progress Report: Yucca Mountain, Nevada,* April 1, 1995–September 30, 1995, Number 13 (Washington D.C.: U.S. Department of Energy/Office of Civilian Radioactive Waste Management, April 1996), p. ES-9., DOE/RW-0486.

57. Robert Craig (chief of the U.S. Geological Survey's Nevada Operations Program), "Drillers Find More Perched Water in Yucca Mountain's Unsaturated Zone," *Of Mountains & Science,* Summer 1995, 106.

58. *Science News* 133, no. 9 (27 Feb., 1988): 139.

59. Odum, in *Environment, Power, and Society*, envisioned nature as a "network nightmare"—out of control when left unmanaged. "Man" was needed as engineer to ensure that the system behave optimally (*Environment, Power, and Society*, 274–76).

60. For more on "cybernetic technological functionalism" and its genealogy see Haraway, *Primate Visions*, particularly "A Semiotics of the Naturalistic Field: From C. R. Carpenter to S. A. Altmann, 1930–1995," 84–111.

61. Loren D. Potter, "Desert Characteristics as Related to Waste Disposal," in Reith and Thomson, *Deserts as Dumps?*, 21.

Chapter 10

1. Odum, *Fundamentals of Ecology*, 1959, 479–80. [My italics.]

2. To insist that one system of meaning be placed along side the other (for instance, traditional Indian and Western scientific), rather than within a hierarchically organized dualism, helps us avoid what Jacques Derrida calls the binary opposition of Western logic.

3. For a theoretical analysis of the naturalization of the dominant ethos (not necessarily scientific), and thus its invisibility as an identifiable entity, see Roland Barthes, *Mythologies*, trans. Annette Lavers (New York: Hill and Wang, 1982). For an analysis of the impenetrability of science from critical scrutiny by those outside its domain, see Jurgen Habermas, *Toward A Rational Society* (Boston: Beacon, 1968) and Helen Longino, *Science As Social Knowledge* (Princeton, N.J.: Princeton University Press, 1990).

4. Chiras, *Environmental Science*.

5. As has been shown by Haraway, *Primate Visions*; Barbour, "Ecological Fragmentation"; Taylor, "Technocratic Optimism"; Evelyn Fox Keller, *Reflections on Gender and Science* (New Haven/London: Yale University Press, 1985); and many others.

6. For instance, Shrader-Frechette argues forcefully that we need to use "*negotiated*, monitored, retrievable storage" for high-level nuclear waste—a "wait and see" strategy so that we have time to attempt to solve some of the uncertainty and inequity problems associated with deep-geologic disposal. Her proposal is founded upon generational responsibility since there is little doubt that, although the twentieth and perhaps twenty-first centuries may not be subject to escaping radionuclides, generations after this will most certainly be. With all the problems that accompany monitored retrievable storage, Shrader-Frechette notes, at least those promoting this option do not misrepresent its capacities as do those promoting deep-geologic disposal. See Shrader-Frechette, *Burying Uncertainty*, 213–251.

7. Alan Burdick, "The Last Cold-War Monument," *Harper's*, August 1992.

Bibliography

Books and Periodicals

Abrams, David. *The Spell of the Sensuous: Perception and Language in a More-Than-Human World*. New York: Pantheon, 1996.

———. "Merleau-Ponty and the Voice of the Earth."w In *Minding Nature: The Philosophers of Ecology*, ed. David Macauley. New York: Guilford, 1996.

Allen, James S. *Atomic Imperialism: The State, Monopoly, and the Bomb*. New York: International Press, 1952.

Ambler, Marjane. *Breaking the Iron Bonds*. Lawrence: University Press of Kansas, 1990.

Austin, Mary. *Land of Little Rain*. New York: Penguin, 1988; originally published by Houghton Mifflin, 1903.

Ball, Howard. *Justice Downwind: America's Atomic Testing Program in the 1950s*. New York/Oxford, UK: Oxford University Press, 1986.

Barbour, Michael G. "Ecological Fragmentation in the Fifties." In *Uncommon Ground*, ed. William Cronon. New York: W.W. Norton, 1995.

Barthes, Roland. *Mythologies*, trans. Annette Lavers. New York: Hill and Wang, 1982.

Bartimus, Tad, and Scott McCartney. *Trinity's Children: Living Along America's Nuclear Highway*. New York: Harcourt Brace Jovanovich, 1991.

Basso, Keith H. "Stalking with Stories: Names, Places, and Moral Narratives among the Western Apache." "Text, Play, and Story: The Construction and Reconstruction of Self and Society," ed. Stuart Plattner, *1983 Proceedings of the American Ethnological Society*. Washington D.C.: American Ethnological Society, 1984.

Baudrillard, Jean. *For a Critique of the Political Economy of the Sign*, trans. Charles Levin. St. Louis, Mo: Telos, 1981.

Beardsley, Tim. "Science and the Citizen." *Scientific American*, April 1994.

Birnbaum, Raoul. "Signs of Power in the Natural World: Indicator Plants in the Wutai Mountains." In *Culte des sites, culte des saints*, ed. Françiscus Verellen. Paris: Ecole Française
d'Extreme-Orient, forthcoming.

Blackburn, Thomas C., and Kat Anderson, eds. *Before the Wilderness: Environmental Management by Native Californians*. Menlo Park, Calif: Ballena, 1993.

Bourdieu, Pierre. *Outline of a Theory of Practice*, trans. Richard Nice. Cambridge, UK: Cambridge University Press, 1972.

Box, Thadius, et al. *Rehabilitation Potential for Western Coal Lands*. Cambridge, Mass:
Ballinger, 1974.

Bramwell, Anna. *Ecology in the 20th Century: A History*. New Haven, Conn.: Yale University
Press, 1989.

Brosius, Peter J. "Negotiating Citizenship in a Commodified Landscape: The Case of Penan
Hunter-Gatherers in Sarawak, East Malaysia." Prepared for the Social Science
Research Council conference, "Cultural Citizenship in Southeast Asia." Honolulu,
Hawaii, 2–4 May, 1993.

Bullard, Robert D., ed. *Confronting Environmental Racism: Voices from the Grassroots*. Boston:
South End, 1993.

Burdick, Alan. "The Last Cold War Monument." *Harper's*, August 1992.

Camilleri, Joseph A. *The State and Nuclear Power: Conflict and Control in the Western World*. Seattle: University of Washington Press, 1984.

Chalfant, W. A. *The Story of Inyo: Its Pioneering, Its Indians, Its Struggles Over Water*. Bishop,
Calif.: Chalfant, 1959.

Chiras, Daniel D., *Environmental Science*, 3rd ed. Redwood City, Calif.: Benjamin-Cummings, 1991.

Churchill, Ward. *Struggle for the Land: Indigenous Resistance to Genocide, Ecocide and Expropriation in Contemporary North America*. Monroe, Maine: Common Courage, 1993.

Cronon, William. *Changes in the Land: Indians, Colonists, and the Ecology of New England*. New
York: Hill and Wang, 1983.

Crum, Steven J. *Po'i Pentun Tammen Kimmappeh/The Road on Which We Came: A History of the
Western Shoshone*. Salt Lake City: University of Utah Press, 1994.

D'Antonio, Michael. *Atomic Harvest: Hanford and the Lethal Toll of America's Nuclear Arsenal*.
New York, Crown: 1993.

Davis, Mike. "Dead West: Ecocide in Marlboro Country." *New Left Review*, no. 200 July/August
1993.

Day, Samuel H., ed. *Nuclear Heartland: A Guide to 1,000 Missile Silos of the United States*. Madison, Wis.: Nukewatch, 1988.

D'Azevedo, Warren L., et al., eds. "Tribal Distribution and Boundaries in the Great Basin." *The
Current Status of Anthropological Research in the Great Basin 1964*.

Desert Research Institute Technical Report Series S–H. Social Sciences and Humanities Publications, no. 1. Reno, Nev.: Desert Research Institute, 1966.

Dorn, Ronald I., and David S. Whitley. "Chronometric and Relative Age Determination of Petroglyphs in the Western United States." *Annals of the Association of American Geographers*, vol. 74, no. 2 (1984).

Dreeson, D.R. "Uranium Mill Tailings: Environmental Implications." *Los Alamos Scientific Laboratory Mini-Report*, February 1978.

Enson, Beth. "The Nuclear Waste Struggle Continues on the Mescalero Apache Reservation." *The
Workbook*, vol. 20, no. 1. Albuquerque, N.Mex.: Southwest Research and Information
Center, Spring 1995.

Epstein, Barbara. *Political Protest and Cultural Revolution: Nonviolent Direct Action in the 1970s
and 1980s*. Berkeley: University of California Press, 1991.

Foucault, Michel. *The Archaeology of Knowledge*, trans. A. M. Sheridan Smith. New York: Pantheon, 1972.

————. "Nietzsche, Genealogy, History," trans. Donald F. Bouchard and Sherry Simon, *The Foucault Reader*, ed. Paul Rabinow. New York: Pantheon, 1994.

Gallagher, Carole. *America Ground Zero: The Secret Nuclear War*. New York: Random House, 1993.

Gerber, Michele Stenehjem. *On the Home Front: The Cold War Legacy of the Hanford Nuclear Site*. Lincoln: University of Nebraska Press, 1992.

Gibbs, Lois, and the Citizens Clearinghouse for Hazardous Waste. *Dying from Dioxin: A Citizen's Guide to Reclaiming Our Health and Rebuilding Community*. Boston: South End, 1995.

Gill, Sam D. *Mother Earth: An American Story*. Chicago/London: University of Chicago Press, 1987.

Golley, Frank Benjamin. *A History of the Ecosystem Concept in Ecology*. New Haven, Connt.: Yale University Press, 1993.

Gould, Jay M. *The Enemy Within: The High Cost of Living Near Nuclear Reactors*. New York/London: Four Walls Eight Windows, 1996.

Grossman, P. Z., and E. S. Cassedy. "Cost Benefit Analysis of Nuclear Waste Disposal." *Science, Technology, and Human Values* 10, no. 4 (Fall 1985): 48.

The Groundwork Collective. "The Illusion of Cleanup: A Case Study at Hanford." *Groundwork*, 4. San Francisco: Groundwork Collective, March 1994.

Grove, Richard H. "Origins of Western Environmentalism." *Scientific American* 267, no. 1 (July 1992).

Habermas, Jurgen. *Toward A Rational Society*. Boston: Beacon, 1968.

Hagen, Joel B. *An Entangled Bank: The Origins of Ecosystem Ecology*. New Brunswick, N.J.: Rutgers University Press, 1992.

Haraway, Donna J. *Primate Visions*. New York: Routledge, 1989.

————. *Modest_Witness@Second_Millenium.FemaleMan©_Meets_OncoMouse(™)*. New York: Routledge, 1996.

————. "The High Cost of Information in Post-World War II Evolutionary Biology: Ergonomics, Semiotics, and the Sociobiology of Communications Systems." *The Philosophical Forum* XIII, nos. 2–3 (Winter-Spring 1981–82).

Harney, Corbin. *The Way It Is: One Water . . . One Air . . . One Mother Earth*. Nevada City, Calif.: Blue Dolphin, 1995.

Havelock, Eric A. *Preface to Plato*. Cambridge, Mass.: Belknap Press of Harvard University Press, 1963.

Hayles, Katherine N. *Chaos Bound: Orderly Disorder in Contemporary Literature and Science*. Ithaca, N.Y.: Cornell University Press, 1990.

Heims, Steve J. *The Cybernetics Group*. Cambridge, Mass.: The MIT Press, 1991.

Historic Preservation Committee of the Timbisha Shoshone Tribe. *The Timbisha Shoshone Tribe and Their Living Valley*. Death Valley, Calif: Death Valley '49ers Inc., Published as Keepsake No. 34 for the 45th Annual Death Valley '49ers Encampment. November 1994.

Hoppe, Richard. "A Stretch of Desert along Route 66—the Grants Belt—Is Chief Locale for U.S. Uranium." *Engineering and Mining Journal* 79, no. 11 (1978): 79–93.

Hulse, James W. *Forty Years in the Wilderness*. Reno: University of Nevada Press, 1986.

Hultkrantz, A. "An Ethnoecological Approach to Religion." *Ethnos* 31: 131–30.

Jorgenson, Joseph G. "The Political Economy of the Native American Energy Business." *Native Americans and Energy Development, II*, ed. Joseph G. Jorgenson. Boston: Anthropology Resource Center/Seventh Generation Fund, 1984.

Keller, Evelyn Fox. *Reflections on Gender and Science*. New Haven, Conn./London: Yale University Press, 1985.

Kelly, Klara Bonsack, and Harris Francis. *Navajo Sacred Places*. Bloomington and Indianapolis: Indiana University Press, 1994.

Kerr, Richard A. "Another Panel Rejects Nevada Disaster Theory." *Science*, 24 April 1992.

Kirby, Kathleen M. *Indifferent Boundaries: Spatial Concepts and Human Subjectivity*. New York/London: Guilford, 1996.

Kitching, R. L. *Systems Ecology: An Introduction to Ecological Modeling*. New York and London: University of Queensland Press, 1983.

Klasky, Philip M. "The Eagle's View of Ward Valley: Environmentalists and Native American Tribes Fight Proposed Nuclear Dump in the Mojave Desert." *Wild Earth*, Spring 1994.

Kuhn, Thomas S. *The Structure of Scientific Revolutions*, 2nd ed. Chicago: University of Chicago Press, 1970.

LaDuke, Winona. "A History of Uranium Mining." *Black Hills/Paha Sapa Report* 1, no. 1 (1979).

———. "Native Environmentalism." *Earth Island Journal*, Summer 1993.

Lefebvre, Henri. *The Production of Space*, trans. Donald Nicholson-Smith. Oxford, UK: Basil Blackwell, 1991.

Lévi-Strauss, Claude. *The Savage Mind*. Chicago: University of Chicago Press, 1962.

Lifton, Robert Jay. *The Future of Immortality*. New York: Basic Books, 1987.

Lilienfeld, Robert. *The Rise of Systems Theory: An Ideological Analysis*. New York: John Wiley & Sons, 1978.

Limerick, Patricia Nelson. *Desert Passages*. Albuquerque: University of New Mexico Press, 1985.

Longino, Helen. *Science As Social Knowledge*. Princeton, N.J.: Princeton University Press, 1990.

Loomis, David. *Combat Zoning: Military Land-Use Planning in Nevada* (Reno/Las Vegas: University of Nevada Press, 1994.

Lovelock, J. E. *Gaia: A New Look At Life on Earth*. Oxford, UK/New York: Oxford University Press, 1979.

Lyotard, Jean-Francois. *The Postmodern Condition: A Report on Knowledge*, trans. Geoff Bennington and Brian Massumi. Minneapolis: University of Minnesota Press, 1984.

Macy, Joanna Rogers. *Despair and Personal Power in the Nuclear Age*. Baltimore: New Society, 1983.

Makhijani, Arjun, and Scott Saleska. *High-Level Dollars, Low-Level Sense: A Critique of Present Policy for the Management of Long-Lived Radioactive Wastes and Discussion of an Alternative Approach*. Takoma Park, Md.: Institute for Energy and Environmental Research, 1992.

———, Howard Hu, and Katherine Yih. *Nuclear Wastelands: A Global Guide to Nuclear Weapons Production and Its Health and Environmental Effects*. Cambridge, Mass.: MIT Press, 1995.

Mander, Jerry. *In the Absence of the Sacred: The Failure of Technology and the Survival of the Indian Nations*. San Francisco: Sierra Club Books, 1991.

Martin, Calvin. *Keepers of the Game: Indian Animal Relationship and the Fur Trade*. Berkeley: University of California Press, 1978.

Merchant, Carolyn. *Ecological Revolutions*. Chapel Hill: University of North Carolina Press, 1989.

———, ed. *Major Problems in American Environmental History*. Lexington, Mass.: D.C. Heath, 1993.

Merleau-Ponty, Maurice. *Phenomenology of Perception*, trans. Colin Smith. London: Routledge & Kegan Paul, 1962.

———. *The Visible and the Invisible*, ed. Claude Lefort, trans. Alphonso Lingis. Evanston, Ill.: Northwestern University Press, 1968.

Miller, Jay. "Basin Religion and Theology: A Comparative Study of Power (Puha)." *Journal of California and Great Basin Anthropology* 5 (1,2): 66–86.

———. "Numic Religion: An Overview of Power in the Great Basin of Native North America." *Anthropos* 78: 337–354.

Misrach, Richard. *Bravo 20: The Bombing of the American West*. Baltimore and London: Johns Hopkins University Press, 1990.

Mitman, Gregg. "From the Population to Society: The Cooperative Metaphors of W. C. Allee and A.E. Emerson." *Journal of the History of Biology* 21, no. 2 (Summer 1988).

Mukerji, Chandra. *A Fragile Power: Scientists and the State*. Princeton, N.J.: Princeton University Press, 1989.

Mumford, Lewis. "The Morals of Extermination." *Atlantic Monthly*, October 1959.

Nafziger, Richard. "Transnational Energy Corporations and American Indian Development." *American Indian Energy Resources and Development*, Development Series no. 2, ed. Ortiz. Albuquerque: Native American Studies Dept., University of New Mexico, 1980.

Nagel, Joan. "American Indian Ethnic Renewal: Politics and the Resurgence of Identity." *American Sociological Review*, 1995, 60 (December: 947–965).

Nash, Gerald D. *The American West Transformed: The Impact of the Second World War*. Bloomington: Indiana University Press, 1985.

Nash, Roderick. *Wilderness and the American Mind*. New Haven, Conn.: Yale University Press, 1967.

Nicolis, Gregoire, and Ilya Prigogine. *Exploring Complexity: An Introduction*. New York: W. H. Freeman, 1989.

Novik, S. *The Electric War*. San Francisco: Sierra Club Books, 1976.

Odum, Eugene P. *Fundamentals of Ecology*, 2nd edition. Philadelphia: W. B. Saunders, 1959.

Odum, Howard T. *Environment, Power, and Society*. New York: Wiley Interscience, 1971.

———, and Elizabeth C. Odum. *Energy Basis for Man and Nature*. New York: McGraw-Hill, 1981.

———, and Eugene P. Odum. "Trophic Structure and Productivity of a Windward Coral Reef Community on Eniwetok Atoll." *Ecological Monographs* 25 (1955): 291–320.

———, and Robert F. Pigeon, eds. *A Tropical Rain Forest: A Study of Irradiation and Ecology at El Verde, Puerto Rico*. Springfield, Va.: U.S. Atomic Energy Commission, 1970.

O'Neill, Dan. *The Firecracker Boys*. New York: St. Martin's Press, 1994.

Ong, Walter J. *Orality and Literacy*. London and New York: Routledge, 1982.

Ostling, Kristen, and Joanna Miller. "Taking Stock: The Impact of Militarism on the Environment." *Science for Peace*, February 1992.

Pagels, Heinz R. *The Dreams of Reason: The Computer and the Rise of the Sciences of Complexity*. New York: Bantam, 1988.

Pines, David, ed. *Emerging Synthesis in Science*. Proceedings of the founding workshops for the Santa Fe Institute, Santa Fe, New Mexico. Redwood City, Calif.: Addison-Wesley, 1988.

Pippin, L. C., R. L. Clerico, and R. L. Reno. *An Archaeological Reconnaissance of the NNWSI Yucca Mountain Project Area, Southern Nye County, Nevada*. Reno: University of Nevada, Desert Research Institute Social Sciences Center publication no. 28, 1982.

Pippin, Lonnie C., ed. *Limited Test Excavations at Selected Archaeological Sites in the NNWSI Yucca Mountain Project Area, Southern Nye County, Nevada*. Reno: University of Nevada, Desert Research Institute, Social Sciences Center publication no. 40, 1984.

Pooley, Eric. "Nuclear Warriors." *Time*, 4 March 1996.

Pratt, Mary Louis. *Imperial Eyes: Travel Writing and Transculturation*. New York: Routledge, 1992.

Ruta, Suzanne. "Fear and Silence in Los Alamos." *The Nation*, 4-11 January 1993.

Quick, Polly, ed. *Proceedings: Conference On Reburial Issues*. Society for American Archaeology and Society for Professional Archaeologists. Chicago, Newberry Library, 1985.

Real, Leslie A., and James H. Brown, eds. *Foundations of Ecology: Classic Papers with Commentaries*. Chicago/London: The University of Chicago Press, 1991.

Regan, Tom. "Environmental Ethics and the Ambiguity of the Native American Relationship with Nature." In *All That Dwells Therein: Animal Rights and Environmental Ethics*, ed. Tom Regan. Berkeley: University of California Press, 1982.

Reith, Charles C., and Bruce M. Thomson, eds. *Deserts as Dumps? The Disposal of Hazardous Materials in Arid Ecosystems*. Albuquerque: University of New Mexico Press, 1992.

Renner, Michael. "Tarnished Armories." *Environmental Action*, May-June 1991.

Rhodes, Richard. *The Making of the Atomic Bomb*. New York: Simon & Schuster, 1986.

Ricoeur, Paul. *A Ricoeur Reader: Reflection and Imagination*, ed. Mario J. Valdes. Toronto/Buffalo: University of Toronto Press, 1991.

Robinson, Paul. "Uranium Production and Its Effects on Navajo Communities Along the Rio Puerco in Western New Mexico." *The Proceedings of the Michigan Conference on Race and the Incidence of Environmental Hazards*, eds. Bunyan Bryant and Paul Nohai. Ann Arbor: University of Michigan School of Natural Resources, 1990.

———. "Review of Recent Uranium Production and Market Trends." Joint Federal Provincial Panel on Uranium Mining Developments in Northern Saskatchewan. Inter-Church Uranium Committee. Saskatoon, Canada, 1996.

Rochlin, Gene I. *Plutonium, Power, and Politics*. Berkeley: University of California Press, 1979.

Rosenthal, Debra. *At the Heart of the Bomb: The Dangerous Allure of Weapons Work*. Menlo Park, Calif.: Addison-Wesley, 1990.

Rothman, Hal. *On Rims and Ridges: The Los Alamos Area Since 1880*. Lincoln: University of Nebraska Press, 1992.

Samet, Jonathan M., et al. "Uranium Mining and Lung Cancer in Navajo Men." *The New England Journal of Medicine* 310, no. 23 (7 June, 1984).

Shields, L. M. et al. "Navajo Birth Outcomes in the Shiprock Uranium Mining Area." *Health Physics* 63, no. 5 (1992).

Shrader-Frachette, K. S. *Burying Uncertainty: Risk and the Case Against Geological Disposal of Nuclear Waste*. Berkeley: University of California Press, 1993.

Shuey, Chris. "The Puerco River: Where Did the Water Go?" *The Workbook*, vol. XI, no. 1. Albuquerque, N.Mex.: Southwest Research and Information Center, 1986.

Skinner, Michael. *Red Flag*. Novato, Calif.: Presidio Press, 1984.

Smith, Anne M. *Shoshone Tales*. Salt Lake City: University of Utah Press, 1993.

Soja, Edward W. *Postmodern Geographies: The Reassertion of Space in Critical Social Theory*. London: Verso, 1980.

Solnit, Rebecca. *Savage Dreams*. San Francisco: Sierra Club Books, 1994.

Stannard, J. Newell. "Survey of Radioecology: Environmental Studies Around Production Sites." *Radioactivity and Health: A History*. Springfield, Va.: Office of Science and Technical Information, 1988.

Steward, Julian H. *Basin-Plateau Aboriginal Sociopolitical Groups*. Bureau of American Ethnology. Bulletin 120. Washington, D.C.: Smithsonian Institution, 1938, 1941.

Stoffle, Richard, et al. *Native American Cultural Resource Studies at Yucca Mountain, Nevada*. Ann Arbor: Institute for Social Research, University of Michigan, 1990.

Szasz, Andrew. *Ecopopulism: Toxic Waste and the Movement for Environmental Justice*. Minneapolis: University of Minnesota Press, 1994.

Taylor, Linda. "Uranium Legacy." *The Workbook*, vol. VIII, no. 6. Albuquerque, N.Mex.: Southwest Research and Information Center, 1983.

Taylor, Peter J. "Technocratic Optimism, H.T. Odum, and the Partial Transformation of Ecological Metaphor after World War II." *Journal of the History of Biology* 21, no. 1 (Spring 1988).

Tedlock, D., and B. Tedlock, eds. *Teachings from the American Earth: Indian Religion and Philosophy*. New York: Liveright, 1975.

Thomas, William. *Scorched Earth: The Military's Assault on the Environment*. Philadelphia: New Society Publishers, 1995.

Turner, Frederick. *Beyond Geography: The Western Spirit Against the Wilderness*. New York: Viking, 1980.

Vecesey, C., and R. W. Venables, eds. *American Indian Environments*. Syracuse, N.Y.: Syracuse University Press, 1980.

Visenor, Gerald. *Manifest Manners: Postindian Warriors of Survivance*. Hanover, N.H.: University Press of New England, 1994.

von Bertalanffy, Ludwig. *General System Theory: Foundations, Development, Applications.* New York: George Braziller, 1968.

Walker, Samuel J. *Containing the Atom.* Berkeley: University of California Press, 1992.

Watson-Verran, Helen, and David Turnbull. "Science and Other Indigenous Knowledge Systems." In *Handbook of Science and Technology Studies,* ed. S. Jasanoff, G. E. Markle, J. C. Petersen, and Trevor Pence. Thousand Oaks, Calif.: Sage, 1995.

Whitley, David S., and Ronald I. Dorn. "Rock Art Chronology in eastern California." *World Archaeology,* vol. 16, no. 2 (1987).

———, et al. "The Late Prehistoric Period in the Coso Range and Environs." *Pacific Coast Archaeological Society Quarterly,* vol. 24, no. 1 (January 1988).

Wheelwright, Jeff. "For Our Nuclear Waste, There's Gridlock on the Road to the Dump." *Smithsonian,* May 1995.

White, Richard, and P. L. Limerick. *The Frontier in American Culture.* Berkeley: University of California Press, 1994.

Wiener, Norbert. *Cybernetics.* Cambridge, Mass.: The MIT Press, 1948.

Williams, Raymond. *The Sociology of Culture.* New York: Schocken, 1981.

Wilson, Alexander. *The Culture of Nature.* Cambridge, Mass.: Blackwell, 1992.

Worman, Frederick C. *Archaeological Investigations at the U.S. Atomic Energy Commission's Nevada Test Site and Nuclear Rocket Development Station.* Los Alamos, N.Mex.: Los Alamos National Laboratory, 1969.

Worster, Donald. *Nature's Economy: A History of Ecological Ideas.* Cambridge, UK: Cambridge University Press, 1977.

Yaeger, Patricia, ed. *The Geography of Identity.* Ann Arbor: University of Michigan Press, 1996.

Yaroshinskaya, Alla. *Chernobyl: The Forbidden Truth,* trans. Michele Kahn and Julia Sallabank. Lincoln: University of Nebraska Press, 1995.

Government Documents

Advisory Committee on Human Radiation Experiments. *Final Report,* Washington, D.C.: GPO, October, 1995. Report no. 061-000-00-848-9.

Bureau of the Census. *A Statistical Portrait of the American Indian Population.* Washington, D.C.: GPO, 1984.

China Lake Naval Weapons Center. "Naval Weapons Center Silver Anniversary." October 1968. Technical Information Department Publishing Division.

———. *Notable Achievements of the Naval Weapons Center.* By R. E. Kistler and R. M. Glen. August 1990. NWC TP 7088.

General Accounting Office. "Nuclear Health and Safety: Examples of Post World War II Radiation Releases at U.S. Nuclear Sites." November 1993. RCED 94-51FS.

Los Alamos National Laboratory. "Infiltration Processes at Yucca Mountain Inferred from Chloride and Chlorine-36 Distributions." By J. T. Fabryka-Martin et al. December 21, 1994. LA-CST-TIP-94-019/Milestone Report 3417.

Monitored Retrievable Storage Review Commission. "Nuclear Waste: Is There a Need for Federal Interim Storage?" *Report of the Monitored Retrievable Storage Review Commission.* Washington, D.C.: GPO, 1989. No. 022-003-01164-1.

National Academy of Science. Committee on Waste Disposal. Division of Earth Science. *The Disposal of Radioactive Waste on Land.* 1957. Washington, D.C. NAS-NRC pub. 519.

Nevada Nuclear Waste Project Office. *Native Americans and Yucca Mountain: A Summary Report.* By Catherine S. Fowler. September 1990. NWPO-SE-026-90.

U.S. Atomic Energy Commission. "Hydrogeologic and Hydrochemical Framework, South-Central Great Basin, Nevada-California; with Special Reference to the Nevada Test Site." By I. J. Winograd and W. Thordarson. *Hydrology of Nuclear Test Sites.* Washington D.C.: GPO, 1975. Geologic Survey Professional Paper 712–C.

U.S. Congress. House Committee on Appropriations. *Energy and Water Development Appropriations for 1995.* 103rd Cong., 2nd sess.

U.S. Congress. House Committee on Energy and Commerce, Subcommittee on Energy and Power. 1989. *Safety of DOE Nuclear Facilities.* 101st Cong., 1st sess. Serial no. 101–1. Washington, D.C.: GPO, 1989.

U.S. Congress. House Committee on Interior and Insular Affairs, Subcommittee on Energy and Environment. 1988. *Nuclear Waste Policy Act,* 100th Congress, 1st sess. Washington, D.C.: Government Printing Office, 1988.

U.S. Department of Energy. "Could Radioactive Materials Get Out of a Repository?" *DOE's Yucca Mountain Studies.* Las Vegas, Nev.: Yucca Mountain Site Characterization Project.

———. *Environmental Impact Statement for a Proposed Repository at Yucca Mountain, Nevada.* July 1995. RW-0364P.

———. *Environmental Management 1995.* February 1995. DOE/EM-0228.

———. *Estimating the Cold War Mortgage: The 1995 Baseline Environmental Management Report.* March 1995. DOE/EM-0232.

———. *Final Programmatic Environmental Impact Statement for Stockpile Stewardship and Management,* September 1996. DOE/EIS-0236.

———. *Nuclear Waste Policy Act, as Amended.* February 1995. DOE/RW-0438.

———. *OCRWM Transportation Report.* June 1995. DOE/RW-0473.

———. Office of Civilian Radioactive Waste Management. "Why Are Scientists Studying Yucca Mountain?" April 1993. DOE/RW-0340P.

———. Office of Civilian Radioactive Waste Management. "Overview—Nuclear Waste Policy Act." DOE/RW-0104.

———. Office of Civilian Radioactive Waste Management. *Site Characterization Progress Report: Yucca Mountain, Nevada, April 1, 1995-September 30, 1995, Number 13.* April 1996. DOE/RW-0486.

———. Office of Environmental Management. *Closing the Circle of the Splitting of the Atom: The Environmental Legacy of Nuclear Weapons Production in the United States and What the Department of Energy Is Doing About It.* January 1995.

———. Office of Environmental Management. *Environmental Management 1995.* February 1995. DOE/EM-0228.

———. *Yucca Mountain Project: Literature Review and Ethnohistory of Native American Occupancy and Use of the Yucca Mountain Region.* By Stoffle et al. OTIS, DOE/NV-10576-21.

———. *Yucca Mountain Project Native American Plant Resources in the Yucca Mountain Area, Nevada.* By Stoffle et al., Wesley E. Niles and Joan T. O'Farrell. November 1989. DOE/NV-10576-19.

U.S. Department of Health and Human Services. *Chart Series Book.* Washington, D.C.: Public Health Service. HE20.9409.988, 1988.

U.S. Department of Interior. *Indian Lands Map: Oil, Gas, and Minerals on Indian Reservations.* Washington, D.C.: GPO, 1978.

———. *Final Environmental Impact Statement for the Jackpile-Paguate Uranium Mine Reclamation Project.* Albuquerque, N.Mex.: Bureau of Land Management, October 1986.

U.S. Environmental Protection Agency. *Radiological Quality of the Environment in the United States.* Washington, D.C.: GPO, 1977. Cited in Churchill, *Struggle for the Land,* 266.

———. *Potential Health and Environmental Hazards of Uranium Mine Wastes.* Washington, D.C.: GPO, 1983.

Interviews and Taped Presentations

(This list does not include interviews conducted with those who requested anonymity.)

Big Pine Paiute Tribe of the Owens Valley tribal elders, group interview. Interview by author, 20 November 1994. Tribal Council Center, Big Pine, California. Tape recording. Author collection.

Bukowski, Grace, director of Rural Alliance for Military Accountability. Phone interview by author, 2 December 1996.

Charlie, Dewey, Inyo county elder Paiute resident. Interview by Iroquois Research Institute. *Land Use History of Coso Hot Springs, Inyo County, California.* Public Works Department, Naval Weapons Center, China Lake, California. Administrative publication number 200, January 1979.

Coghlin, Jay, program director, Concerned Citizens for Nuclear Safety, Santa Fe, New Mexico. Phone interview by author, 9 December 1996.

Edwards, Debbie, USGS hydrologist, USGS Headquarters, Las Vegas, Nevada. Phone interview by author, August 1996.

Esteves, Pauline, acting tribal chairperson for the Timbisha Shoshone. Interview by author. 22 November 1994. Timbisha Shoshone Village, Death Valley, California. Tape recording. Author collection.

Fasano, Gregory A., senior environmental scientist with SAIC/Yucca Mountain Project. Interview by author, 17 October 1994. Las Vegas, Nevada. Tape recording. Author collection.

Don Hancock, Southwest Research and Information Center. Phone interview by author, 17 June 1997.

Harney, Corbin, spiritual leader of the Western Shoshone Nation. Interview by author, 15 February 1995. Santa Cruz, California.

Hirschberg, Susan, waste and contamination director for Concerned Citizens for Nuclear Safety, Santa Fe, New Mexico. Phone interview by author, 30 March 1995. Tape recording. Author collection.

Johnson, Karl, technical director for Nevada's Nuclear Waste Project Office. Phone interview by author, October 1994. Tape recording. Author collection.

Moapa Paiute tribal elders, group interview by author, 18 April 1995. Moapa Paiute reservation, Nevada. Tape recording. Author collection.

Miller, Lalovi, Moapa Paiute elder. Interview by author, 18 April 1995. Moapa Paiute reservation, Nevada. Tape recording. Author collection.

Moose, Bertha, Big Pine Paiute Tribe of the Owens Valley tribal elder and cultural resource tribal contact. Interview by author, 20 November 1994. Big Pine, California. Tape recording. Author collection.

Moose, Gaylene, Bishop Paiute Tribe of the Owens Valley tribal member. Interview by author, 20 November 1994. Big Pine, California. Tape recording. Author collection.

Paiute and Shoshone individuals, remembering Coso Hot Springs. Interviews by Iroquois Research Institute. *Land Use History of Coso Hot Springs, Inyo County, California.* Public Works Department, Naval Weapons Center, China Lake, California. Administrative publication number 200, January 1979.

Purley, Dorothy A., Laguna Pueblo tribal member. Interview by author. 16 September 1995. Paguate Village, New Mexico. Tape recording. Author collection.

Rambeau, Clara, Big Pine Paiute Tribe of the Owens Valley elder. Interview by author, 20 November 1994. Big Pine, California. Tape recording. Author collection.

Rosse, William, Jr., chairman, Environmental Protection Committee, Western Shoshone National Council. Interview by author, 10 October 1994. Cactus Springs, Nevada. Tape recording. Author collection.

Samalar, Evelyn, Moapa Paiute elder. Interview by author, 18 April 1995. Moapa Paiute reservation, Nevada. Tape recording. Author collection.

Sanchez, Virginia, Western Shoshone Director of Citizen Alert Native American Project. Presentation taped by author, 15 April 1995. Healing Global Wounds gathering at Mercury ("Peace Camp"), Nevada. Tape recording. Author collection.

Shuey, Chris, Southwest Research and Information Center. Phone interview by author, 19 November 1996.

Zabarte, Ian, high-level nuclear waste contact for the Western Shoshone National Council. Interview by author, 24 October 1994. Cactus Springs, Nevada. Tape recording. Author collection.

Zabarte, Ian, high-level nuclear waste contact for the Western Shoshone National Council. Interview by author, 10 October 1994. Indian Springs, Nevada. Tape recording. Author collection.

Zucco, Marion, Big Pine Paiute Tribe of the Owens Valley tribal member. Interview by author, 20 November 1994. Big Pine, California. Taped recording. Author collection.

Newspaper Articles, Newsletters, and Radio Broadcasts

Albuquerque Journal, 16 December, 1993.

———, 4 April 1992.

Albuquerque Tribune. 13 April 1993.

Anchorage Daily News, 7 February 1994.

Aviation Week & Space Technology, vol. 140, no. 24 (13 June 1994).

China Lake (Calif.) Rocketeer, 8 November 1963.

The Circle, vol. 16, no. 4 (April 1995).

———, vol. 15, no. 8 (August 1994).

———, vol. 16, no. 10 (October 1995).

———, vol. 16, no. 1 (January 1995).

Citizen Alert Newsletter, vol. 2, no. 1 (March 1996).

Enchanted Times, Summer 1993. (Albuquerque, N.M.: All People's Coalition, Los Alamos Study Group).

———, Fall/Winter 1993.

Gallup (N.M.) Independent, 18 July 1989.

Geotimes, January 1989.

———, August 1991.

Horizons, National Public Radio, 1993. (Radio broadcast)

Las Vegas Sun, 21 June 1994.

Milwaukee Journal, 11 October 1993.

Mother Jones, October 1996.

Native American Smoke Signals: Voice of the Nations, vol. 1, no. 5 (August 1993).

———, January, 1994.

New York Times, 18 November 1990.

———, 22 October 1993.

———, 5 March 1995.

The Nuclear Reactor, vol. 3, no. 1 (February/March 1994). Concerned Citizens for Nuclear Safety.

———, vol. 3, no. 2 (Santa Fe, N. M., May/June 1994).

———, vol. 3, no. 3 (September/October 1994)

———, vol. 4, no. 1 (Early Spring 1995).

Of Mountains & Science, Summer 1995.

———, Winter 1996.

The Radioactive Rag, vol. 4, no. 1 (Santa Fe, N.M., Winter-Spring, 1992). Concerned Citizens for Nuclear Safety.

Reno Gazette-Journal, 7 June 1994.

The Ridgecrest (Calif.) News Review, November 1993.

The Rocketeer, 27 July 1995.

San Francisco Chronicle, 2 February 1995.

————, 2 April 1995.

San Francisco Examiner, 30 January 1994.

San Jose Mercury News, 4 April 1995.

————, 27 April 1995.

————, Tuesday, 2 May 1995.

Santa Cruz City on a Hill Press (University of California), 16 March 1995.

Science News, 133, no. 9 27 Feb., 1988.

Southwest Indigenous Uranium Forum Newsletter (Gallup, N.Mex.), September 1993.

Terrain, Summer 1995.

Washington Post, 8 December 1993.

Western Shoshone Defense Project newsletter, vol. 4, no. 1, Winter/Spring/Summer 1996.

Western Shoshone National Defense Project. *Newe Sogobia Is Not For Sale!* Crescent Valley, Nevada.

Unpublished Materials

The Navajo Health Authority. "Neoplasms Among Navajo Children." Grant proposal. Window Rock, Ariz.: 24 February 1981.

Masco, Joseph. "Nuclear Reservations: Plutonium and 'National Security' in Post-Cold War New Mexico." Presented at the American Anthropology Association Annual Meeting, Washington, D.C., 15–19 November 1996.

Rawles, Richard. "Cybernetics Killed The Cat." Paper, University of California, Santa Cruz, 1993.

Sharrock, Susan R. "A History of the Indians of Nevada from First White Contact to the Reservation Period: Extracted from Eye-Witness Accounts." Unpublished paper, 1 June 1967.

Stevens, Robert Henry. (Osage Nation) "Sacred Landscapes: Continuity and Change." Paper presented at the 11th Annual American Indian Conference, University of California, Los Angeles, 7 October 1995.

Copyright Information

Index